# *The* CHICKENSHIT CLUB

WHY THE JUSTICE DEPARTMENT FAILS TO PROSECUTE EXECUTIVES

JESSE EISINGER

SIMON & SCHUSTER

*New York London Toronto Sydney New Delhi*

Simon & Schuster
1230 Avenue of the Americas
New York, NY 10020



First Simon & Schuster hardcover edition July 2017



*Interior design by Ruth Lee-Mui*

Manufactured in the United States of America

1 3 5 7 9 10 8 6 4 2

Library of Congress Cataloging-in-Publication Data is available.

ISBN 978-1-5011-2136-4
ISBN 978-1-5011-2138-8 (ebook)

*For Sarah*

# CONTENTS

# AUTHOR'S NOTE ON SOURCING AND METHODS

TO REPORT AND WRITE THIS STORY, I RELIED ON thousands of pages of court documents, journalistic and academic accounts of events, internal government documents, emails, transcripts, and hundreds of hours of interviews with hundreds of current and former prosecutors, Congressional staffers, and other government officials and regulators, defense attorneys, bankers, investors, corporate executives, academics, lobbyists, consumer advocat and others.

I spoke with most of the people named in this book. For those v not speak to me, I contacted them, or attempted to contact them, them to tell their story. Many of the sources I spoke to did not w names used. Most former prosecutors continue to work in the law want to threaten their careers by speaking out publicly. I have not attributed much in the book to protect my sources. Furth sourcing for specific chapters can be found in the Notes section

The book's dialogue comes from documents or the best recollections of participants. Where I could, I tried to contact as many people in a given meeting or scene to confirm what was said. States of mind often come from the speaker, but also from documents or conversations where the speaker contemporaneously relayed to others what was said. The reader should not infer that I spoke to that person.

# INTRODUCTION

THE DEPARTMENT OF JUSTICE IS A LOOSE FEDERation of ninety-four offices around the country, each a realm unto itself, run by a US attorney who is almost untouchable by headquarters in faraway Washington, DC. Of all those offices, the Southern District of New York, located at the bottom tip of Manhattan, has the smartest and ablest prosecutors in the land. Any alum of the office will be happy to verify that.

The Southern District's founding, in 1789, predates that of the Department of Justice itself. The office held its first criminal trial in 1790, which lasted a day. The first US attorney convicted two men of conspiring to destroy a brigantine and murder its captain and a passenger. The second US attorney simultaneously served as mayor of New York City. Today the office specializes in the most complex and difficult criminal cases: corporate white-collar fraud, often securities law violations. Insiders relish its nickname: the "sovereign" district, for its penchant for claiming jurisdiction over any such case from any corner of the United States, the other ninety-three offices be damned.

Prosecutors in the Southern District have the strongest résumés from the best schools. They should inspire trust when they stand up in court to say, "I represent the government of the United States of America." But it takes something even more to get to the Southern District; something more personal. Someone somewhere—a top partner at a law firm, a respected judge or professor—had to send the signal. That sign indicated the candidate wasn't just special; he or she was a superstar in the making. The Manhattan US Attorney's Office launched the careers of judges and legal giants of every kind; politicians (New York City mayor Rudolph Giuliani and Representative Charles Rangel); cabinet secretaries (Henry Stimson, the US secretary of war under presidents William Howard Taft, Franklin Delano Roosevelt, and Harry Truman); a US attorney general (Michael Mukasey); FBI directors (Louis Freeh); and two Supreme Court justices (Felix Frankfurter and John M. Harlan II).

In January 2002, early in the George W. Bush presidency, the White House appointed James Comey the fifty-eighth US attorney for the Southern District of Manhattan. Comey was a Southern District alumnus with a record of serious prosecutions. He helped prosecute the Gambino Mafia family in the late 1980s and (after he'd left the Manhattan office for Richmond, Virginia) the 1996 Khobar Towers terrorist bombing in Saudi Arabia.[1] The staff, worried that the Bush administration would appoint a political operative, felt relieved. The prosecutors hadn't wanted to lose his predecessor, Mary Jo White, the first (and only) woman to have been US attorney for the Southern District of New York. She had served for almost nine years. She had been so loyal to her charges and such a stubborn guardian of the office's prerogatives that the attorneys in the office would have run through the Corinthian columns that held up the Foley Square courthouses for her.

When Comey arrived for his first day in 2002, he received a resounding ovation. Then he did something unusual. Comey took several months to feel out the office where he'd been a prosecutor a few years earlier, meeting new attorneys and learning what kinds of cases they were making.

After Jim Comey had finished his months-long listening tour, he decided to give a speech to the criminal division. He made his debut during a regularly scheduled meeting, held in the evening in what the assistants called the Old Courthouse in lower Manhattan. The staff gathered in a courtroom where trials took place. Assistant prosecutors piled into the spectator benches. These lawyers were the nation's elite, most of them in their twenties and early thirties. From youth, they had been the highest achievers and hardest workers. They had summered as associates at the most powerful law firms. They had clerked for the finest judges. In the coming years, many of the attendees became star prosecutors and top partners at major law firms. Members of the Southern District at that time included Preet Bharara and David Kelley, both successors to Comey and White as US attorneys for the Southern District; Ben Lawsky, who would become the top New York State financial regulator; Neil Barofsky, the future overseer of the federal bank bailout program in the wake of the 2008 crisis; and Ronnie Abrams and Richard Sullivan, future judges.

Usually held monthly, the meeting had a certain formula. First, supervisors rounded up office news. Then they'd go through the box score, where someone would read off who had a trial, what the trial concerned, and whether the office had won or lost. By tradition, whoever ran the meeting made special note of a prosecutor's first trial. Regardless of whether the rookie had won or lost, everyone would applaud. Prosecutors say that that inauguration gave them chills. They'd made it.

If there was anything Comey might be better at than Mary Jo White, it was giving a speech. Though her prosecutors worshipped her, White was so tiny, a fire hydrant could obscure her. She could not hold crowds rapt. Comey, by contrast, at six foot eight, towered, and he liked to perform. His delivery carried a humility practiced enough to suggest he knew he was good at it. He had used his talents so often to keep the jury's attention with jokes, knowing references, and pithy turns of phrase. Now he had to enthrall a courtroom of prosecutors. Overachievers all, the office's attorneys wanted to impress, to feel the chill, to know they had made it.

"Before we read off the box score, I have something to say," Comey said. "We have a saying around here: We do the right things for the right reasons in the right ways."

All the assembled prosecutors had heard that exhortation in some variation, from Comey in the hallways or in smaller meetings, and from other chiefs.

Then Comey asked the seated prosecutors a question: "Who here has never had an acquittal or a hung jury? Please raise your hand."

The go-getters and résumé builders in the office were ready. This group thought themselves the best trial lawyers in the country. Hands shot up.

"Me and my friends have a name for you guys," Comey said, looking around the room. Backs straightened in preparation for praise. Comey looked at his flock with approbation. "You are members of what we like to call the Chickenshit Club."

Hands went down faster than they had gone up. Some emitted sheepish laughter.

"If it's a good case and the evidence supports it, you must bring it," Comey told his troops. "I know it can get crazy in court. You feel stressed when the judge is pounding on you. When that happens, you can all take a deep breath. I don't want any of you to make an argument you don't believe in. I want you to believe that you are doing the right thing. Make the right decisions for the right reasons."

Comey had laid out how prosecutors should approach their jobs. Prosecuting wrongdoers is an awesome responsibility, to be undertaken carefully and judiciously. But prosecutors—unlike other lawyers—are not simply advocates for one side. They are required to bring justice. They need to be righteous, not careerist. They should seek to right the biggest injustices, not go after the easiest targets. Victory in the courtroom should be a secondary concern, meaning that government lawyers should neither seek to win at all costs nor duck a valid case out of fear of losing. Federal prosecutors should not be judged on their trial record, whether they are criticized, or what the political consequences might be of their prosecutions. Comey wanted his prosecutors to be bold, to reach and to aspire to great cases, no matter their difficulty.

Ben Lawsky, a young prosecutor in the office when Comey gave his speech, recalls the inspiration from the meeting many years later. He had been waiting with trepidation for the box score because he had lost his first trial. Comey came to his case: "Ben Lawsky. First time out of the box and out of the Chickenshit Club!" Everyone applauded. Lawsky swelled with relief and pride.

## BOOM, BUST, AND CRACKDOWN

America's economic history has unfolded in a series of booms followed by busts followed, crucially, by crackdowns. After the stock market crash of 1929, congressional hearings channeled public outrage and resulted in landmark laws regulating Wall Street and creating the Securities and Exchange Commission in 1934. A few years later, the new SEC helped put the head of the mighty New York Stock Exchange (NYSE) in prison. Though inconsistent, the SEC over the intervening decades emerged as one of the most respected government regulatory bodies. The SEC is the country's most important corporate regulator, overseeing publicly traded companies and the nation's capital markets. The agency has civil powers, and must team up with various offices of the Department of Justice when a securities law violation turns into a criminal investigation. After the go-go years of the late 1960s, the SEC worked closely with the Southern District to take on top law firms, top accounting firms, and top executives who had helped perpetrate corporate frauds. After the savings and loan scandals of the 1980s, when hundreds of small banks across the country failed due to reckless real estate loans, the Department of Justice prosecuted over a thousand people, including top executives at many of the largest failed banks. After the Michael Milken–run junk bond boom and blow-up of the late 1980s, prosecutors spent years digging up evidence of stock manipulation and insider trading at major investment banks and law firms, prosecuting some of the most powerful Wall Street figures of the era. In the early 2000s, the burst Nasdaq bubble revealed a corporate book-cooking pandemic. Top officers from giants such as Enron, WorldCom, Qwest Communications, Adelphia, and Tyco International ended up in prison. Recklessness and stupidity fuel booms, but usually so do crimes.

By contrast, after the 2008 financial crisis, the government failed. In response to the worst calamity to hit capital markets and the global economy since the Great Depression, the government did not charge any top bankers. The public was furious. The bank bailouts and lack of consequences for bankers radicalized both ends of the political spectrum and gave rise to two of the most potent social movements of our time: the Tea Party and Occupy Wall Street. Anger about the lack of Wall Street accountability seeded disenchantment with Obama. The 2016 insurgency of Vermont senator Bernie Sanders, who challenged front-runner Hillary Clinton almost up to the doors of the Democratic Convention, demonstrated the anger that remained on the left years after the apex of the crisis, undergirding mistrust about Clinton. She had given friendly, fateful, and highly compenstated speeches to investment banks. While a Republican president had presided over the crisis and a Democratic one had saved the financial system, Hillary Clinton, Obama, and the Democrats could not claim to be the protectors of the working class and the scourges of investment bankers. That was due, in large measure, to the lack of corporate prosecutions. According to a *Wall Street Journal* analysis of 156 criminal and civil cases brought by the Justice Department, the Securities and Exchange Commission, and the Commodity Futures Trading Commission against ten of the largest Wall Street banks since 2009, in 81 percent of the cases, the government neither charged nor even identified individual employees. In the remainder, the government only charged forty-seven low and midlevel employees. Merely one was a boardroom-level executive, whom the SEC charged civilly.[2]

In his own incoherent and superficial way, Donald Trump rode anger about Wall Street throughout his campaign, railing at bank power. He closed his campaign by hinting poisonously about a cabal of global bankers rigging the system. He assailed politicians who were "owned" by Goldman Sachs: first Ted Cruz in the primary and then Hillary Clinton in the general. The Republican platform called for breaking up the big banks by returning to the Glass-Steagall Act, the Depression-era law that split commercial banking from investment banking, a reflection of resentment about the government bailout of the financial system as bankers wriggled free. (No sooner had Trump taken office then he rushed to stuff members of that cabal into his White House and cabinet. He and the Goldman alumni who advised him moved within days of taking office to unravel Dodd-Frank and loosen restrictions on corporations generally.)

It's commonplace to observe that no top bankers from the top financial firms went to prison for the widespread malfeasance that led to the 2008 financial crisis. It's such a socially acceptable opinion that no less than an inside-the-Beltway figure than the former chairman of the Federal Reserve, Ben Bernanke, said (after he was safely out of office) that more bankers should have gone to prison. But the problem is worse than that.

Today's Department of Justice has lost the will and indeed the ability to go after the highest-ranking corporate wrongdoers. The problem did not begin in the aftermath of the 2008 crash—and it has not ended. Prosecutors don't simply struggle to put executives for "Too Big to Fail" banks in prison. They also cannot hold accountable wrongdoing executives from a gamut of large corporations: from pharmaceuticals, to technology, to large industrial operations, to retail giants.

James Comey's exhortation came at the beginning of a dramatic and little-understood shift in how the government prosecutes white-collar corporate crime. After the post-Nasdaq-bubble prosecutions of the early 2000s, the Justice Department began to suffer fiascos, losses in court, damning acts of prosecutorial abuse, and years of intense lobbying and pressure from corporations and the defense bar to ease up. Prosecutors lost potent investigative tools and softened their practices, changes that have made it harder to gather evidence and conduct even the most basic investigations. Compounding this issue, the Justice Department has been hurt by budget constraints. The FBI, which usually conducts investigations for the department, shifted resources to antiterrorism efforts in the wake of 9/11. The Justice Department has kept track of white-collar cases only since the early 1990s. In the four years from 1992 through 1995, white-collar cases averaged 19 percent of overall cases. In the four years from 2012 to 2015, that number had fallen to just under 9.9 percent. The Department of Justice wasn't just going after fewer cases, but easier cases, contrary to Comey's admonition. In that same period, the conviction rate was slightly higher: 91 percent in the 2012–15 period, compared with 87 percent in the early 1990s.[3]

Meanwhile, judges all over the country embarked on newly generous interpretations of the law, broadening corporate and executive rights and privileges, narrowing white-collar criminal statutes, and repeatedly overturning federal prosecutors in notable white-collar cases. The Supreme Court has expanded the rights of corporations in the most potent, visible fashion, but lower courts have contributed to the trend. Over the last decade, while draconian when it came to street criminals, the courts have repeatedly read the US Constitution expansively when the government tried to charge corporations or their top executives. Congress sat by, failing to recognize the problem, much less propose legislative solutions.

To compensate for these changes, the Department of Justice shifted from targeting individual corporate executives with trial and imprisonment. Instead, prosecutors switched to a regime of almost exclusively settling with corporations for money. In these negotiations with corporations, prosecutors discovered they had great leverage.

Since 2001, more than 250 federal prosecutions have involved large corporations. These include some of the biggest names in corporate America: AIG, Google, JPMorgan Chase, and Pfizer among them.[4] The majority of these have been negotiated deals, not indictments. From 2002 through the fall of 2016, the Justice Department entered into 419 such settlements, called deferred prosecutions and nonprosecution agreements, with corporations. There had been just 18 in the preceding ten years.[5] Meanwhile, corporate prosecutions fell. The Justice Department prosecuted 237 companies in 2014, 29 percent below the number in 2004.[6] These prosecutions tended to be of tiny, inconsequential companies.

Large and powerful corporations, under the advice of their expensive defense lawyers, were eager to appear cooperative and wrap up investigations quickly, before prosecutors uncovered more damning information. They could pay settlements with other people's money: that of their shareholders. Since the early 2000s, changes in the business of law accelerated. Big Law corporatized white-collar criminal defense, working more often in symbiosis with prosecutors than as adversaries. These lawyers, not the government, conducted extensive and lucrative investigations, delivering their findings to the government and moving on to the next. Prosecutors, for their part, could generate headlines with eye-popping dollar amounts and set themselves up for lucrative careers in the private sector. And they hadn't had to go to court to prove their case. The bigger the penalties, the more headlines they grabbed, and the more appealing they became to the prosecutors who could name their price.

These settlements did little to deter corporations from breaking the law. "Over 50 percent of the most serious fraud and larceny culprits were recidivists," writes University of Virginia law professor Brandon Garrett, a rate "about the same as robbery and firearms offenders and far higher than drug traffickers." Five years before the BP Deepwater Horizon explosion in 2010, the British oil and gas company had the Texas City refinery disaster.[7] ExxonMobil has been convicted four times since 2001 of environmental crimes. In recent years, Pfizer, the pharmaceutical behemoth, has suffered every form of government crackdown that prosecutors can imagine, short of the ultimate sanction of being put out of business. Pfizer and subsidiaries have had two convictions, two deferred prosecution agreements, and a nonprosecution agreement.

Corporate settlements were easier to reach than indictments of individuals, particularly top executives. The Justice Department shifted away from white-collar prosecutions. In 2016 the Department of Justice brought the lowest number of white-collar cases against individuals in twenty years, on track for just 6,200 cases, down more than 40 percent from 1996—despite population and economic growth.[8] Though companies pledged cooperation with follow-on investigations of individuals, usually no one from a company that signed a deferred prosecution went to prison. In two-thirds of cases involving deferred prosecutions or non-prosecutions of public corporations between 2001 and 2012, according to Garrett, the company was punished, but no employees were prosecuted.

Of the thirty-one publicly listed firms convicted in the same period (thus not including those who reached a settlement), Garrett counted the leaders of those companies who went to prison: four CEOs, one chairman, one president, and one CFO.

Investigations and prosecutions of people are much more difficult than going after corporations. Prosecutors began to see probes of single human beings, one by one by one, as a slog; nasty trench warfare that carries a risk of humiliation if they lose. Investigations of individuals consume more time. Investigators must work slowly, first going after lower-level employees and then flipping them against their bosses. To their bosses at the Department of Justice, prosecutors who pursue individuals appear less productive. Investigating top executives at large corporations is more difficult because they insulate themselves from day-to-day decision making. Prosecutors find it harder to accumulate the evidence necessary to prove their cases beyond a reasonable doubt. And individuals have greater incentive to fight prosecutors.

Defaulting to a settlement with a corporation without prosecuting individuals corrodes the rule of law. Settlement culture validates the critiques of both sides. Companies argue that the government has extorted them into forking over money for unproven crimes. They say they cannot contest allegations because regulators hold the power of life or death over them. The public, meanwhile, sees corporations writing checks to make charges disappear.

Settlements have another downside: they weaken prosecutorial skills. Over time, prosecutorial aversion turns into lost knowledge. Settlement culture breeds investigative laziness and erodes trial skills.

Corporate power is at a zenith in America, and business has privileges not seen since the Gilded Age. Executives make more money than ever. Corporate profits are at record highs. The courts are expanding corporate rights, as companies exert great political power and dominate our policy discourse. But the most valuable perquisite corporate officers possess is the ability to commit crimes with impunity. Such injustice threatens American democracy.

Today the justice system is broken. Over the decade after Jim Comey's speech, his words failed. The Justice Department succumbed. The department avoided the biggest cases. It became fearful of losing and lost sight of its fundamental mission to make this country a just place. James Comey would have no way of knowing it at the time, but his sermon to the Southern District prosecutors could have easily been a eulogy for the courage he hoped to muster. The Chickenshit Club's ranks in the years ahead would only grow.

## *Chapter One*

# "THERE IS NO CHRISTMAS"

ON A GRIM DAY IN SEPTEMBER 2003, WITH HURricane Isabel brewing off the East Coast, federal prosecutor Kathy Ruemmler prepared for the government's third interview with an Enron witness. The investigation into the top officers at the collapsed energy giant was stalled. Ruemmler knew the prosecutors had to flip someone.

She had just joined as the youngest member of the Enron Task Force, the special SWAT team the Justice Department had assembled to dig into what had been one of the richest and most admired companies in the world. Now it had been revealed to be one of the biggest frauds in American business history. At a passing glance, the thirty-two-year-old assistant US attorney looked fresh faced and friendly, with her shoulder-length blond hair and clothing that was a step up from the typical government servant's. But she had a steeliness that she could wield at will. Her warm blue eyes hardened when she was deposing a witness.

Her teammate in those days was Sam Buell. Before joining the task force, Buell, thirty-nine, had prosecuted Boston mob cases. He was tall and clean cut. His short, reddish hair framed a wide, gentle face that sat above broad shoulders. Buell, the son of schoolteachers, had grown up in Milton, Massachusetts, outside of Boston. Self-deprecating and easygoing, he looked like a favorite high school math teacher. Witnesses liked him in spite of themselves. Buell and the task force had been laboring over the case for months now. They were going after Jeff Skilling and Ken Lay, Enron's top officers. Ruemmler and Buell spent most of their time shuttling from DC to Houston, where the two of them would drive from their dingy government-rate hotel rooms to an abandoned space at the top of Houston's run-down federal courthouse, a 1960s-era squat white cube in the middle of downtown Houston.

They passed through building security unencumbered. Here it was already 2003, and they still didn't even have BlackBerrys. Upstairs, their clunky computers balanced on cardboard boxes atop chipped metal desks. The whole place was so run-down that it was fodder for jokes. A defense attorney bringing a tony client for an interview once cracked, "It looks like an OSHA violation in here!" During the first winter, most of them had come down with miserable respiratory infections. Were the offices infecting them? Or was it just the pressure of their task? They had no document management system and no way even to email the FBI agents assigned to the investigation, who were just a few blocks away. With this pathetic setup, they were taking on an infernally complex company in the most important corporate fraud case in memory, against a legion of defense lawyers from the best firms in the world.

The country had invaded Iraq six months earlier. Madonna kissed Britney Spears and Christina Aguilera on the MTV Video Music Awards show. The American tennis star Andy Roddick won what would be the only major tournament of his career: the US Open championship. But Ruemmler barely noted outside events, significant or trivial. She had no time for anything but the case. During these eighteen-hour days, when she could only sneak in a frozen pizza and a shower, Ruemmler would sometimes marvel that she had ended up here. She had grown up in Richland,

Washington, a rural corner of the Northwest, where both of her parents worked at the giant Hanford nuclear facility on the Columbia River, her father as a computer engineer and her mother in a toxicology lab. Unlike most of her Justice Department colleagues, Ruemmler hadn't gone to an elite eastern college. She'd been thrilled to get into the local University of Washington, and before she left to attend Georgetown University Law Center, she had been out of the Northwest only three times.

Yet Ruemmler had landed a plum job: assistant US attorney; a federal prosecutor in the DC office. She'd been handling violent crime and narcotics cases when Leslie Caldwell, head of the Enron Task Force, reached out. Ruemmler hadn't had much experience prosecuting financial fraud. She'd been reading the papers and coming across the same phrase: if normal financial fraud was "algebra," the articles intoned, Enron was "advanced calculus." She felt intimidated. But Caldwell assured her the Enron Task Force would be only a six-month detail.

Twice, the Enron prosecutors had brought in one of their most promising witnesses, Dave Delainey, the head of Enron's energy trading division. He'd stuck with his story, brushing aside questions from the prosecutors and the FBI agent assigned to this part of the investigation. They weren't giving up, though, and that morning they felt certain they had discovered a dangling thread that might help them unravel his story.

As Ruemmler and Buell went through the many emails Delainey had sent to his head trader, they found a huge gain the company had made trading in California's energy markets in the late 1990s. Enron didn't want to tell shareholders it was a volatile trading shop. Instead, the company line for Wall Street had been that Enron was a stable, fast-growing operation. CEO Jeff Skilling had downplayed Enron's trading, once saying on CNBC that it was "just a small portion" of its business.[1] Enron was just a "logistics" business, he'd say, meaning that Enron helped speculators but wasn't one itself. A big trading gain, such as the one Ruemmler and Buell discovered, hinted at the reality. Speculation dominated the company's culture and contributed an outsized portion of its profits. Once, after a trader had lost close to a half billion in one day, Skilling came down to the trading floor and exhorted the traders to "man up." Get back out there and make more trades. Win it back.

Instead of having Enron disclose those trading profits, Delainey and his executives hid them. They stashed the millions of dollars of earnings and created a cover story: it was setting aside those profits for a possible legal settlement.

Ruemmler and Buell had figured out that this reserve, this "cookie jar," was a lie. Poring over the company's intentionally complicated and messy financial statements one more time, they'd noticed that a year after creating the reserve, Enron had lost millions in another division and dipped into that money—reserved for legal costs—to cover the losses and make it look like it had made money that quarter. That accounting hocus-pocus was illegal, and Delainey and his top trader had emailed about it. But they'd used a lot of trader jargon, and the emails were vague enough that a jury would need them decoded. The prosecutors understood how the scam had been pulled off but believed they couldn't prove it yet.

Delainey could explain that little scam, but that's not why they needed to flip him. Complex white-collar investigations required finding "rabbis" to guide you through the transactions. Even the smartest outsiders couldn't rely on the documents. They were conducting an old-fashioned investigation. They needed someone on the inside. If they could flip Delainey, they could take the prosecution all the way to the top. They could begin to build a case that Jeff Skilling had lied to investors and the public.

## ALL BULLSHIT

That led them, in the middle of the hurricane, to haul Dave Delainey and his expensive lawyers into a windowless conference room in the Bond Building in Washington, DC, for a third time.

Buell and Ruemmler and their expert FBI agent had new verve; they took command of the interview from the start. Buell had a hunch Delainey wanted to cooperate. Getting him over to their side, however, required breaking down his instinct to deny and minimize his culpability. Delainey had long been an Enron true believer. A clean-cut Canadian, he'd been awed by the testosterone-flooded Enron trading culture. Hard-charging, sure, but they weren't—couldn't be—criminals.

Few corporate white-collar fraudsters—not egregious Ponzi schemers or boiler room operators but perpetrators at large, respectable companies—start out thinking they will commit a crime. As one academic study, "Why Do They Do It?: The Motives, Mores, and Character of White Collar Criminals" put it, most white-collar criminals are "individuals who find themselves involved in schemes that are initially small in scale, but over which they quickly lose control."[2]

They tell themselves, "I'll just do it this quarter so we don't miss the number, and then I'll stop it and undo what I've done." They don't think of themselves as crooks. It's just a short-term fix. Then they use the device again and again until they have no choice but to keep up the charade. They start rationalizing what they're doing. It may be aggressive, but it's not wrong. It's not theft. The bad guys aren't lying just to prosecutors. They are lying to their shareholders, their colleagues, and their families. And they are lying to themselves.

The prosecutor's job is to crack through that self-justification and self-delusion. That's what Ruemmler and Buell were going to do that morning, in that room, with Delainey.

The two stuck with their plan to stay calm, to both be the good cops, and keep asking questions about the emails. They would reason with him, confronting him with the evidence, though selectively, to test his credibility. Their advantage was that Delainey didn't know exactly which documents interested the prosecutors, as well as who else from Enron was talking and what they were saying. As Ruemmler and Buell ground him down on the emails, his story began to collapse. A couple hours into the conversation, it happened: Delainey glanced over and signaled a silent plea for help to his lawyers: John Dowd of Akin Gump and a promising young associate named Savannah Guthrie, who would later coanchor the *Today* show.

Dowd was a legend, one of the premier defense lawyers in the country. Big and aggressive, he'd vow to fight the government from every rampart in Washington. He had some quirks. Using just two fingers, he'd bang out his emails in twenty-eight-point purple Comic Sans font. "*Who He?*" he'd email-bellow to his associates. He toned it down for Buell, who saw a familiar character in Dowd, a brash and street-smart working-class Bostonian. They would chat about the Red Sox. Dowd was no intellectual, but he was savvy and knew how to help his clients. Buell and Ruemmler made it clear where the email evidence was taking Dowd's client. The attorney understood it perfectly.

Dowd asked if he and Guthrie could confer with their client and then left the room.

They were gone for about fifteen minutes. When they came back in, Ruemmler noticed that Delainey's demeanor had changed. He now slumped in his chair. A moment passed in silence. He then spoke—mumbled, really: "It was all bullshit."

As Kathy Ruemmler snuck a quick a look at her partner, she saw the smallest of smiles on his face.

## GEORGE BUSH AND "KENNY BOY"

When Enron filed for bankruptcy in December 2001, the implosion devastated a major US city, Houston, both economically and psychologically. *Fortune* magazine had named Enron "America's most innovative company" six years straight for having changed the way that gas and electricity moved around the country. The magazine *CEO* had named Enron's board one of the top five in America.[3] Former secretaries of state Henry Kissinger and James Baker had lobbied for the company. Nelson Mandela had come to Houston to receive the Enron Prize for Distinguished Public Service.

The Enron scandal reached all the way to the president and vice president of the United States. George W. Bush and Dick Cheney had run in the same business and social circles as the Enron executives. Bush's family had made its money in Texas energy; Cheney, only a few years earlier, had been the CEO of the energy services giant the Halliburton Company, then based in Dallas. Ken Lay, Enron's founder, was a longtime Bush family friend and major Republican donor. Bush, as is his way with intimates, had given Lay a nickname: "Kenny Boy." Lay had once hosted a fund-raiser for Senator John Ashcroft, a Republican from Missouri, who was expected to make a bid for the 2000 presidency. Now Ashcroft was Bush's attorney general, the top law enforcement officer in the United States.[4]

The country fell into recession in late 2000. It was reeling from the bursting of the biggest stock market bubble the world had seen, which had inflated through most of the 1990s before collapsing mercilessly in March 2000. Over the next few years, new companies reported accounting problems with alarming regularity: Tyco, Adelphia, HealthSouth, WorldCom. But Enron's collapse was the most spectacular. The pandemic of corporate greed and criminality felt so consequential that it wasn't outlandish to think that Enron's failure might be the seminal financial event of a generation.

Enron's significance would recede, however, and the lessons it holds for white-collar enforcement would be forgotten. Despite Enron's political might, the US government aggressively investigated the fraud at the energy trading company and prosecuted dozens of individuals, including the top officers of the company. Lay, Skilling, and Andrew Fastow, the chief financial officer, were all found guilty. Skilling and Fastow went to prison; Lay would have gone, too, but he died of a massive heart attack in 2006, just three months before his sentencing. In all, the government charged thirty-two people associated with the Enron frauds, including Wall Street bankers who'd facilitated the deceptions.[5] The government did indeed take down rogue executives not that long ago.

Many people look at the crimes at Enron, WorldCom, Adelphia, Tyco, and the generation of post-stock-market-bubble-bursting prosecutions and think the crimes were so egregious that the prosecutions must have been easy. But that's only with the benefit of hindsight. What Kathy Ruemmler, Sam Buell, and the rest of the Enron Task Force did was not simple and never inevitable. If the task force hadn't had resources, time, intelligence, and patience, Lay and Skilling may not have been prosecuted at all or could have easily been acquitted. The prosecutorial team went up against the best defense lawyers in the country. The public brayed for faster action. The team had its share of stumbles, blowing some of its trials. Lay didn't use email; Skilling rarely did. So the government lacked direct, incriminatory evidence of their guilt. But in the big cases, the task force prevailed. These were not accidents. The Enron prosecution team made smart strategic decisions, secured necessary resources, learned from their mistakes, used aggressive tactics, and ran the major trials well.

Despite this success, the Justice Department took the wrong lesson from Enron. Over the next decade, the task force's legacy, at least for the subsequent leaders of the Justice Department, lay more in its mistakes than its successes. Courts reversed the government in key cases. The defense bar and Justice Department officials came to view the Enron prosecutors as reckless and abusive rather than sufficiently aggressive to meet the prosecutorial challenge. Today it's an open question whether the Justice Department would be capable of taking on Enron the same way the task force did.

## ASSEMBLING THE TEAM

In the early years of the George W. Bush administration, its Department of Justice compiled a sterling record of corporate prosecutions. Larry Thompson, Bush's first deputy attorney general, understood that the DOJ had to respond assertively to the unfolding crisis. Thompson joined the administration in 2001, just as the corporate accounting scandals were breaking. Stock markets were collapsing. The public was furious. By the end of its run, the early Bush-era Department of Justice had prosecuted almost every major accounting fraud from the early 2000s. Not just Enron but also WorldCom, Adelphia, Global Crossing, and Qwest Communications among them. At the state level, the Manhattan district attorney prevailed in cases against the top corporate officers of Tyco.[6]

Prosecutors took losses, too. They weren't taking on the easiest cases and juicing their stats with easy victories. One of the more unfathomable losses was the acquittal of Richard Scrushy, the head of hospital and rehab clinic operator HealthSouth. Prosecutors charged him with thirty-six counts, including securities fraud and conspiracy in connection with a $2.7 billion accounting fraud. They flipped multiple former employees against Scrushy, including the HealthSouth CFO, but a hometown jury found him not guilty.[7] A year later, in a separate case, a federal jury found Scrushy guilty of bribery.[8] Thompson understood the risks and tolerated losses. In his view, they were the price of ambition.

A fair and lifetime law-and-order man, Thompson conferred with Michael Chertoff, the head of the criminal division at "Main Justice," as the Washington headquarters of the Department of Justice is known. They both emphasized the public need for "real-time" prosecution for white-collar cases. They believed the public deserved action and defendants deserved speedy resolutions. But the strategy was also practical. White-collar cases could languish for years, a poor way of conducting any investigation. The evidence trail grows cold, memories fade, and defense lawyers have time to formulate their client's stories and tactics. Prosecutors needed to maintain momentum. Thompson and Chertoff understood that with the Enron debacle, the public would be bothered with slow justice. That there might be no justice—no prosecutions at all—never even occurred to anyone.

In early 2002 Thompson and Chertoff feared that the Enron case was already a mess. Several US Attorney's Offices had separate pieces of the investigation. Main Justice oversees the other offices but does not direct each about its investigations. The criminal division in Washington also conducts its own investigations into securities fraud, antitrust violations, public corruption, and civil rights. Prosecutors coordinate probes but do not conduct them. Every investigation has agents, usually from the FBI. Often other government regulators, including the SEC, have only civil enforcement powers. For criminal matters, they work with the Justice Department. Since the Southern District of New York took on most of the corporate and securities fraud matters, it had the closest relationship with the SEC. In early 2002 the Southern District vied to take all the Enron cases for itself, but Thompson and Chertoff wouldn't allow that. The Southern District, in a pique, removed itself entirely.

With the Southern District out of Enron, nobody seemed to know who was in charge of what. The government's document requests deluged the company. Robert Bennett, the Washington power lawyer, then with Skadden, Arps, Slate, Meagher & Flom, which represented Enron, called up Larry Thompson's office and told them he wanted to cooperate but didn't know with whom he should deal.[9]

Main Justice realized that the Houston office of the Justice Department had too many professional and personal conflicts of interest and had to recuse itself from prosecuting the company. Thompson, FBI Director Robert Mueller, and Chertoff mulled the problem. Should they assign a special prosecutor to head up all the cases? Do nothing and let the US Attorney's Offices work the cases on their own? Chertoff had been a US attorney in New Jersey and had worked under Rudolph Giuliani when Giuliani was the US attorney in Manhattan. Chertoff likened US attorneys to ship captains: they mapped their own courses. Chertoff knew that US attorneys felt free to heed or ignore distress flags from shore. He'd done it himself. They were not autonomous, but they took direction from Main Justice reluctantly. Top Justice Department officials in Washington were political appointees. The responsible ones took care in offering direction in order to not be seen as meddling politically in investigations.

Chertoff argued to Thompson that these cases were too important for Main Justice to leave them up to individual US attorneys. When he was the US attorney in Atlanta, Thompson had overseen a drug task force with another US attorney, the future Alabama Republican senator Jeff Sessions, who would become the US attorney general in 2017. He believed task forces worked, though not by magic. They shared information and investigative techniques. A task force focused prosecutors and gave them clear priorities. After that, it was pick-and-shovel work on the case, flipping low-level soldiers to get to the capos.

All the officials in the conversation understood that a task force with prosecutorial powers had some inherent weaknesses. It faces enormous pressure to emerge with some kind of charge, leading to abuses. (Similar problems plague independent prosecutors.) The public has made up its mind. Prosecutors need courage not to bring cases as the spotlight shines. The more cases a task force can bring, the better. It's difficult to wind up the operation. Worse, a task force has few checks and balances. A US Attorney's Office has institutional knowledge and a decision-making structure; a task force operates in a vacuum.

But Thompson thought he might ward off those bad outcomes with his gentle persistence. The top officials created the President's Corporate Fraud Task Force to supervise the efforts of the various offices around the country. They identified approximately ten big cases for it to oversee. Thompson made weekly calls to the heads of the offices to make sure prosecutors were working them and to make it clear that he cared. Thompson had a soft and inviting disposition. He didn't direct anything. He just let them know he wanted to hear the status. His bedside manner was deceptive. He would "stay on their asses," as one Department of Justice official put it.

Main Justice also created the elite operation to go after Enron specifically. In early 2002 Chertoff got to work on forming the Enron SWAT team. Mueller recommended the stoic Leslie Caldwell to head the team. He had worked with her in the San Francisco US Attorney's Office, where she led the securities fraud unit. Caldwell, then in her early forties, maintained a soothing calm. She carried an air of someone who'd had years of practice cracking jokes that only she might hear or get. Her formative prosecutorial experience had been in the US Attorney's Office in Brooklyn, the Eastern District of New York, where she had overseen mob prosecutions. She liked to say that back then the rooftops of Brooklyn were for stashing bodies, not kale gardens.[10] Eastern District prosecutors liked to think they were scrappier than those in the Southern District in Manhattan. Eastern District "mafia"—prosecutors loved to identify themselves as mafiosi from certain offices—dominated the Enron investigative team.

Caldwell brought in Andrew Weissmann as her deputy. In many ways, he was her opposite: loud, aggressive, flamboyant. "Your client is a lying sack of shit!" he'd yell at defense lawyers. Caldwell, who had worked with Weissmann in Brooklyn, admired his trial brilliance.

Caldwell then turned to Sam Buell, with whom she'd worked in the Eastern District. Buell was then working up in Boston, having spent three grueling years on the Whitey Bulger case, the notorious Boston mobster wanted in connection with nineteen murders, among other crimes. He'd been on the lam for sixteen years before being captured in 2011. Caldwell had attended Buell's wedding. When she called about the task force job in early 2002, Buell didn't have to think about it. He knew he was in. His wife, a corporate lawyer who had left the workplace to raise their children, encouraged him. Buell had little white-collar experience. He'd done only some low-level corporate fraud work—a money-laundering case or two. But he understood that prosecutors couldn't shy from difficult cases. After attending law school at New York University, he had clerked for Jack Weinstein, a legendary federal district court judge famous for resolving mass tort cases involving Agent Orange and asbestos. From Judge Weinstein, Buell drew the lesson that nothing is too complex or too big. These people committing the crimes weren't smarter than you; they, too, had to learn it all at some point.[11]

But it always helped to have some expertise on hand. So Caldwell recruited Tom Hanusik from Main Justice. Hanusik, an SEC enforcement lawyer in the mid-1990s, had a knack for financial investigation. He loved combing through complicated documents and identifying dodgy deals. With the addition of one other prosecutor, the team—smart, young, ambitious, and energetic—was set. They were all intimidated to take on a fraud so sprawling and complex. Eventually the Enron Task Force would have about forty FBI agents and an average of ten prosecutors assigned to it full-time, bringing cases over the next half decade.

At least to the public, the task force didn't get going fast enough. The prosecutors anticipated that Enron's defense lawyers would argue the company may have been aggressive but had technically adhered to the law. The defense would point out that lawyers and accountants blessed the company's actions. Indeed, that was true. Prosecutors needed to move cautiously. They had to sift through the complexities to find the potential crimes. However, the public and the press did not understand or sympathize.[12] The press assailed the government for moving too slowly and letting the perpetrators walk. CNN's Lou Dobbs, then one of the most influential business journalists, started running an Iran-hostage-like daily count noting there hadn't been Enron indictments. The CNBC show *Kudlow & Cramer* would ask, Who is in the pokey? Buell saw cohost Larry Kudlow spout some nonsense about how this case should be as easy as locking up someone for dealing drugs on a street corner. Jeffrey Toobin, CNN's legal analyst, swung the other way. Explaining how difficult it was to make white-collar cases, he predicted that neither Skilling nor Lay would go to prison.[13] Tom Daschle, the Senate majority leader, called on the Justice Department to explain why it hadn't indicted anyone.[14]

When prosecutors turned lower-level executives or pressed seemingly tangential cases, the media would report as if the investigations into Skilling and Lay had stalled. But the talking heads misunderstood what was going on. The prosecution team was moving deliberately, moving the lower-level cases to build the evidence to go after the top Enron officers. Privately, team members wondered, Would they get there?

They would. Though the trials were long, arduous, but full of good breaks, prosecutors won guilty verdicts against the key architects of the Enron fraud through working three main witnesses: Delainey, Fastow, and company treasurer Ben Glisan Jr. They were the government's best witnesses, its Virgils through the labyrinthine off-balance-sheet deals and accounting shenanigans. The investigators and prosecutors would rely on dozens of executives, victims, experts, witnesses, and countless documents to prove their cases beyond a reasonable doubt. But the government needed Glisan, Delainey, and Fastow. Without all three, the Enron Task Force likely would have failed.

Prosecutors took a different path to work each of the three: Delainey cooperated in a traditional fashion, in exchange for leniency; Fastow reached a nontraditional agreement in which he cooperated without receiving a reduced sentence; Glisan cooperated reluctantly but voluntarily while serving time.

## THE FASTOW FLIP

The outside world was helping the government, providing a road map for the prosecutors. Journalists were breaking stories. The Enron board of directors had ordered an internal investigation into what had caused the collapse. The three-person panel of independent directors, headed up by William Powers Jr., the dean of the University of Texas Law School, came out with its report on February 1, 2002, only two months after the bankruptcy. The report detailed the self-dealing at Enron, the dubious transactions, and the lax oversight, blistering top management.

The first big case the Enron Task Force brought, in March 2002, was against Arthur Andersen, Enron's accounting firm, for obstruction of justice. The case consumed Caldwell, Weissmann, and Buell. Meanwhile, Tom Hanusik could work in relative peace to start building Enron cases. In the Powers report, Hanusik saw an intriguing reference to how a British investment bank, NatWest (National Westminster), had helped in a suspicious Enron transaction. He retrieved the emails behind the deal and saw right off how damning they were. They outlined NatWest's effort to help Fastow and Michael Kopper, his young right-hand man, create an off-balance-sheet entity to hide Enron debt.

By the summer of 2002, he had charged three NatWest bankers with wire fraud in the first of many Enron cases, seeking their extradition. To outside observers, it seemed tangential. But Hanusik understood he was essentially publishing a banner headline in a newspaper meant for one man. His message came through. The young Kopper read where Hanusik's investigation was leading. Just three weeks later, Kopper came in. Hanusik had scored the first Enron cooperator. Kopper would help the Enron Task Force start building its case against Fastow. But there was another important signal from the case, a message sent by the indictment of Arthur

Andersen as well: prosecutors weren't going just after Enron executives. They were going after the bankers and accountants who enabled Enron. These prosecutors understood the ecosystem of corporate fraud.

On August 21, 2002, Kopper entered into a plea deal for up to fifteen years. (He was later sentenced to three years and a month.) The deal created a way to get to Fastow, the most obvious target for initial investigation. Fastow had been a wunderkind, rising to become Enron's CFO in his thirties. He was the mastermind behind the most troubling aspects of the Enron frauds: its off-balance-sheet vehicles. In October 2002 the task force indicted Fastow. He pleaded not guilty.

Larry Thompson, the deputy attorney general, and Robert Mueller, the FBI director, held a press conference to celebrate the accomplishment. Thompson laid out his approach in clear and simple terms, not heard often in the constipated confines of an official Washington media gathering. "Our strategy is really straightforward. We aim to put the bad guys in prison and take away their money," he said.[15]

Skilling and Lay were blaming Fastow for the corporation's fraud and collapse, like parents who leave the keys to the liquor cabinet when they go away for a weekend and then blame the teenagers for getting drunk. The task force scoffed. But the executives' position helped them. They knew Fastow's cooperation would be necessary to get Skilling and Lay.

Over the course of the next several months after they indicted him, Fastow stayed as mute as a mob soldier, despite all the damning evidence the task force had assembled on him. The government needed to bring more pressure. Weissmann, with Caldwell's nod, metaphorically put a drill to his knees. On May 1, 2003, the task force indicted Fastow's wife, Lea, charging her with filing a false income tax return. Both Fastows faced the prospect of being in prison and away from their young children. Lea came from a prominent Houston family. She had lost her reputation and standing. Now she stood to lose her liberty.

Fastow wasn't so insensate that he didn't care about his wife. He came in. His lawyer John Keker was a profane and argumentative legend who ran his own boutique practice. Keker sometimes screamed and swore at the prosecutors. True to her style, Caldwell remained calm and let him run on like a three-year-old until he tired himself out. Keker proclaimed he never allowed any of his clients to cooperate. Of course, if it served their interest, he would. For Fastow, it did.

On January 14, 2004, more than two years after Enron declared bankruptcy, prosecutors struck an uncommon deal. Both Fastows pleaded guilty. Andrew pleaded guilty to one count of conspiracy to commit wire fraud and one count of conspiracy to commit wire and securities fraud. He pledged to forfeit tens of millions of dollars and to no longer seek the millions in compensation he claimed Enron owed him. Vitally, Fastow stated that other top executives shared his culpability:

> I and other members of Enron's senior management fraudulently manipulated Enron's publicly reported financial results. Our purpose was to mislead investors and others about the true financial position of Enron and, consequently, to inflate artificially the price of Enron's stock and maintain fraudulently Enron's credit rating.[16]

Fastow agreed to a ten-year sentence. The agreement stipulated he would not request a reduced sentence, even if he were particularly cooperative with prosecutors. To impugn the prosecution's witnesses, defense attorneys highlight the leniency deals witnesses have received to persuade the jury they are likely self-serving liars. Caldwell, Weissmann, and Buell's agreement with Fastow blunted the defense's ability to argue that Fastow was lying about Skilling and Lay in order to get off more easily. Eventually the judge would sentence him to only six years in prison.

## THE GLISAN GAMBIT

Kathy Ruemmler, the young up-and-coming star, joined the task force after Fastow's indictment but before his plea deal. Getting the CFO was great, but they needed much more evidence to bring Skilling and Lay to justice. She and Buell flipped Delainey in September 2003. When he stopped lying and came around, they worked his information for a month before he pleaded guilty. She and Buell reached a traditional cooperating witness arrangement with him: He did so in exchange for a deal to keep the charges minimal. Ruemmler could worry that the defense would attack the deal later. For now, she and Buell had to drain Delainey of everything he knew, which was plenty about Skilling. The key for the Enron prosecutors—for prosecutors of any white-collar crime—was to keep the pressure on. Nobody knew who the Feds were interviewing. Nobody knew who was talking and who wasn't. The day Delainey pleaded, Skilling transferred $10 million to O'Melveny & Myers, his defense firm.

"Good," thought Ruemmler. "He understands exactly how much danger he's in."

The final one of the big three, Enron treasurer Ben Glisan, cooperated in a different fashion: reluctantly. On September 10, 2003, Glisan pleaded guilty. He went straight to prison for his five-year sentence, the first former Enron executive to be locked up. Glisan wouldn't cooperate. He wanted no agreement. Instead, he said he would do his time. He made a decision that his children were young, and if he had to be sent away, he wanted to serve now rather than after a protracted legal battle.

Glisan's position at Enron was so important, he could be a font of damning evidence—if he wanted to be. So prosecutor Andrew Weissmann gambled. Just a few months into his sentence, Weissmann brought Glisan from prison to put him in front of the grand jury. Ruemmler marveled. All the young team members did. It was ballsy, because Weissmann had no indication that Glisan would be helpful. The move carried a huge risk: Glisan might offer testimony exonerating Skilling or Lay. And it would all be on the record for the grand jury.

A *Houston Chronicle* reporter guarded the grand jury every day. Prosecutors didn't want Glisan's presence before the grand jury to leak. US marshals snuck him in through a back door in his green jumpsuit. Weissmann immunized him from further prosecution, but that was the extent of the deal. He would have to serve his prison time no matter what he said. Then the task force deputy director started in with his questions, right in front of the grand jury. Would Glisan understand all he had to do was tell the truth? He did. He was candid. Weissmann put him on the stand for days. Glisan was fantastic.

Each evening after the sessions, the team went out to dinner. Ruemmler couldn't believe what Glisan was saying in court. He understood every deal. He could place Skilling and Lay in the room during crucial conversations. "Shit, I have to go talk to this guy," she said. Weismann beamed. Glisan would later be a star witness in both the Ken Lay trial and Ruemmler's other trial against Merrill Lynch executives who had allegedly helped Enron disguise a loan as revenue, known as the Nigerian barge trial. (The deal had taken place off the coast of the African country.) Glisan would be immunized at both.

The Nigerian barge trial was delayed till the fall of 2004. Ruemmler and an FBI agent rented a cheap Buick to go see Glisan in prison. Kathy had never seen a car with chillers on the seat to keep the driver cool in the Texas summer. Bastrop Federal Correctional Institution, a low-security prison, sits a couple hours from Houston. When she approached the gray, sprawling compound, surrounded by barbed wire and huge floodlights, Ruemmler thought, "Every prosecutor should spend a lot of time in prisons." They should know where they were sending people and how serious it was to strip them of their liberty.

Prisoners don't want to be snitches. Ruemmler's meeting with Glisan had to be secretive. The prison concocted a cover story to get the former Enron executive out of his cell and sneak him into the warden's office. Dressed in his olive drab prison garb, he was nervous. But the former company treasurer soon relaxed and became introspective, though never bitter. He wasn't overly helpful or ingratiating, nor too eager or vindictive. Ruemmler and Buell came to respect him, impressed by his recall and command of detail.

Glisan was a patient teacher. He had kept careful notebooks of all of his meetings and deals. Ruemmler went through every entry with him. It was trial gold. He corroborated everything. Glisan would go over a certain Enron off-balance-sheet vehicle. It was maddeningly complicated. Finally, Ruemmler would exclaim, "I get it!" The next morning, she'd wake up and realize she no longer understood it anymore. She'd need another session. She knew she'd never have to go into this level of detail at trial, but the defense team had their knives at the ready for evisceration if her jury-friendly version was so dumbed down that it was even slightly wrong.

Glisan had damning information on Skilling. But more important, he had damning information about Lay. He made the Enron Task Force feel confident enough to bring a case against Enron's founder. On July 7, 2004, the Enron Task Force indicted Lay, charging him with eleven counts, including securities fraud and making false statements. He pleaded not guilty, calling a press conference to proclaim his innocence and portray himself as a victim of the fraud. Andrew Fastow had betrayed his trust "and betrayed it very, very badly," he said. "There is no CEO that I'm aware of" who could possibly know about every decision lower-level employees make. They rely on the advice of lawyers, bankers, and accountants. "Now, there may be some superman somewhere that thinks they know everything going on in their company in every department, in every level, in every country, and every employee. But I think that would be very unrealistic."[17]

Top corporate executives would continue to make versions of this argument for the next decade, especially in the wake of the 2008 financial crisis. Ignorance equaled innocence. Lay's defense might have worked if prosecutors had charged him with masterminding Enron's accounting frauds. But they were too smart and built a different case.

## THE DARK PERIOD

By the second half of 2004, the young prosecutors of the Enron Task Force faced tough times. Leslie Caldwell had left the team in the spring. Sam Buell left as well. He had never moved from Boston, getting on a plane every week for two years. His second child was born while he was working the case. He regretted barely seeing her.

Disarray started to cost the team. Sean Berkowitz, a prosecutor on the team, and Ruemmler were exhausted. Sometimes they doubted they would ever be able to bring the big cases. There were no smoking guns. Would juries buy their theory? They both entertained leaving the task force. Then, in mid-2005, Weissmann beat them to it, announcing his resignation. Berkowitz was appointed director. He asked Ruemmler to be his deputy. The two were stuck in the task force and stuck with a mess. For all of his brilliance and gutsiness, Weissmann had been no manager. Roles weren't defined. The task force had no focus as it was trying to prepare for the big trials of Skilling and Lay. The prosecution teams weren't even set.

Berkowitz had joined in December 2003, shortly after Ruemmler came on board. Thirty-six at the time, he had been going through a bad patch. A graduate of Harvard Law School, he had spent the last five years working in the Chicago US Attorney's Office, most recently for US Attorney Patrick Fitzgerald. But he was getting divorced from his wife, a prosecutor in the same office. Desperate to get out, he went to Fitzgerald to see if there was anywhere he could go. Fitzgerald recommended him for the Enron team. Berkowitz had little familiarity with Enron or the investigation, but he had some corporate prosecution experience. He took it.

Weissmann had resigned during the trial of executives from Enron's broadband unit. It wasn't going well. Enron had created a division to market broadband Internet service. It was unsuccessful in reality but profitable on paper, because Enron booked revenue and earnings right when it signed a deal, long before the actual money came through. Early on, the task force had devoted significant resources and people to probing the broadband unit. That expenditure of money and time looked good on July 30, 2004, when Ken Rice, the CEO of the unit, pleaded guilty to one count of securities fraud. The next month, the chief operating officer of the unit pleaded guilty.

The task force had also charged five executives of its broadband unit for overstating the strength of the division's business. On April 18, 2005, the trial of the five executives began. It dragged on for months. Members of the prosecution team—which didn't include Berkowitz or Ruemmler—clashed. They got bogged down in debates about the viability of the technology.

In July the jury acquitted the executives on some counts and got hung on the rest. The judge declared a mistrial.

Now director, Berkowitz, normally calm and congenial, felt spooked. Cases that had looked like fortresses began to appear vulnerable. The sprawling defense teams kept filing motion after motion, loosing their catapults. He and Ruemmler realized they didn't have enough people and help. The resource deprivation was inexplicable. How could the department have set up this team with such public celebration but not given them the tools to win?

The FBI had an ancient document management system. Task force prosecutors had to call up the FBI, ask it to search a term, and wait. Three days later, they'd get the documents—usually. Enron was both the first massive electronic discovery investigation and the last of the old style, with paper discovery, manual searches, and files in cabinets. After one such failed search, Ruemmler reamed out the FBI agents and then came into Berkowitz's office and slumped in a chair.

"What's the matter? Why can't they handle it, Berko?"

All Berkowitz could think was, "When is this going to end?"

They needed to alert the higher-ups. Berkowitz and Ruemmler went over to Main Justice to meet with John Richter, the acting head of the criminal division. They sat in a windowless conference room. Sean and Kathy beseeched him.

"We are going to lose this case and lose it spectacularly," Ruemmler warned.

"Okay, okay, I hear you," Richter said. "What do you need?"

"Everything," Berkowitz said.

They rattled off their requests: document support, graphics support, trial support. They needed a jury consultant. They needed more bodies to deal with all the defense motions. The defense would motion to change the venue, citing experts and polling data. Were they supposed to stand up there with nothing in response and say, "That's wrong. Trust us, Judge"?

Berkowitz and Ruemmler also analyzed what had gone wrong with the broadband trial. A defense attorney summed it up: "Never prosecute a complex, overreaching 192-count case in midsummer in Houston, Texas, against a passel of good lawyers."[18] From now on, the task force would keep it simple. Prove everything and drop anything you can't. Try to prevent the defense from getting down into the detailed muck that puts jurors to sleep. They were such common, obvious mistakes but so easy to make. Prosecutors did it all the time.

Berkowitz focused the task force. The priority was the big trials. Weissmann had wanted to do everything, to take every case, to bask in the publicity. Now they just needed to focus on bringing Skilling and Lay to justice.

## THE CASE AGAINST SKILLING

The government had less evidence against Lay than Skilling and had brought lesser charges. Ruemmler and her team headed up the cases against Skilling and Richard Causey, Enron's chief accounting officer. She didn't want the Lay case stapled to it. The Causey and Skilling cases cohered. The two executives had engaged in a conspiracy to commit securities fraud between December 1998 and December 2001. The problem was that Lay wasn't CEO for the entire period. He had founded the company but then ceded the operation to Skilling in February 2001. He had come back in August 2001, when the company turned from darling to joke, the stock was dropping, and the business was crumbling. In the period before that, Lay had been the chairman of the company, but he wasn't an engaged leader.

Finally, the team realized Skilling and Lay had to go together. The cases had many of the same witnesses. The prosecutorial strategy would be to show how senior management conspired, as Lay took over the lies from his protégé. Berkowitz brought Ruemmler around. They planned to try the top three officials at the same time.

Worried about the weakness in the Lay case, the Enron Task Force layered on the charges against him. In doing so, they made a small mistake that would have significant consequences for corporate white-collar prosecutions in the coming years. The prosecutors wanted to explain to the jury that Lay had lied to his employees. It was an easy-to-understand charge: he was saying one thing publicly but another privately. When he made a big show of buying Enron stock for his own account, he told the public he was a net buyer of the stock. But he had an undisclosed plan to sell portions of his Enron shares on a regular basis. And he was selling more than he was buying. Lay had committed securities fraud.

Prosecutors charged Lay with another crime in addition to securities fraud. Public officials have a duty to provide citizens with their "honest services." They deprive the public of their honest services when they take bribes or kickbacks or engage in deals to enrich themselves. In the 1970s and 1980s, prosecutors had begun to apply the same standard to executives of publicly traded companies. The honest-services charge, a part of the mail and wire fraud statutes, was useful. In basic frauds, the criminal steals from the victim. But there are whole categories, such as bribery or kickback schemes, in which criminals might enrich themselves that don't involve direct theft. The victim is the employer or the public, which has an intangible right to honesty. Prosecutors liked the charge because juries grasped it easily. They could explain that executives had a duty to do their best for their shareholders, to take the best deal they could and not to enrich themselves at the shareholders' expense.

The government charged that Lay, in pumping up morale with his deceptions about the state of Enron's health while selling secretly, had deprived Enron's employees and shareholders of his honest services. Adding honest-services fraud was overkill. The government's other charges were sufficient. But the prosecutors sought to bring overwhelming force, which would ultimately expose the government to mistakes.

Adding the honest-services charge to Lay meant adding it to Skilling, too. They had no way of knowing, but the gamble would later cost the Department of Justice. In 2010 the Supreme Court would reverse that part of the sentence, determining that the government used the honest-services charge too broadly. In doing so, the highest court stripped prosecutors of a significant weapon for battling corporate fraudsters.

## FUCK YOUR FIREARMS TRAINING

On May 27, 2005, for his thirty-eighth birthday, Sean Berkowitz ran a ten-mile race. As he ran, he reflected on the crazy year, but he could see the finish line. By the time his next birthday came, the trial would be done. "We will have won or lost, but either way, it will be over," he thought.

The weeks up to the trials were tense. The prosecutors moved to Houston and lived in cheap corporate apartments. They barely slept. One day, an exhausted Ruemmler walked over to ask an FBI agent to join a meeting the next day. He said he couldn't do it because he had firearms practice. What? What?!? Ruemmler walked over to the bullpen, where all the FBI agents were piled on top of each other in their cramped cubicles. She stood at the hinge of their L-shaped room so everyone could see her. Color rose on her neck.

"Everyone listen the fuck up!" she yelled. The agents looked up.

"You think this is a big fucking case? Do you? This is the biggest fucking case of your lifetimes! This is the biggest corporate fraud in US history! The whole fucking world is watching this trial. There are no dentist appointments. There is no Christmas. There isn't firearms training, okay?" Ruemmler asked if they would like her to call Bob Mueller, the head of the FBI, to see what he thought of their firearms training. If any of them left any thread unexplored and lost, she warned, that person would regret it for the rest of his life.

Berkowitz sat there smiling. It was Ruemmler's *Glengarry Glen Ross* moment. The FBI agents, tough guys, were cowed and impressed. The head of the group screamed back, "This is bullshit! We are working our asses off, Kathy, and you know it!" But no one took off for firearms practice or anything else until the trial was over.

Berkowitz and Ruemmler figured the defense strategy would be to argue that prosecutors were criminalizing aggressive business decisions. The Enron refrain was that the government was attacking the company for its innovations and risk taking. Executives liked to say, "You can always tell who the pioneers are, because they're the ones with arrows in their backs."[19]

They also understood that the defense would want to drag them into the boring arcana during the trial. The defense team longed for nothing more than long debates between expert witnesses about accounting standards. To counter the my-eyes-glaze-over defense, the team focused on the Big Lie. The stories Skilling and Lay told about Enron publicly were different from reality. They used everything—every witness, every piece of evidence—to reinforce that narrative of duplicity. Even the trial graphics reflected the distinctions between what the executives told the world and what they knew to be the truth.

Berkowitz and Ruemmler and the team set about ridding the trial of anything debatable. They reduced the witness list to sixty-two from seventy-nine and trimmed counts against Skilling.[20] If something Enron had done smelled wrong but could be depicted as just a bad business decision, they excised it. They concentrated all their energy on the gut punches—actions everyone would agree were wrong. Berkowitz, in one of his highest moments, had discovered a perfect example. During the crucial second quarter of 2000, Enron had been a penny short on the earnings-per-share estimates. Missing by a penny would be a calamity for the stock. Shareholders expected Enron to outdistance estimates by miles, not fall short. Berkowitz had gone to Enron headquarters to look at the corporate ledger. Sure enough, right in the corporate books was a reserve that had been whited out after the close of the quarter. A $21 million reserve had been changed to $14 million and then to $7 million. Skilling had needed the earnings to make the number. Berkowitz had found a key piece of evidence of crimes.

The cases were going well now. On the eve of the trial, they got a big break: Causey, the former chief accounting officer, capitulated, pleading guilty. Berkowitz and Ruemmler celebrated. The case against Causey, while crushing, was full of detail and arcana. Now they could drop a ton of material from the trial. They met for six hours and went through everything they could. They cut out evidence, mourning the loss of some of their favorite pieces of research. They had a perfect, clear fraud with an off-balance-sheet entity called Mariner Energy. To meet earnings estimates one quarter, Enron had raised the value of the asset even though nothing had changed with the underlying business. It was just a pure accounting maneuver.

"Can we tie this to Skilling and Lay?" Berkowitz asked.

"No," sighed Ruemmler.

"It's gone," he said.

Then Ruemmler and Berkowitz and the prosecutors asked an audacious question: Could they get away with not even putting Andrew Fastow on the stand? Fastow could be expected to deliver damning accounts of Skilling's and Lay's complicity. No one knew the dodginess of the off-balance-sheet arrangements better than the former chief financial officer. Who better to refute that Fastow was the sole mastermind than Fastow? On the other hand, he came across as a creep. That mop of hair and boyish insouciance! Ruemmler couldn't stand being in the same room with him. The defense team would find him so easy to attack. He was an admitted liar; the principal schemer. It was so easy to imagine a jury turning against him. Then again, if they didn't put him on the stand for at least a bit, it might look strange—as if they were hiding something. They finally decided to have him testify but briefly, reducing his role at trial to the minimum.

After that meeting, what would have been a seven-month trial became a four-month trial. Crucially, the Enron Task Force had stripped out any evidence or testimony that didn't involve Lay and Skilling. Had Berkowitz and Ruemmler left that material in the trial plan, the defense would have been able to argue that if Lay and Skilling didn't know about that, how could the jury be so confident that the top officials knew about the other bad deals?

Even with all their preparation, they had to worry about the jury. Every jury is a fickle beast. Lay was a friendly old grandpa, with a goofy smile, godliness on his sleeve, and as Texan as they come. Skilling was everyone's idea of a businessman in a country that worships tycoons. On the other side, Berkowitz was a northerner, a bulldog, with a big, prominent brow set in a scowl. And he was named Berkowitz. The other lead prosecutor who would be doing the trial with them, the ramrod John Hueston, just seemed to have a way of pissing off everyone. Ruemmler had a better shot with that room. She was a Texas-approved blonde and favored high heels. But would that Houston jury go for a lady lawyer grilling Lay?

On January 30, 2006, more than four years after Enron had collapsed, the Lay and Skilling trial began. In late February, about four weeks into the trial, Dave Delainey took the stand. Ruemmler had known him for years now. She knew he would be calm and credible. Skilling had viewed him as a candidate to be CEO of the company at one point.[21] As she hoped and predicted, he was the strongest government witness yet. He admitted his own wrongdoing. He told the jurors that Enron played "fast and loose" with the accounting rules, testifying that Skilling attended meetings where they hid losses and rigged the numbers. He told them how when he had objected to one attempt to hide losses in an executive meeting, Skilling fixed on him and asked, "What do you want to do?"

The judge in the trial had allowed the lawyers to roam around the courtroom. Ruemmler got close to the jury box, almost touching the bar. She asked, "What did you take that to mean?"

"Get in line," Delainey said. It was the worst thing he'd ever been a part of, he said. "I wish on my kids' lives I could have got up and stepped away from the table that day."[22]

Ruemmler paused, sneaking a look at the twelve jurors, so close to her. Having listened to so much complexity and tedium, they grasped it. She had her black-and-white, right-and-wrong moment. Delainey might as well have said, "That's when I knew we were committing a crime."

Enron was not a volatile trading shop, Skilling had told the public. Ruemmler brought on Delainey to destroy that notion, and he did. He testified that Enron's wholesale energy unit's trading gains and losses swung wildly. The unit had lost $551 million in one day in late 2000, a sum that exceeded the unit's entire profits from the previous year. Earlier that same month, it had made $485 million in a day.[23] In what may have been the most damaging anecdote, Delainey testified about the time he told

Skilling that his retail energy trading unit had created up to $300 million in "reserves": money stashed away for future use. Skilling, Delainey said, came over and hugged him.[24] Delainey fingered Lay as well, telling jurors he had told the chairman about how he was hiding losses of its retail energy line in its wholesale division.

As Ruemmler expected, Delainey stood up well on cross-examination. Skilling's defense lawyers tried to emphasize that no one had used the word *fraud*; that these business decisions were inherently ambiguous and subject to judgment. Delainey wouldn't have it. "Everyone in that room knew exactly what was going on," he insisted.

John Hueston took the lead in the Lay trial. He had rescued the Lay investigation, shifting toward examining the CEO's misleading statements as Enron faced the crisis of shareholder confidence in the summer and fall of 2001.[25] Still, the case against Lay was weaker, leading to tension on the trial team. Hueston and the other prosecutor working the case weren't getting along. Some on the team felt Hueston didn't take direction or suggestions well. He had a chin-up bar in his office and a sign that read "Play like a champion today." As he left his office, he'd jump up and hit it.

During the trial, even the judge seemed to take an open dislike to Hueston. He was a crack trial lawyer and had built a convincing case, but people on the team worried about the Lay case. The agents often teased Ruemmler that she was obsessed with Skilling and neglected Lay. Now an FBI agent came up to Ruemmler to beg, "Can you please mention Mr. Lay?" during one of her rounds with another witness. After she did, the FBI team sent her flowers, in sympathy for how tough it must have been for her. Ruemmler and Berkowitz prayed that good evidence and Hueston's intelligence and skills would triumph over any irritation the jury might feel.

The cornerstone of a successful white-collar defense is putting the accused on the stand. The jury wants to hear from defendants, to take their measure. The team knew they would have to crack Lay's and Skilling's manicured personas. The Lay PR team was rolling. To generate sympathy, Lay's wife, Linda, went on the *Today* show. Weeping, she told America that she and Ken had "lost everything" and were "fighting for liquidity."

The Lays were still living in a $7 million Houston penthouse and owned $20 million in other real estate at the time.[26]

Lay had the better shot of beating the government. Not only had he been removed from the details and not been active at the company at the time the bulk of the crimes were committed, but he had also been charged with fewer crimes. The prosecutors and the media expected Skilling to be short-tempered, easily rattled. He had a bullying streak. One time in the hallways, he passed Ruemmler and snarled, "Figured out the business yet, Kathy?"[27]

But the jury didn't see that Jeffrey Skilling. On the stand, he was authoritative and precise, parrying prosecutors calmly. The trial ordeal wore more on the older man. When Lay took the stand, he was arrogant and querulous. At one point, he even barked at his own lawyer, George McCall Secrest Jr., "Where are you going with this, Mr. Secrest?"

On cross-examination, Lay was even worse. Hueston raised his conflicts of interest. Lay hadn't disclosed an investment in a company owned by an ex-girlfriend of Skilling's. He had unloaded tens of millions of shares of Enron stock. His defense was that he was meeting margin calls, but Hueston showed he could have met those in other ways. And Hueston homed in on how Lay had called government witnesses, accusing him of tampering.[28] Lay was infuriated. The jury took note.

In late March 2006, about eight weeks into the trial, Ruemmler brought on Ben Glisan, the former treasurer, as her closer. All of the prosecutors suffered frayed nerves and little sleep. Right before Glisan's testimony, one of Hueston's team came up to Ruemmler to request that she ask the witness about some complicated accounting issues. She had enough to handle as it was. It had taken her months to master the accounting material she was planning to cover. Now this? But Glisan was the Christmas tree: all the team members wanted to hang their last piece of evidence on him.

"Are you fucking kidding me?" she screamed.

"It's no big deal!" yelled the other prosecutor.

"You are out of your mind."

Berkowitz, ever calm, mediated. They decided she would ask him some limited questions about the topic.

As Ruemmler expected, Glisan was an excellent witness. He put Lay and Skilling in damning meetings, identifying their incriminating admissions. Glisan buried Lay. He said he told Lay and the company's finance committee that the company's liquidity was "strained"—that Enron was having trouble funding its ongoing operations. The next day, Lay told employees at a companywide meeting that Enron's fundamentals were the "strongest they have ever been" and that liquidity was "strong." Glisan testified that Fastow warned Lay that the company would need to be restructured or sold. Five days later, Lay told *BusinessWeek* magazine that the company was "probably in the strongest and best shape it's ever been."

Ruemmler looked over at Lay and saw him seething, redder than a sunburned rancher. Lay's lawyer would deride Glisan as a "trained monkey," but the jury was siding with the monkey.

Berkowitz's mother came to visit and to watch the closing arguments. In the evening, after the defense's summation, she came to his office. He noticed that she was following him around.

"Sean," she said, "they made a lot of good points today."

"I know, Mom."

"Sean, there's a lot riding on this," she said.

"Yes, I know, Mom."

"Sean," she said. She paused. "I'm worried."

"Mom, I've got this!"

His mother needn't have worried. The government had put on a devastating trial. It was easy for the jury. After jurors deliberated for six days, Lay was found guilty on all counts against him; Skilling was convicted on nineteen of twenty-eight counts.

Lay was self-righteous to the end, declaring his innocence, wrapping himself in the mantle of religion. He also told the press and supporters gathered outside the courtroom, "I have a very warm and loving and Christian family . . . Most of all, we believe that God, in fact, is in control, and indeed, he does work all things for good for those who love the Lord. And we love our Lord."

• • •

Enron was the most spectacular corporate implosion of the period. The government had, in fits and starts, done its job. The Justice Department had made the case a priority, allocating just enough money, resources, and people to the task. The team knew it had to flip executives and not rely solely on documents. Prosecutors came and went from the team, but the team's focus stayed the same, so it could weather departures. The team members had investigated aggressively, keeping maximum pressure on the targets such as Fastow. They took risks, as with Glisan. They were persistent, not giving up when Delainey stonewalled them in the first two meetings. They went after not just Enron executives but also their enablers on Wall Street and the company's accountants. The task force overcame losses, learning to run trials better. It focused on simple and clean story lines, and created a model for complex white-collar investigative and prosecutorial work. Houston's economy recovered, and American corporate accounting had a period of relative cleanliness.

But the Enron prosecutions led to a weaker Justice Department. After the Enron prosecutions came a backlash against aggressive government action, led by corporations and the defense bar. The courts overturned several Enron verdicts. The Justice Department began to lose the institutional knowledge necessary to bring such complicated corporate cases successfully. The DOJ would turn against task forces, forgetting the Enron successes. It would not centralize decision making. Prosecutors began settling with corporations. The Justice Department steered away from going after the enablers of corporate fraud: bankers and accountants. By 2016, the Justice Department did not approach cases the way it had with Enron. Its ability to hold corporate executives accountable for their actions suffered as a result.

The most unfortunate lesson learned from the Enron Task Force experience came from its first success. The team's first victory in court was its most consequential. The business lobby, the defense bar, and even today's Justice Department came to believe that the government had made a grave mistake. It had convicted Arthur Andersen.

## *Chapter Two*

# "THAT DOG DON'T HUNT"

BEFORE THE ENRON TRIALS—BEFORE KATHY Ruemmler and Sean Berkowitz joined the task force—just as the team was created, Michael Chertoff, the head of the criminal division at Main Justice, assigned its first case: Arthur Andersen. Andersen, one of the remaining Big Five accounting firms, had audited Enron's books. In the fall of 2001, Andersen employees destroyed documents to cover up how enmeshed the two companies were. Congressional hearings revealed documents related to the Andersen shredding. The media attacked the story like white blood cells ganging up on a diseased organ. The Justice Department realized it had to investigate. Chertoff called up Leslie Caldwell, the head of the task force, to tell her to work the Andersen angle as hard as she could.[1] After several weeks of work, the Department of Justice concluded that the government could prosecute the storied and stalwart accounting firm. The task force wanted to avoid such a serious move if it could. On Sunday, March 3, 2002, Arthur Andersen executives and its legion of lawyers came to meet

Chertoff and the Enron team to encourage this line of thinking: please go easy.

Such meetings have rituals. The principals on both sides bring large retinues. The defense team comes as a supplicant and does most of the talking. The important meetings happen in windowless conference rooms with austere and formal furniture and lined with law tomes that haven't been cracked. This Sunday conference took place at the Robert F. Kennedy Building in Washington, a white neoclassical pile with Art Deco flourishes that takes up the block between Pennsylvania and Constitution Avenues and Ninth and Tenth Streets.

Andersen's CEO Joseph Berardino rushed back from a business trip to Japan to join his lawyers for the meeting. But he wasn't the lead orator for the company's performance. That role fell to Robert Fiske Jr., a renowned former US attorney for the Southern District of New York. Fiske, then seventy-one, worked at the New York law firm Davis Polk & Wardwell, the grayest graybeard on the Andersen side. They did not come more patrician than Fiske.

Chertoff, then forty-eight, belonged to the generation behind Fiske, but they had similar pedigrees and prosecutorial experience. Despite Chertoff's Ivy League education (Harvard College and Law School degrees and a Supreme Court clerkship), he cultivated an image as a tough guy. Talking him out of an idea shared odds with finding a clean politician from his home state of New Jersey. *One L,* Scott Turow's semifictional account of attending the first year of Harvard Law, depicted a student, modeled after Chertoff, who engaged in an argument with a professor for two days straight. Tall, with dark rings around his eyes and thin cheeks, Chertoff had the forbidding look of the Sam the Eagle Muppet.

As a US prosecutor in New Jersey in the early 1990s, he had overseen the Crazy Eddie corporate fraud case, one of the biggest corporate scandals of its time. Run by Eddie and Sam Antar, Crazy Eddie was a discount electronics chain with a famous TV pitchman touting prices that were "INSANE!" But the Antars had been falsifying the company's inventory and its books. Before working that case, Chertoff had, as an assistant in the Southern District in the mid-1980s, spearheaded several cases against the New York Cosa Nostra, including the Mafia Commission trial that included crime bosses "Big Paul" Castellano and "Fat Tony" Salerno as initial defendants. When Chertoff was promoted, Salerno cracked that Chertoff owed him a thank-you note.[2] In 2001 he became Bush's first head of the Justice Department's criminal division.

When Chertoff had been at the Southern District in the mid-1980s, his boss, Rudolph Giuliani, had introduced the "perp walk" to the white-collar world. FBI agents frog-marched Wall Street Masters of the Universe off the trading room floor in handcuffs, their pictures snapped by waiting news photographers. Deterring corporate crime, Giuliani believed, began by making the penalties personal.

But in the decade between the Michael Milken and Ivan Boesky insider trading and the stock manipulation scandals and prosecutions of late 1980s and the 2000s, the Department of Justice had begun a subtle shift in its approach to corporate crime. Prosecutors began to believe it wasn't enough to go after individuals. They saw that corruption ran all through Drexel Burnham Lambert, Milken's investment banking firm. They indicted Drexel; the company went out of business. Rotten corporations were not different from Mafia organizations. They could corrupt an honest person.

Fiske and his right-hand man, Denis McInerney, attended the Justice Department meeting to prove otherwise. They presented their case, pointing out that only a small group of employees had destroyed documents. The wrongdoing was isolated. If the Justice Department indicted the firm, the Davis Polk lawyers said, Andersen would go out of business. "Death, death, death," Fiske intoned. Chertoff scoffed. He reminded the lawyers he'd been a mob prosecutor who'd taken on cases of actual life and death.[3] He asked, Would Andersen automatically lose licenses to operate if it were to be indicted? The Andersen lawyers looked at one another and then had to admit that, no, it wouldn't be automatic.

Arthur Andersen was not an ice cream company, unsophisticated about corporate investigations. It was in the business of working with large companies in litigation, for God's sake, Chertoff thought. Proper handling of documents was a core aspect of its business.

The firm was a recidivist as well, as Chertoff explained to Fiske and McInerney. Enron was not the only problematic Andersen client. The SEC had recently put Andersen on probation for past auditing negligence involving Waste Management, the garbage removal giant. The firm had pledged not to break the securities laws again. This time the penalty had to be severe. Chertoff told Andersen lawyers the Justice Department wouldn't take a deal without an admission of wrongdoing.

Gauging the response to its tough stance, Chertoff and his Enron Task Force were getting the sense that nobody on the Arthur Andersen team thought the government dared take the firm to trial. Chertoff, decisive and straightforward, never wrong and never in doubt, lectured Fiske and McInerney and the Andersen executives: "You guys were the auditor for the biggest accounting scandal in modern times. We can't let that go away. Don't doubt that we will take you to trial." Then Chertoff made a pronouncement. He wanted to make it clear that the evidence was devastating. He straightened and said, "If we take this case to trial, we are taking head shots."[4]

## "ALMOST INCOMPREHENSIBLE"

Arthur Andersen was built on a legend of stalwart midwestern ethics. Arthur Edward Andersen, a Northwestern University professor of accounting, founded the firm in Chicago in 1913. He drew its motto from his Norwegian mother: "Think straight, talk straight." In a story that would pass into firm lore, Andersen himself refused to change an accounting decision for a client, no matter how lucrative the business was. "There is not enough money in the city of Chicago," he is supposed to have said.

Over time, Andersen's consulting division began to grow faster than its auditing business. Consultants came to dominate the firm. Unglamorous auditors merely looked over a company's books. Consultants had lucrative relationships, sitting at the right hand of CEOs and advising them on strategy. The firm expected the number crunchers to push consulting business. Ethics receded. The firm's employees called themselves "Androids," a moniker that elevated fitting in and sacrificing for the company.[5] This conformity ameliorated Andersen's accounting standards.

Even before the stock market crash of 2000, investors and regulators worried about the bubble and accounting excesses. In 1998 President Bill Clinton's chairman of the SEC, Arthur Levitt, gave a speech titled "The Numbers Game," in which he declared, "We are witnessing an erosion in the quality of earnings and, therefore, the quality of financial reporting. Managing may be giving way to manipulation; integrity may be losing out to illusion." Levitt was particularly critical of the auditing profession. The industry was an oligopoly, with five big firms dominating the business of handling large corporations' books. The industry had no regulator. Instead, it shared a body of self-governance called the Public Oversight Board. In essence, they policed each other. Deloitte & Touche had only recently conducted a peer review of Arthur Andersen. The accounting firm emerged cleanly.[6]

Come March 2000, the dot-com boom that had taken up the last half of the 1990s came to a spectacular end. Stock market plunges reveal fraud. When the tide goes out, you get to see who is swimming naked, as Warren Buffett said famously. In the five years following the crash, thousands of companies restated their earnings.[7]

The SEC, struggling to deal with the volume of fiascos, started making noises about investigating the accounting industry. It asked the Public Oversight Board to investigate whether the firms kept auditors, who oversaw corporate books, independent from the consultants at the same firms, who advised companies on strategy. In response, in early May 2000 the industry stopped funding for the Oversight Board.[8]

The accounting profession had lost its way. Arthur Andersen was one of only five major accounting firms. While all of them had problem clients, the list that Andersen had compiled stood out for its length and variety. The company paid out more than $500 million to settle lawsuits between 1997 and 2002, much more than its fraternal accounting firms.[9] In 2002 alone, Andersen clients WorldCom, Sunbeam, Boston Chicken, and Qwest had to restate billions in earnings. In 1998, after revealing a massive financial fraud that falsely inflated its profits, Waste Management had to take what was then the largest restatement in corporate history: $1.7 billion.[10] Andersen had been its auditor.

The SEC settled its securities fraud investigation with Arthur Andersen and three partners years later, in June 2001, just months before Enron's bankruptcy. In the fashion of the regulatory time, the company did not admit anything (though it was prohibited from denying wrongdoing).

So egregious was the Waste Management scandal that the SEC sanctioned Andersen, too. The accounting firm entered into a consent decree—a binding agreement—permanently enjoining the firm from violating securities laws again. It was the first time the SEC had ever accused a top accounting firm of securities fraud because of bookkeeping failures.[11] The SEC found that Andersen partners had not only known that Waste Management's financial statements were inaccurate but also had enabled the company's financial shenanigans. During the SEC investigation, Andersen promoted one of the partners who had contributed most to helping the fraud, making him the firm's head of global risk management. In this role, he would write a new document retention policy that provided the framework for the later Enron file destruction. This policy stated that information gathered or considered in connection with Andersen work should be culled and "only essential information to support our conclusions should be retained."[12]

Astonishingly, Andersen kept Waste as a client, and Waste kept lavishing the firm with fees. In 2000, the year before Enron's collapse, the company paid Andersen $79 million in fees. Only after Enron imploded did Waste Management, not Andersen, sever the relationship.[13]

Andersen's wrongdoing had gone back years. In 1996 the firm faced the threat of criminal prosecution. But it settled federal charges over accounting fraud at Colonial Realty Co., a real estate company that had been looted by its partners. Earlier, Andersen received a light censure from the state of Connecticut, where Colonial was based, barring the firm from a narrow portion of its business activities in the state for two years. Punishments such as these were equivalent to a tossed snowball on a passing semi.[14]

In May 2001 the SEC charged Sunbeam's celebrity CEO, Al "Chainsaw" Dunlap, nicknamed for his relentless cost cutting, and an Andersen auditor with perpetrating a "massive financial fraud." The accounting games Sunbeam was playing, with Andersen's help, had come undone in the late 1990s. The company restated its earnings.[15]

Andersen faced thirteen major state and federal investigations over accounting frauds in the years before and just after Enron. Among them: McKessonHBOC, Global Crossing, Supercuts, and the Baptist Foundation of Arizona, then the largest bankruptcy of a nonprofit in history.[16]

Bernie Sanders, then the left-leaning congressman from Vermont, excoriated an Andersen partner at a hearing of the House Financial Services Committee on July 8, 2002:

> Arthur Andersen failed in their audit of WorldCom. You failed in the audit of Enron. You failed in the audit of Sunbeam. You failed in the audit of Waste Management. You failed in the audit of McKesson. You failed in the audit of Baptist Foundation of Arizona. What was Arthur Andersen doing? I mean, how do you—it is incomprehensible to me that a major accounting firm can have such a dismal record in trying to determine what the financial health of a company is. It's almost beyond comprehension.[17]

## THE GREAT ENABLER

Enron hired at least eighty-six accountants who had worked at Andersen, including Richard Causey, the firm's chief accounting officer, and Ben Glisan, the company's treasurer. (Both eventually went to prison for their roles in the Enron fraud.) More than top Wall Street banks and law firms, Andersen was Enron's great enabler.

Myriad Andersen employees either worried about the energy trader or looked the other way. "Enron is continuing to pursue various structures to get cash in the door without accounting for it as debt," one Androit warned colleagues in 1998.[18] Andersen had labeled the client "high risk." Auditors said Enron had a "dependence on transaction execution to meet financial objectives." They wrote that the company relied on "form over substance" transactions.[19] At one point, to make its quarterly earnings, Enron borrowed money from Merrill Lynch but disguised the transaction as a trade (with Merrill's full understanding of the dodginess). Andersen threatened Enron: if the company unwound the sham trade, the energy trader would have to restate its earnings. Sure enough, Enron unwound the trade right away in the next quarter. But Andersen didn't follow through on the threat, and Enron did not restate.[20]

Andersen employees warned repeatedly about Enron's accounting, but the high-level partners ignored them. A top Andersen accountant and member of its Professional Standards Group, a body that issued rulings on thorny accounting questions, campaigned against Enron's accounting but was routinely ignored by David Duncan, Andersen's partner in charge of servicing Enron, and the rest of his Houston team. Duncan, an Andersen lifer who had taken over the Enron account at the age of thirty-eight, had become enmeshed with the company, becoming close friends with executives.[21]

In March 2001 Bethany McLean's story in *Fortune*, "Is Enron Overpriced?," came out. The piece didn't uncover the fraud, but it crushed the fantasy and wounded the company irrevocably. Critical stories, revealing questions about the company's business, came out all summer. Investors sold. Hedge funds shorted. By early fall, Enron had lost control over public perception, and the fraud unraveled.

On October 9, 2001, Nancy Temple, an Andersen lawyer in the Chicago office, wrote a memo saying it was "highly probable" there would be an SEC investigation. She added that there was "probability of charge" for Andersen for violating the cease and desist order over Waste Management. The next day, an Andersen executive gave a presentation to the

Houston team explaining the document retention policy and that everything that wasn't an essential part of the audit file should be destroyed. Two days later, on October 12, Temple sent another reminder, which would become famous: "It might be useful to consider reminding the engagement team of our documentation and retention policy." Any sentient professional understands what that hint means.

On October 16, 2001, Enron announced that it would reduce its shareholders' equity—a common measure of a company's value—by $1.2 billion. Astonished by the size of the wipeout, Enron investors fled and the stock crashed. In an email, Temple suggested "deleting some language that might suggest we have concluded [Enron's] release is misleading." Andersen had indeed determined that Enron was being misleading but wanted any hint of that excised so that the public didn't see it. Temple asked for her name to be taken off a document. Being named, she complained, "increases the chances that I might be a witness, which I prefer to avoid."

The SEC opened an inquiry the next day, officially requesting information from Enron officials. Two days later, on October 19, Enron notified the Andersen audit team about the SEC's probe. Top Andersen partners scrambled an emergency meeting the next day. Two days after that, on October 22, Andersen's engagement team, which headed up the audit of the company's books, spent the day at Enron headquarters.

On October 23, six days after the SEC had launched its Enron inquiry, Andersen's Houston team started its enormous document destruction program, overseen by Duncan, the lead partner on the Enron account. In a matter of three days, the firm shredded more documents than were usually destroyed in a year. It also deleted around 30,000 computer files and emails.[22] On just one day, October 25, in an orgy of policy compliance, Andersen employees obliterated 2,380 pounds of documents, compared with the average of about 80 pounds a day.[23] One executive testified at trial that he told Duncan he could not delete an email about a conversation with Sherron Watkins, an Enron whistle-blower. Duncan deleted it anyway.

Andersen would receive the SEC's official subpoena for Enron-related records only on November 8. That notice prompted an Andersen secretary to send out an emergency email the next day: stop the shredding. The firm had been "officially served."

## THE PR FIASCOS

Andersen's chief executive, Joseph Berardino, was new to his role. He'd just ascended to CEO in January 2001, after Andersen spun off its consulting business, now called Accenture. Partners pushed him to attack. His PR advisors tried to save him from the partners' bad instincts.

The first tack of Andersen messaging was an audacious campaign of denial and misdirection. The *Wall Street Journal* op-ed page was, as ever, at the ready to provide a platform to defend corporations and undermine the government. On December 4, 2001, just weeks after the festival of shredding, Berardino wrote an opinion piece in which he called Enron a "wake-up call." A wake-up call, that is, to reform some rules, somewhere, sometime. He presented the same arguments that bankers would make only a few years later after the 2008 crisis. Enron, he wrote, "made some bad investments, was overleveraged, and authorized dealings that undermined the confidence of investors, credit-rating agencies, and trading counter-parties."

Berardino continued: "Enron's collapse, like the dot-com meltdown, is a reminder that our financial-reporting model—with its emphasis on historical information and a single earnings-per-share number—is out of date and unresponsive to today's new business models, complex financial structures, and associated business risks."[24]

The problem wasn't fraud, but something else. There may have been recklessness. There may have been some stupidity. But at bottom, went the argument, was a lack of updated financial disclosure rules and a failure of government to keep up with innovation.

Critics mocked Berardino's self-serving and blinkered argument. But when bankers and defense attorneys made versions of the same argument in the wake of the 2008 financial crisis, they convinced official circles. The crisis, these people parroted, involved overly complex, overly risky, but nonetheless legal activities. The crisis might warrant changes, the argument went, but prosecutions were too blunt an instrument to solve the problem. The reasoning persuaded many people after 2008, including prosecutors and regulators.

After news of Andersen's document destruction emerged, Billy Tauzin, then a Republican representative from Louisiana and chairman of the House Energy and Commerce Committee, decided to investigate. The committee subpoenaed documents. Tauzin was one of the accounting industry's stalwart friends in Congress. (Intimate with the drug industry as well, he left later to head PhRMA, the main lobbying group of the pharmaceutical industry.) When, in 2000, SEC chairman Arthur Levitt pushed rules to prohibit firms from consulting and auditing the same companies, Tauzin and others blocked the reforms.[25] But now the 2002 midterms were coming up. The accounting scandals made corporate friendliness briefly toxic. Tauzin and his fellow Republicans had to distance themselves from their erstwhile allies to protect their places in Congress.

In late January 2002, just ahead of the hearings, Berardino accepted an invitation to appear on the TV news program *Meet the Press*, hosted by the aggressive Tim Russert. The PR advisors had counseled against it, but his partners urged him to accept. CNBC would be a better option, the PR team suggested; it was a friendlier and more familiar format. Berardino wasn't a politician who had been on television hundreds of times. Undeterred by his botched foray into opinion writing, he decided to go on air. Berardino fumbled. Enron failed "because the economics didn't work," he told Russert. The PR reps cringed.

During the early, intense period, Andersen's law firm Davis Polk made a call that the Andersen team would come to believe was a significant error. Davis Polk had discovered the email deletions and brought them to the attention of the Justice Department.[26] Now Tauzin requested any materials about the document destruction. In response to the congressman's request, the firm advised Andersen to give over everything en masse. The executives took the firm's advice. The law firm didn't even interview any employees before handing over the documents, as far as several Andersen employees knew. Andersen executives felt Davis Polk had been overly cooperative. Lawyers must have legitimate reasons for not turning over documents from their clients for an investigation, but they have enormous leeway to slow the process down.

The result of the disclosure was a press bonanza. Reporters scored leaks, and Andersen faced unrelenting daily stories based on its internal documents. Patrick Dorton and Charlie Leonard, public relations specialists, hunkered down in their own small office in Andersen's quarters on K Street in Washington to head up crisis response. Dorton was young, only thirty-two years old, and had come from a PR position in the Clinton White House. He'd held his breath when he made his salary request. Andersen, to his disbelief, topped it. Having just left the torrid pace of the DC mire, he expected a sleepy job. Leonard, who ran his own PR consultancy, won the position by bringing in a shirt on a hanger and promising to stay in the office overnight during the crisis if needed. The firm set up a website and a war room and a rapid response team, all part of a reportedly $1.5 million PR campaign—a fortune at the time. The Andersen media frenzy would be nothing like either had ever seen or would ever see again.

They girded daily to save Andersen. Mornings were quiet. Then in midafternoon, the phone lights went berserk, and they entered into verbal combat with reporters. The Enron scandal—and often Andersen—was front-page and evening-broadcast news almost every day for months. Multiple reporters from the same papers would call. Dorton and Leonard would clash late into the night, when international reporters took over after the American reporters closed their pieces. The two would leave the office around midnight, have martinis across the street, and get ready to do it again the next day. This kind of media scrum doesn't exist anymore. Today fewer reporters would cover such a story, and they wouldn't pay attention as intently for as long.

In the early months, Dorton and Leonard battled leaks. Every reporter would tell Andersen's reps the same opening statement: "I just got a document." Dorton and Leonard figured it was coming from Congressman Billy Tauzin's people—a gotcha every single day. They would scramble to find the document among the firm's trove and interpret it, but it was so late in the day that the responses were often perfunctory. Tauzin was killing them.

Tauzin's House hearings were held in January 2002. The PR folks knew they would be dangerous. To get ahead of the news, Andersen fired David Duncan, the lead partner on Enron who had overseen most of the document destruction. In its press release, the firm accused Duncan of having "directed the purposeful destruction of a very substantial volume of documents—and in doing so, he gave every appearance of destroying these materials in anticipation of a government request for documents." Rather than placate critics, Andersen's release infuriated people further. The company appeared to be shirking the blame by making it seem as if the document destruction were an isolated event orchestrated by one person. (Many of the emails and other damning information about the document destruction emerged later.)[27]

But it was even worse from the lawyers' standpoint: Andersen had just admitted wrongdoing. Sure enough, when the hearings started, the representatives couldn't beat their colleagues fast enough to express their umbrage. Tauzin topped them, warning the Andersen witnesses that they would likely face criminal charges.[28]

## JUST A COST OF DOING BUSINESS

With the Andersen furor raging, the Department of Justice forged ahead with its investigation. Through the early months of 2002, Andersen, under the influence of attorney Bob Fiske, the Davis Polk eminence, made a show of cooperating with the investigation. Andersen insisted to the government that it was taking the investigations and need for reform seriously. In late January, Berardino brought in Paul Volcker, the former Federal Reserve chairman and one of the most respected figures in finance, to propose a reform program. But Andersen kept bungling its efforts. The partners were too split and didn't act on Volcker's proposals. Many partners were too busy forming escape plans.

In negotiations, the Justice Department made it clear it was seeking tough sanctions. Despite ostensibly cooperating with the government, Andersen held to a bright line in the talks: the firm would not admit any wrongdoing. Andersen remained so adamant because its problems were not just federal. Connecticut, where the Colonial Realty scandal had taken place, was making dangerous noises. The company fretted that other states would start following suit.

Over a series of meetings with the Justice Department in the spring of 2002, Arthur Andersen's lawyers often made their client's situation worse by continuing to insist that the firm was so vulnerable to any reputational hit that the Justice Department must be lenient.

"Isn't the SEC going to do something here? That's going to hit the firm's reputation," Chertoff asked.

Clients and investors "don't care about the SEC," Fiske said. Prosecutors felt he was almost nonchalant, shrugging off the entire thing. He explained that the agency's rebukes were routine for the company. Companies viewed the law as a tackling dummy to push aside. Companies habitually entered into agreements with the SEC without being forced to admit anything. They were insignificant punishments, and they didn't change the conduct. The prosecutors realized: fines are just a cost of doing business.

Chertoff was enraged, in large measure because the lawyer was right. Fiske might have been trying to flatter prosecutors about their importance compared with the SEC but had inadvertently sent another message: the firm's regulatory oversight was toothless. Davis Polk was treating the regulator with the same contempt that Andersen had when it destroyed documents. Something had to change, Chertoff thought.

He grew impatient with the parade of Andersen lawyers. In another meeting, Richard Favretto, lead lawyer from the Chicago firm Mayer Brown, stood up and screamed at Chertoff that Andersen was "too big" to indict. The markets would drop by 25 percent, he warned. Chertoff was furious but remained calm. He stood, too. The son of a rabbi from New Jersey, Chertoff punctuated his words. "If you are telling me that we cannot indict Arthur Andersen because it is too big," he told Favretto, pausing for dramatic effect, "well, in this building, that dog don't hunt!"

"Where the fuck did that come from?" thought Enron Task Force member Tom Hanusik, silently cheering Chertoff on.

Andersen and its lawyers found Chertoff unreasonable. They tried to appeal to his higher-ups. Fiske requested a meeting with Larry Thompson, the deputy attorney general. Thompson was talking with Chertoff often multiple times a day. He wanted the two parties to resolve their differences but supported Chertoff in his stalwart fashion. Thompson believed that he shouldn't meddle in underlings' investigations or decisions, and so he turned down Fiske. But Andersen didn't stop there. The firm engaged in a nice bit of "bullet lobbying": a technique in which a company enlists not an expert but someone close to the target, like a college roommate.

Early in his career, Thompson had been a young lawyer at Monsanto, where he met a young, black conservative lawyer named Clarence Thomas. Later, during Thomas's confirmation hearings for the Supreme Court in 1991, he met John Danforth, then a US senator for Thompson's home state of Missouri. Now Andersen hired Danforth to defend the firm in its fight with the government. Danforth had left the Senate with a glistening reputation to become a corporate lawyer, but he had no particular expertise in accounting shenanigans. When Danforth requested a sit-down, Thompson assented. They had an awkward meeting, mentee listening politely. Danforth repeated the Andersen line: the indictment would destroy the company and throw the markets into chaos. Thompson remained unmoved. He wouldn't intervene.

Still, prosecutors were cautious. If they could reach a settlement, rather than having to indict, they would do so. Chertoff and the Enron team offered a deferred prosecution agreement to Arthur Andersen. In such a settlement, an outside attorney appointed by prosecutors might monitor the corporation. Such a settlement is less serious than an immediate indictment. By making this offer, government lawyers stuck to Chertoff's nonnegotiable point: the company needed to admit wrongdoing. That was the bare minimum. Arthur Andersen refused.

The entire Enron Task Force gathered in the Main Justice offices to vote on the indictment. Prosecutorial teams often take such informal head counts. Prosecutors had demanded an admission of wrongdoing. They couldn't call up Andersen and say, "Just kidding!" There had to be something behind the threat. All but one member of the task force favored the indictment. On March 7 the grand jury delivered a secret, sealed indictment of the firm. A week later, Larry Thompson announced the news publicly.

Negotiations continued nevertheless. Many would come to argue that it was the indictment—not the eventual guilty verdict—that put Andersen out of business. But Andersen didn't go out of business upon indictment; it continued to negotiate with the Justice Department.

The experience seared the Davis Polk lawyers. Fiske and his junior colleague McInerney thought the Justice Department was unreasonable and found Chertoff intransigent. It was wrong to indict the firm, they believed. It would kill Andersen. And for what? The wrongdoing had been committed by only a limited number of people. Not only was Davis Polk about to lose the argument, but also Andersen was shunting the firm aside for other lawyers. The humiliation affected McInerney in particular.

For the trial, Andersen brought in another lawyer to be its local counsel: Rusty Hardin, a legendary Texas defense attorney with a colorful aw-shucks style sure to charm a Lone Star State jury. Hardin began to take control of Andersen's defense. In early April he became infuriated about what he thought were government leaks to reporters. He called Caldwell, who was just settling into her position as director of the Enron Task Force. Hardin liked Caldwell. However, he couldn't stand Weissmann. Ever the bulldog, Weissmann had sent Hardin a letter saying that if he didn't stop talking to the media and making misrepresentations, he would seek sanctions against him. Hardin composed a response:

*Dear Andrew,*

*I thought you would like to know that some idiot is writing me letters and signing your name. You might want to investigate.*

*Regards,*
*Rusty*

Davis Polk and Mayer Brown talked him out of sending it.

Now Hardin let loose. "What the hell is this in the paper?" he yelled at Caldwell. "What are these leaks? You know as sure as hell as I do that Andersen tried to get a deferred prosecution agreement, and Chertoff denied it!"

Caldwell responded as she did to all defense lawyer histrionics, in her measured tone:

"All I can tell you is that it didn't come from my team."

"I know where it comes from. It comes from that asshole you work for."

On April 5, 2002, Hardin flew to DC. The gang was there: Davis Polk's Denis McInerney, lawyers from Mayer Brown, Andersen executives, and in-house lawyers. They met with Caldwell, with Weissmann on the phone. The Andersen lawyers thought they had a deal: Andersen could get a deferred prosecution agreement. The firm wouldn't have to admit guilt but instead to a narrow set of "mistakes."[29]

Hardin flew back to Houston. When he got off the plane, he received bad news: Chertoff had vetoed the deal and chewed out the task force members. The final offer: a nonprosecution agreement, but Arthur Andersen had to admit wrongdoing.

Chertoff felt emboldened. Earlier that day, the task force secretly wrung a cooperation agreement out of David Duncan, the Andersen partner in charge of the Enron relationship. He would testify for the government in its trial with Andersen. Duncan pleaded guilty on April 9.

Arthur Andersen dared the Justice Department to make the hard decision. The government team believed Andersen had done something wrong and that the prosecution was just. They couldn't be cowards. They had to go all the way to trial.

Hardin put up a formidable fight. Almost all the witnesses were former Andersen employees. To a person, they were hostile to the prosecution, resentful that their firm had been put out of business. Hardin, in contrast, was his folksy self, soothing and friendly on cross-examinations. But when the jury was excused and out of the room, he flew into histrionics, attacking the prosecutors, the judge, the outrageousness of it all. Davis Polk's McInerney played his second fiddle, with unrelenting technical arguments on the law at every turn, enervating the prosecutors. The entire firm of Davis Polk seemed to be taking the case personally. Low-level associates came to the courtroom just to hear the decision being read. Sam Buell, who had conducted the trial with Andrew Weissmann, looked over and saw the young lawyers grimacing at him.

The jury was, as juries often are, quirky. The members struggled with their deliberations, asking whether it was necessary for them to agree unanimously on which employee was guilty. Judge Melinda Harmon instructed that while they all needed to believe someone at the firm "acted knowingly and with corrupt intent," it didn't matter if they all agreed on who that person was.

The jury returned its guilty verdict the next day of deliberations, its tenth day. The instruction turned out not to be particularly significant. The jury agreed unanimously that Nancy Temple, the lawyer, had been the "corrupt persuader." She had intended to obstruct the government's investigation when she told Duncan to cut out any suggestion that Andersen disagreed with Enron's characterization of its earnings and also when she asked him to delete her name from the memo, worried that she might be called as a witness in any future Enron litigation.[30]

Trials are not about arriving at larger truths or depicting the whole story. Andersen partners, lawyers, representatives, and supporters would continue to maintain that the prosecution was unjust and abusive. Many would point out that the firm and its partners had not been accused of accounting fraud, as if that were the only measure of culpability. Andersen had to attest to Enron's financial health. Auditors sign off that books are presented "fairly, in all material respects," as the language goes. But Enron wasn't healthy at all; its business wasn't viable. Enron's lie required Andersen's complicity. It was immoral, it was a dereliction of professional duty, and it was criminal in the colloquial sense of the word. Now Arthur Andersen was criminal in the narrow legal sense of the word, too. But the verdict would not last.

## THE HUMAN FACE

Arthur Andersen had become the exemplar of a corrupt enterprise. It had been handmaiden to serial corporate fraud. It had engaged in a document destroying cover-up. The accounting industry held, as a principle, that a profit-seeking profession could advise CEOs but would also tell them the truth when they were pushing the numbers too far. Andersen fouled that ideal.

Congress acted. George W. Bush had entered office in 2001, inheriting an economy in recession. The GOP was the party of big business, and big business was rotten. Republicans had energetically pushed financial deregulation throughout the 1990s.[31] Now they reacted in classic law-and-order fashion. Many old-line Republicans regarded the scandals with revulsion; a violation of the rules of capitalism. Belief in pure markets required that people play by the rules, in the naïve and idealistic view. "The vast majority of CEOs in America are good, honorable, honest people who have nothing to hide," President Bush said at a July 2002 press conference. "It's the few that have . . . created the stains that we must deal with." Bush would repeatedly discuss the coming criminal crackdown. "We'll vigorously pursue people who break the law" to restore confidence to the American people, he said.

The Bush administration proposed tougher punishments and called for moral behavior to reassert itself, perhaps magically, in the corporate boardroom. "America's greatest economic need is higher ethical standards," the president asserted. Having proposed an enforcement personnel cut in an earlier budget, Bush, bowing to political pressure, now reversed himself, calling for Congress to approve a hundred new enforcement staffers.[32]

The Democratic Party regarded prosecutions as secondary and insufficient. Its response was to push legislation that emphasized systemic regulation. Democrats proposed more statutory powers for prosecutors, but they argued that rot was pervasive, requiring the broad solutions of legislation and regulatory oversight. Their view was that the problem was not that corporate accounting was bad at a few firms. Corporate America needed an overhaul. The left wing of the party, in particular, rejected the rotten-apples thesis or the notion that moral suasion was the correct path. The liberal Democratic senator from Minnesota, Paul Wellstone, responded to Bush's speeches by saying, "I don't think the president or the administration gets what this is really about." The need for legislation "goes way beyond Enron, goes way beyond WorldCom. The American investing public has lost its confidence in this corporate system."[33]

In July 2002 Congress passed a would-be landmark law, Sarbanes-Oxley, named after Maryland Democratic senator Paul Sarbanes and Ohio House Republican Michael Oxley. Sarbox, as it came to be known, required corporations to have tighter internal bookkeeping controls. Chief executives and chief financial officers had to certify their companies' books. Over objections, lobbying, and corporate resentment, the law set up a new overseer for the accounting profession: the Public Company Accounting Oversight Board. There was a period of optimism about Sarbanes-Oxley. Some believed the new rules would grant regulators and prosecutors powers of legal oversight. Law professor Kathleen Brickey predicted, "Sarbanes-Oxley firmly puts Andersen's legal and factual arguments to rest while placing broad power in prosecutors' hands."[34] She was wrong.

Instead, Andersen became the great symbol of unjust white-collar prosecution. Andersen was the improbable terrain on which the American business and legal lobby chose to fight against the excesses of federal prosecutorial power. Those forces prevailed.

Andersen's legal and PR teams fought tough, occasionally distorting facts and impugning prosecutors' motives. Andersen honed its PR message, and its employees mobilized. They marched on the Justice Department offices in Washington. They held rallies in Houston and Philadelphia. They donned orange T-shirts and wrote letters to their elected officials. Legendary college basketball coach John Wooden wrote an open letter to President Bush. They took out full-page ads in the major newspapers. Andersen executives petitioned US ambassadors across the world to warn them that the local offices might close. Chertoff even had to change his email address because of the deluge. After Berardino resigned, the interim CEO began making more television appearances. Andersen's PR executives capitalized on the mobilization, announcing that any Andersen employee who wanted could speak to the press.

The Enron Task Force prosecutors weren't moved by the publicity stunts. But the notion that there were tens of thousands of employees at risk became indelible. When Andersen condemned the verdict against the firm, it decried what would happen to "a firm of twenty-six thousand innocent people." (The number would be reported variously; sometimes it was twenty-eight thousand.)

Initially, the media was Andersen's implacable enemy. The horde of reporters covering the firm rooted for its collapse, the Andersen team thought. Dorton and Leonard figured a way to counter it. Then at CNN, the conservative host Lou Dobbs was fighting a ratings war with CNBC. Nothing stokes cable ratings like a sustained campaign of outrage. The PR masters assigned an Andersen executive to check in with Dobbs's show every day. Dobbs embraced Andersen, hammering the Feds for having gone after the accounting firm while supposedly letting Enron executives off. Andersen had its first media ally.

The company's lawyers argued that government had abused the grand jury process by disallowing Andersen from putting its case in front of the body. Defense attorneys have no right to present evidence to a grand jury, which renders the typical grand jury a one-sided process run by prosecutors. In a departure, the Justice Department invited Andersen lawyers to submit exculpatory evidence to the grand jury. They didn't respond. Nonetheless, the press echoed the claim. The *Wall Street Journal* reported, "The government didn't give Andersen a chance to present its case to the grand jury investigating the firm."[35]

One of the best spokesmen for the beleaguered employees of Arthur Andersen was Rusty Hardin, as its counsel. Davis Polk and Mayer Brown were cautious about talking to the press, but the charismatic defense attorney thought their approach was absurd. He courted the media.

Hardin had new talking points. Andersen would no longer concede anything. The new company line was daring, since Andersen partner David Duncan had pleaded guilty and Andersen itself had admitted wrongdoing in a press release. Hardin dismissed all that, insisting that no Andersen employee did anything wrong. None had destroyed documents to obstruct the government. They were just routinely clearing out materials. Hardin contended that Andersen was a victim of politics. He targeted Chertoff, a Justice Department political appointee. A company's biggest nightmare, he would say, was to fall under criminal investigation amid a public fury and have to watch as politicos refused to acknowledge any rules. In the media before and during the trial, Hardin switched Andersen's line on Duncan, no longer blaming him but transforming him into a victim of government pressure who didn't believe what he was saying. Andersen partners thrilled to Hardin's resolve. One employee would say later that he had helped the firm "find its heart."

Andersen's voice mattered more than its heart. All that work Dorton and Leonard did in their PR war room may not have kept the firm alive, but it had succeeded. Through an intentional strategy, they had put a human face on Andersen. No longer was Andersen about accounting fraud. It now stood for the government putting a major American company out of business. The firm, its PR team, Andersen, the corporate lobby, and the defense bar succeeded by changing the subject.

## ANDERSEN'S LEGACY

The notion that the indictment was solely responsible for putting Andersen out of business is a myth. (Technically, Andersen surrendered its accounting license but never filed for bankruptcy.) Between 2001 and 2010, no publicly traded company failed because of a conviction, the attorney and scholar Gabriel Markoff has found. According to him, "[T]he risk of driving companies out of business through prosecutions has been radically exaggerated."[36]

The Andersen indictment and trial verdict accelerated Andersen's downfall. The Justice Department moved uncharacteristically fast, making the government susceptible to accusations it overreacted in haste. Michael Chertoff, who pushed the indictment, saw his reputation sag later as the head of the Department of Homeland Security, overseeing the botched response to Hurricane Katrina in 2005. Chertoff had violated the unwritten rules of corporate criminal negotiations. He was not a man of proportion. The prosecution was a reminder that government power is awesome and consequential.

But clients were fleeing before the indictment because of the profound reputational damage Andersen had suffered as Enron's auditor. The document destruction and the previous accounting settlements combined in a toxic swirl of irreparable harm. In the weeks before the indictment, major clients such as Merck & Co., Freddie Mac, SunTrust Banks, and Delta Air Lines all abandoned the firm. In the end, Arthur Andersen faced 175 shareholder suits. Partners had every incentive to dissolve the firm to avoid paying up in those civil settlements. Even if Enron had not killed Arthur Andersen, WorldCom would have. Ten days after the Andersen verdict, the giant telecom darling revealed a multibillion-dollar accounting fraud. WorldCom's auditor? Arthur Andersen.

Nonetheless, years later, Arthur Andersen and its supporters would righteously point out that the firm was never convicted of accounting fraud.[37] Critics of the prosecution make two potent arguments: The first was that the innocent, low-level employees who had nothing to do with wrongdoing suffered the most. High-level partners, for the most part, got new jobs easily. The law, however, cannot condone crimes simply because there are collateral victims. A convicted murderer's family might suffer, too. The second contention was that indicting Andersen would tie the hands of regulators and prosecutors. They would become overly cautious for fear of putting one of the now–Big Four firms out of business. In a case against KPMG in the following years, that prediction came to pass.

Then the government suffered a blow. In May 2005, three years after the prosecution, the Supreme Court reversed the verdict in a unanimous vote. The court determined that trial judge Melinda Harmon's instructions were overly generous to the government, failing to make clear that the prosecution had a burden to demonstrate that Andersen executives intended to obstruct justice when they destroyed or instructed others to destroy documents. The judge overseeing the Andersen trial had been inconsistent. At one point, she had told the jurors that they needed to find that Andersen employees committed fraud knowingly. At another, she had told the jurors that "even if [Andersen] honestly and sincerely believed that its conduct was lawful, you may find [it] guilty." The Supreme Court called this instruction a crucial error. People need to know they are doing something wrong to commit a crime. The judge's instructions "failed to convey the requisite consciousness of wrongdoing," Chief Justice William Rehnquist wrote in his opinion. "Indeed, it is striking how little culpability the instructions required."

Today legal observers argue over the ruling. Several aspects of the Supreme Court ruling are odd. Andersen had been charged under a statute that, by the time of the ruling, was no longer relevant. In July 2002, a month after Andersen's conviction, Congress passed Sarbanes-Oxley. The new law closed loopholes related to obstruction of justice and document destruction, making the actions that Andersen had taken illegal in the future. So why did the Supreme Court, as overburdened as it is, pick up this case, considering a statute that had been euthanized by Congress? The court rarely takes on issues that have been already resolved by the legislature. Given that the Enron Task Force took flak for its overzealous approach, some prosecutors interpreted the highest court's action as a warning to the government not to be so aggressive again.

The case against Andersen was overwhelming. The firm destroyed documents, with one partner pleading guilty. The firm did not go out of business undeservedly. Moreover, the prosecution did not lead to any economic or financial crisis, as the firm and its lawyers warned. The SEC had begun contingency planning for Andersen's collapse, worried about the cascading effect that it would have on investor confidence as corporations scrambled both to switch auditors and clean up their accounting. The agency had even brought together Enron creditors, pensioners, and shareholders to try to push a modest settlement with Andersen to avoid its collapse. After the indictment, however, markets didn't crash. Corporations just found other auditors. In the following months and years, investors the world over came back into the American capital markets. Most of the cashiered Andersen workers and partners found work quickly. The victory of Andersen PR's efforts is all the more improbable given that the greatest fears about the consequences of Andersen's prosecution went unrealized.

Yet opinion turned. In the later years of the 2000s and 2010s, top Justice Department officials invoked Andersen when discussing corporate investigations, certain that the government had gone too far. Expressing a commonly held belief, the former US attorney in Manhattan and future SEC chair Mary Jo White said in 2005:

> The Justice Department came under a lot of criticism for indicting Arthur Andersen and putting it out of business.
>
> That was justified criticism.
>
> What has happened is that since Arthur Andersen, the Justice Department, to its credit, has focused on the awesome collateral consequences of moving against an entire entity criminally. The stigma of that, the reputational hit of that, is too severe for most companies to survive. And so, they have turned to what they consider to be a lesser sanction with lesser collateral consequences.[38]

By the end of the aughts, top Justice Department officials didn't even have to mention the firm by name. Everyone knew what they were talking about. Lanny Breuer, who held the same role as Chertoff a half decade later as the Obama administration's criminal division head, indicated in a speech on September 13, 2012, the caution with which the department approached corporate prosecutions:

> [T]he decision of whether to indict a corporation, defer prosecution, or decline altogether is not one that I, or anyone in the Criminal Division, take lightly. We are frequently on the receiving end of presentations from defense counsel, CEOs, and economists who argue that the collateral consequences of an indictment would be devastating for their client. In my conference room, over the years, I have heard sober predictions that a company or bank might fail if we indict, that innocent employees could lose their jobs, that entire industries may be affected, and even that global markets will feel the effects. Sometimes—though, let me stress, not always—these presentations are compelling. In reaching every charging decision, we must take into account the effect of an indictment on innocent employees and shareholders, just as we must take into account the nature of the crimes committed and the pervasiveness of the misconduct. I personally feel that it's my duty to consider whether individual employees with no responsibility for, or knowledge of, misconduct committed by others in the same company are going to lose their livelihood if we indict the corporation. In large multinational companies, the jobs of tens of thousands of employees can be at stake. And, in some cases, the health of an industry or the markets are a real factor. Those are the kinds of considerations in white-collar crime cases that literally keep me up at night, and which must play a role in responsible enforcement.[39]

The Andersen case ushered in an era of prosecutorial timidity when it came to taking on the largest corporations in America. The response to the financial crisis of 2008, which took down the nation's largest banks and put the global financial system at risk, stands in contrast to the post-Nasdaq-bubble accounting-fraud emergency. Central banks poured in trillions of dollars in extraordinary lending. But fear for the fragility of the system dominated the political discourse and tormented Department of Justice officials.

Democrats, in possession of the White House and Congress by 2009, sought systemic solutions, as they had during the Sarbanes-Oxley debate. Congress passed a gigantic (though arguably insufficient) stimulus bill and moved on to writing and passing the Dodd-Frank Wall Street Reform and Consumer Protection Act, a sweeping piece of financial reform legislation. The left mobilized to push specific pieces of law to protect individuals from predatory finance, to make the financial system safer, and to pull unregulated areas of finance under government supervision.

Here and there, elected officials called for greater enforcement. But the Obama administration did not emphasize that aspect of crisis response. Aside from a few speeches, the White House took little concrete action on the prosecution of white-collar crime. Attorney General Eric Holder did not mobilize a major law enforcement response right away. Prosecutions, they seemed to hope, would take care of themselves. But they wouldn't, in no small measure because of the Arthur Andersen prosecution.

Today prosecutors remain reluctant to indict large corporations for fear of driving them out of business. In the decade following the accounting firm's conviction, the Department of Justice would overhaul its approach to corporate prosecutions, moving to settlements over charges. The strategic shift came without any strategy or plan. A Pyrrhic victory for Andersen, the firm's prosecution was only too real a triumph for corporate America. Andersen had to die so that all other big corporations might live, free of prosecution.

*Chapter Three*

# THE SILVER AGE

WHITE-COLLAR CRIME HAD TO BE INVENTED. Even the phrase needed to be coined, generally attributed to a sociologist, Edwin Sutherland, who came up with it in the late 1930s. Sutherland cofounded the Institute of Criminal Law and Criminology at Indiana University Bloomington and published his classic work, *White Collar Crime*, in 1949, a year before his premature death. Sutherland wrote that such crimes were "committed by a person of respectability and high social status in the course of his occupation," nonviolent, economic crimes of fraud, collusion, or deception. Often it is not obvious the behavior is criminal. Embezzlement is as easy to understand as purse snatching. But securities manipulation is a more abstract concept.

The government prosecuted little white-collar crime in the first three decades of the twentieth century. "The business of America was business; there was a certain lack of zeal for punishing business behavior," writes historian Lawrence Friedman of this period.[1] The crash of 1929 and the

Great Depression spurred a white-collar crackdown. Between September 1929 and July 1932, stocks listed on the NYSE lost more than 80 percent of their value, a decline from $90 billion to $16 billion. Wall Street's prestige collapsed. The political debates then followed a pattern similar to that of the early 2000s, in the wake of the technology stock bubble implosion, and in the aftermath of the 2008 financial crisis. Democrats proposed bills almost immediately after the 1929 crash to regulate corporate financial statements and trading activities. President Herbert Hoover maintained for three years that there was "doubtful constitutional authority" to regulate markets.[2]

The government found prosecuting corporate criminals difficult. The Feds went after Samuel Insull, whose electric utility collapsed during the 1930s amid pyramid-scheme-like borrowings, indicting him for mail fraud and bankruptcy law violations. Turkey extradited him. Tried three times (once in 1934 and twice in 1935) and defended by a legendary defense lawyer of his time, Insull was found not guilty on all counts. The acquittals disgusted Sutherland, who explained that he then began his study of the "apparent disregard" the legal system had "for the serious harm white-collar crime caused."[3]

In 1933 Congress created the SEC and the FDIC (Federal Deposit Insurance Corporation) after the famous Senate hearings from early in the year, known as the Pecora investigation. Ferdinand Pecora, an Italian immigrant, lawyer, and chief counsel of the Senate's banking and currency committee, led public inquiries into Wall Street stock manipulations, outrageous banker salaries, snug deals between banks and their executives, and tax evasion. Wealthy investors and Wall Street bankers had created stock pools to manipulate stock prices and conduct phony trades. In one egregious scenario that Pecora uncovered, Albert Wiggin, the chairman of Chase National Bank, had shorted his own company's stock, profiting in the crash. Such bets against one's own company were not then illegal.

In the first hundred days of the new administration of Franklin Delano Roosevelt, Congress inched forward with new regulations. It passed the Securities Act of 1933, a modest law requiring that sales of certain securities be registered with the Federal Trade Commission. The law disappointed reformers. The liberal *New Republic* denounced it, complaining, "The bankers rewrote the bill."[4] Meanwhile, the Wall Street and business lobbies attacked it from the other side as a complex monstrosity that would curtail economic recovery, hinder issuance of securities, and damage American competitiveness by sending corporations abroad to issue stocks and bonds. "It seems hardly necessary to burn down the house to exterminate vermin," wrote a corporate attorney.[5] Major Wall Street firms went on strike, refusing to issue new securities.

Felix Frankfurter, the jurist and close advisor to FDR, took to the pages of *Fortune* to assure the business class that the law was "modest," which it was. Frankfurter was a disciple of Louis Brandeis, the legendary lawyer and longtime Supreme Court Justice who shaped the regulatory ethos of the era more than any other. A Jeffersonian, Brandeis railed against "bigness"—monopolies and powerful Wall Street banks—and promoted the benefits of transparency, saying famously, "Sunlight is said to be the best of disinfectants; electric light the most efficient policeman." Frankfurter once maintained that the 1933 Act was simply a "belated and conservative attempt to curb the recurrence of old abuses."

Unassuming as it was, the '33 Act was merely the first installment of reform. The next year, Congress passed the much more sweeping Securities Exchange Act of 1934, which went far beyond the earlier law. It established the SEC and gave the new agency the power to regulate the stock exchanges, prohibit manipulative trading practices, and regulate corporate disclosures. The 1934 act bestowed the most important securities enforcement law: Rule 10b-5, which prohibits market manipulation.

Still, over the next several decades, the government's efforts to crack down on corporate crime were haphazard. Academics, lawyers, and regulators debate whether business is better controlled through "regulation" or "enforcement." Not all bad behavior is criminal, especially if the rules haven't caught up to the innovations made by malefactors.[6] And not all criminal behavior is pervasive in an industry. Is it better to lay down rules and guidelines for all companies and enforce them civilly, with fines and sanctions? Or is it better to investigate individual crimes, one by one, with the possibility of prison time for individuals? Which way is more effective? More efficient? Through the 1940s and 1950s, prosecuting corporate crime was not a priority.

Indeed, there has never been a golden age of white-collar prosecutions. The rich and powerful have always been rich and powerful. But there have been silver ages. Robert Morgenthau ushered in one of them. Morgenthau was US attorney for the Southern District of Manhattan from 1961 to 1970. After his election in 1968, President Richard Nixon asked him to resign. He refused, saying it degraded the office by making it seem like a patronage position. After a struggle, Morgenthau reluctantly left the job, soon after running unsuccessfully for governor of New York State. These were the go-go years in the stock market, an era of takeover frenzy and bubbly equities. Prosecutors felt the influence of the political and cultural tumult of the era. They, too, questioned the establishment.

Before Morgenthau, federal prosecutors focused on nailing Ponzi schemers, penny stock pump-and-dump or boiler room operations—grubby securities crimes committed by two-bit reprobates. That is, if they enforced securities violations and corporate crime at all. Morgenthau surrounded himself with young hotshots and turned their attention to a higher class of criminal. "How do you justify prosecuting a nineteen-year-old who sells drugs on a street corner when you say it's too complicated to go after the people who move the money?" he once asked.

Morgenthau created the securities fraud unit, now amended to the Securities and Commodities Fraud Task Force within the Southern District. Under his watch, prosecutors targeted prominent Americans who had illegal Swiss bank accounts, as well as the prominent financier (and major donor to Democratic candidates) Louis Wolfson for selling unregistered securities. They also prosecuted James Landis, a former chairman of the SEC and dean of Harvard Law School, for income tax evasion. He also went after Roy Cohn, the power lawyer who had been Joseph McCarthy's right-hand man. Responding to Cohn's complaint that Morgenthau had a vendetta against him, he said, "A man is not immune from prosecution merely because a United States Attorney happens not to like him."[7] Before Morgenthau, it was the office's informal policy not to prosecute lawyers who enabled financial crimes. Morgenthau changed that.[8] In one of the first cases of its kind, he charged accountants at Lybrand, Ross Bros. & Montgomery who'd certified the fraudulent financial statements of a vending machine company. (Nixon would later pardon the accountants.)[9]

After Morgenthau left his post as the head of the Southern District, his successors continued his legacy through the 1970s. Morgenthau had inspired them but was now competing with them as Manhattan's district attorney, using state laws to go after major companies, especially Wall Street. Robert Fiske, who served as US attorney of New York's Southern District from 1976 through 1980, built a reputation almost as great as Morgenthau's. (Fiske then took up his position at the law firm Davis Polk & Wardwell, where he would wind up defending Arthur Andersen decades later.) Under Fiske, the Southern District tackled more ambitious cases against organized crime, corrupt politicians, and corporate criminals. The office began to hire women as criminal prosecutors. Previously, they were believed to be too delicate for the scuzzy worlds prosecutors attacked.

Morgenthau's influence reached down to Washington, forcing the Securities and Exchange Commission to begin enforcing securities fraud more doggedly. Through the 1950s and 1960s, the SEC had focused on whether companies filed their books in orderly fashion. Now the SEC began to realize it needed to police fraud. In the early 1970s, the commission created its first enforcement division. By 1974, the SEC had its own legendary enforcer tormenting corporations: Stanley Sporkin.

## SPORKIN'S COUCH

In the 1970s, every corporate lawyer in Washington, DC, knew about the couch. High-priced Wall Street lawyers from Simpson Thacher & Bartlett, or Weil, Gotshal & Manges, or Shearman & Sterling would be ushered into his small government office and placed in uncomfortable chairs. Stanley Sporkin would be there, sitting on the end of the couch.

In 1974 Sporkin became the SEC's director of enforcement. Sporkin had been at the agency since the early 1960s. He became that rare creature: the superstar bureaucrat who overshadows his superiors and becomes an untouchable political force. By the end of his run at the SEC in 1981, Sporkin had become a hero regulator, feared by corporate America. He became one of the most accomplished figures in the history of corporate regulation. He would come to be known as "the Father of Enforcement."[10]

Wedged deep in the ugly couch's cushions, Sporkin gave birth to securities law enforcement. The piece of furniture had a hideous array of yellows, greens, and blacks, faded yet still resembling nothing found in nature. There wasn't anything the least bit countercultural about Sporkin, but the couch was downright psychedelic. "The ugliest piece of furniture ever created by man," thought Harvey Pitt, who, as the wunderkind general counsel of the SEC, worked closely with Sporkin. One day toward the end of his tenure, Sporkin arrived at the door to Pitt's office and declared that he was ready to get rid of it. The general counsel couldn't believe it. Sporkin told Pitt he was going to donate the couch to the government. Pitt replied, "Stanley, on behalf of the government, we refuse."

Sporkin had unfailing instincts for bad deeds, and he treated everyone he was investigating the same: gruffly. In meetings, Sporkin would lean all the way back, his tie separating so that both ends framed his Falstaffian midsection. He would break ice with his molars and then appear to shut his eyes, which were then encircled with dark bags. Looking at him, one couldn't quite tell if they were open or not. His head would droop, his chin resting on his chest. The corporate lawyers—worldly, seasoned interlocutors—would be discombobulated. Did Sporkin expect them to continue their presentation? Pitt would watch, noticing "they had carefully prepared their pearls of prose that they had no interest in having him miss." They kept pleading for their clients because they could think of nothing else to do.

Then Sporkin would bolt upright. He had caught something. In his crusty and triumphant manner, he would ask a question. The lawyers would look at one another. He had just detonated their argument. He'd fingered the hole. They had fallen yet again for his Columbo routine. They were in Sporkin's power now.

Stanley Sporkin grew up in Philadelphia, the son of a federal judge. He stayed in state for his college education, attending Penn State University. Then he enrolled in Yale Law School. In addition to his law degree, he became a certified public accountant. Too combative, though, he wasn't made for private practice. He joined the SEC in 1961 as a young attorney. Just as Morgenthau spurred the Southern District to go after more ambitious crimes, Sporkin and his softer-spoken mentor Irving Pollack transformed the agency.[11]

In the 1960s, the SEC had few regulatory weapons. Even more debilitating, agency attorneys did not confront big, respectable Wall Street firms. Overturning such timorousness, Sporkin and Pollack inspired the young attorneys in their unit. In the old days, if the SEC found that a broker at the Salt Lake City office of the prestigious Merrill Lynch had bilked a client, it would sanction him or, at most, his office. Sporkin argued that the agency should bring an action against Merrill Lynch as a whole.

Sporkin had nothing close to absolute power. The SEC staff needed to bring its case in front of the five commissioners of the agency—political appointees who vote on all enforcement matters. The investment bank's lawyers presented their case to the commissioners, which historically gave the banks a sympathetic hearing and undermined the staff. Merrill Lynch would object, saying it was just a few rotten apples in Utah.

But Sporkin began consolidating his position at the agency. When Pollack became a commissioner, Sporkin replaced him as the head of enforcement. Now he had full control over the enforcement division and a reliable friend on the commission.

In his new role, Sporkin was a whirlwind. His huge office was the size of two conference rooms. The couch moldered in one area. He had a desk across the way, and tables and chairs. He would hold three or four meetings in there at a time, moving from one to the other. The enforcement staff was small then, made up of about a hundred lawyers. (Today the enforcement staff has more than 1,300 people.) He might interact with each lawyer at least once a week. The young attorneys couldn't understand how he got through the amount of material he did. Sporkin's briefcase sat next to his secretaries. Lawyers prepared memos, sticking them in the briefcase. By the next morning, Sporkin had read them and scribbled something illegible in the top right corner. Only his secretary could decipher Sporkin and render him into English. When the lawyers received a "Good boy," they were happy.

Sporkin couldn't be bothered by interruptions such as meals. He treated eating not as a pleasurable diversion but as a utilitarian necessity. He needed more energy. He ate in his office but made no concession to the food in his mouth. He talked straight through it. He often ate Jell-O with fruit in it. Peter Clark, then a young SEC lawyer, remembers Jell-O and bits of fruit flying everywhere, onto the floor and into the couch. That's where it remained. One day, a staffer caught some movement from under the couch. "Stanley, Christ almighty, there's a mouse!" a staff attorney cried. Sporkin barely looked up.

Sporkin inspired creativity and instilled loyalty. His charges had the freedom to pursue investigations. Sporkin wanted his lawyers to reach for the best and broadest cases they could bring. They loved him. And they feared him. When Sporkin wanted to talk to a staffer, he wanted him that second. Sometimes the staffer wasn't ready to meet with Stanley. Where's so-and-so? Get him here! Stanley would bellow. No one could hide for long. During one such hunt, Peter Clark went to the bathroom, and, sure enough, Sporkin's prey was in there, at the urinal to Clark's right. Boom, the door flew open, and it was Sporkin. The lawyer panicked and did what came to mind: he turned left to face him. Clark realized the flustered attorney had urinated down Clark's leg.

His staff's dread was nothing compared with the fear that Sporkin instilled in corporate America. Companies vilified him hysterically, as if he were bent on seizing the means of production for the proletariat, and not a midlevel bureaucrat attempting to enforce rules long on the books.

They whispered about his uncouth tactics and took the SEC to court. In 1976 the business lobby won a significant Supreme Court victory. The high court ruled, in *Ernst & Ernst v. Hochfelder*,[12] that to prove securities manipulation, a violation of the SEC's Rule 10b-5, regulators had to prove "scienter": the legal term, from Latin, for knowledge. Securities law violators had to know they were actively violating (or consciously disregarding) the law. Sporkin was characteristically nonchalant: "If they want to scienter, it's no problem—we'll give them scienter!"[13]

Sporkin's bravado aside, the verdict provided a key building block for white-collar legal defense, driving a significant wedge between the legal treatment of white-collar criminals and so-called street criminals. White-collar cases became harder to prove. Bad actors adopted the defense that they didn't understand they were doing anything wrong, especially if lawyers and accountants had signed off on their actions. In complex securities litigation, or in cases where the whole corporation was systematically perpetrating a crime, the high court now supplied a pathway for plausible deniability. In a federal criminal case, the Department of Justice must prove knowledge beyond a reasonable doubt. The SEC only needs to prove it based on a preponderance of the evidence. Proving scienter to either standard was never easy, Sporkin's shrug notwithstanding.

But Sporkin was never friendless. For a time, Republicans and Democrats alike protected him. The SEC's enforcement flourished under Republican leadership and Nixon's Republican administration. Sporkin himself confounded political ideology. A registered Republican, he switched to become an independent at the peak of his public career. As regulator and jurist, Sporkin opposed corporate power. Yet he viewed tough enforcement as a conservative, capitalist value. "The premise I operate on is that this is the greatest country the world has ever known, that the freedoms we have and the free enterprise system are the reasons it's so good, and that you cannot afford to compromise those freedoms," Sporkin told a reporter.[14]

Sporkin had allies as diverse as the rock-ribbed Reagan conservative William Casey, who'd gotten to know him as chairman of the SEC, and William Proxmire, the quixotic liberal Democrat from Wisconsin. He was also backed by President Ronald Reagan's first Treasury secretary, Donald Regan, a former Merrill Lynch CEO and the kind of Republican who wanted to keep markets clean for capitalism. A vein of skepticism about the sharpies from New York ran through both parties, among midwesterners, southerners, and even some northeastern Rockefeller Republicans. Early in the Reagan era, a Republican SEC commissioner, Daniel McCauley, declared, "Wall Street is a cesspool of hanky-panky and the biggest gambling casino in the country."[15]

In Congress, Proxmire grilled incoming commissioners about their views regarding Sporkin—and then made them pledge not to fire him. Sporkin was untouchable.[16] The status made him a despised figure in certain legal and corporate circles.

Sporkin couldn't understand what they were complaining about. He regularly tried to soothe sensitive corporate souls. He gave interviews to the business press that he was moving away from the "traditional adversarial system." He did not relish bringing fear, regarding himself as judicious and reasonable. In the mid-1980s, after Sporkin had left the agency, he shared a limo with a young commissioner, Joseph Grundfest, and Gary Lynch, the agency's new enforcement director.

On their way to a conference, Sporkin explained to Lynch that if he wanted to do his job right, he needed to have the correct combination of *rachmones* and *sechel*. Lynch, of Irish stock, looked blank. Sporkin encouraged him to try to pronounce the Yiddish. Lynch made an attempt. Sporkin and Grundfest broke out in laughter. Grundfest thought he might lose his tonsils. *Rachmones*, Sporkin explained, is a nuanced notion. It means compassion, mercy, empathy, pity, concern—all stirred in a chicken soup with a lot of schmaltz. *Sechel* is curiosity and knowledge, but not just for knowledge's sake. It means common sense and wisdom, not just book learning.

But Sporkin understood that the SEC couldn't investigate and take every company and scofflaw to court. It had too many companies to oversee and too many securities law violations to chase. The agency could never examine every company or investigate everything fully. Publicly traded companies had more lawyers, more accountants, and more resources. Why not co-opt this power, Sporkin thought?

So he did. He made the companies work for the government. He took an obscure regulatory weapon few used: the consent decree, settlements with companies and executives to head off any trial. These were binding, legal agreements a regulator would reach with a regulated entity. Under Sporkin's consent decrees, the defendants did not have to admit wrongdoing, but they promised not to do anything bad again. Often they had to set up compliance programs and departments to demonstrate how serious they were.

In the beginning, companies settled with the government and then went out of the building to proclaim their innocence. They said they were settling with the SEC to make the charges go away. The posture infuriated Sporkin and the agency. In 1972 the SEC amended the agreements to disallow any denial of the charges. "No-admit, no-deny" settlements came to be.[17] Over time, the SEC became an addict. The agency would become almost unwilling or unable to enforce laws without relying on consent decrees. The agency seemed incapable of getting an admission of guilt and unwilling to go to trial except in the easiest cases. By the 2000s, no-admit, no-deny settlements would be both habitual and toothless. Arthur Andersen entered into one but continued its lax practices.

No company could go public without the help of law firms, investment banks, and accounting firms. These firms gave companies access to public capital through bonds and stocks. What if the SEC made these advisors their agents? Sporkin believed that if there was fraud, how could the lawyers, investment banks, and accountants *not* be complicit? If they didn't know, what the hell were they doing anyway? He realized that if the SEC started sanctioning these gatekeepers, the government could force them to police the fraudsters and the violators. The professionals had more to lose. Clients would come and go, but their franchises depended on their reputation and their licenses. The SEC would stand at the chokepoint. He called this practice his "access theory."

Years later, in 1985, Sporkin became a federal district court judge in Washington, DC. In 1990 he presided over the Charles Keating case. An extraordinary fraud, Keating helped loot the Arizona savings and loan bank he ran. He had been a major donor to both Republicans and Democrats, such as Senators John McCain and John Glenn, and a benefactor to the Republican Party. In an unusual move that delighted legal observers and the media covering the case, Sporkin grilled Keating during one of the legal tussles. Over five hours, Sporkin questioned the defendant, treating him gruffly one moment and genially the next. With his glasses resting on his brow, he stretched back in his chair at the bench and peered up at the ceiling—while continuing to bear down on Keating.[18] At one point during the trial, Sporkin asked a series of questions that would become famous in legal circles:

> Where were the professionals . . . when these clearly improper transactions were being consummated? Why didn't any of them speak up or disassociate themselves from the transactions? Where also were the outside accountants and attorneys?[19]

He had summed up the animating theme of his career. In 1964 Henry Friendly, the distinguished jurist, put it in more baroque terms: "In our complex society, the accountant's certificate and the lawyer's opinion can be instruments for inflicting pecuniary loss more potent than the chisel or the crowbar."

One evening in November 1973, Sporkin, still at the SEC, did what the rest of the nation was doing: he turned on his television set to watch the Watergate hearings. He saw testimony about the Committee to Reelect the President, known as CRP, or "CREEP." Corporations such as the Minnesota Mining and Manufacturing Company, the Goodyear Tire & Rubber Company, Gulf Oil, and many others had set up slush funds to funnel illegal campaign contributions to President Nixon to help his reelection in 1972.[20] He learned that Gulf Oil had established two offshore subsidiaries to fund bribes. Walking into the office on Monday, Sporkin declared to his deputies, "Goddamn it, how are they hiding this money? We have to do something about it."[21] He sent an SEC attorney to Gulf Oil. It only took the man a day: Gulf Oil had set up the two subsidiaries and made the funds that went to the two subsidiaries small enough that the accountants weren't interested in it.

At the time, bribery of foreign officials was not illegal in the United States.[22, 23] Sporkin, a certified public accountant in addition to being a lawyer, had a flash of brilliance: How were the companies recording these bribes on their books? Was there a line item for "bribery"? Everything material had to be disclosed in SEC filings. The materiality test is a key concept in securities law. Usually regulators must demonstrate not just that there was a violation but also that the violation matters for the company's finances and for shareholders. Of course, there was no such disclosure. American corporations weren't insane. They didn't reveal the amount of bribery they did in their official government filings. The Gulf Oil slush funds were absent in the company's books and records. It was a classic Sporkin maneuver. He'd gone to law school with luminaries and Washington power brokers. Why should they be the creative ones? he thought. They are brilliant and inspired in defending their clients. Why can't government lawyers use their imagination in bringing cases against their clients?[24]

Companies were leaving materially relevant information out of their filings, filing misleading books and records with the agency. Shareholders had a right to know. How much business came from bribes? If they didn't pay bribes, how much business would they have without them?

Until that point, the SEC brought few actions against corporations over disclosure failings, focusing instead on making the markets more honest and emphasizing securities law violations such as stock manipulation (and two-bit manipulations at that). At first, the commissioners looked askance at Sporkin's initiative and squeezed him on his budget. They argued it was unseemly for the regulator to probe into the inner workings of corporations. It wasn't what the SEC had been envisioned to do, critics argued. But Sporkin pushed his settlements through with support from his mentor Irving Pollack on the commission. Soon the SEC was regularly fining companies for bribery abroad. Sporkin was changing and broadening the notion of how regulators could define their mandate.

Bribes were often relatively small, especially compared with the revenue and profits of the biggest corporations in the country. Corporations argued that the payoffs didn't "materially" affect the company's revenue or profits. Sporkin redefined *materiality*. When these bribes became known, he noted, the companies' share prices would often fall. Investors found even these small bribes important. Sporkin added a moral dimension to what constitutes thorough disclosure. A company could participate in an activity that, while small compared with the bottom line, could hurt its reputation if revealed.

Without a sufficient budget, Sporkin realized he needed help. He turned to corporations themselves. He made companies investigate themselves and turn themselves in for foreign bribery in exchange for leniency. Sporkin invented the self-examination as a regulatory tool. A corporation typically appointed a special review committee. The new committee often hired an accounting firm and a law firm, which conducted the investigation and submitted reports to the board of directors. Then the corporation would come hat in hand to Sporkin and the SEC to confess its sins.

Sporkin foresaw the implications. His approach sacrificed pure accountability, since companies avoided serious punishment through cooperation. He was providing law firms with a huge new revenue stream. Companies could not always be trusted to confess everything. In mid-1973, around the same time that Sporkin began his initiative at the SEC, Archibald Cox, the special prosecutor in charge of investigating Watergate, had set up an amnesty program for companies to come clean about their illegal Nixon campaign contributions. Cox was forced to bring extra charges against Gulf Oil and Ashland Oil when it turned out they hadn't fully disclosed their activities in the initial investigation.[25] Nonetheless, Sporkin figured it was better to get three-quarters of what he'd like than nothing at all.

Even without bringing a full measure of justice to a wrongdoing corporation, Sporkin changed behavior—and won notoriety. An *Atlanta*

*Journal-Constitution* article about him carried the headline "He Terrorizes Wall Street." The agency sought disgorgement of profits to defrauded investors. The SEC appointed special directors and monitors at corporations. The agency took on some of the biggest names in corporate America: Robert Vesco and his looting of Investors Overseas Service (Vesco would flee the US, eventually landing in Cuba, where he lived out his years as a fugitive); George Steinbrenner, the principal owner of the New York Yankees, for failing to record illegal campaign contributions; and C. Arnholt Smith, for his misuse of funds of the US National Bank of San Diego. A few years later, his SEC charged Bert Lance, director of the Office of Management and Budget in the Jimmy Carter administration, with securities fraud in connection with a Georgia bank he'd run.[26] In pushing bribery investigations, Sporkin prevailed on his Senate friend William Proxmire to sponsor a law to make bribery of foreign officials illegal. In 1977 Congress passed the Foreign Corrupt Practices Act (FCPA).

Sporkin could not rely solely on company cooperation. As an enforcer, the SEC needed more serious help. Though Sporkin used the courts to get wrongdoers to disgorge ill-gotten profits, freeze assets, and submit to oversight, the SEC had no ability to fine corporations for violations. To prosecute crimes, he needed allies at the Department of Justice. The Southern District had an effective monopoly on white-collar enforcement at the time. Main Justice and other offices around the country played little role. So Sporkin looked north and discovered friends in the Southern District of New York. He found one prosecutor particularly excited about his brand of justice; a brilliant, young, and aggressive lawyer eager to attack corporate and securities scofflaws: Jed Rakoff.

## "TRY A THIN CASE HERE"

Jed Rakoff loves the law. He loves it as the guardian of society's morality. He loves its endless complications. He loves the history and tradition. He is a student of statutes and great legal careers and has worked to create one for himself. When he isn't writing or practicing earnestly, he relaxes by lampooning the courts with tender doggerel. He knows the law from every side. He took criminals to court as a prosecutor, won their exoneration as a defense attorney, and delivers prison sentences heavy and light as a US Federal District Court judge. Most of all, he loves that the law is alive. Prosecutors, defense attorneys, judges, and scholars change the country every day.

After college, Rakoff earned a graduate degree at Oxford University and dabbled with the notion of becoming a historian, writing his master's thesis on Mohandas Gandhi. Eventually deciding to do something with a greater practical effect on the world, he attended Harvard Law School. In 1969 he watched student protestors take over a campus building, but he was not a politico or a hippie. Rakoff never even tried pot.[27] He entered law reluctantly, inclined to follow his true love: musical comedies. With a friend who composed the music, they started on a musical about P. T. Barnum but got only as far as the first act. They thought they could work during the day at their jobs and write the musical at night, a notion they soon discovered was ridiculous.

Law school mesmerized him. Good lawyers excelled at analysis. They argue the facts when the facts are on their side and argue the law when it favors them. The old joke is that when neither is on their side, good lawyers bang the table, but Rakoff had come to his own view of legal greatness: the brilliant lawyer recasts the question so that the case raises an issue of principle that had not appeared in previous cases. Reimagining the law was the way to win otherwise unwinnable cases.

Rakoff's professors forced him into understanding that on most issues, there were two defensible positions. Other people, no matter how professional, intelligent, or accomplished, tended toward absolutism. Lawyers, however, learned that cases are rarely simple. One side is completely right or wrong only infrequently. Rakoff delighted in these complexities. Years later, in 1996, nearly twenty-seven years after graduating from law school, Rakoff became a judge. He had to learn anew that, after all the arguments have been made and despite all the nuances, he had to make a decision.

After graduating from Harvard Law and a short stint in private practice, Rakoff joined the Southern District of New York in 1973 as a federal prosecutor. Young Rakoff had the luck to arrive at a moment of creative ferment in white-collar criminal law. John "Rusty" Wing, the guy down the hall, had just indicted the recently departed attorney general of the United States, John Mitchell, and the secretary of commerce, Maurice Stans, for trying to impede a Sporkin SEC investigation into Robert Vesco, in exchange for a secret donation to Nixon's reelection campaign. With Wing as his mentor, Rakoff learned to tackle big cases. All of the young prosecutors understood, Rakoff as much as any of them, that to succeed, they had to be a champion. To be a champion, they had to take down the biggest target. To do that, they needed to get into the fraud unit. That's where you could go up against the highest-profile criminals defended by the most famous and top-notch defense attorneys. Most prosecutors wouldn't leave the office until they won such a case. In 1978, five years after he had joined the office, Rakoff became head of the unit.

Rakoff worked as hard or harder than anyone in the office, but not in the mornings. During trials, colleagues tended to arrive well before him. Rakoff tortured them by making them wait, often showing up just as the judge was arriving. He had often stayed up late into the night, studying the mail fraud statute. His fellow prosecutors all relied so frequently on the mail fraud statute that Rakoff decided to write the seminal piece on its history and uses. Rakoff read every mail fraud case he could find. Colleagues would walk by his office and see stacks and stacks of articles overwhelming his desk and piled high above his chair. He did so much research that he decided to break the articles into two parts. He finished part one, the history. His colleagues delighted in the opening lines of Rakoff's subsequent 1980 law review article, "The Federal Mail Fraud Statute (Part 1)": "To Federal prosecutors of white-collar crime, the mail fraud statute is our Stradivarius, our Colt .45, our Louisville Slugger, our Cuisinart—and our true love. We may flirt with RICO, show off with 10b-5, and call the conspiracy law 'darling,' but we always come home to the virtues of 18 U.S.C. §1341," he wrote. After the history, he planned to bring it all up to date in part 2. His friends teased him about his progress. Rakoff, usually prolific but ever busy, never managed to get to it.

Rakoff dreamed of becoming a judge. He watched the great ones carefully. He came to admire US District Court Judge Milton Pollack (no relation to the SEC's Irving Pollack). A Lyndon Johnson appointee, Pollack was one of the finest securities law experts in the country and a great courtroom strategist. He awed Rakoff with his mastery of legal intricacies, but the young prosecutor saw that Pollack had flaws. The judge wanted cases to go the way he thought they should go. In his rulings, Pollack would tip the balance as much as he could. He would launch the occasional question to witnesses from the bench under the guise of clarification. The inquiries would turn the case around.

On occasion, when Rakoff had a trial before Pollack, he would get a call in the early evening, after the secretaries had gone home: "This is Milton Pollack," the judge would say before asking, "Have you considered such and such procedural motion?" Trapped, Rakoff would have to hear him out.

"Judge, I will certainly take that under account," Rakoff would reply. The next day, he'd bring that motion.

He always felt uncomfortable about Pollack's "helpful" advice, which other prosecutors received as well. They were blatant ethical violations. Rakoff used to disclose the tips to his defense counterparts, but they were often too afraid to complain to Judge Pollack. Rakoff reported these late-night advisories to his chiefs. He regretted not asking Pollack to refrain. Eventually, when he became a judge, Rakoff placed Pollack's portrait up in his chambers, along with his other legal heroes, such as Robert Fiske. But Pollack's fervor for results provided Judge Rakoff with a model of what not to do.

As the head of the fraud unit, Rakoff continued his office's fruitful relationship with Washington and Sporkin and his SEC. Sporkin possessed uncanny instincts for criminal behavior. When he smelled something beyond a civil enforcement matter, he referred the case to the Justice Department for investigation. Rakoff was in awe. Once he heard Sporkin hear out the mitigations and obfuscations of a high-priced lawyer and his white-shoe client. He looked up from the couch. "Thank you," said Sporkin. "But I don't believe a goddamn word you just said." The young Rakoff couldn't go to a cocktail party without being buttonholed by a defense attorney or an executive denouncing Sporkin: He's just an ideologue. He's destroying the fabric of our business community. He's just after headlines. He can't distinguish between real misconduct and lapses in judgment. He's mistaking the messengers for the people who commit fraud. Rakoff defended him with vigor.

One day in the late 1970s, Sporkin called the Southern District. He wanted clearer insider trading rules. Always on the lookout for a good test case to bring criminal charges, he thought he'd found one in Vincent Chiarella, an employee for a financial press. The press printed materials for corporate takeovers but encrypted them to conceal the company names. Chiarella cracked the code, gaining early access to the takeover information and trading on it.

Rakoff was skeptical. Chiarella was something of a schnook, he thought. Juries might be sympathetic toward such a low-level guy. Sporkin insisted that it was the first chance they'd had in years to get the damn thing decided. And he said they could win.

Which they did, although Chiarella's conviction was eventually overturned by the Supreme Court in 1980. The court ruled he had no fiduciary relationship with the companies. But sometimes losses create progress. Despite the defeat, the path toward codification of insider trading laws had started. Over the next decade, the SEC and the Justice Department began bringing more successful insider trading cases.

Sporkin and Rakoff understood that insider trading constituted only a minor part of what a full enforcement program would cover. Sporkin was revolutionizing the agency, expanding the SEC's mandate and attacking regulation with new vigor. Rakoff and the Southern District continued what Robert Morgenthau started and brought ambitious cases.

In 1972 Sporkin brought the National Student Marketing Corporation fraud to the Southern District. The prosecution became one of

Rakoff's formative cases, where they put Sporkin's access theory—going after the corporate gatekeepers—into action. The company was a fraud, but Sporkin and the prosecutors believed they should go after the abettors: accountants, lawyers, and investment bankers that held the gates to the capital markets open to fraudulent companies.[28]

Cortes Wesley Randell, a young social fixture and entrepreneur around Washington, DC, known for his yacht, mansion, and Learjet, founded National Student Marketing. One of the hottest stocks in the go-go stock bubble years of the late 1960s, the company promoted itself as a distribution channel for the untapped college market, selling students coffee mugs, discount cards, and assorted tchotchkes and services. After National Student Marketing went public in 1968, its stock price soared from $6 a share to $140 a share within two years, attracting investors such as Bankers Trust, the Morgan Guaranty Trust Company of New York, and the endowments of Harvard and Cornell Universities.

But Randell was a slick face man, running a fraud with his lieutenants. Like many stock promotions, it was built on a series of acquisitions. The company only appeared to be growing swiftly. Randell had falsified the books, claiming profits from transactions for which it never billed (calling them "unbilled receivables") and income from subsidiaries it had never acquired.[29] When the shenanigans were revealed, the stock crashed. The SEC began to investigate, and, soon after, Sporkin called up to New York and referred the case to his friends at the Southern District for criminal investigation. In 1975 Randell pleaded guilty to four counts of stock fraud and was sentenced to eighteen months in prison—of which he ultimately served eight—and was fined $40,000. (Corporate fraud sentences and fines were lower back then.)

With Randell punished, the Southern District focused on professional abettors: the company's lawyer and its Peat Marwick accountants. National Student Marketing issued a false proxy in conjunction with a merger, claiming profits in the period when it had losses. In preparing the proxy statement, accountants from Peat Marwick composed a letter detailing the differences between the accounts the public saw and the real ones, and sent it to Marion Epley III, a partner at the old-line Wall Street firm White & Case. Epley did not require the accountants to explain the financial maneuvers in its public disclosures.

One of the accountant's lawyers brought him into the office for an interview, as a demonstration of his client's willingness to cooperate. The accountant argued he never intended to do anything wrong, the threshold to prove a crime. Defense lawyers often contended that accountants couldn't be held responsible for frauds. They could be duped as easily as anyone. Accountants were supposed to make sure that the books were consistent with accounting principles. The prosecutor investigating the case, Harold "Skip" McGuire Jr., and his fellow assistant US attorneys had heard that line from accountants and were sick of it.[30] The defense lawyer escalated his plea to the US attorney at the time, but got rebuffed.

As always, the question in a white-collar investigation was whether there was any intent to commit a crime. A midnight contract tipped it for McGuire. He discovered that on the last day of a crucial quarter for National Student Marketing, the accountants had been in the office at night, waiting to sign off on the books. A few minutes before the stroke of midnight, voila, a contract arrived. It was one of the unbilled receivables, signed by Randell himself, and it saved the quarter. The company swung to a profit from what otherwise would have been a loss. The accountants had to suspect how dodgy these deals were. McGuire liked the accountant who led the National Student Marketing audit. He considered him a decent guy and knew he had not set out to commit fraud. He'd caved to the pressure. But that didn't matter.

To push the investigation forward, McGuire zeroed in on breaking a third Peat Marwick auditor on the National Student account, to get him to flip on the top two. The accountant didn't flip right away. He didn't break under threats of prison. Threats worked rarely, a reason why Rakoff would later be skeptical as Congress ratcheted up mandatory minimum sentences for white-collar crimes.

Instead, Rakoff took different approaches. Sometimes he appealed to lower-level executives under criminal investigation as their father confessor; their agent of redemption. Other times he worked their gripes, the prosecutor becoming the outlet for a slighted employee to seek revenge against bosses. Now and then, Rakoff had a tinge of conscience about manipulating lower-level corporate middlemen. They were vulnerable. Judges, who had much greater leeway in sentences then, might give them a harsh term despite their cooperation. Was the risk worth the greater good? "Am I playing God too much in pushing them in one way or the other?" he worried. The power of prosecution was awesome.

McGuire and the Southern District charged two Peat Marwick accountants with crimes. McGuire then left the Southern District for private practice. He handed the case to those who would handle the trial: Frank Velie, a trial specialist, and Rakoff. Peter Fleming, who had worked under Morgenthau and was now a defense attorney, had represented a person tangentially related to the National Student Marketing case. He came into the Southern District offices one day, stretched out his long legs and propped his feet up on Frank Velie's desk, and asked him what the trial strategy was going to be. Such was Fleming's reputation for brilliance in the courtroom that they said of him, "Any good defense counsel can shed tears in summation for a client. Only Fleming can shed tears for the government." He went on to become one of the preeminent defense attorneys of his day. Fleming was coming off a spectacular 1974 victory against his old office, having won acquittals for Mitchell, the former attorney general of the United States, and Stans, the former secretary of commerce.

Before Velie could answer, Fleming supplied his own advice: "Try a thin case here, Frank." That meant honing it down to the essentials, just as Sean Berkowitz and Kathy Ruemmler would do in their Enron trials decades later. If one witness says something, don't call a second to say the same. Don't get bogged down in minutiae. If a case is overly complicated, it requires weeks upon weeks of evidence and a parade of witnesses that alone create reasonable doubt in the minds of jurors. Velie and Rakoff culled their evidence, exhibits, and witness list. The trial lasted just three weeks. The strategy worked. The jury found both accountants guilty.

The SEC brought charges against National Student Marketing's outside lawyer, Marion Epley III of White & Case and the son of the former president and chairman of Texaco. The SEC took the position—all the more remarkable for its obviousness today—that securities lawyers owed a duty to the investing public and not just to their clients. The agency built the case on a landmark theory: even if the lawyers and accountants had not actively aided and abetted the fraud, they had remained silent as their client made false representations.[31, 32]

Sporkin was furious that the Southern District didn't charge Epley criminally. For three long days, the Manhattan prosecutors had put him in front of the grand jury, the legal body used to conduct legal proceedings, produce documents, and take testimony from witnesses. The Southern District used grand juries frequently in corporate white-collar cases, unlike today, but it was rare to put someone under questioning that long. When the office passed on charging Epley, Sporkin screamed—at the line attorneys, at their bosses, and all the way up to the US attorney. Grand jury secrecy rules prevented the prosecutors from sharing what Epley had said when testifying, so they couldn't explain their thinking to the apoplectic Sporkin.

The accountants appealed. Both hired star defense counsel, who pushed the higher court to throw out the convictions. In a draft response to the defense, Rakoff exceeded the page limit on appeals. Audrey Strauss, the head of the Southern District's appellate efforts, urged him to cut it down. Rakoff insisted the appeal needed every one of his points. Strauss argued back that the judges would hate it, but Rakoff couldn't be moved from any word, comma, or footnote. Giving up on the length, Strauss insisted on one point: "At the very least, you have to clean up the split infinitives," she told him. This set off the young prosecutor—son of an English teacher—who took pride in his writing.

"You're totally wrong!" Rakoff cried. He explained that the rule against split infinitives was just a bizarre invention by some pedants in the late nineteenth century to have English mimic Latin, in which infinitives are one word. All the great authors—Shakespeare! Faulkner!—split the infinitive. Rakoff and Strauss, who remain close friends, yelled at each other through the halls of the US Attorney's Office, fighting over grammar. Finally, Strauss gave up. Today in his courtroom, Judge Rakoff has strict length rules for briefs and comes down on any lawyer who runs over them.

During the appeal, the Second Circuit dangled victory to both sides like a child holding food above a dog's mouth. The higher court first reversed the prosecution of the second, lower-level Peat Marwick accountant. Then it reversed its reversal to restore the prosecution's victory. Then it reversed again. The Southern District had fought hard, but it was over. Rakoff comforted himself that charges against the main accountant had been upheld. Adhering to the gentlemen's rules of the game at the time, Rakoff called the defense attorney and told him, "You've won. We won't appeal again."

Just a few years later, President Jimmy Carter pardoned the main accountant, Anthony Natelli, who later went on to become a prominent Washington, DC, real estate developer.[33] And so it was a mixed verdict. The government had alerted the business community that white-collar criminals, including accountants, could face the threat of prosecution. But the Second Circuit's reversal and the presidential pardon muddied the message. Nevertheless, because of Sporkin's censure of Epley, a legal scholar would write by the end of the decade that the case "may well be one of the most significant cases on legal ethics in the history of the American legal profession."[34]

## *Chapter Four*

# "UNITEDLY YOURS"

EARLY MONDAY MORNING ON FEBRUARY 3, 1975, ELI Black climbed into the back of his company car, greeted his chauffeur with a cheerful hello, and inquired about his weekend. The driver, James Thomas, responded cordially and drove his boss down from the Upper East Side to his office in the Pan American Building in Midtown Manhattan.

Business wasn't going well for Black. He was the chairman of United Brands, parent company of United Fruit, which in turn owned the Chiquita banana brand. United Fruit had dominated Central America in the middle of the century—we owe the term "banana republic" to the company—but by the early 1970s, the business had gone off. In 1970 Black had maneuvered to merge United Fruit into a company he owned to create United Brands. An orthodox rabbi who came from ten generations of rabbis,[1] Black had left the clergy to become a financier. He worked at Lehman Brothers before embarking on a career buying and selling companies. He had pledged to turn around United Brands, and not just financially. He trumpeted his company's good morals, boasting in his 1973 letter to shareholders that its "changing image" had been noted in articles in the *New York Times*, the *Chicago Daily News*, and the *Boston Globe*. One reporter gushed, "It may well be the most socially conscious American company in the hemisphere."[2]

His turnaround stalled, however. Revenue continued to fall, and losses mounted. Several Central American countries, noting how the Organization of Petroleum Exporting Countries (OPEC) had become a successful market power, created their own cartel to control the banana market. The new Unión de Países Exportadores de Banano (UPEB) raised tariffs on banana multinationals, hammering United Fruit. Desperate, Black counteracted the measures.[3]

Now the consequences of his tactics were becoming clearer. Thomas pulled the car up to let Black out. He asked Black whether he would need him during the day.

"No, Jim, today will be an in day," Black replied.

Black was the first to arrive in the office that morning. He walked through the long hallway on the forty-fourth floor to his office, small and modest by the standards of CEO corner offices. It had a contemporary rust-colored wooden desk on chrome legs. Abstract paintings by his wife lined the walls. On his desk, he kept a picture of his son, Leon, then at Harvard getting his MBA. (Leon Black would become a billionaire financier himself, founding the giant private equity firm Apollo Global Management.) The senior Black went in. He slid the bolt, double locking it, and then locked the rarely used metal door right beside the wooden door.

Black went to the window, made of quarter-inch-thick plate glass, and raised the venetian blinds. He swung his attaché case through the window, shattering the glass onto the street below. Carefully, Black picked shards of glass out of the window frame. "He apparently didn't want to cut himself," a police officer said later.

A half hour later, the chauffeur came up to Black's office. He knocked. There was no answer. He knocked louder. He banged on the door and called out to Black. Worried, Thomas fumbled for his key and tried the door. He couldn't get it open because of the sliding bolt. He went to another office and got a secretary to call Black's office. Still nothing. Now panicked, he slammed against the door with enough force that he broke it down and rushed in. By then, on the terraced section of Park Avenue below, police officers had found the body.[4, 5]

Something about Eli Black's leap didn't seem right to Stanley Sporkin. The explanation couldn't be that he had been working too hard, as his friends speculated. Sporkin had his enforcement attorneys open an investigation. They soon discovered what been going on at United Fruit, one of Black's most prominent business holdings. It was the kind of activity a man like Black would never want to become public.

A few months earlier, in August 1974, a United Brands executive had met with the Honduran economics minister, who was acting on behalf of that country's president,[6] at the Fontainebleau Miami Beach—the once-swanky hotel where Frank Sinatra, Dean Martin, and the rest of the Rat Pack had partied in the 1950s. The executive wanted to get rid of the banana tariff crippling United Brands's business. The minister was willing to consider the request. He asked for $5 million.[7]

The executive was not authorized to commit such a sum. He checked with Eli Black to see if the chairman would condone such a sizable bribe. Black told him to counter with an offer for half. The Honduran economics minister accepted graciously. Soon after, United Brands sent the first half of the payment, $1.25 million, through its European subsidiaries into a numbered account at the Credit Suisse in Zurich.[8] In exchange, Honduras agreed to lower the banana tariff and extend favorable property terms for twenty years.[9]

After unearthing the details of the arrangement, Sporkin called the Southern District to say he had a hot one. Prosecutors were intrigued. The actions were bad; the evidence—internal corporate correspondence, wire transfers—was strong. But the case presented them with a dilemma.

The US Attorney's Office in Manhattan went after individual criminals, not corporations. The way to deter corporate crime was to put culpable executives in prison. In this case, that executive was dead. The prosecutors could always bring a case against the company, but the Justice Department regarded that kind of action as useless. What was the point? A company, after all, could not go to jail.

The office took that position even though it had the law on its side. The ability for the government to prosecute corporations dates to a 1909 Supreme Court ruling, *United States v. New York Central and Hudson River Railroad Company*. In that case, the high court recognized, for the first time, a notion of corporate criminal responsibility. Two railroad employees had charged a sugar company a secretly discounted rate, a violation of a law that proscribed railroad side deals and favoritism. The company had countered the government with an argument that companies continued to make over the next century whenever they faced legal jeopardy: to "punish the corporation is in reality to punish the innocent stockholders, and to deprive them of their property without opportunity to be heard, consequently without due process of law."[10] In turning back that entreaty, the court showed that corporations had been held criminally liable often through history.[11]

Under the Supreme Court's unanimous decision, a company could be held accountable for the actions of a sole employee. To be liable, the employee had to be shown to have been acting within the scope of his or her official corporate duties with the aim of helping the company. It did not matter if the actions violated corporate policy. The employees were "clothed with authority" of the corporation. If "the invisible, intangible essence or air which we term a corporation can level mountains, fill up valleys, lay down iron tracks, and run railroad cars on them, it can intend to do it, and can act therein as well viciously as virtuously."[12] For decades after that ruling, however, prosecutors rarely charged corporations—especially large ones—with crimes, focusing instead on individuals.

After Eli Black's suicide, the Southern District debated what to do about United Brands over the next several years, an argument that consumed Rakoff and his mentor and friend Rusty Wing. They hashed out the various issues with their boss, the US attorney Robert Fiske.

In Rakoff's day in the Southern District, prosecutors had to make the opposite case from the one that government lawyers make today: sometimes it is necessary to go after a corporation. Today prosecutors lean toward sanctioning companies. They all say they want to go after individuals first and foremost, but they find it difficult to identify and prosecute culpable individuals.

While Rakoff and Wing agreed in principle that individuals were the priority, the two young prosecutors argued that United Fruit's bribery was too blatant to be dismissed. Rakoff pointed out to Fiske that their friend Stanley Sporkin had begun a national debate about bribery at corporations. The Southern District could help.

When the two prosecutors and their wives vacationed together in the Caribbean for a week, they sent Fiske a postcard. Rakoff, obsessed with the case, put in elliptical references to the investigation and closed it waggishly, "Unitedly Yours." Finally, after years, they prevailed on their boss. The Southern District charged United Brands with conspiracy and five counts of wire fraud. The theory was a classic Rakoffian feat of far-reaching imagination.

For the charge against United Brands, Rakoff and Wing combined two legal concepts. Prosecutors could charge American companies for frauds committed abroad. An American company selling fraudulent stamps to Canadians could be indicted in the United States. Rakoff combined that notion with a second piece of the puzzle. He and Wing took an old concept and repurposed it marvelously. It was possible to charge corrupt public officials with depriving their constituents of their honest services, the same charge prosecutors would use fatefully with Enron's Lay and Skilling. Public officials were not permitted to enrich themselves at the expense of the public. Rakoff and Wing used the charging theory, but in this case, they argued the violation was that the Honduran foreign minister had deprived his country's citizens of his honest services. United Brands had helped him do it.

Hence a charge for United Brands. The defense bar, unsurprisingly, was outraged. Wealthy and prominent investors had acquired United Brands after Black's suicide. They came in to plead their case. They explained to Rakoff and Wing that they had nothing to do with the fraud.

"It's going to murder us in Honduras. All the Honduran workers who work for us are going to lose their jobs. The company is going to be anathema," the investors told the prosecutors. Robert Morvillo represented United Brands. Portly and short, looking like an unmade bed, Morvillo was just starting to become the legend of the defense bar he would later be. He had taken the traditional route to criminal defense work, forming his own boutique. Only a few years earlier, he had been the chief of the fraud unit at the Southern District. There he had regularly said to his underlings, including Rakoff, "Corporations don't commit crimes, people do." Now he was back, making that plea to Fiske, the US attorney. The prosecution theory was a stretch and deeply unfair, he said. It would hurt only the current, innocent shareholders and the creditors. It would cause job losses. Fiske listened but rejected the petition.

Rakoff and Morvillo were friends, so Morvillo's zealous defense didn't bother him. He collected friends from all corners of the legal world. He and Morvillo would hammer each other during the day and then go to Gassner's, a restaurant near Foley Square where all the lawyers gathered. They would talk about their families, joke, and drink together. The legal bar was smaller then. Everyone who was anyone knew all the other anyones.

Morvillo gave up the fight on United Brands, but in wily fashion. On a sleepy summer day in July 1978, he walked into court and had United Brands plead guilty to all six counts for a grand total fine of $15,000. United Brands put out a statement that the company "had voluntarily disclosed" the facts more than three years ago—which was true only insofar as it had volunteered the information when Sporkin asked for it. "Management had concluded that it was far better to settle with the government for this modest amount than to engage in prolonged litigation," the company said, sounding not particularly contrite.[13]

Rakoff and his colleague walked out to the courthouse to denounce the statement. They pointed out that none of the senior executives involved in the bribery had been dismissed. Though some had left the company, they had done so voluntarily. Others remained.

That was that. The story ran buried on page D3 of the *New York Times* the following day. Was it a victory or a defeat? Despite the meager media coverage, Rakoff felt the point was made. Congress cited United Brands when it passed the Foreign Corrupt Practices Act, a law that is still used to go after the bad practices of corporations as powerful as Halliburton, Alcoa, Daimler, and Siemens. But in some ways, any chance for accountability died with Eli Black.

## THE END OF THE SPORKIN ERA

In 1980 Ronald Reagan was elected president. The onetime actor and two-term governor of California ran on the notion, as he would put it in his first inaugural address, that "government is not the solution to our problem; government is the problem." Stanley Sporkin, the consummate government problem solver, was vulnerable. With Reagan in power, Sporkin's critics rounded on him and his agency. The new president planned to lacerate its budget by 30 percent over three years and slash the enforcement division from two hundred people down to fifty.[14] Reagan's new SEC chairman, John Shad, the first Wall Street executive to head the agency in fifty years, told the world that the SEC would refocus on securities crime such as insider trading. It's not that Sporkin didn't believe in insider trading enforcement. After all, he and Rakoff had put together the Chiarella case, one of the pioneering criminal insider trading cases. But Shad's message was clear. The *New York Times* reported that the legal world understood Shad's shift of focus was code for turning away from Sporkinesque enforcement actions against bad corporate behavior.[15]

The Reaganites rolled back many Sporkin-era reforms and softened the agency's enforcement. The new top SEC officials dropped an investigation into Citicorp, the giant bank that was a precursor to today's Citigroup. SEC investigators had found that for seven years, senior management directed operations that circumvented and violated tax and foreign exchange laws of other countries. The case was shelved because the Citi violations weren't, the agency now said, "material."

The new Reagan SEC loosened up disclosure requirements for smaller companies. The agency allowed Wall Street investment banks to lower their capital requirements. Such a move permitted the banks to take greater risks and make more money, while making them less sound. And the new chairman, Shad, publicly supported weakening Sporkin's baby: the FCPA antibribery law.

Sporkin was exhausted from fighting the SEC commissioners. Underneath the gruffness, he never relished the criticism. Though Sporkin couldn't be fired, his friends understood that the new regime sought to make him miserable. William Casey, his old friend and the former chairman of the SEC, called him. Reagan had just appointed Casey to be head of the CIA.

"Stanley, how would you like to be the general counsel of the agency?"

In an unlikely move, Sporkin took the job in April 1981. Upon Sporkin's departure from the SEC, Milton Gould, a legendary defense litigator who had clashed with him, offered grudging praise: "He's despotic, offensive many times, but he's instilled a little morality in the business community."[16] From his deathbed a few years earlier, Manuel Cohen, who had served as SEC chairman before working as a prominent corporate lawyer, wrote to Sporkin, "The thing that has given me great pleasure is to bring to a meeting with you an inside general counsel or CEO who has heard you are a devil or madman and then hear him report to his board that you are hardly an unreasonable person."[17] Others were less laudatory. A Stanford University law professor would chastise him for his "rampant prosecution mentality."[18] Later, Senator Alfonse D'Amato of New York would call Sporkin "a steamroller" who had "gone too far" during his days at the SEC.

As a federal district court judge, he continued to enjoy piercing corporate power. In 1991 he pressed the government to make Exxon's settlement more generous to native Alaskans after the 1989 *Exxon Valdez* ran aground in the state's Prince William Sound, splling nearly eleven million gallons of crude oil. Sporkin warned prosecutors that they shouldn't allow Exxon to escape "on the cheap."[19] In 1995 Sporkin rejected the US government's settlement with Microsoft over antitrust violations. He branded the company "a potential threat to the nation's well-being" and called the settlement "too little, too late."[20] An appeals court rebuked the maverick for his ruling.

Meanwhile, Rakoff started to think about leaving the Southern District. What would be his next step? Briefly, the new administration considered him as a possible replacement for Sporkin as the new SEC director of enforcement. But it didn't want a Democrat.

## THE WILY GOTCH GETS 'EM

Before the 1970s, the biggest and most prestigious law firms did not do criminal defense work. Criminal defense lawyers worked at boutiques. Gentlemen and elite lawyers from great schools did not participate in such a grubby business. But with the new focus from Morgenthau, Fiske, and Sporkin on top corporate officers, there was a need for top defense attorneys.

The legal world adapted. White-collar criminal defense started to look like a business that was not only respectable but also lucrative. Peter Fleming, a Morgenthau lieutenant, had been the first, moving to Curtis, Mallet-Prevost Curtis, Colt & Mosle in the 1970s. A few years later, Rusty Wing left the Southern District for Weil, Gotshal & Manges. At his farewell party, the office roasted him. Rakoff penned doggerel in the form of a children's poem, warning Wing to beware a mysterious ghoul:

> Now Rusty proved a courtroom pro,
> A prosecutor's panacea.
> His words were as cool as this past week's snow,
> Yet as catchy as gonorrhea.
> Win, lose, or draw, he held all in awe,
> With never a flub or a botch.
> So who would have guessed it was simply a test
> For his future at Wily Gotch.

Cause the Wily Gotch'll getcha though you don't even shout.
Yes, the Weil Gotshal getcha if you don't watch out.

In 1980, a few years after Wing left, Rakoff, too, made a pioneering move, going to a top law firm to start a white-collar criminal practice. He joined Mudge Rose Guthrie & Alexander, where Nixon had worked in the 1960s when he was temporarily out of politics, having lost the California governor's race. The transformation of the business of law was inexorable. Top firms no longer looked down on representing white-collar executives accused of crimes. As prosecutors turned away from focusing on individual prosecutions to probing companies in the following decades, Big Law's criminal defense business got better.

For this lucrative line of fees, Big Law owed much to Stanley Sporkin. Radical and far-reaching as he was, he inadvertently ushered in today's softened regulatory approach. Still overmatched and underfunded, government overseers leverage their authority through compliance mechanisms: corporations police themselves. When they fall under regulatory scrutiny, companies often conduct internal investigations ahead of the government. They hire law firms. The government requires corporations to cooperate. Cooperation yields settlements. Rarely do companies have to admit wrongdoing. Sporkin had imagination and righteousness and tempered assertiveness. Under his watch, the amnesty model worked. But something was lost in translation. The system was fragile. Who serves in government matters. What they believe and how they approach their jobs can be the difference between being tough or being soft. By the mid-2000s, the Sporkin innovations had become perverted.

*Chapter Five*

# THE BACKLASH

In 1994 Mary Jo White's Southern District made the most significant advance in corporate prosecutions in the modern era, forming the first deferred prosecution agreement, or DPA, a special kind of settlement with a company. The office didn't plan it. Beyond the one agreement, they put little thought into what they had done. No one understood that they were creating the model for twenty-first-century corporate law enforcement.

Before the first DPA, the Department of Justice's prosecutorial approach to corporate enforcement evolved slowly. Jed Rakoff's United Brands case in the 1970s was something of a one-off. Prosecutors continued to focus on individuals, rarely contemplating corporatewide enforcement measures until the late 1980s. During the 1980s and 1990s, fear of street crime brought policing and penal changes. Congress and the states passed punitive laws about street crime, increasing prison terms, establishing mandatory minimum sentences, and building the modern prison complex. The movement touched corporations, too. Corporations skated too easily for their wrongdoing. Potential fines were small, as the government realized with United Brands. The profits from illicit activities dwarfed the penalties, neutering any disincentive power they might have.

In the mid-1980s, Congress authorized the creation of the US Sentencing Commission to examine prison terms and codify norms to correct the arbitrary punishments meted out by unaccountable judges. First, in 1989 the commission's guidelines for individuals went into effect, establishing a point system for how many years of prison a convicted criminal might get, based on the seriousness of the misconduct and a person's criminal history. In 1991, amid public and congressional outrage that sentences for white-collar criminals were too light and fines and sanctions for corporations too lenient, the Sentencing Commission expanded the concept to cover organizations. It formalized the Sporkin-era regime of offering leniency in exchange for cooperation and reform. The new rules delineated factors that could earn a culprit mercy. In levying a fine, the court should consider, the sentencing guidelines said, "any collateral consequences of conviction."[1]

"Collateral consequences" was, and remains, an ill-defined concept. How worried should the government be if a punishment causes a company to go out of business? Should regulators worry about the cashiering of innocent employees? What about customers, suppliers, or competitors? Should they fret about financial crises? From this rather innocuous mention, the little notion of collateral consequences would blossom into the great strangling vine that came to be known after the financial crisis of 2008 by its shorthand: "too big to jail." Prosecutors and regulators were crippled by the idea that the government could not criminally sanction some companies—particularly giant banks—for fear that they would collapse, causing serious problems for financial markets or the economy.

As the Sentencing Commission wrote rules for punishing organizations, the Southern District of New York also fumbled for a solution to corporate investigations. In 1992 the office, under White's predecessor, reached an agreement not to file charges against Salomon Brothers, in a case in which traders tried to corner the market for US Treasury bonds.

The office deemed the investment bank's cooperation earnest and complete, so it dismissed the charge upon settling. It did one more similar settlement.

Two years later, in 1994, prosecutors were trying to salvage a flailing case against Prudential Securities. For more than a decade, Prudential brokers steered clients, mainly small investors, into inappropriately risky investments. Brokers pitched them as safe, and they were—but not for the investors. The partnerships served as reliable vehicles for transferring fees to Prudential. Clients had collectively lost more than $2 billion.[2] Yet Southern District prosecutors realized that any Prudential criminal case would face significant problems. Much of the malfeasance had taken place years earlier. Memories were fading, evidence yellowing. The SEC had already settled its civil case a year before, so the agency wasn't generating new evidence. Prudential had a charming CEO who convinced prosecutors of his desire to turn around the company's corporate culture. While no one at the office would admit it publicly, the Southern District was concerned it wouldn't prevail at trial. Prosecutors wouldn't tell Prudential that, obviously. What to do? In a meeting of White's top advisors, her top lieutenant, Shirah Neiman, tossed out an idea: "What about trying a deferred prosecution agreement?"

Until then, such agreements had been used only in street crime. They began in the 1930s as a method of dealing with first-time juvenile defendants. There might be some mitigating circumstances—the criminal had stolen medicine for his sick mother—that might require something less than a full conviction. It was a middle ground between dropping charges and a draconian sanction.[3]

White wasn't enthusiastic, but she couldn't see any other option. She approved the deferred prosecution agreement, the first with a large company. In late October 1994 the Department of Justice filed criminal charges against Prudential Securities but then held off on pressing them on the condition that the firm adhere to reforming itself. The Department of Justice made the company put $330 million into a fund for the investors, doubling the fund that the SEC had set up the previous year. White said that she and her office made the decision not to indict formally out of fear for what would happen to Prudential's eighteen thousand employees and to its clients.[4]

The company accepted a monitor: a law partner who had left his position as a federal judge in the Southern District. He went on Prudential's board of directors and reported to the Manhattan US Attorney's Office over the next three years. Something about the deal rankled Neiman and White; justice had been served underdone. After Prudential, Mary Jo White's office didn't do any corporate deferred prosecutions for the rest of her tenure, which ended in early 2002.

Other US Attorney's Offices around the country did, however. Defense attorneys complained that prosecutors demanded a DPA even before they opened cases. "Some offices really didn't have the evidence to indict a company, but they would threaten them with prosecution and then offer a deferred prosecution if the company cooperated," Neiman would say later. White "rued the day we came up with this idea."[5]

The defense bar worked the new system. Lawyers complained to any official who would listen that they were being extorted into an agreement before the government had amassed evidence to support its suspicions. Defense attorneys, however, would also accept deals when offered early because they stopped an actual investigation. By the mid to late 1990s, defense bar complaints reached Deputy Attorney General Jamie Gorelick and other high-level officials in President Bill Clinton's Justice Department. There seemed to be no rules. What were the policies? What were the factors they considered? The defense bar wanted written guidelines for prosecuting corporations. Gorelick ordered up a memo to codify the approach.

White and Neiman felt a memo was unnecessary. Of course the defense bar knew what the factors were; they were the same in every case. Any settlement came about if there was appropriate cooperation, and defense lawyers understood whether the cooperation was full and sincere. Neiman and White considered the defense bar's complaints ridiculous. A memo was not only unwarranted but also dangerous. Anytime you write down something, clever lawyers can take advantage of it. Defense lawyers would just start arguing about what it did and didn't say.

But the memo was going to happen with or without the Southern District. So Mary Jo White, facing a turf threat on her hands, directed Neiman to go to Washington to make sure the politicos didn't screw up the policy.

White's emissary prosecuted without discrimination, legally and in the hallways—against defendants, their counsel, judges, and Justice Department colleagues, subordinates and superiors alike. Neiman grew up in a modern Orthodox Jewish household in Brooklyn and Queens. Her mother was a concert pianist and piano teacher and her father an intellectual of Jewish history. She went to Ramaz, the Orthodox day school on the Upper East Side; Barnard for college, and then Columbia Law School, where there were only 23 women in her 1968 graduating class of 304. She served on law review.

After law school, Neiman clerked for two federal district court judges, where she began a romance with the courtroom. One of her judge's cases was against a Weather Underground fellow traveler who had helped plant bombs across the city. The day of the trial came, and she sat among the spectators, impatient for it to begin. The prosecutors and the defense team rose to go into the judge's chambers. To her horror, she realized they were going to settle. She was crushed.

By the late 1960s, Neiman had decided to go to the US Attorney's Office in the Southern District. She spoke with the attorney in charge of hiring and told him she wanted to go to the criminal section. The man informed Neiman that the Southern District did not hire women in the criminal division. For years, women had served in the civil division of the Southern District but Robert Morgenthau (as had his predecessors) blocked them from being criminal prosecutors. She said she knew about the policy.

"Are you going to make an issue of it?" he asked.

"Yes, I do intend to and want to make an issue of it," she replied.

It was 1969. While her application process wound through the system,

Morgenthau left in 1970, and Whitney North "Mike" Seymour took over as US attorney. The judge she clerked for, Milton Pollack, one of the most respected federal district court judges of the day, called up Seymour and recommended that he hire one of his great clerks to the criminal division. Seymour told him, "Great! Send him over." "It's not a 'him,'" Pollack replied.

The head of the office's criminal division asked Neiman to lunch at a Chinese restaurant. She had recently stopped keeping kosher and had never been to one before. The food disgusted her. She ordered what he ordered but didn't eat. She remembers him asking her three questions: Will you be able to get along with the FBI agents? Will you be able to handle the blue language in the Thursday criminal division meeting? Will juries believe you?

She was furious. Such sexist, ridiculous questions. Years later, Neiman barely remembers her answers. Of course she could get along with agents and handle any bad words! And why wouldn't juries believe a woman? She went back to her office, and, assuming she wasn't going to get the job, called her contact at a law firm that had recently offered her a position and accepted. Ten minutes later, US Attorney Seymour called and said, "How would you like to be the first woman in the criminal division of the Southern District of New York?" She told him she'd have to think about it over the weekend.

Neiman took the job. Of course she did. When she was sworn in, the *Daily News*, the *Times*, and the *New York Post* all covered it. According to one account, some of her new colleagues sat in the back and said, "All right, let's go to McSorley's." The bar was in the news because it didn't allow women. A collection of pioneering women criminal prosecutors would soon follow her.

Three decades later, Neiman was still at the Southern District. She was an obsessive, telling the *New York Sun* once that she worked "twenty-two hours a day." People believed it. She mastered arcane areas, particularly tax law, making her invaluable. She was curt, short-tempered, and unapproachable, but able. Young prosecutors would rather face down an Islamic terrorist or a Mafia boss than have to deal with Neiman.

Though more often right than wrong, she was missing a diplomacy gene. Neiman recognized that her colleagues held her to a different, double standard. Aggressiveness in a male prosecutor was praised and rewarded; she was criticized for it. She wasn't a pushover but, as she saw it, no more so than many of her male colleagues. When Rudolph Giuliani was a US attorney in the 1980s, he'd banished her physically, moving Neiman to an office on the other side of the floor. In the 1990s, Mary Jo White retrieved her back from Siberia to serve as her chief advisor. Neiman did not fear delivering bad news or wielding a shiv in a turf battle. White could arrive on the scene and be the placating hero in the wake of Neiman's "violence."

Now, in 1999, Neiman had another job to do for White: to help shape the new corporate prosecution guidelines. Putting aside her disdain, she did her typical mountain of research, looking at White's speeches, case law, and her own history and institutional knowledge. Neiman arrived in Washington with an outline of the factors that prosecutors should think about before bringing charges against a company. These made up the heart of what would become the Holder memo, named after Eric Holder, who was then deputy attorney general under Janet Reno. Holder himself had little to do with drafting it. Of the many people on the memo's working committee, Neiman was the most forceful.

The Holder memo, signed on June 16, 1999, wasn't policy; it provided only guidance for prosecutors. But it was the first effort by the Justice Department to enumerate principles for charging corporations. In corporate prosecutions, the Holder memo first laid out the usual factors: prosecutors needed to consider "the sufficiency of the evidence, the likelihood of success at trial, the probable deterrent, rehabilitative, and other consequences of conviction." But it went further than that. It proposed eight other factors prosecutors could consider when deciding whether to indict a corporation:

1. the seriousness of the offense and risk of harm to the public;
2. the pervasiveness of wrongdoing at the company;
3. the corporation's history of similar conduct;
4. the corporation's timely and voluntary disclosure of the wrongdoing and its willingness to cooperate in the investigation, "including, if necessary, the waiver of the corporate attorney-client and work product privileges";
5. the existence and adequacy of the corporation's compliance program;
6. the corporation's remedial actions;
7. the collateral consequences, "including disproportionate harm to shareholders and employees not proven personally culpable"; and
8. the adequacy of noncriminal remedies.

The new elements essentially changed how the law would be enforced. The Supreme Court had allowed corporations to be prosecuted as legal persons since the 1909 *New York Central & Hudson* decision. The Holder memo conceded something that had been influencing prosecutorial decisions about corporate indictments since Mary Jo White's Prudential DPA: corporations are different from individuals. The memo was an admission that the government did not desire or seek a corporate indictment as a matter of routine.

How to get sufficient cooperation bedeviled the department. Companies evaded investigations and hid wrongdoing even as they made a show of cooperating. For years, big businesses hid behind attorney-client privilege to conceal facts and bad behavior. They shielded questionable conduct by invoking privilege, rendering details of suspect dealings by top executives inadmissible in court.[6]

When companies came under federal scrutiny, they typically paid the legal bills for its executives, hiring some of the nation's best law firms, which were expert at slowing or even killing inquiries. When multiple executives fell under suspicion, their lawyers would often sign joint defense agreements allowing them to share with one another what they had learned about the Feds' case.

Since these maneuvers hindered the government's investigations, Neiman and her memo-formulating colleagues sought to explain to the corporate world and the defense bar that this behavior would not be tolerated anymore. Their tactics had become a form of obstruction of justice. To reverse this slide, the Holder memo authors laid out what cooperation meant. If necessary, they wrote, companies would need to waive corporate attorney-client privilege. Such privilege is rule of evidence that protects clients from having their lawyers use the information they gave them against them in court. A bedrock principle of ethical conduct that predates the American legal system, lawyers treat attorney-client privilege as sacrosanct.

For the first few years of its existence, the Holder memo, including the attorney-client privilege waiver language, wasn't controversial. Then came the Thompson memo.

## THOMPSON GETS TOUGH

After the Arthur Andersen prosecution in 2002, Deputy Attorney General Larry Thompson was preoccupied with how to rein in corporations and fend off critics of his aggressive Justice Department. Political advisors in the George W. Bush administration began to worry. Corporate executives told White House aides that the Justice Department was demonizing business. The Enron Task Force was too aggressive. Corporate executives weren't used to being treated this way—and by a Republican administration! In early 2002 the president summoned Thompson to the White House. The deputy attorney general and FBI Director Robert Mueller met with the president in the Roosevelt Room of the White House. The two of them decided not to talk legal theory with him; instead, they showed him the evidence prosecutors had amassed in investigations such as the Enron case. Thompson, with short gray-flecked hair and rimless glasses, spoke in his stately manner, barely above a whisper, laying out the evidence.

George Bush seemed stunned. His trusted advisors explained how executives, some of whom he knew personally, like Ken Lay, made up numbers and lied to the public. The president could no longer condone what was happening at corporations. At the end of the presentation, he turned to Mueller and Thompson and dashed the hopes of his political and economic advisors. Bush said, "Bobby and L.T., continue what you are doing." It was just what a law-and-order man like Larry Thompson wanted to hear.

Born in 1945, Larry Dean Thompson grew up in Hannibal, Missouri, Mark Twain's hometown. His mother was a cook who worked in various private homes; his father worked as a railroad laborer. Neither had more than a high school education. Missouri was segregated, so Thompson attended an all–African American school through the eighth grade. For vacations, Thompson's father would get free passes on the railroad, taking the family all over the Midwest. Even in ostensibly integrated places, they couldn't count on being able to find a hotel that would put them up. The Thompson family relied on an informal network of African American families to board them when needed. Such experiences hadn't left him embittered. He recalled the acts of kindness and equity. Thompson played basketball and football for his integrated high school. Once, when a restaurant in town refused to serve him, his coach and teammates declined to eat there without their black teammate.

In his preintegration schools, Thompson's teachers employed a strict, rigid style. Sometimes they would tell him he had to be better than white students. One year, at a citywide spelling bee for students from all four schools in town—three white and one black—Thompson came in second. His teachers didn't praise him, they assailed him. He was going to be a failure because he didn't work hard enough, they said. Thompson loved them for it. He liked to say that he never knew he was "quote-unquote 'disadvantaged' " until he was a college sophomore taking sociology classes, and his professors taught about class stratification in the United States.

Thompson had little notion of politics in his youth. But by 1964, he'd read *The Conscience of a Conservative* by Senator Barry Goldwater, the conservative insurgent and Republican candidate for president in 1964, and found an ideological home. He didn't care for Goldwater's stance against the Civil Rights Act of 1964, but otherwise, the views of the Arizona firebrand grabbed him. Thompson never thought that expecting the government to support people was right; he would point out to people that it was the government that had enforced segregation. The conservatives he came to know treated him more like an individual, he felt, while the liberals patronized him.[7]

He graduated from Culver-Stockton College in Canton, Missouri, in 1967, earned a master's degree in sociology from Michigan State University, and then went on to the University of Michigan Law School, graduating in 1974. Thompson's first intense involvement in politics came in 1980, when he became a soldier in the Reagan revolution. An associate at an Atlanta law firm, King & Spalding, Thompson campaigned for Mack Mattingly, the first Georgia Republican to be elected to the US Senate since the post–Civil War Reconstruction period. Two years later, thanks to Mattingly, Thompson was drafted to become the US attorney for the District Court for the Northern District of Georgia. He was thirty-six years old.

As a prosecutor, Thompson came to believe that white-collar crime could be just as serious as blue-collar street crime. It sapped the economy and created an uneven playing field. A sense that no one was above the law fired him. As a US attorney, he heard all kinds of excuses. He liked a thought experiment: a drug dealer is caught, say, in Brooklyn. The dealer says, "I gave a lot of money to charities in the Eastern District of New York. I'm willing to resolve this problem, but I'm not going to plead guilty to a crime. I want a civil resolution. You can take my money and give it to the charities. You can do all kinds of things. You can do all kinds of things to me, but I cannot agree to a criminal resolution."

It was preposterous. This country put kids in prison for carrying drugs. But the United States should accept corporate bigwigs going free because the company settled with the Justice Department? He was so mild-mannered that all he would say was that this state of affairs bothered him. Larry Thompson allowing that something "bothered" him was the equivalent of a normal person overturning a table.

Both Shirah Neiman and Larry Thompson were steely about white-collar crime. They believed that the priority of prosecutors should be going after individuals. Perhaps not coincidentally, both were outsiders: a pioneering woman and an African American Republican.

Thompson never once doubted the necessity of indicting Arthur Andersen. The accounting firm had been so truculent that the prosecutors had to indict. He believed in the decision. But the prosecution had stirred outrage, forcing him to respond.

Just as Neiman and the Southern District had to respond to pressure from the defense bar to help craft the Holder memo, Thompson had to turn his attention to the same questions over how the department approached corporate prosecutions. He and his team decided to revise the Holder memo.

The result, known as the Thompson memo, came out on January 20, 2003, six months after Arthur Andersen had been found guilty. The only substantive change was a new factor to consider, number eight of nine: "The adequacy of the prosecution of individuals responsible for the corporation's malfeasance." Thompson still wanted prosecutions of individuals to be the government's priority. Additionally, the Thompson memo formalized the policy outlined by its predecessor, the Holder memo. That memo was only advisory, but US Attorney's Offices around the country had to follow Thompson. In his preface, Thompson emphasized how necessary the guidelines were. Companies, he wrote, purport to cooperate while impeding exposure of the full account of a company's wrongdoing.

The Thompson memo offered a deal. It was not intended to be a generous one. Companies could win Brownie points for being cooperative. Prosecutors could push companies to waive their attorney-client privilege and share detailed materials with the government. They needed to cooperate with the prosecutions of individuals. And they had to eschew tactics such as joint defense agreements, in which the various counsels for various targets of investigation share information about government tactics and prosecutorial knowledge. Sophisticated companies with their sophisticated lawyers had defenses when the government began to investigate. The government wanted to tear those down.

Thompson had a goal for prosecutors and a message for business. He wanted to make certain that the Justice Department wasn't going to indict a corporation willy-nilly, even though it could by law. He wanted to make sure, however, that companies understood what they had to do. Pervasive bad behavior, a lack of contrition, a phony compliance program—his Department of Justice would treat these transgressions sternly. Members of the white-collar bar howled in outrage.

## THE THOMPSON ATTACKS

By the middle of 2003, Thompson was getting attacked from both sides. Corporate America was furious about how aggressive the Justice Department had been in its investigations and prosecutions following the Nasdaq crash. The public and the media, however, wanted immediate gratification. In an interview on CNBC in June 2003, a host asked Thompson what was taking so long. Just that month, Martha Stewart had been charged with obstructing justice in an insider trading probe. "The CEOs in the most notorious scandals still haven't been charged. Why is it that we see Martha Stewart marching into court, but not Ken Lay, Jeff Skilling, Bernie Ebbers?" (Ebbers was the cofounder and CEO of WorldCom. He would be convicted of fraud and conspiracy in 2005 and is currently serving a twenty-five-year prison term.)

Thompson responded: "We're looking at the facts of these investigations, and we're going to let the facts take us to the people that are involved in these matters. We don't want to be engaged in any kind of what I would call a lynch mob mentality. We're going to proceed professionally, methodically, but most importantly, thoroughly."[8] He repeated the "lynch mob" line in a press conference the next month. It was an unfortunate metaphor for a man who had grown up in segregated Missouri.

Like Stanley Sporkin, he preferred to play down his tough approach, while remaining serious about prosecuting individual wrongdoers.

A more powerful backlash against the Justice Department's aggression began to take shape. The corporate lobby and the defense bar began to attack the Justice Department's new policies for corporation prosecutions. They could not attack prosecutors for going after corrupt and unsympathetic Enron, WorldCom, or Adelphia executives. The soft underbelly of the Thompson memo was the demand for companies to waive their attorney-client privilege. When a company waived its privilege over an investigation, it delivered all of the law firm's materials to the government, including details of employees' meetings with lawyers—such as transcripts of interviews the lawyers conducted. Understanding how much exposure the materials might contain, law firms and companies sought to protect them.

The corporate lobby waited. Memories of Arthur Andersen's crimes receded, supplanted by the company's PR narrative. In September 2004, a little more than two years after Andersen's indictment, the American Bar Association began its push against the Justice Department. The ABA created a task force on the attorney-client privilege problem, focused on rolling back the government's policies. (The SEC had a similar directive.)

The ABA helped form a coalition with business lobbyists and trade organizations, including the Business Roundtable and the US Chamber of Commerce, as well as the Association of Corporate Counsel and the National Association of Criminal Defense Lawyers. Even the American Civil Liberties Union (ACLU) jumped into the coalition protecting the rights of corporations. The coalition lobbied and railed against aggressive prosecutors, but there was no serious effort to quantify the extent of the problem. The research was junk science. The studies had classic indicia of push-polling, with leading questions. And the respondents were more likely to have been investigated, skewing the results. The Justice Department's antagonists conducted online surveys, without random samples, making the results scientifically invalid. In one survey from 2005, the coalition found that 50 percent of respondents under investigation had waived privilege.

Of course, this meant that even with a self-selected group, the other half did not. In a subsequent study, the coalition conceded, "[S]ince we are not an independent surveying company or statisticians, we can make no proffer that the sampling is statistically significant or representative of the entire profession." As a legal scholar would write later, the surveys "were not conducted with even minimal rigor, at least tested by the standards required in academic circles." She concluded there was no evidence of the claimed abuses.[9] Nevertheless, Congress cited them in criticizing the Justice Department.

The *Wall Street Journal* editorial page joined the campaign with enthusiasm. In one editorial, it denounced the Thompson memo as an institutionalized method to threaten a corporate "death sentence." One 2006 op-ed labeled it "the odious Thompson memo."[10] Thompson often shared the page's politics but fell out with the paper over its attacks.

Even Mary Jo White, who had traded in her post as US attorney for a partnership at the powerful New York law firm Debevoise & Plimpton, became a zealous Justice Department critic. In 2005 White gave a speech titled "Corporate Criminal Liability: What Has Gone Wrong?," opining, "On the federal level especially, the sweep of corporate criminal liability could hardly be broader." She conceded:

> I must bear my share of responsibility for how government prosecutors are today using the easy prospect of corporate criminal liability and the Thompson memorandum to inject themselves too deeply into the business of corporate America and to dictate how companies must respond to government investigation. But, having now been on the receiving end of these measures in my representations of companies in criminal investigations, I have seen the light and urge that some prosecutors should change or at least moderate how they are treating companies in criminal investigations.[11]

Thompson left the administration in August 2003, becoming general counsel for PepsiCo the following year. He attended meetings of the

American Bar Association, despite its task force devoted to rolling back his memo. People brazenly said to him, "Larry, we know you really didn't mean to write it this way. You're a pretty good guy." Then they would continue, denouncing the memo. The same happened at the US Chamber of Commerce and the National Association of Criminal Defense Lawyers meetings. Thompson felt uncomfortable and patronized. "Such an outcry over the mistreatment of these poor corporate executives!" he thought. Even assuming that prosecutors were a little too aggressive with them, well, law enforcement gets tough with targets sometimes, he figured. Big companies and big lawyers could handle it.

In a clever touch, defense attorneys couched their arguments against Thompson as a way to *help* the Department of Justice in its investigations. They argued that the language suggesting that companies waive attorney-client privilege intimidated employees, forcing them to clam up during internal probes. In a September 2006 letter to then US attorney general Alberto Gonzales, various Republican and Democratic luminaries wrote in support of proposed revisions. Among them were former attorneys general, including Dick Thornburgh; deputy attorneys general, such as Jamie Gorelick; and onetime solicitor generals Theodore Olson and Kenneth Starr. "By making waiver of privilege and work-product protections nearly assured, the department's policies discourage personnel within companies and other organizations from consulting with their lawyers, thereby impeding the lawyers' ability effectively to counsel compliance with the law," the letter claimed.[12]

Gorelick, who had ordered up the precursor memo to Thompson, which also had the attorney-client privilege language, was now working in the private sector as a partner defending corporations at WilmerHale. Larry Thompson thought the effort silly and cynical. Critics summoned no evidence to back up their wild claims. He thought that Washington groups were trying to show corporations how much they were in their corner to whip up outrage and generate donations. Thompson had become a fund-raising tool.

Around that time, he read about a small scandal out of Los Angeles

County. Cops were arresting Latino men, taking them into custody, and giving them their Miranda rights on a giant screen that had been mounted in a holding pen. Then the police asked the arrestees to sign papers saying they understood what had just been displayed before them. Could they have grasped their rights? Who knew if they even spoke English? Few, if anyone, objected to the police practice. At the same time, people on the Beltway conference and cocktail circuit and up and down the Amtrak Acela Express corridor raised their collective voices over corporate executives getting their rights trampled. Drug dealers, mobsters, terrorists—there was no outcry about any other class of potential criminal except corporate executives.

Thompson was in his office at Pepsi when an old acquaintance, Chris Christie, the US attorney in New Jersey, called him. "I want to give you a heads-up of what's going on here. Can we have lunch?" They met in the Trump International Hotel and Tower on Columbus Circle.

Christie told him some bad news: the furor over the Thompson memo had the White House scared. In its early years, when Thompson was there, the Bush administration refrained from meddling in Justice Department decisions. Now Alberto Gonzales was attorney general. He had never adjusted to the transition from having been White House counsel, acting like a political operative rather than the head law enforcement officer in the land. Christie told Thompson that some Justice Department politicos were preparing to renounce the Thompson memo.

US attorneys around the country were angry. They thought the memo brought corporations to the negotiating table. Christie led a group of US attorneys, never the most easily mobilized group, to prevent the withdrawal of the memo. (Christie had a spotty history with corporate prosecutions. Critics charged he doled out lucrative corporate monitorships to friends. In one case, he had Bristol-Myers Squibb donate to his alma mater in exchange for a settlement with the drugmaker. At Main Justice, top officials were deeply concerned about the deal, which made it appear as if a US attorney was using his office to benefit an institution close to him. The Justice Department changed the rules to prevent such arrangements. In another deal, Christie gave John Ashcroft, the former attorney general, a monitorship that ended up being worth as much as $52 million for his firm, far more than initially anticipated.)[13]

Congress mobilized to make waiver requests illegal. The Justice Department could not tolerate this legislative branch incursion on executive power. Caving, the Bush appointees set to work revising the Thompson memo. On December 12, 2006, Paul McNulty, who was now in Thompson's role as deputy attorney general, announced a change. The new policy called for carefully weighing the benefits and costs to an investigation of a waiver before requesting one. Now, before any such request, prosecutors had to obtain permission from their US attorney, who in turn needed sign-off by the head of the criminal division of Main Justice.[14]

In his letter introducing the new policy, McNulty wrote that the Justice Department had "experienced unprecedented success in prosecuting corporate fraud during the last four years." But corporate officials had been complaining, he wrote. "Many of those associated with the corporate legal community have expressed concern that our practices may be discouraging full and candid communications between corporate employees and legal counsel."

McNulty and the late-era Bush Justice Department had now embraced the criticisms from the defense bar and the corporate lobby.

The McNulty memo had new language, extolling attorney-client privilege, calling it "one of the oldest and most sacrosanct privileges under US law." But the memo also explained that such waivers could be crucial in helping investigations, helping the government evaluate "the accuracy and completeness of the company's voluntary disclosure." The critics were not placated. They wanted a complete rollback.

## *Chapter Six*

# PAUL PELLETIER'S WHITE WHALE

IN SEPTEMBER 2002 A YOUNG LAWYER NAMED Michael Atkinson had just left a lucrative partnership at a comfortable law firm to join Main Justice, where he was thrown together with a senior prosecutor named Paul Pelletier to investigate PNC Bank. In 2001 PNC had conducted some complex deals to get soured assets off its balance sheet, arranged by a secretive division of the giant insurance company AIG called AIG Financial Products. The deals were shams. AIG Financial Products took no risk, parking the assets for a fee so that PNC could make its books look better for investors and regulators. The deals had unraveled, and now Atkinson and Pelletier were to begin their probe.

First they flew up to Pittsburgh and then took a cab to the FBI offices in a new and (by government standards) lavish building just outside the city. Atkinson was getting a chance to do what he wanted when he joined the government: dig into complex corporate crime and expose bad executives. He was meeting the FBI for the first time. He wouldn't necessarily have admitted it, but yeah, he felt almost giddy.

The two men arrived in the lobby and signed in. Then they sat, waiting. A half hour passed. Pelletier, who had a raspy voice and an assertive South Boston accent, blond locks, and Ray-Bans often dangling from his Croakies, grew increasingly agitated. The senior prosecutor had a sprawling network throughout the Department of Justice. He'd been around. Now he had a sense of what was coming in Pittsburgh: a turf battle for the PNC case. An FBI agent had called down to a Justice colleague in Miami to get the book on Pelletier before the meeting. Unbeknownst to the FBI agent, the colleague happened to be a buddy of Pelletier's and tipped him off. Pelletier shrugged it off. "Yeah, they said they're gonna give me an ear douche about the case." "Ear douche"? That was a new one for Atkinson, and he wasn't sure what the hell it meant. Soon he would learn there were many Pelletierisms. "Don't let them fugitate!" he'd say, warning his prosecutors not to let their targets get out from under their surveillance. When people didn't want to hear what you were saying, for whatever reason, you had to give them an ear douche to break through that waxy buildup so that they would understand they had no choice but to do it Pelletier's way.

After more than an hour of waiting, the agent came to bring Atkinson and Pelletier upstairs to a conference room. The two prosecutors figured out what had been going on as they waited. The FBI agent, an FBI supervisor, and a staff attorney for the Pittsburgh US Attorney's Office had been sitting there talking this whole time! They were conspiring to keep Main Justice out of the case. PNC was a nice target for them, a chance to get on the *Pittsburgh Post-Gazette*'s front page—maybe even the *Wall Street Journal*—and they'd be damned if Washington was going to muscle in on them. His expectations confirmed, Pelletier sat listening to the FBI supervisor talk about the case, not bothering to hide his impatience and irritation. The supervisor explained that Pittsburgh—the local FBI and the US Attorney's Office—would take the lead on the case. They weren't even sure they needed Main Justice.

Pelletier could handle only about ten minutes. "There's no fucking way you are taking the lead on the case," he snarled. "You wouldn't know where to fucking begin with this, but it doesn't matter because you guys aren't even going to be on the case. You guys have a conflict. You are going to be recused. It's going to be our case! Not yours. Do you want to talk about how we can get this investigation going, or are you going to have us sit around for another hour? And by the way: *fuck you*!" Pelletier roared.

"No, fuck *you*!" the FBI supervisor screamed back.

Atkinson stared. This meeting had gone sideways faster and more completely than anything he'd ever seen in the private sector. Weren't they all on the same team?

Sure enough, Pelletier was right. The Pittsburgh office was recused. The US attorney had a conflict of interest. It became Atkinson's and Pelletier's case. The investigation of PNC began a years-long quest for Pelletier to bring AIG to justice. AIG became his white whale. He would bring some charges and win some battles, but the Department of Justice did not succeed in changing AIG's culture or deterring its aggressive and often lawless behavior. By 2008, AIG Financial Products had blown up due to its exposure to risky assets it had not disclosed adequately, helping to bring down the global financial system. Pelletier and his colleagues would investigate AIG all over again, probing the same people. That investigation would be thwarted, too, thanks, he was convinced, to his bosses at the Department of Justice rather than a lack of sufficent evidence against the AIG Financial Products executives.

## DO YOUR J.O. GODDAMN B.

Pelletier had just come up to Washington from the Miami US Attorney's Office, where he had been the chief of the white-collar unit. Charming the secretaries, chatting with the security guards, scowling at the supervisors, inquiring after everyone's family, Pelletier was, most said, a prosecutor's prosecutor. "Paul came out of the womb divisive. Nobody has ever had ambivalent feelings about Paul," says Guy Singer, a former colleague and admirer. To those who loved him, he possessed a romantic nobility, pure and apolitical. The head of the criminal division, Josh Hochberg, recruited him to solve a problem.

Main Justice had long been an also-ran to the Southern District of New York. The Southern District got the biggest, most important cases, especially corporate fraud matters. Main Justice supervisors tended to farm out their prosecutors to help other offices. These prosecutors didn't have much trial experience themselves and therefore avoided taking their cases to court, compounding their weakness. Instead, they sought to settle cases—or failed to conclude them altogether. Hochberg wanted to change that by improving the quality and skills of his assistant prosecutors. He went around the country looking for trial dogs: lawyers who thrived in front of juries. He didn't care about pedigree. He wasn't out to create a collection of graduates from the best law schools. He saw that Miami's US Attorney's Office was successful. The office took a different approach than the Southern District, however. In Manhattan, they were deliberative and hierarchical. But down in Miami, the office hired street-smart lawyers and gave them freedom. Few of the attorneys had attended the most prestigious institutions in the country. The office motto was "If it's a choice between perfect and fast, choose fast." Paul embodied the Miami approach. Pelletier wasn't rash, and he wasn't thoughtless, but he is a creature of action. "Don't fuck around. Make a goddamn decision and move forward," he would say.

Hochberg had gotten to know Pelletier because he'd been sending prosecutors to work with him in Miami, to get litigation experience. Pelletier resisted Hochberg at first. No way he'd have his trials saddled with a bunch of useless clods from DC. "It was more of a pain in the ass than it was worth, and I'd be spending time training his prosecutors instead of working my cases," Pelletier says. Hochberg took care to send down his brightest prospects, and, in the end, Pelletier came to think it hadn't been as bad as he'd expected. They'd even been helpful occasionally.

Pelletier had been telling Hochberg for months that there was no way he was going to leave Miami. He was having too much fun. In one of their discussions, Hochberg told him the fraud section at Main Justice had fifty lawyers and fifteen indicted cases going on right then.

"Fifty indicted cases—five-oh? Or fifteen—one-five?" Pelletier asked. Fifteen, Hochberg repeated, or about one for every three lawyers. "Fifteen!?!? Get the fuck out of here." Over the course of thirteen years in Miami, Pelletier had handled more than a hundred trials, about twenty of them white-collar, including health care and money-laundering cases.

If Pelletier was a true-blue, full-blooded prosecutor, he was an unlikely one. Born August 21, 1956, he'd grown up in Dighton, Massachusetts, a working-class town of 3,500 south of Boston, the fourth of eleven children. After the tenth child, his mother, Marge, had two miscarriages. Her doctor told her, "Your body is telling you 'No more.' " But she thought she had a lot more love to give and adopted a child, choosing one from the *Boston Globe*'s weekly feature of an "unadoptable child." Brian, the eleventh, had juvenile-onset Huntington's disease and died young. Pelletier's father was a manager of a Sears, first in Fall River, Massachusetts, and then in Newport, Rhode Island. After raising her children, Marge went back to school to become a registered nurse.

Paul worked from a young age and studied on a strictly voluntary basis. From age eleven, he worked at Bradshaw's Food Products, a chicken farm that also distributed to the local bars. He and his brother Mike made pickled eggs. They'd boil them, peel them by rolling them up and down on a washboard, put them in the brine, and then deliver them. They'd do about two thousand eggs each day after school. They'd also pickle just about anything that could be pickled: Polish sausage, onions, pigs' feet, ham hocks, lamb's tongue, tripe. Paul started out earning $1 an hour.

One day in 1970, one of their sisters—Mike and Paul can no longer remember which one—was watching *What's My Line?*, the popular TV game show where a panel of wisecracking B-list celebrities tried to guess the occupation of each guest. She said to Mike and Paul, "You guys have got a really stupid job. Why don't you write in?" When they dismissed her, she wrote in on their behalf. They got on the show. To get to New York, they flew from Providence, making them the first members of the Pelletier family to fly. The show taped in the Ed Sullivan Theater. Mike was fifteen, and Paul was thirteen. They got to meet actress Sandy Duncan and comic Soupy Sales. When they got back, they told everyone, generating predictable skepticism from their classmates. Several months later, when the episode aired, they became local heroes for a moment. Officials made an announcement about the appearance over the school PA system. The local newspapers covered the episode.

Paul devoted much of his childhood to avoiding getting caught. He evaded the nuns; only the slower kids got caught by them. But the police managed to nail him a couple of times. One night, at age fifteen, Pelletier went to a party where his hockey coach had bought a beer keg for the players. Soon the keg ran out. Paul and a friend got into his VW Beetle to drive to a bar. Paul had bought it recently for $50 in anticipation of getting his learner's permit. The car had no plates yet. Their plan, made in the haze of a few beers and with teenage logic, was to drive down back roads with the headlights turned off to avoid detection.

He and his buddy drove across the town line to Taunton to the bar. No one knew the name of it, but it had a big sign displaying the words "Open Hearth Inn." (It would later burn down.) As Pelletier and his friend pulled into the bar's parking lot, a cop was driving out. He looked at them skeptically and flashed his lights. The officer got out and wandered over, telling the boys that the vehicle had no license plates. Paul turned to his friend and exclaimed with a look of shock, "Someone must have stolen them!" Asked for his license and registration, Paul responded by saying that he must have left them on his bureau at home. The cop took the two down to the station, where they watched *The Munsters* on TV.

Meanwhile, back at home, Paul's brother Mike was sneaking in past his curfew. He had just gotten to the top of the staircase when the phone rang, waking the household. Their father ambled out of bed to answer it. It was the Taunton police. Their dad looked at Mike and said, "Get your jacket on. We're headed to police station, and I'll deal with you later."

"I was fuming," Mike says. "To this day, I believe I would have made it to my bedroom past my curfew if the phone didn't go off."

Small-time justice being what it was, the cop was prepared to let Paul off, thanks in part to the teenager's smooth talk. As they drove home,

Mike, still furious, turned to their father and, with all the innocence he could muster, said, "Dad, I think I can smell alcohol. Do you think Paul has been drinking?"

A few years later, Pelletier would become an unlikely cop himself. He had attended Catholic schools, finishing by graduating from Providence College in 1978. During college, he developed a vague notion to go into public service. He figured becoming a lawyer might help. But he had no money for law school. His jobs pickling at Bradshaw's and tending bar at the Rusty Scupper didn't provide enough. One day all of Pelletier's buddies came to the bar to announce that they were going to take the test to become local cops in Dighton. When he heard it paid well, he took the test with them.

Pelletier posted the highest score and got the sole position open. He wasn't a full-time police officer but a "special" cop, assigned to scut work such as traffic and security details. For about a year and a half, he worked for the police at the Taunton dog track, his only collar coming when a guy tried to submit a phony trifecta ticket. When he held the shotgun to protect the accountants as they tallied up the track's daily take, he got an extra dollar. Soon he'd had enough and saved enough. It was time to go to law school.

New England School of Law in Boston admitted him—not one of the more prestigious institutions in the city, much less in the country. But by the end of Pelletier's first year, he was on law review. After two judicial clerkships, he managed to get hired into the tax division of Main Justice in 1984, working the southern region. Young prosecutors started in sleepy locales so that they couldn't do much damage. If they showed promise, they could work up to a slightly less sleepy one. Pelletier started in Birmingham, Alabama, getting thrown into three jury trials in the first six months.

In 1989, after a few years of working his way up the bureaucracy, he landed in a genuine hot spot: Miami. These were the *Miami Vice* years, the stylized show that glamorized the world of cops and drug dealers. For a young prosecutor, the city provided a cornucopia of crime, and anyone with some brains couldn't help being successful. After four and a half years of tax fraud cases, he moved over to the Miami US Attorney's Office and soon was handling narcotics cases. "It was a beautiful time to become a federal prosecutor," Pelletier recalls. In 1986 Congress passed a law criminalizing money laundering. The US Sentencing Commission put in new guidelines, and legislatures passed mandatory minimum punishments and new forfeiture laws. Prosecutors had new weapons. Previously, Miami prosecutors specialized in picking up what Pelletier called "roadkill": small-time cases that could be tied up quickly. Now with the new tools, the Miami office started targeting more serious criminals. Pelletier and his colleagues started going after big drug organizations. Over the coming decades, prosecutors would abuse these tools, but in the early years, he says, "This leveled the playing field. I got fifty-year sentences on people who deserved fifty-year sentences."

Pelletier's flamboyant manner was suited to the place and time. He made the *Guinness Book of World Records* for a period for having pulled off the largest-ever illegal-drug-cash seizure: $200 million. Newly ambitious, prosecutors started to go after the drug lawyers; clearly, they assisted in the crimes. In the Miami office, there was a gentlemen's agreement among the lawyers on the defense side and the older prosecutors. Prosecutors did not pursue their fellow attorneys. But the young firebrands, including Pelletier, threw out the old norms. They started pursuing defense lawyers for aiding and abetting money laundering. They prosecuted "Dirty Mel" Kessler, who once joked, "I have more cash than Burger King," and who'd helped hide $9.5 million in drug money.[1] Some of the first money Pelletier seized was an envelope of cash found on Kessler.

Pelletier got a tutorial on how to build a case against an enterprise. He learned how to move up the chain from the low-level dealers to the kingpin. He swept up everyone, including the lawyers. He used the new federal rules—such as the threats of the mandatory minimum sentences and pretrial detention—to force them to cooperate against their bosses. Ultimately, he could take out the whole organization.

Seeking a greater challenge, Pelletier wanted his office to go after bankers, lawyers, and corporate professionals, not just drug organizations and their shifty counsel. In 1997 Pelletier became the head of the white-collar unit. Five years later, he conducted a big Medicare fraud trial with a colleague, Kirk Ogrosky. On one side were three prosecutors. On the other were fifteen defense attorneys representing twelve defendants, including several physicians, pharmacists, and clinic owners. It was a nasty, hard-fought trial. The defense alleged misconduct and motioned for mistrial. Even as Pelletier and his colleagues pressed the case hard, Paul stayed affable. He cracked jokes and buoyed his fellow prosecutors and agents. The jury seemed to love him.

After months, the jury returned its verdict. The prosecutors won, convicting most of the defendants. After hearing the verdict, one of the now-felonious doctors walked over to the prosecutors' table. He scowled at Ogrosky and then walked past him to Pelletier. The two of them looked at each other. Then the doctor gave Pelletier a big hug. "I hated what the guy did, so I just tortured him, and the jury brought him to justice. It was weird, but I think it was out of respect," Pelletier explains.

His Miami superiors wanted Pelletier to clean up the division. The white-collar unit had too many, as Pelletier put it, "RIPs": people "retired in place." One time he began a campaign to get rid of a prosecutor who was, in Pelletier-ese, "vociferous in his incompetence." Paul was belittling and public about it. Do your "J.O. Goddamn B.!" he'd cry.

But it was the government, and personnel decisions happened slowly. After the targeted prosecutor made such a serious mistake that it jeopardized a prosecution, Pelletier thought they had enough to get rid of him. The head of the unit called Pelletier and another supervisor into his office. He told Pelletier that he was prepared to move the young assistant out of the section. Then he told Pelletier to be more respectful toward him. The supervisor left the office. Pelletier, fuming that he'd been upbraided in front of another prosecutor—and for something about which he was right—walked to the door, shut it, and locked it. Then he exploded. "I will fucking kill you! Never fucking do that to me again in front of my charges!"

Pelletier developed a reputation as a good boss, an effective leader, and a savvy manager of investigations. "He never once talked about winning. There was never an 'attaboy' for getting a judge to do big sentence," remembers Ogrosky. "It was always about doing the right thing." Pelletier was teaching a crucial lesson to young prosecutors. When confronted with a tough case that they worried they couldn't win, their inclination would be to cut a deal. But Pelletier told them to resist. If the prosecutor believed the person was guilty and if the evidence was sufficient, the government should bring the case—even if it might lose at trial. If evidence is insufficient, Pelletier would say, of course don't indict that case. That happens. Witnesses disappear. They change their stories. But if you believe in the evidence and you lose at trial, well, that's the justice system.

## CHASING AIG

Josh Hochberg had been watching Pelletier for several years. The fraud section needed his talents and attitude. Hochberg prevailed on Pelletier to come up to Washington. When he left Miami, his supervisors joked that half the defense bar wanted him disbarred, while the other half feared him. In July 2002 Pelletier joined Main Justice with a fancy title: special counsel for litigation.

A few months later, Pelletier met Mike Atkinson. Pelletier came away impressed. Smart and serious, Atkinson had left a big-time law firm job to come work for the government. That put him on the right side of things, in Pelletier's view.

After the turf battle with the Pittsburgh US attorneys, Pelletier and Atkinson settled into investigating PNC and its enablers. AIG Financial Products, a mysterious division of the insurer, sold the vehicles to the bank. Ernst & Young, the auditor, signed off on the deals. Financial deregulation was the watchword of the moment. Bank regulators, such as the Federal Reserve and the Office of the Comptroller of the Currency, freed banks of strictures. AIG was even less subject to government oversight than banks. States regulate insurance. They could not rein in a sprawling multinational like AIG. Maurice "Hank" Greenberg, the founder, CEO, and chairman of the insurer, reigned as one of the last of the Imperial CEOs, tightly controlling his behemoth organization. He had built AIG into the world's largest insurer, obsessed with AIG's daily stock price as a mark of his wealth and accomplishment. AIG Financial Products was a rogue within the rogue, a secretive skunkworks operation. AIG FP didn't manage investments and it wasn't a bank; it didn't help companies with shares or mergers. It wasn't subject to any regular regulation whatsoever.[2] The operation pushed "innovative" products, a term that in financial markets tends to mean regulatory arbitrage, exploiting a loophole in government rules.

Pelletier and Atkinson knew they wanted to target culpable individuals. They would investigate the three companies involved, including Ernst & Young, but to investigate all three at once was to investigate none. So they started with PNC. The bank had done three such deals with AIG FP involving a total of $762 million in assets. PNC and AIG FP created a new entity, "off" PNC's balance sheet, to hold on to the souring assets. The key element to make the deals acceptable to PNC's auditors was that an independent third party—in this case, AIG FP—needed to invest in the newly created company. AIG FP was supposedly in control of the vehicle, not PNC. Ostensibly, the deal conformed to the rules about such vehicles at the time. But the deals had a slick element: AIG FP got fees that equaled its investment, plus a little bit, and PNC took all the risk. PNC wasn't getting rid of the assets in any meaningful sense. If the value of the assets fell, PNC took the losses; if it rose, PNC retained the gains. AIG wasn't taking any true risk, nor could it get any rewards. This arrangement violated the rules. When it revealed the vehicles and unwound them, PNC admitted that it had overstated earnings by 38 percent, or $155 million.[3]

The PNC executives who had carried out the deals told government investigators that they were not accounting experts. They all said they'd relied on Ernst & Young to clear the accounting for the transactions and relied on AIG Financial Products for the representations. In fact, PNC had shopped to find a law firm to give the okay. For one transaction, it went first to a New York law firm. When the attorneys there didn't give the bank the answer it sought, it went to a hometown Pittsburgh firm, which it judged correctly as likely to be more amenable. Another time it went to a Washington law firm, which also wasn't fooled. PNC jettisoned that firm's unpleasant opinion and went back to the Pittsburgh firm.

The PNC chief financial officer was sophisticated. A former E&Y partner, he defended himself by saying that PNC and he had relied on the E&Y partner for advice on whether the deals were okay. So it was up to Pelletier and Atkinson to show that PNC had either misled the accountant, or that it had done something contrary to the advice from E&Y, or that E&Y knew they were sham transactions. The accountant was unflappable, however. He continued to maintain that PNC had transferred risk. That was true only in the most technical sense. But AIG wasn't dumb enough to take even an unlikely risk of loss; its real risk of loss was somewhat akin to that of a meteor wiping out its headquarters.

PNC may have used the steroids, but AIG Financial Products was the doctor. It had been going around the country shopping the products to dozens of financial firms. Only PNC took the insurer up on the deals. Other financial firms raised concerns about whether the transactions would conform to accounting rules.[4] AIG didn't bother mentioning those doubts in any of its other sales pitches, including the ones it made to the Pittsburgh bank.

The head of AIG Financial Products was a little-known executive, Joseph Cassano, who displayed his scrappy working-class background ostentatiously. He did not attend an Ivy, but Brooklyn College with financial aid. He worked his way out of back offices at investment banks until he arrived at that emblem of Gordon Gekko–like 1980s ambition, Drexel Burnham Lambert. Cassano joined right at the beginning of the decade. In 1987 he moved to AIG Financial Products, becoming head of the unit in 2001.

With total control at AIG Financial Products, he blessed the PNC products. But Pelletier and Atkinson uncovered no clear evidence that Cassano or other top executives knew that they were sham transactions.

Cassano and the top AIG executives had "advice of counsel" defenses. Lawyers and Ernst & Young had signed off on the deals. Having the professionals okay a deal doesn't exonerate a fraudster, but it makes proving a case more difficult.

Throughout Pelletier and Atkinson's investigation, the Federal Reserve and the Office of the Comptroller of the Currency—PNC's regulators—were hostile. Financial regulators had embraced the deregulatory era as zealously as any government overseer, if not more so. In one video conference call, Fed officials tried to convince the prosecutors that there had been no fraud in the transactions. Again Pelletier shouted down government colleagues: "There is plenty of evidence of fraud here, and we are going to pursue it!"

What made the regulatory hostility particularly bizarre was that the prosecutors found evidence that PNC had misled them. The bank submitted to the regulators backdated accounting correspondence. When the regulators expressed concern about the first two deals, the bank accelerated the completion of the third one without telling them. The regulators tsk-tsked PNC, thinking that should be the end of it. They urged the Justice Department to overlook such blatant disregard, worried that if PNC were prosecuted, investors might panic. There might be a run on the bank, and the fear might spill over to other regional banks or even large institutions. Punitive action was too dangerous for the bank and the system. Herbert Biern, then a top banking supervision official at the Fed, requested a meeting with Justice Department officials. He sat down with Michael Chertoff, still head of the criminal division, as well as Pelletier and Atkinson, among others. Biern worried that PNC would lose its banking licenses if charged. He insisted that the Fed and the OCC had dealt with PNC adequately and, more important, quietly.

Chertoff had just come off of the successful Andersen prosecution. Though he was beginning to feel the backlash to his department's aggressive treatment of the accounting firm, the Fed's stance infuriated him. It stirred the same Andersen emotions. Now, however, the resistance came from inside the government, not a company's paid advocates. Chertoff told Biern that if the Justice Department "can't bring these cases because it may bring harm, then maybe these banks are too big." It was a prescient warning.

In the end, the Department of Justice did not indict PNC. It wouldn't risk going through Arthur Andersen again. Chertoff vented at Biern and the other regulators, but caution prevailed. In June 2003, about nine months into the investigation, PNC entered into a deferred prosecution agreement but continued to operate. Pelletier felt content with the DPA. He liked that Chertoff backed him and wanted to go after individual executives anyway. Neither man perceived the larger picture: the deferred prosecution era had arrived.

After embracing a more recalcitrant legal strategy, AIG FP signed its own DPA in November 2004. The company paid just over $126 million in fines and disgorgement of profits. Pelletier and Atkinson were satisfied. The department assigned AIG a monitor, James Cole of the law firm Bryan Cave.[5] Cole would go on to become a deputy attorney general in the Obama administration Justice Department. AIG bore Cole's costs. He communicated with the board of directors and produced regular reports, which weren't made public. Cole was required to examine only narrow aspects of the financial firm's business, and he expected initially to keep an eye on the firm for just a year. As deferred prosecution agreements went, it was strict. But it did not have an appreciable effect on the culture at AIG Financial Products. Nobody there was fired. "All show and no go," they said in the Department of Justice. AIG periodically called Pelletier to complain about Cole's high billings. Meanwhile, Cassano went on to consolidate his power and influence over the company.

## *Chapter Seven*

# KPMG DESTROYS CAREERS

On June 27, 2006, Justin Weddle was in his office on the sixth floor of One St. Andrew's Plaza in southern Manhattan when he learned that a judge had called him a liar.

Weddle, an assistant US attorney for the Southern District of New York, read the ruling that had just come down from United States District Judge Lewis A. Kaplan. He had his door closed, thank goodness. He couldn't face anyone. Was everyone in the entire Southern District reading this decision right now? He was a member of the special club of Southern District criminal prosecutors. Weddle had been there when Jim Comey had given his famous Chickenshit Club speech. He and his colleagues did the right things in the right way for the right reasons. Upstanding, he never even liked practical jokes. He hated April Fools' Day. He tried not to be self-righteous about it because he understood that nobody could tell the truth all the time, but he had become a lawyer to uphold—okay, this idea was corny, but Weddle believed it—truth and justice. With a ready smile, pug nose, and blond hair, the assistant US attorney looked more like a gregarious schoolboy than one of those prosecutorial cowboys who did what needed to be done to get the bad guys. Nobody would mistake him for a bully.

Yet that's not the way Judge Kaplan saw it. The judge thought the government had strong-armed people, stripping them of their rights, and coerced cooperation as it investigated the way that the accounting firm KPMG had set up tax shelters for wealthy Americans. Kaplan wrote that the government, including Weddle, had let "its zeal get in the way of its judgment" in pressuring KPMG to stop paying the attorneys' fees for former KPMG executives under investigation. The company had no choice, the judge believed. It was fighting for its corporate life, negotiating with a "proverbial gun to its head."[1] Judge Kaplan hadn't wanted to go that far. But he felt Weddle and the other Southern District prosecutors had not only interfered with the executives' constitutional right to counsel but also misled him. Weddle read on, as Kaplan assailed the prosecutors, writing that they had been "economical with the truth." He was sitting in his office, experiencing the greatest catastrophe of his professional life.

Weddle had been killing himself on this case. KPMG, prosecutors came to believe, had sold illegal investments, knowingly designing them to help wealthy American clients avoid taxes while allowing them to claim to the IRS that they were investment vehicles. By the government's reckoning, it was the largest criminal tax case ever brought. KPMG had created at least $11 billion in phony tax losses, which cost the United States at least $2.5 billion in uncollected revenue.[2] The degree of difficulty in putting together this case dwarfed anything Weddle had worked on before. The tax shelters were monumentally complex, full of exotic derivatives. The prosecutors believed they were sham transactions with no purpose but to exploit the accounting rules.

But to prove such an assertion beyond a reasonable doubt for a jury was going to be like translating Aramaic into Mandarin and then English. Multiple law firms had signed off on them. They had no whistle-blower. Prosecutors did not have a big internal investigation into KPMG, served up by some top law firm. No employee had flipped or started giving the government evidence. The investigators had no wiretaps. All the charged executives were upstanding citizens in their communities. To bring the perpetrators to justice would take hard work, brilliance, and every good break available. Weddle always knew the case might be hard. It never occurred to him that it might be his undoing.

The KPMG case, which Weddle would say was bigger than Enron, began to implode. The debacle would reach beyond this one case. In its aftermath, US senators readied bills to roll back what they saw as prosecutorial overreach. The Department of Justice rushed to change its policies covering investigations of corporations and their executives. The Arthur Andersen indictment, the post-Nasdaq-bubble prosecutions, and the Thompson memo had generated a backlash that had been building for years. Now KPMG was a further blow. After the case fell apart, defense attorneys could fight investigations more effectively. As a result, the Justice Department had a harder time prosecuting top executives.

## "TRY AN HONEST ANSWER!"

The Internal Revenue Service began investigating KPMG's tax shelters in early 2002 during a season of corporate crime and punishment, when the probes into Enron and Arthur Andersen were just starting. The IRS issued nine summonses to KPMG. The firm did not comply fully. In July 2002 the government had to go to court to enforce them. A few months after that, the Senate's Permanent Subcommittee on Investigations, under its chairman, Senator Carl Levin of Michigan, started a probe. The PSI held public hearings in November 2003, revealing KPMG's misdeeds. The firm's fees were even paid based on the taxes saved, not the investment returns generated. Its executives had come off terribly in front of the Senate, alternatively combative and evasive. In one memorable exchange, a KPMG partner, under attack from Levin, told the senator, "I don't know how to change my answer."

"Try an honest answer," Senator Levin replied.[3]

After the hearings, KPMG decided it needed a new, more conciliatory approach. The firm hired Bob Bennett, the quintessential Washington superlawyer. Bennett had followed a path similar to that taken by Southern District pioneers Peter Fleming, Rusty Wing, and Jed Rakoff, who had gone on to start white-collar practices at major firms. Bennett had been in the US Attorney's Office for the District of Columbia in the 1970s, and foresaw the coming boom in white-collar work. Corporations didn't want to hire "Fifth Street Lawyers," as the low-rent criminal counsels were called. They would be drunk by lunchtime. He left for a boutique firm to do white-collar criminal work. There he built a powerful practice, and in 1990 he jumped to Skadden, Arps, Slate, Meagher & Flom with fourteen others to build up Skadden's white-collar practice. He represented giant corporations such as Boeing and Northrop Grumman, and marquee individuals such as Reagan's secretary of defense Caspar Weinberger, during the Iran-Contra arms-for-hostages affair; Clark Clifford, during the Bank of Credit and Commerce International money-laundering and bank secrecy scandal; and served as President Bill Clinton's private attorney during the Monica Lewinsky scandal. By 2002, Skadden had become the most profitable law firm in the country, ranked tenth by profits per partner.[4]

Portly and formidable, Bennett presented himself with a casual charm. He advised his new client KPMG to start showing the government it was cooperating; KPMG pushed out three senior executives. Bennett's initial efforts weren't enough, however, to prevent the IRS from referring the case to the Justice Department for criminal prosecution in early 2004. Back then, all complex tax cases found their way to Shirah Neiman, chief counsel to the United States attorney in the Southern District of New York. She brought in assistant US attorneys to help, including office veteran Stanley Okula and a young gun, Justin Weddle.

Weddle had grown up in Chappaqua, New York, and gone to Columbia Law. From there he'd worked at Debevoise & Plimpton, one of the top Manhattan firms. But he wanted to conduct trials and put away criminals. A partner he worked for wrote Weddle's recommendation letter for a position at the Southern District. Weddle got to see the letter. The partner had written to Mary Jo White, then the US attorney: "As you and I discussed, Justin is a star."

In 1999 he joined the Southern District under White. After a brief stint in Manhattan, he worked out of the suburban office of the Southern District in White Plains, New York, in the general crimes unit. White Plains is a beatdown, where a prosecutor may have seventy cases going at once. When a guy gets arrested, you have to find out what happened, write the complaint, and go to court, all in a matter of about three hours. Day after day, it was exhaustion, but if you screwed up, at least you screwed up small. After a little bit, you moved up to a better class of cases with more sophisticated crimes. In 1999, when Weddle was twenty-nine, he scored his first big one: working on the prosecution of Al Pirro, the husband of the Westchester County district attorney at the time, Jeanine Pirro, for tax fraud. Pirro often attended her husband's trial, sitting in the front row of the visitors' gallery.[5] Weddle became careful. When he drove through Westchester, he kept to the exact speed limit, heeded all the traffic rules, and kept an eye to the rearview mirror. He did not want to give the local cops any excuse. The government convicted Pirro of thirty-four counts of tax evasion and conspiracy.[6]

Few prosecutors can master the complexities of tax law. If they were honest about it, most would admit they wouldn't even want to try. Now Weddle had developed some expertise. Eventually anyone who touched taxes at the Southern District worked with Shirah Neiman.

## "UNDER A MICROSCOPE"

In early February 2004 Weddle had just finished a long and grueling tax trial. He was about to vacation in Spain with his wife and young child, when Neiman called and told him that the KPMG case had been referred for criminal investigation. He had been following the Senate hearings only casually. "You're going to be in charge," she said. Weddle received the full Neiman tornado, as she rattled off the thousand tasks he needed to do.

Soon after, they scheduled a meeting with Bennett and KPMG.

Neiman, Okula, Weddle, and some others held a strategy meeting. Neiman was hot to send subpoenas. "We don't want them destroying documents," she said. Arthur Andersen had just done that. Neiman turned to Weddle: "What about the attorneys' fees?"

"Why?" he asked.

"It's in the Thompson memo."

The Thompson memo, as had the Holder memo before it, outlined how prosecutors should view corporations paying lawyers' fees for the executives:

> Another factor to be weighed by the prosecutor is whether the corporation appears to be protecting its culpable employees and agents. Thus, while cases will differ depending on the circumstances, a corporation's promise of support to culpable employees and agents, either through the advancing of attorneys' fees, through retaining the employees without sanction for their misconduct, or through providing information to the employees about the government's investigation pursuant to a joint defense agreement, may be considered by the prosecutor in weighing the extent and value of a corporation's cooperation.[7]

Many prosecutors did not focus on who was paying for counsel, worried that they were interfering in the relationship between the accused and their counsel. Aggressive prosecutors, however, believe that the practice of firms underwriting legal fees is a form of hush money. Former deputy attorney general Larry Thompson told me, "If you sit there and think these corporations are paying for the employees' choice of lawyer, and not sometimes simply to keep the employees quiet, then you believe in the tooth fairy."

On February 25, 2004, the government and KPMG held a giant meeting in New York. Weddle had gotten back from Spain and was battling jet lag. Everyone wanted to be there: IRS agents from Washington, Justice Department supervisors from New York and DC, and an army of

Skadden lawyers, including one former IRS commissioner. The Southern District takes up several floors of One St. Andrew's Plaza. Most of them are messy, with stacks of books everywhere. The offices have little wooden desks. The conference rooms have hand-me-down, mismatched chairs. The important and formal meetings are held in the eighth-floor library, with leather chairs, elongated wood tables, law books all around, and no windows. This room is where the government met with KPMG.

Bennett had asked for the meeting, as a gesture of goodwill, but he had trepidation. Bennett felt corporate investigations were legalized extortion. He would counsel angry chief executives who wanted to fight: "Rise above principle. If you don't, you won't have a company left."

As everyone settled into their seats, Bennett seemed to indicate he expected the government to start, but Weddle warily invited him to proceed. "This is your meeting, Bob. What would you like to say to us?" The dance began. KPMG and Skadden wanted to figure out how serious the Southern District was, how much it knew, what its plans were, and how amenable it was to negotiating. The prosecutors wanted to give no indication of any of that, while pressuring the company to take the matter as seriously as open-heart surgery and to be as cooperative as a Border collie. Running with Weddle's invitation, Bennett and the Skadden team laid out the apocalyptic scenario. Pursuing this matter could put KPMG and its eighteen thousand employees out of business.[8] Arthur Andersen had upward of twenty-eight thousand. An indictment would not just be bad for the firm, but also could wreak havoc with the capital markets, throwing corporate bookkeeping in disarray as companies scrambled to find other auditors. The standard playbook. The Skadden lawyers urged the prosecutors to promise that they would consult the SEC and other regulators before acting.

The prosecutors emphasized that the investigation was at an early stage. No one had decided what to do yet. Weddle could honestly say he knew little about the KPMG case. The office was just seeking information. But they were stern about expecting cooperation. The prosecutors had reason to be wary: the company had not cooperated with the early

IRS investigation, and executives had been confrontational in the senate hearings.

Bennett, seeking to minimize any sanction, emphasized that KPMG had a whole new attitude. Then the two sides had fateful exchanges about whether KPMG would pay the attorneys' fees for any indicted employees. The prosecutors had received an anonymous tip: KPMG had given its outgoing deputy chairman, Jeffrey Stein, a huge severance package. That was a generous way to treat someone who would be a major focus of the investigation. It contrasted with KPMG's insistence that it was taking the probe seriously and willing to punish wrongdoers. Neiman warned KPMG and the Skadden lawyers that the firm shouldn't "reward misconduct." Weddle and Okula understood the warning in the context of the anonymous tip; KPMG and Skadden took it to mean something else: the prosecutors were warning the company that the government would view KPMG as uncooperative if it continued to lay out the attorney payments for current and former employees.

Weddle asked about the company's plan regarding fees. A lawyer for Skadden, Saul Pilchen, piped up, "Why do you ask?" According to what Pilchen recorded in his notes, Weddle responded, "if u have discretion re fees—we'll look at that under a microscope." For an exchange that would change Weddle's life, it was barely noticeable. He wouldn't think anything of it coming out of the meeting and soon forgot all about it.

Combined with Neiman's admonition not to reward wrongdoers, the microscope comment solidified Bennett's and KPMG's sense that the firm had no choice but to cut off the executives under scrutiny. Bennett played cool. "We may have a legal obligation to pay the fees," he said. It turned out that the company had not indemnified its executives, and therefore the accounting firm was not legally bound to pay their attorneys' fees. The following month, KPMG took what it considered to be the government's hint. The firm announced a new policy: it would cap each executive's attorney's fees at $400,000, on the condition that the executives cooperated with the government's investigation. If they were charged, KPMG would cut them off. In reality, the move was in KPMG's interest: it made the company appear cooperative with the government, helped preserve the institution, and, as a bonus, saved some money.

KPMG's cooperation continued to be desultory. In an August 2004 meeting with the Southern District, the prosecutors brought up the issue of deputy chairman Stein's generous severance package. Despite pledges that it was taking the probe seriously, the company was doling out generous golden parachutes to potential malefactors. At that time, KPMG and Skadden knew something even more concerning: the legal fees paid out to Stein had exceeded the $400,000 threshold the company itself had set up. Nobody told the government.

## MR. BENNETT GOES TO WASHINGTON

At the beginning of 2005, almost a year after that first meeting, the Southern District began preparing for discussions with Skadden and KPMG to resolve the investigation. US attorney David Kelley was about to leave his job and wanted the corporate aspect of the investigation finished. Kelley made it clear: if KPMG had committed a crime, the Southern District had to bring charges against individuals, too. Weddle put together a memo about what to do. He tried to figure out the contours of resolving the case. What was KPMG going to pay? What was KPMG going to say? What will the charge be? Should they indict or not? The case was moving forward, and his career was on track. His second child, a daughter, had just been born in late 2004.

But there were, at least in retrospect, harbingers of what would come. In one conversation during this process, IRS lawyers warned Weddle that KPMG prosecution would run into roadblocks. When he asked why, they told him that the Andersen prosecution had become a political sticking point in Washington. Weddle couldn't understand what they were talking about; Andersen had nothing at all to do with KPMG, he thought.

From Bennett's point of view, talks weren't going well. The Southern District was still sounding bellicose. He wanted the possibility of indictment off the table. In one discussion, Neiman said about KPMG, "Well, maybe they should be put out of business." On March 2, 2005, KPMG and Skadden met with David Kelley. As Bennett extolled the amount of cooperation his client had offered, Kelley interrupted, "Let me put it this way: I've seen a lot better from big companies."[9]

Internally at the Southern District, Neiman held the hardest line on how to resolve the case. If they weren't going to indict KPMG, then they sure should secure a guilty plea. The company had engaged in egregious behavior. It conducted a multiyear, multibillion-dollar fraud on the United States that had been orchestrated and approved at the highest levels of the organization.

Kelley agreed. He sent a letter to Bennett with his final decision: KPMG could plead guilty to one count of conspiracy. There would be no indictment. A few days later, Bennett wrote back. The prosecutors read it over and marveled at its audacity. Bennett took pages to say . . . nothing. He was elegant and gracious. He thanked Kelley for sending the letter and said they looked forward to continuing the negotiation. What? The prosecutors were nonplussed. Kelley was informing the company of a decision, not continuing the conversation. The Southern District had said that if KPMG rejected the deal, it would indict. Kelley sent another letter affirming his decision.

The New York prosecutors didn't appreciate that Bennett, the Washington power broker, was working hard in the capital. He requested a meeting with James Comey, who had been elevated to deputy attorney general. When Bob Fiske requested a meeting with Larry Thompson on the Andersen matter, Thompson had refused. By contrast, Comey, who not so long ago had talked so tough as a US attorney in the Southern District, agreed to the meeting.

Finally, on May 5, 2005, in anticipation of meeting with Comey, KPMG cut off former chairman Stein's attorney's fees. The firm also terminated a consulting agreement it had with Stein under his severance package. Skadden thought it would help with its pitch to the government.

On June 13, 2005, KPMG and Skadden met with Comey.[10] Bennett told the officials that KPMG couldn't afford an indictment or guilty plea.

The Justice Department officials didn't need any reminding about what happened to Arthur Andersen, but Bennett brought it up anyway, pressing his case. "It's not fair" to indict the company, he said, asking, "Who will do the books and records for all of these major companies?" The American capital markets would be down to three accounting firms. Bennett and the other attorneys pointed out that KPMG audited the financials of the Southern District of New York.

After months of fruitless talks with New York, Bennett's pleas ripened in Washington. Comey consulted with Attorney General John Ashcroft, and the Department of Justice blinked. Comey asked the Southern District prosecutors to return to the negotiating table.

"Ashcroft can't be responsible for putting another accounting firm out of business," Comey told the Southern District prosecutors.

"They are two totally different cases!" Neiman replied. "We would try to help them avoid that."

This edict removed the Southern District's leverage. Any further threat was empty, because Skadden understood that Main Justice was too scared to allow a KPMG indictment. There went the Manhattan prosecutors' ability to indict KPMG or wring out a guilty plea. Neiman fumed.

Judge Kaplan later would accuse the prosecutors of strong-arming KPMG as it begged for its life. Begging? KPMG and Skadden had gone over their heads to the top. On August 29, 2005, the company secured a deferred prosecution agreement with the Southern District.[11] The government charged the firm with one count of fraud, but it was deferred, per the agreement. KPMG paid a $456 million fine. Weddle and the team were happy that the agreement included a tough statement of facts detailing the wrongdoing (to which KPMG stipulated). KPMG admitted that its partners "assisted high-net-worth United States citizens to evade United States individual income taxes on billions of dollars in capital gain and ordinary income by developing, promoting and implementing unregistered and fraudulent tax shelters."[12] KPMG further conceded how it worked. Its partners engaged in a two-step: They prepared representations for wealthy clients that mischaracterized the way the shelter deals worked. Then they wrote opinion letters that approved the transactions, based on those false representations.

Judge Kaplan would later regard the agreement as a significant punishment. He wrote that if KPMG did not comply with the terms of the DPA, "it will be open to the risk that the government will declare that KPMG breached the DPA and prosecute the criminal information to verdict." Kaplan did not know that Comey and the other top Department of Justice officials had no will to carry out such a prosecution. Comey had joined the Chickenshit Club. As KPMG, Skadden, and the Department of Justice understood, the DPA would be the final sanction against the accounting firm.

## "ECONOMICAL WITH THE TRUTH"

The KPMG settlement may have been unsatisfactory, but the Southern District prioritized bringing culpable individuals to justice. On the same day that it announced the deferred prosecution agreement, the government indicted nine people involved in the KPMG tax shelters—eight of them former KPMG executives. Later, the figure would rise to eighteen individuals, including seventeen ex-KPMG executives.

By the spring of 2006, KPMG defense attorneys began to argue that the government had violated the indicted executives' Sixth Amendment rights (which grant the accused the right to a lawyer and fair treatment in court) by pressuring KPMG to stop paying their legal fees. In April 2006 the *Wall Street Journal* editorial page attacked the prosecution, singling out Weddle by name.[13] Stung, he brought it to the new Southern District US attorney, Michael Garcia, first thing in the morning, not wanting the US attorney to read it himself. Garcia just laughed. "That's awesome. Frame it," he said.

Prosecutors weren't worried initially. Judge Kaplan seemed to think the fee issue unimportant. A Clinton appointee, he had never been a prosecutor, but the government considered him a friendly judge. Kaplan felt comfortable overseeing complicated litigation. He had been brought in as a mediator on complex insurance disputes surrounding the September

11, 2001, terrorist attacks on the Twin Towers. He presided over the litigation over the diabetes drug Rezulin, which had contributed to patient deaths. Prosecutors in the KPMG case began to worry, however. In May 2006 Kaplan held a hearing to discuss the issue, and it didn't go well for the government. Kaplan seemed sympathetic to the accused.

Kaplan had been at the New York law firm of Paul, Weiss, Rifkind, Wharton & Garrison for twenty-four years before his judicial appointment. He kept close friendships with its lawyers, once serving as a character witness for a retired partner who had been disbarred for pilfering more than $500,000 from a family trust.[14] Another fellow partner, Mark Belnick, underwent a terrible ordeal at the hands of the government. Prosecutors indicted Belnick, who had left Paul, Weiss to become the general counsel of the conglomerate Tyco International, for stealing millions in unauthorized bonuses and loans from the company. Belnick won acquittal, but not before his reputation had been ruined.

On June 27, 2006, Judge Kaplan put out his decision in the *United States v. Stein* case. Weddle sat in his office at One St. Andrew's Plaza, oblivious to what would soon happen. Shirah Neiman saw Kaplan's wife in the gallery and worried, thinking it was a sign that the judge thought what he was about to do was noteworthy. Sure enough, Kaplan's ruling excoriated the government. Kaplan concluded, "The government's assertion that the legal fee decision was made without 'coercion' or 'bullying' by the government can be justified only by tortured definitions of those terms." He ruled that prosecutors violated the rights of the KPMG case defendants. He assailed the tenets of the Thompson memo and what he saw as prosecutorial overreach. "The government let its zeal get in the way of its judgment," he wrote.

Many employees have an expectation that they will be indemnified against legal fees incurred during investigations of work-related activities. A reporter in a libel case almost always does. Kaplan pointed out that cops sued in wrongful-arrest cases and nurses in malpractice cases do as well. But a reporter accused of murder or a nurse accused of theft does not have that expectation or right.

Kaplan expanded this notion, ruling that KPMG violated the employees' constitutional right to counsel: "Everyone charged with a crime is entitled to the assistance of a lawyer. A defendant with the financial means has the right to hire the best lawyers money can buy. A poor defendant is guaranteed competent counsel at government expense. This is at the heart of the Sixth Amendment." Changing the argument from a question of tax evasion to a matter of constitutional principles turned out to be a brilliant strategy.

The judge ended his opinion with a note of restrained fury at what he perceived as the misbehavior of Weddle, Neiman, and others in the Southern District. "The government was economical with the truth in its early responses to this motion. It is difficult to defend even the literal truth of the position it took in its first memorandum of law." The government, he wrote, had not come clean about what it had said about the fees and when it had said it. He called out Weddle for a response to the court that "was far from the whole story." Kaplan believed Weddle made the "under a microscope" comment. The statement confirmed to the judge that the prosecutors were pressuring the firm to cut off the accused executives. (Skadden's Saul Pilchen had conceded that his notes weren't necessarily verbatim. Weddle never thought he had said it. He and his colleagues said they had no recollection of the phrase.)

In explaining her actions, Neiman had told the court that her "rewarding misconduct" comment referred to federal sentencing guidelines, not specifically to KPMG's payment of its executives' lawyer bills. Kaplan dismissed this assertion as implausible. He felt what they had said to him was "misleading." The judge warned, "There should be no recurrence."

The Southern District was outraged, particularly bitter that Kaplan had singled out prosecutors. After he read the opinion, Weddle went to meet Michael Garcia. All the top people had gathered to decide what to do. The Kaplan ruling was a problem for the case and the Southern District. Weddle wasn't quite listening to the discussion. When he did speak up, he concentrated on not letting his voice break. Garcia insisted he wanted to make a statement. He backed his prosecutors and took the rare and bold move of writing a letter to Kaplan protesting his decision. He also wrote a response, correcting what he perceived as factual errors and asking Kaplan to take out the names of the prosecutors and his criticisms of them. Weddle felt relieved and grateful. But Kaplan rejected the request.

The next year, in the summer of 2007, the KPMG fiasco reached its peak. Kaplan, with what he wrote was "only with the greatest reluctance," threw out the cases against thirteen of the sixteen indicted KPMG executives. He wrote that the prosecutorial misconduct "shocks the conscience," going on to say that prosecutors "deliberately or callously prevented many of these defendants from obtaining funds for their defense that they lawfully would have had . . . This is intolerable in a society that holds itself out to the world as a paragon of justice."[15] In August 2008 a three-judge panel of the Second Circuit Court of Appeals upheld Kaplan.[16] "The government's threat of indictment was easily sufficient to convert its adversary into its agent. KPMG was not in a position to consider coolly the risk of indictment, weigh the potential significance of the other enumerated factors in the Thompson memorandum, and decide for itself how to proceed," wrote the court.[17]

## KILLING THOMPSON

After Judge Kaplan's ruling in the Stein case, the Justice Department, already on the defensive over the Thompson memo and its perceived overreach on Arthur Andersen, entered a furious rearguard action. The judge had attacked the Thompson memo. Three distinct and nuanced issues—an aggressive prosecution that helped put Arthur Andersen out of business; attorney-client privilege; and rights of accused executives to the payment of their attorneys' fees—became one: prosecutors were out of control. The usual corporate defenders, such as the *Wall Street Journal* editorial page and the US Chamber of Commerce, seized on the KPMG case to deliver their kicks to the vulnerable department over all three issues. Congress listened.

In the fall of 2006, the Senate Judiciary Committee held hearings on the Thompson memo and prosecutorial abuse, featuring the supposed victimization of KPMG.[18] Senators Patrick Leahy, Democrat of Vermont, and Arlen Specter, then still a Republican from Pennsylvania, thought that the Justice Department abused corporations. Leahy wanted the Justice Department to change voluntarily, reluctant to meddle with the executive branch through legislation. Specter was more aggressive. In December he introduced a bill that reversed Thompson memo policies. Specter's legislation called for prohibiting prosecutors from demanding waivers of attorney-client privilege or from using the information about whether companies were paying for employees' legal fees in making charging determinations.[19]

The new deputy attorney general, Paul McNulty, and his colleagues saw the bill as a dangerous incursion of the legislative branch on its powers. He understood that he had to act before Congress did. Five days after Specter introduced the Senate bill, McNulty issued a new memo about corporate prosecutions. Under the new rules, if a federal prosecutor wanted to ask a corporation to waive its privilege, it would have to get permission from higher-ups at the Justice Department.

Critics weren't mollified. McNulty hadn't gone far enough. In August 2008 his replacement, Mark Filip, pulled back prosecutorial powers further. Today the new post-KPMG, post–defense bar revolt Justice Department standards prohibit prosecutors from even asking companies to waive their attorney-client privilege. Inquiring about who is paying fees is forbidden. The Thompson memo has been buried.

Corporations and the defense bar routinely argue that government investigations are tantamount to extortion exercises. Once an investigation commences, the company has no choice but to give in. Employees might fear that their corporation will turn them over to law enforcement. If the government also nudges companies to strip them of their livelihoods and stop paying legal fees, isn't that an abuse of people who are presumed innocent? Kaplan's ruling can check corporate abuse of its employees, even top executives.

But the Supreme Court has ruled more than once that the constitution does not provide a right to the best defense money can buy, as Kaplan held. People have a right to competent and effective counsel. In two similar cases in 1989, *United States v. Monsanto*[20] and *Caplin & Drysdale, Chartered v. United States*,[21] the court ruled that the government can seize assets from an accused criminal, even if those funds were earmarked to pay for legal fees. In the *Caplin* case, a law firm had been paid by an accused drug dealer. A lower court forbade the drug dealer from transferring any assets that the government would potentially seize, but the drug dealer, before he was indicted, did so anyway. The law firm brought a case arguing that its payments should be exempt from the seizures. The court ruled against the law firm, saying that the forfeiture did not violate the drug dealer's Sixth Amendment rights.

In the context of street criminals and the indigent, courts have deemed an astonishing array of circumstances not violations of the Sixth Amendment. As Berkeley Law professors Charles Weisselberg and Su Li point out, the courts have upheld a variety of circumstances that interfered with indigent and street criminals' ability to secure competent counsel. The court has ruled it does not violate the rights of the accused if his court-appointed attorney is an alcoholic who drinks heavily at trial and is arrested for driving under the influence on his way to court. The high court has deemed that a cap of $1,000 for an appointed lawyer's out-of-court work doesn't violate the Constitution, even in a death penalty case. The court has written that no violation has occurred if one court-appointed lawyer replaces another, even when the client is unable to form a "meaningful relationship" with her new lawyer. Though there may be a legal argument for Kaplan's ruling in the KPMG case, Weisselberg writes, "To people steeped in ordinary criminal cases, *Stein* is downright odd, if not otherworldly."

The government forces accuse drug dealers and mobsters to forfeit money that might otherwise go to their defense. In many racketeering cases, in which defendants are accused of participating in a conspiracy, the government can seize or freeze assets, even if the action renders the accused so poor that they cannot afford their own lawyer. Courts have held that such seizures don't violate the constitutional rights of the accused. Such crimes are often as sophisticated and complicated as corporate white-collar cases.

The Justice Department defended its actions by arguing that KPMG's executives have no right to use "other people's money" for their defense. Kaplan rejected the argument. He contended it was an unstated expectation of their employment. Kaplan wrote in those drug and Mafia cases, that the government was seizing ill-gotten gains. But an executive's gain may be just as ill gotten, and an accused drug dealer may be as innocent as an accused executive. Even many experienced white-collar crime experts, including judges and prosecutors, persist in seeing differences between the two classes of criminal. Many believe that such defendants are entitled to a defense attorney from a certain echelon. Top executives receive representation from the finest firms. The courts and the legal system show no inclination to protect the indigent's right to counsel.

Even if Judge Kaplan's ruling was correct, did he have to throw out the prosecution, preventing the Southern District from trying to prove its case? Due to his ruling, the accused KPMG executives now had access to the lawyers of their choice—some of the best and most expensive lawyers—whose bills would be footed by their former employer. Any harm from the government's meddling would have been undone, but the cases could have gone forward in court.

The KPMG case, Weisselberg argues, can be perceived as a victory of a company against the unfair pressure and power brought to bear by the government, a justified reassertion of Sixth Amendment rights. It could be interpreted as an example of how the government is outdueled and outgunned in court. Or, he suggests, it could be read as a fight, predominantly by major law firms, "to preserve a funding stream for a lucrative and growing area of practice—in essence, protecting the ability of law firms to receive compensation through indemnification and advancement."[22]

The fight over privilege waivers and the rights to counsel for corporate executives was a seminal white-collar battle of the mid-2000s. The

Kaplan decision and the rollback of the Thompson memo, justified or not, hurt the government's ability to investigate and prosecute corporate cases. Prosecutors could no longer try to pressure companies into waiving privilege, to stop paying for attorneys' fees for accused executives, or to forego joint defense agreements, where lawyers representing different clients share information. The information highway from defense attorney to defense attorney reveals the prosecutorial strategy, allows the defense to prepare and coordinate, and gives time for executives to get their stories straight.

In 2005 the Supreme Court took up *United States v. Booker*, a case that challenged mandatory sentencing guidelines, which gave judges strict rules that bound them to assign specific sentences to the guilty. A federal jury had convicted a drug dealer of a crime that came with a set sentence of ten years to life. But at sentencing, the judge decided to increase the sentence to thirty years to life, based on a preponderance of evidence that the defendant possessed even more crack and had obstructed justice. The high court affirmed the ruling, and in so doing, restored judges' discretion over sentences. Some judges now assign lighter white-collar sentences than before. When prosecutors negotiate with midlevel executives, the executives are more inclined to take their chances than to plead guilty or plea bargain, prosecutors say. While mandatory sentences were pernicious, and judicial discretion is generally a good thing, one unintended result is that corporate executives are now harder to flip.

The courts took other useful weapons against corporate fraud away from prosecutors through the decade. In a 2010 ruling involving the Jeff Skilling case, the Supreme Court narrowed a law that prosecutors used to get the Enron executive, called the honest-services fraud statute. The court restricted the use of the provision to only the most egregious forms of fraud, such as bribery and kickbacks, disallowing the charge for grayer types of corporate malfeasance.[23] After the *Wall Street Journal* broke a story in 2006 about widespread corporate stock-option backdating—revealing that executives had enriched themselves by backdating stock-option grants to have lower, more favorable prices—the SEC and the

Justice Department investigated more than a hundred companies. The San Francisco office started a Stock Options Backdating Task Force. Dozens of companies restated their books and scores of executives lost their jobs. The prosecutions mostly fizzled. One of the biggest criminal stock-option backdating cases, against the co-CEO of Broadcom Corp., collapsed amid prosecutorial misconduct. Several other cases were dropped after the Skilling Supreme Court ruling.

Across the country, districts geared up to address the rampant stock-option backdating scandal. Over the next several years, various US Attorney's Offices brought myriad cases. Some prosecutors had success, but most cases fizzled. Several were overturned on appeal. Prosecutors were even reprimanded for abuse.

And there were cultural changes, which pushed prosecutors to settle rather than go after individuals. The Southern District of New York believed in prosecuting individuals, not settling with corporations. The case harmed Neiman's, Okula's, and Weddle's careers. The risk of going after individuals in complex corporate cases was already high. Now it became stratospheric. The KPMG case gave prosecutors one more incentive to seek a corporate settlement rather than risk prosecuting individuals.

In the post–Thompson memo world, giant companies press their advantages in settlement negotiations. When necessary, corporations and their counsel reach into the corridors of power to be heard and win results. Defense lawyers fight evidence discovery requests, using liberal claims of attorney-client privilege. Courts rarely hear about these battles, and the media hardly covers them. At the least, these fights slow down investigations. Delays are defendants' friends.

The Justice Department failed to grasp the implications of the decade's legal changes. No single modification in the law or policy was momentous, and some have restored defendants' rights. Together, however, they have added up to a significant—and largely unrecognized—blunting and removal of prosecutorial tools in white-collar corporate investigations. These fights exposed how much the government depends on corporate cooperation to conduct its investigations. But cooperation flows from pressure and leverage. The Justice Department's defeats and retreats have shifted the balance of power to defense lawyers.

## BANISHED TO ROMANIA

The KPMG case scarred the Southern District prosecutors. Shortly after the Judge Kaplan opinion, Jed Rakoff took Shirah Neiman to lunch at Antica Roma in Chinatown. She was livid at Judge Kaplan, her vituperation the verbal equivalent of a clenched fist, Rakoff felt. Kaplan had attacked her integrity. Neiman was unpopular within the office, so her colleagues had mixed feelings about her slapdown. To the extent that they saw anyone making a mistake or being too aggressive, they blamed her and not Weddle. As a prosecutor's prosecutor, she never had many friends on the defense side. Her former boss turned star defense attorney, Robert Morvillo, decrying a white-collar criminal system that had become overly harsh, told *American Lawyer* magazine that she had become "more and more rigid." Another legend, Stanley Arkin, went further, telling the publication that Neiman was "the exact opposite of what you want in a career prosecutor."[24]

Stan Okula, Weddle's KPMG colleague, continued to work at the Southern District, but he struggled to preserve his reputation. Judges would later accuse him of lying to them as well, further damaging his reputation.

By the fall of 2007, the KPMG case was still going on, even though most of the indictments had been thrown out. Kaplan put off the trial for the remaining defendants. Weddle just couldn't take it anymore. It's not uncommon for prosecutors to hand off cases after a couple of years. He had held on longer than usual to seek vindication, but now he was done, exhausted and shattered. His boss understood and acceded to his request to get off the case. The *Wall Street Journal* initially reported that he had been removed from the case, mortifying him.[25] The paper ran a correction six weeks later to say he'd left voluntarily.[26] In all the tax shelter cases, the Southern District had gotten $1.3 billion in criminal penalties and dozens of felony convictions. Weddle could argue that the government had scored a victory. All the major professional services firms had been helping the richest Americans dodge taxes. The Department of Justice had put a stop to these techniques. But the accused firms and defendants had come after him and his fellow prosecutors, and they had scored a hit.

Weddle put himself on the market. He still thought as a Southern District prosecutor that he would land a job rapidly. He had not grasped the ramifications of Kaplan's ruling. Firms, including his old firm Debevoise & Plimpton, said they had no positions available. The legal world took its revenge.

One day he saw a job listing to be a Department of Justice resident legal advisor in Romania. For some reason, the opportunity jumped out at him. He could go there, thousands of miles from New York, to build back his career. It might be exile or banishment, but so what? He went to Bucharest to become a diplomat, helping coordinate law enforcement cooperation in Southern Europe. After more than two happy years, a friend at a big law firm called about a job. The firm flew him back. He made it through several interviews. Then the talks stopped mysteriously. He had no word and no idea what happened. It turned out that a lawyer for a bank that had been subject to some of Weddle's tax shelter investigations called up the firm and told them not to hire him. Finally, in 2014 he landed a white-collar defense job at a firm in New York.[27] The KPMG case still weighs on him. Even a decade later, discussing the case could leave him visibly hurt and breaking down.

*Chapter Eight*

# THE HUNT FOR AIG

AIG COULD NOT STAY OUT OF TROUBLE. After pursuing the PNC-AIG Financial Products for two years, from 2002 to 2004, the Department of Justice and Paul Pelletier spent the next frustrating six years trying to corral what they were convinced was the serially law-flouting insurance company. The next big case against AIG involved one of the biggest names in American business: Warren Buffett, one of the richest men in the world, and his giant industrial and financial conglomerate, Berkshire Hathaway.

In February 2005 Tom Hanusik, the accounting and white-collar expert who had rejoined the criminal division of Main Justice from the Enron Task Force, began investigating a questionable insurance transaction between AIG and General Reinsurance Corporation, one of Berkshire Hathaway's companies. Gen Re specialized in selling insurance to other insurance companies, known as reinsurance, and dabbled with exotic derivatives and other complicated financial deals. The SEC and Eliot Spitzer, the New York State attorney general, also began to investigate.

Hanusik went down to Richmond, Virginia, for a meeting with prosecutors at the Eastern District of Virginia and power lawyer Ron Olson, of the firm of Munger, Tolles & Olson, for materials. (Charlie Munger, the vice chairman of Berkshire and a founding partner of the firm, is a charming and curmudgeonly billionaire who has long played second-fiddle to Buffett's grandfatherly Oracle of Omaha act.) Olson delivered a binder of documents to the prosecutors.

Hanusik didn't have anything to do that evening, so when he got back to his hotel room, he opened up the binder. He spent two hours just putting the disorganized documents in chronological order. Then he went through them. By the end of the night, he realized what he was reading. The next day, Hanusik met again with Olson and thanked him for the materials. "Maybe I'm mistaken, but do those documents show a half-billion-dollar sham transaction?" he asked Olson. Two weeks later, Hanusik was interviewing people about the case.

Every investigation requires agents. Usually they come from the FBI, but in white-collar cases at the time, the Justice Department often drew agents from the Postal Inspection Service, a vestige from when white-collar crime often carried a mail fraud charge. Postal inspectors were a secret weapon of the Justice Department. Agents were frequently certified public accountants and experts in complex financial shenanigans. Throughout their history, the inspectors had cracked bank and train robberies. In the early 1970s, they proved that the letter written to author Clifford Irving allegedly awarding him exclusive rights to ghostwrite reclusive millionaire Howard Hughes's autobiography was a fraud (as was the manuscript, which Irving and a writer friend invented wholesale, with no involvement whatsoever from Hughes, who then sued both Irving and his publishers). The late 1980s brought investigations into insider trading, and the unit was also instrumental in putting televangelist Jim Bakker in prison after his ministry collapsed in a sex and fraud scandal.[1] By the mid-2000s, however, the US Postal Service faced desperate finances and squeezed the budgets of the inspection units.

Hanusik and a postal inspector named James Tendick worked the case, interviewing other top AIG and Gen Re executives. They brought in Buffett for an interview in the Woolworth Building in downtown Manhattan, giving him a "queen for a day" proffer. Under such an agreement, the government immunizes a witness temporarily to free him up to speak frankly. Buffett gave good shtick but was otherwise unhelpful to the investigation. The Oracle did help himself, though, managing to convince the prosecutors that he knew little about the details of the transaction.

Despite having no luck with Buffett, Hanusik and Tendick began to excavate what had happened. The autocratic chairman and CEO Hank Greenberg led AIG. He had his insurance company manage its earnings to the penny a share, never daring to miss Wall Street estimates. If the Street was paying attention to another financial performance measure, it appeared to the prosecutors that Greenberg had his company massage those figures as well. In 2000, analysts and investors worried that AIG was manipulating the money it reserved to pay out insurance claims, a measure called "loss reserves." Investors want to see the loss reserves going up in conjunction with new business. If the company isn't reserving, it may face big losses in the future from all the new insurance contracts it is writing today. Even though AIG was writing new insurance business at a good pace, loss reserves were falling. Investors thought AIG might be drawing down its reserves to boost its earnings.

In October 2000, to quell the disquiet, Greenberg called up Ronald Ferguson, the head of Gen Re. The two struck a deal: AIG entered into two sham transactions with Gen Re worth $500 million—deals designed to appear like insurance but, in fact, were merely loans to AIG. For its part, Gen Re charged a secret fee and AIG took on no risk. Thus, the deal boosted AIG's loss reserves without it taking a hit to earnings. Greenberg would insist that the deals he discussed were not shams and that he did not order a risk-free transaction. Like Buffett, but less credibly, he contended that they didn't know the details.[2]

Spitzer remained unconvinced and pressured the AIG board to get rid of Hank Greenberg. In March 2005 he succeeded: the board forced the CEO to step down from the company he'd built. In his tenure as New York attorney general, Spitzer regulated the financial world aggressively, often outpacing and embarrassing the Feds. (He also got in the way. In another AIG investigation, he immunized an executive, inadvertently stymying a Department of Justice probe.) In May AIG said it realized that there hadn't been any transfer of risk and restated its earnings for the entire period the deal had covered.

Meanwhile, Hanusik pounded away on the criminal case. He had learned from Michael Chertoff that the most important factor in a white-collar investigation was to keep the momentum going. In early June Hanusik reached plea agreements with two executives from Gen Re. Now the government had two executives who would testify that they knowingly helped AIG misstate its finances. The prosecutors also had tapes, containing evidence they viewed as dynamite. The tapes indicated that executives understood the deals were about manipulating earnings and not substantive insurance transactions. Proving that executives knew what they were doing was wrong is the single biggest challenge of any white-collar case. Elizabeth Monrad, then General Reinsurance's chief financial officer, said on tape that the company would have "a tough time getting the accounting they want out of the deal" in a November 2000 conference call. Monrad said, "These deals are a little bit like morphine. It's very hard to come off of them."[3]

The AIG–Gen Re probe started promisingly. But the saying at the department is "Big cases, big problems." Usually that means political problems within the bureaucracy. AIG–Gen Re was as big as they come. Plenty of offices had a tangential claim to jurisdiction on the case and wanted in. The deputy attorney general's office is in charge of adjudicating Department of Justice turf battles. Paul McNulty, then the US attorney for the Eastern District of Virginia, pushed to participate in the case. Hanusik wasn't happy. Adding a new prosecutor meant getting him or her briefed on the complexities, slowing momentum. Sure enough, an assistant US attorney named Ray Patricco was added. The prosecutors waded through the tar of the investigation as the prey fled. Hanusik fretted that the executives weren't feeling enough pressure.

## "INDICT AND GOOD THINGS WILL HAPPEN."

After securing the plea agreements, Hanusik left the department to go into private practice. Colleen Conry, then a ten-year veteran of the Department of Justice, with several highly complex litigations on her résumé, picked up the case. Paul Pelletier, now the deputy chief in the fraud section, thought highly of her. She felt the same about him. Conry leaned on Pelletier for advice.

Pelletier emphasized that on such a serious case, the department had to go after the highest-ranking culpable people. He and Conry believed they could deter executives from committing white-collar crime if they saw their colleagues go to jail. Pelletier hadn't been able to prosecute individuals in his previous case against AIG over the PNC matter, but he wanted the department to concentrate on individuals here. The two of them knew what that meant: an enormous commitment of time, energy, agents, and money. Pelletier helped Conry game out who should be included in the initial indictments. Was there clear evidence each executive intended to do something wrong? What were the weaknesses of the case? How will the defense counter?

Pelletier was tearing a swath through Washington just as he had done in Miami. His mantra was "Thin to win," the great trial wisdom that Peter Fleming had advocated in the United Brands case decades earlier. Pelletier advised prosecutors to bring simple charges and few of them. Hold short trials with only the necessary witnesses. Make matters as clear for the jury as you can. He'd hear prosecutors expecting a three-month trial and, without knowing anything more about the case, predict they were going to lose. Invariably, they did. "Anything over six weeks, the trial turns into a shit-show, and you risk losing the jury," he says.

But the key to a good trial was a good, strong investigation. Pelletier had an adage: "Indict and good things will happen." In white-collar cases, it's too easy for a prosecutor to keep investigating, ever so deliberately, fearing there is something he or she doesn't know while hoping that somewhere lies a nugget of golden evidence to uncover. This resulted in investigations that lasted years, until the case was so old that all the department could do was plead out this or that little scrap and claim victory. The Pelletier motto was the antidote. In Miami, they said in law enforcement, B-plus work brings A-plus results. His troops thrilled to the Pelletier Way, while supervisors and the genteel defense bar did not. The attitude posed hazards. The gambling prosecutor risks losing. Sometimes it's necessary to cancel membership in the Chickenshit Club, as Jim Comey had laid out in his famous speech. But supervisors did not like it. And an aggressive prosecutor attracted criticism—not only from the defense bar, but sometimes also from judges or the media.

For the most part, prosecutors and defense attorneys, especially in Washington and New York, speak a common language. They understand that they negotiate for a living. Each side stakes out an extreme position and then works its way to the middle. It was comfortable and well understood. Paul Pelletier didn't speak that tongue. He didn't understand it or believe in it. He didn't seek the defense bar's approval. He might not be able to make and keep friends from the defense bar, but he was a damn good friend to good prosecutors. He had a knack for putting together investigative and trial teams, for motivating and supporting people, and for bringing cases to fruition. If you couldn't do that, you were a "paycheck thief," and he devoted himself to driving you out of government.

In 2005–06 Pelletier supervised the Jack Abramoff case, in which the Department of Justice prosecuted for corruption one of the most powerful Republican lobbyists and his network of businessmen and politicians. The fraud section teamed up with the sleepy Public Integrity Section to carry out the investigation. (Internally, the section was called PIN, but Pelletier called it PIS: "Prosecutors Interested in Sleeping.") The case involved politically fraught and sensitive work. In such an investigation, the best protection prosecutors have against accusations of partisanship or bias is to do what they always do. That came naturally to Pelletier. He didn't know any other way to conduct prosecutions.

But he was lost when trying to manage the delicate internal politics.

Pelletier remained in a constant state of fury at what in his view was some of his colleagues' frequent incompetence. At one point, the front office, where the political appointees resided, gathered the teams together to get them to make nice. Pelletier's younger colleague, Guy Singer, was, to Paul's mind, overly deferential to the other guys. Pelletier listened for a while as Singer agreed to this and agreed to that. Singer was happy enough to make minor concessions to get what he wanted out of the meeting. Pelletier did not have that gene. He could feel his neck tightening and his ears flushing in consternation. As the meeting droned on, he sent a note to Singer: "If you agree one more time, I am going to rip off your head and shit down your neck."

In the summer of 2004, the FBI requested the fraud section's help in its investigation of Qwest Communications, a darling telecom company out of Denver that had engaged in accounting fraud that boosted revenue by $3 billion. The local US Attorney's Office in Colorado had just lost a related trial that put a subsequent case against the CEO, Joseph Nacchio, in jeopardy. Pelletier and his colleagues determined the office had the wrong theory. Prosecutors wouldn't be able to make an accounting fraud case, but they could indict Nacchio for having dumped over one hundred million shares when he knew that the company wouldn't hit its earnings targets. In December 2005 a grand jury indicted Nacchio on forty-two counts of insider trading.

Pelletier thought forty-two counts far too many. But what was done was done. He helped the prosecutors on the trial tighten up their case to make it a six-page indictment and reduce the trial to finish within the magic six-week window. In April 2007 they won, convicting Nacchio on nineteen of the forty-two counts. He was sentenced to six years in prison. But with white-collar executives, it's always difficult to make these cases stick through the appeals process. The defense teams throw endless resources and efforts at challenges. In March 2008 a Tenth Circuit US Court of Appeals panel reversed the conviction. Pelletier had little doubt the panel had gotten it wrong. The department was ready to give it up, but he relentlessly pestered the appeals lawyers and the Solicitor General's Office in the Department of Justice. He argued to push the case to take it "en banc": to a session in front of the entire court rather than the three-judge panel. His instincts turned out correct. In February 2009 the full Tenth Circuit appellate court reversed its panel, reinstating both the conviction and the sentence. Nacchio served more than four years in prison.

When Josh Hochberg, a studious and mellow career prosecutor, left as head of the fraud section in 2005, Pelletier wanted the promotion. As Alice Fisher, head of the criminal division, mulled her choice, Pelletier assumed the role as acting chief. Anyone else would have moderated his style, quieted down on occasion, and broken bread with his enemies within the department. Not Pelletier. He rampaged through his investigations, backing his people and making sure they all knew what he thought of them.

Fisher couldn't bring herself to put him in charge. She brought Pelletier in to the office and sat him down. She offered him the principal deputy position. "Let's celebrate," she said and pulled out a bottle of wine.

"Celebrate? Put that bottle away! I wasn't coming here to find out I flunked!" Pelletier said. He couldn't hold back tears. The job went to his friend, another career prosecutor, Steven Tyrrell.

## FLY UP TO HARTFORD

Prosecutors brought indictments of four Gen Re executives in February 2006, including the former CEO of Gen Re and the chief financial officer. But Colleen Conry was having problems getting along with the Eastern District's Ray Patricco. The assistant US attorney kept suggesting that he could go over her head and hinting that he was friends with Paul McNulty, the former US attorney in the Eastern District of Virginia—who was now deputy attorney general at Main Justice. Pelletier tried to defend Conry, but she wanted off the case. He set about trying to fix the AIG–Gen Re investigation.

The defendants wanted to move the venue from Virginia to Connecticut, where Gen Re was based. A third US court district got involved,

Connecticut, which, of course, meant it had to put its people on the case as well. Now it was a clusterfuck, squared.

In late summer 2006, Pelletier found a Main Justice prosecutor, Adam Safwat, to put on the case. Safwat, who had just joined from the Delaware office, had experience investigating white-collar and corporate fraud. He was a perfect Pelletier foil: even-keeled where Pelletier was emotional, and he had a fetish for detail, while Pelletier could see the big picture.

The prosecutorial team spent the rest of the year putting the case together, arguing about strategy with the other offices as much as they spent investigating. Safwat and Pelletier had little respect for Patricco. They weren't alone. The agents working this case were also unimpressed with the Virginia and Connecticut folks. On one call, the squabbling was so acute, the postal inspector James Tendick yelled out, "Guys, what the fuck is going on here? Get your shit together!"

In the spring of 2007, Safwat and Pelletier flew up to Hartford for a meeting with Patricco to go over pretrial conferences and motions. The two arrived around midnight and jumped into a taxi to go to New Haven for their meeting the next morning. Pelletier took out a little notebook. Over the next forty-five minutes, they sketched out trial strategy and fixed the witness list. Initially, Patricco and another prosecutor had identified seventy people as potential witnesses. The prosecutors wouldn't have gotten to the main focus of the trial for two or three weeks—intolerable for a jury. Safwat and Pelletier whittled the list down to ten. Patricco proposed starting with agents describing which documents they'd compiled and where they'd obtained them. Amateur stuff, they thought!

Pelletier and Safwat argued that they needed to start with their main cooperator and, in the first half hour, have him lay out the fraud up front to the jury. Then, after the jurors have heard the prosecution narrative, they could backfill the chronology and fill in the witnesses as necessary. Research suggests jurors make up their minds in the first moments of a trial and then interpret the remaining evidence in a way that confirms their initial impression.

They didn't settle the matter at the meeting, however. It took knocking heads for the rest of the year before Pelletier and Safwat prevailed in setting the case strategy they had outlined in the cab ride.

## SCANDAL AND CRONYISM

As Pelletier and Safwat continued with their prosecution of AIG and Gen Re, problems roiled the Department of Justice. In February 2005 George Bush appointed Alberto Gonzales to succeed John Ashcroft as attorney general. Cronyism and incompetence marked his short tenure of two and a half years. In November 2007, two months after Gonzales had stepped down, the Justice Department's Office of the Inspector General decried the lack of confidence in the institution. He cited scandals such as the administration's political purge of US attorneys after Bush's reelection in 2004 and the department's improper hiring practices for career positions. At the time, only three of eleven presidentially appointed top Justice Department positions were filled.[4]

White-collar prosecutions suffered from not just a leadership vacuum but also a resource drain. During the years after 9/11, the Department of Justice took money and people away from white-collar investigations, and that shift continued through Gonzales's tenure. The FBI transformed from a domestic investigative body to an international intelligence agency, focused primarily on terrorism. In May 2002 the FBI revamped its priorities and shuffled its staff accordingly. In a list of its top ten priorities, the agency listed first: "Protect the United States from terrorist attack." Number two was "Protect the United States against foreign intelligence operations and espionage." Coming in at seventh, after cyber crime and public corruption: "Combat major white-collar crime."

Between 2000 and 2004, the FBI moved 1,143 field agents from traditional areas—including drugs, organized crime, and white-collar crime—into terrorism. Notionally, the bureau's number of white-collar agents fell only by about 120. But in addition to the formal reassignments, the agency reduced the workload of 1,200 agents who remained in the traditional areas so they could help with terrorism probes. The shifts affected about a quarter of all agents.[5] The Postal Inspection unit, which had been so helpful to the Southern District and Main Justice, retreated from complex corporate fraud investigations. The Post Office changed course to have its remaining agents investigate simple mail fraud. As a result of the leadership vacuum during this period, the Department of Justice struggled with white-collar cases because of prosecutorial inexperience and incompetence, and because it overreached in its notions of what was criminal.

Another scandal began brewing in July 2008, during the waning months of Bush's second term. A grand jury returned a seven-count indictment of the powerful and long-serving Alaskan senator Ted Stevens for failing to disclose hundreds of thousands of dollars in gifts, including home renovations, from a local businessman. As Bush left office and Obama came in, the case fell apart. Prosecutions operate under a set of rules to preserve the constitutional rights of the investigated and accused. The government must give the defense the evidence it is relying on to build its case, called Jencks material, after a 1957 Supreme Court case. More significantly, the government must give over all exculpatory information it uncovers to the defense, or so-called Brady material, after a 1963 Supreme Court case. The Giglio rule, from a related 1972 Supreme Court case, holds that prosecutors must tell the jury about any deals they have made with witnesses not to prosecute in exchange for testimony.

Eventually the court found that prosecutors in the Stevens case violated the Brady and Giglio rules. The judge threw out the case. Eric Holder would request in 2009 that the judge dismiss the Stevens charges. Tragically, in the fall of 2010, one of the prosecutors on the case committed suicide. In 2012 a court-appointed special prosecutor would write that at least two federal prosecutors had "intentionally withheld and concealed" evidence from the defense team that would have helped the late senator's defense. (Stevens lost a bid for reelection in 2008 and then died in a plane crash two years afterward.) Lower-level prosecutors were blamed. Supervisors escaped. The message was clear: be cautious in any high-profile case. All prosecutors worried a little about losing cases. But the Stevens debacle held a more acute lesson: a trauma like that might destroy your career and drive you to suicide.

## PELLETIER SAVES THE TRIAL

In January 2008, as the department's chaos swirled, Pelletier's and Safwat's trial of five executives—four from Gen Re and one from AIG—began. When the prosecutors got to court, it was hard not to be intimidated. Defense lawyers love to talk up the might and terror of government power, which is true in some respects. But in this case, there were five defense teams. The cables for the computers blotted out the legs of the tables. An army of associates, administration, support helpers, and jury experts sat behind the lead lawyers. At the opposing table sat the handful of poorly paid government workers who didn't get along very well.

Ray Patricco took the testimony of the star cooperator from Gen Re, senior vice president Richard Napier. Patricco started off with the Pelletier model—getting him to lay out the fraud—but then seemed to forget about the jury. He walked Napier through dozens of documents; so much material that the jury was visibly slack jawed. During a break, one of the defense attorneys joked with a member of the prosecution team, "Please save us from this misery!" At another point in the trial, after a long and detailed session with another witness, Patricco pulled out yet another binder of materials. A juror rolled his eyes as if to say, "Oh my God, here we go again!"

During Napier's initial testimony, Patricco pushed the witness just a little further than the Gen Re executive had been before, to recall facts over which he did not have full command. The defense pounced. On cross-examination, Reid Weingarten, who was representing Gen Re executive Elizabeth Monrad, exposed Napier. Weingarten was defense bar royalty, having represented numerous CEOs and cabinet officials. In a small-world connection, Weingarten had hired Patricco to be a junior lawyer on his team at his firm, Steptoe & Johnson.

Now Weingarten outflanked his one-time protégé. On the stand, Weingarten forced Napier to acknowledge some mistakes. Though the Gen Re executive didn't recant his allegations, the defense damaged his credibility. After the cross-examination, the prosecution team and the agents huddled in a room. They were miserable. Patricco lay dazed on a couch. Another prosecutor fumed about how Napier had botched matters for them.

Pelletier calmed down everyone. He sketched out how to do the redirect, in which the prosecution gets a limited chance to revisit the issues the defense brought up in the cross-examination. Pelletier walked through how to focus the questions and how to deal with the way the defense impugned Napier's credibility. Patricco's redirect was effective.

The prosecutors jockeyed for position throughout the trial. Initially Pelletier had responsibility for the final rebuttal, but Patricco wanted it, too. The US attorneys from Connecticut, the Eastern District of Virginia, and the head of the criminal division, Alice Fisher, held a conference call with the prosecutors and agents. She resisted, but they decided to give the rebuttal to Patricco.

During the rebuttal summation, Patricco made a humanizing argument: that the fraud hit the stock price. He argued, "Behind every share of [AIG] stock is a living and breathing person who plunked down his or her hard-earned money and bought a share of stock, maybe to put it in their retirement accounts, maybe to put it in their kids' college funds, or maybe to make a little extra money for the family."

This line was a mistake. The prosecution's argument was not predicated on the notion that the fraud had caused shareholder losses. Instead, the prosecution's argument was that the fraud mattered to shareholders—that it was "material." The distinction was significant but fine. Each was a different charge requiring different proof. This passage would haunt the prosecution on appeal.

Despite the tensions and the mistakes, the government brought the trial to a close in five weeks, just at the margin beyond which Pelletier believed the government lost a jury. They hadn't lost this one. In late

February 2008 the jury returned a resounding victory for the government, convicting all five defendants on all counts.

The prosecutors considered this victory only the first step. Pelletier and Safwat wanted to move up the ladder to the higher executives. They wanted to convict Greenberg, though understanding that it would be difficult. After the trial, they wanted to charge Joseph Brandon, who had been a senior executive at Gen Re when the transaction happened and had been briefed on it. Brandon was promoted to CEO in 2001 and appeared to understand the deal's contours. Brandon was a golden boy at Berkshire Hathaway, mentioned as a potential successor to Buffett. He was a big target. Patricco argued against charging Brandon, fearing the evidence wasn't solid enough. The government never charged him.

Hank Greenberg eluded them. The onetime CEO appointed an AIG executive, Christian Milton, to be the point man on the deal. He was convicted at trial but did not flip to give evidence against Greenberg, his chief executive. Pelletier and Safwat believed the sentences for all five were too light—"country club" sentences. Former CEO Ferguson received two years. The former CFO Monrad got eighteen months. Others got off similarly. Pelletier urged the teams to immunize the guilty executives and put them before the grand jury, forcing them to explain under oath what they knew about Greenberg's role. That was how to work up to the top of the corporation. But the other offices rejected the tactic, arguing the evidence didn't support the effort and thwarting Pelletier's ambition. In 2017 a ninety-one-year-old Greenberg finally admitted the transactions distorted AIG's books (though he still contended he had not committed fraud), in a settlement after a twelve-year-long court battle with the New York State Attorney General's Office.

Pelletier and Safwat also began negotiating with Gen Re itself. The sides had one sticking point. Even though he had not been chief executive at the time of the deal with AIG, Brandon, the current Gen Re CEO, had known about it. Pelletier and Safwat explained to the company and its attorneys that the government could not enter into a resolution with Gen Re if the company had the same CEO who had been there for the fraud.

They never came out and said that the company needed to get rid of him, but—come on!—the board shouldn't oppose the concept, they thought. Instead, the defense team cried foul, citing the KPMG case.

From then on, Safwat and Pelletier became ultracautious in every conversation with Gen Re and AIG's counsel. Prosecutors avoided any mention of lawyers' fees, joint defense agreements, and the employment status of the executives under investigation. They were working in the post-KPMG, post–Thompson memo world. Eventually, on January 20, 2010, prosecutors reached a nonprosecution agreement with Gen Re, which paid more than $90 million. The company admitted that its senior management knew the point of the deal was to enable AIG to falsely report increasing loss reserves to both the public and the SEC.

Years later, the Gen Re–AIG case ended in frustration. On August 2, 2011, a panel of judges on the Second Circuit Court of Appeals overturned the convictions of the Gen Re–AIG executives. Dennis Jacobs, a George H. W. Bush appointee and leading libertarian on the court, wrote the ruling, determining that prosecutors had overreached in attributing stock market losses to the particular frauds they hoped to prove. Judge Jacobs manifested hostility to almost every securities law prosecution, in the eyes of the government, at least. He deemed stock charts presented in the trial prejudicial, writing they "suggested that this transaction caused AIG's shares to plummet 12 percent during the relevant time period, which is without foundation, and (given the role of AIG in the financial panic) prejudicially cast the defendants as causing an economic downturn that has affected every family in America." There was only one problem with this assertion: the timing was wrong. The trial had taken place in early 2008, concluding in February—a full eight months before the financial crisis hit. It would have been impossible for the jury to have been prejudiced by an event that had yet to happen.

By now, Pelletier had left the Justice Department for private practice. Safwat argued that the department should go en banc, to ask for the entire Second Circuit to review the case and panel's decision, just as Pelletier had in the Nacchio case. Instead, the Solicitor General's Office advised against asking the panel to reconsider. The panel corrected its factual error but upheld its decision. The Department of Justice could have then petitioned the whole court, but didn't. It could have taken the case to trial again, but there was no appetite. A signature white-collar success had also come undone.

## THE AIG HUNT CONTINUES

Before the disappointment of the loss on appeal, while Pelletier and Safwat were buried in their Gen Re–AIG investigation and trial, the global financial bubble began to feel pinpricks. Housing prices peaked in 2006, and mortgage securities began to tumble in value starting early the following year. AIG started taking losses on its mortgage securities later that year. In February 2008 the company reported a loss of $5.3 billion, the worst quarterly deficit in its history, going back to 1919. Few investors or analysts understood why the company was taking losses. PricewaterhouseCoopers (PwC) was about to report that the AIG books had a "material weakness": a warning that investors cannot rely on a company's numbers. AIG was hemorrhaging money on subprime mortgage securities.

Safwat and Pelletier saw the news as they waited for the jury verdict in the AIG–Gen Re case. They reached out to the company and the SEC for more information. Safwat dug in. Soon after returning to DC, he went into Pelletier's office and told him they had to investigate.

"Is this just a valuation argument?" asked Pelletier. Cases about the value of assets on the books were notoriously difficult. These instruments did not trade, so the value had to be estimated. The prosecution could hire an expert witness to determine the value but the defense would counter with an expert of its own. The jury would then just shrug its shoulders.

"No, Paul, it's not. I can't quite put my finger on it, but it's something unusual. Something very wrong happened here."

Pelletier nodded. "Yeah, let's go see."

For five years, off and on, Paul Pelletier had investigated crimes at AIG. The epicenter of AIG's current mortgage problems was AIG

Financial Products, the London-based derivatives factory. Pelletier knew the unit well. He had investigated AIG FP during his probe of the PNC off-balance-sheet deals. Back then, the government hadn't been able to find enough evidence to prove that the top AIG FP executives had committed crimes. Now it looked as if AIG FP was involved in still more dodgy activity. Again, Paul Pelletier would be investigating a man soon to become notorious as one of the people most responsible for the 2008 financial crisis: Joseph Cassano.

*Chapter Nine*

# NO TRUTH AND NO RECONCILIATION

PAUL PELLETIER WAS THRILLED WHEN THE Obama people came in to the Department of Justice. Though he was a Massachusetts liberal Democrat to his core, it wasn't political. He despised incompetence and was only too happy to bid good-bye to late-era Bush "clowns." Department of Justice offices are split between the "front office" people and the line prosecutors. The front office is composed of political appointees and the staff (those whom Pelletier derided as "tourists"). In most Justice Department district offices, the distinction between the front office and the staff attorneys is thin. Those offices are smaller than Main Justice. The US attorney and his staff typically have a hand in the details and major decisions. By dint of their physical distance from the capital, they are less vulnerable to Washington meddling. In DC, by contrast, the dividing line between the front office and the career staff is, by tradition, thicker. Good political appointees cross it rarely to get into the particulars of investigations.

The tourists all came and went, using Pelletier's beloved department to move on to positions of greater prominence. But that did not mean they were all equal. Some were competent and some were not. The last batch from the Bush administration was among the worst. He expected the Obama lot to be vastly superior.

The financial crisis had hit its peak in September 2008, with Lehman Brothers collapsing, AIG requiring a bailout, and Bank of America taking over Merrill Lynch. Bush Treasury secretary Henry Paulson, the former chief executive of Goldman Sachs, worked with Federal Reserve Chairman Ben Bernanke and the head of the Federal Reserve Bank of New York, Timothy Geithner. By October, they'd injected hundreds of billions of dollars into the major commercial and investment banks, to shore up their capital.

Barack Obama had campaigned on hope and change, but when he took office, fear and anger convulsed the country. His administration had to first deal with a collapsing global financial system and an economy plunged into the worst recession since the Great Depression. He strove for continuity, appointing Geithner as his Treasury secretary. Bernanke was a holdover at the Fed, with a year left on his first term. In February 2009, with the president's push, Congress passed its stimulus plan, which would total over $800 billion.

Markets bottomed in the spring of 2009 but then began to settle down. The crisis subsided, though the economy plunged into a severe recession. Gross domestic product (GDP) fell 6.3 percent in the fourth quarter of 2008. Unemployment peaked at 10 percent in October 2009. Wall Street appeared to be changed forever. Bear Stearns had been taken over by JPMorgan Chase. Lehman Brothers had evaporated. Mortgage banks such as Washington Mutual failed. Countrywide Financial Corporation, a mortgage bank, had cratered and, like Merrill, been taken over by Bank of America. AIG was a ward of the federal government, as were Fannie Mae and Freddie Mac.

Everyone—government officials, bankers themselves, investors, regulators, prosecutors, defense lawyers—expected a serious postcrisis crackdown.

What shape would it take? There would be regulatory reform of the financial system, but there would also be prosecutions, certainly. What were the crimes? Who would go to prison?

President Obama appointed Eric Holder attorney general. He had been the deputy attorney general under Clinton's attorney general, Janet Reno. Holder had spent the last eight years at Covington & Burling, the quiet Washington power broker law firm. When Holder returned to the building in early February 2009, there was jubilation. People streamed out of their offices and peered down the stairwells. They clapped and shouted. Alberto Gonzales had been a fiasco. Michael Mukasey, Bush's last attorney general, had been better, but he was seen as a short-timer—an older judge who never had the pulse of the organization. Holder was respected from his time as deputy attorney general under Reno. He had a reputation within the building for professionalism. He was straightforward.

But the new Obama people got off to a slow start. The Senate did not confirm David Ogden, the deputy attorney general, until March. Lanny Breuer did not take his position as the head of the criminal division until April. Up in New York, Preet Bharara wasn't sworn in as US attorney for the Southern District until mid-August. Surprisingly, given the historic financial collapse, Obama's top Main Justice appointees and their staffers had little to no experience with complex white-collar fraud. Breuer had never been a federal prosecutor. Ogden was not a seasoned criminal prosecutor like Larry Thompson, but a partner from the powerful Washington law firm WilmerHale. Although cerebral and respected, he had little criminal prosecution experience. Staff prosecutors grumbled that the front office appointees were clueless about how to make complicated corporate criminal cases.

The Obama administration's front office would not adhere to the hands-off tradition. The political appointees wanted specifics on Main Justice's important cases. They lived in the weeds of the criminal investigations, following each development and questioning each decision. For as much as they obsessed about the minutiae of Main Justice's cases, they neglected the activities of other US Attorney's Offices, letting them find their own way.

Meanwhile, the administration and the newly installed Democratic Congress set about reforming the financial system to prevent future crises. Dodd-Frank, eventually passed in July 2010, provided technocratic solutions to calamitous economic and social upheaval. Democrats had helped push financial deregulation through the 1990s. Now they set about fixing it, in an effort they viewed as without distracting ideology, consciously rejecting appeals to populist fevers. What use was it to seek "Old Testament vengeance," in Timothy Geithner's phrase?[1]

Instead of doling out punishments, the Democrats engineered preventive measures to stave off similar future crises. In Dodd-Frank, the Obama administration and the Democratic Congress created the ultimate exercise in precision legislation. Sprawling through every corner of the financial world, the law did the opposite of similar legislation from the early twentieth century that reined in business and finance. The Securities Act of 1933 and 1934 had simple language and simple concepts but overweening ambition and structural overhaul. The law made manipulation of securities illegal—while leaving the definition of *manipulation* unspecified. Now, however, the world seemed more complex. Democrats, especially those with elite educations, thought they needed to solve problems in more sophisticated fashion. They wrote a law that tried to imagine any and all financial problems and apply a solution. It called for the regulatory agencies to craft hundreds of arcane rules to define the parameters of the new laws.

K. Sabeel Raman, a scholar at Brooklyn Law School, writes:

> Successive waves of liberal governance reform—from the Clinton administration's "reinventing government" initiative, to the Obama administration's emphasis on cost-benefit analysis and transparency—share a common problem: they prioritize "good" government over "democratic" government. This liberal vision of governance reform does not address the root challenge raised by critics on both the

> left and right today: the fear that government is ineffective, unresponsive, or unduly influenced by business and economic elites."[2]

Dodd-Frank was the emblem of such a flawed approach.In this context, prosecuting individuals seemed like a blunt and crude response. It fed the populist mob, as Geithner had suggested in his famous quote. But it solved nothing. When it came to punishment, the Obama administration's approach seemed to take cues from truth-and-reconciliation movements. The financial crisis had been dealt with quickly and aggressively, from the administration's point of view. But the public didn't get truth—not in any satisfying fashion. The public saw a corrupt bargain: bailouts and exonerations of bankers for unexplained and unspecified crimes. Reform without prosecution undermined the credibility of the reform. Paul Pelletier rued the day the Obamanauts came.

## EVERYONE CALLED HIM "LANNY"

Like Eric Holder, Lanny Arthur Breuer joined the Justice Department from Covington & Burling. There had been some talk that Breuer might be appointed White House counsel to the president, a role he'd had under President Clinton. When Breuer was passed over, White House Chief of Staff Rahm Emanuel, who had gotten to know Breuer during the Clinton years, pushed to make him head of the Justice Department's criminal division.

Breuer was the sort to be referred to by his first name, by friends, enemies, and people who didn't know him alike. "Lanny" was used in affection and to deprecate and infantilize. Breuer is garrulous and open, with a nasally voice that exudes earnestness. He could be warm. But in his role, he carried the air of a man who couldn't decide if he preferred to be loved or respected and was trying too hard to be both. He hated direct confrontations. If a subordinate got angry with him, he'd pretend not to notice, patting the person's arm and saying, "Everything's all right." Then he'd walk away as quickly as he could.

Born in 1958, Breuer grew up in Elmhurst, Queens. His parents were both only children. His mother lost her parents and extended family in the Holocaust. She fled Germany for Holland on September 1, 1939, the day the Nazis invaded neighboring Poland, igniting World War II. Because Lanny was born fourteen years after his brother, a family joke held that he was conceived on the night of his brother's bar mitzvah. A wiry kid, Breuer played rugby at Columbia College. He stayed to attend Columbia Law and then took a job at the Manhattan district attorney's office under Robert Morgenthau for four years in the late 1980s. He liked to tell the story of what his mother said when he told her he was taking a job at the DA's office. After he mentioned the famous sons in the office—Andrew Cuomo, Dan Rather Jr., Cyrus Vance Jr.—she replied, "Them? They should go to the DA's office. You? You should go to a firm." His brother, who became a doctor, countered the advice: "You've never had any money. You won't know what you are missing."

From the DA's office, Breuer went to Covington & Burling, spending about a decade at the prestigious firm. In one of his higher-profile cases, he represented a gay marine, Justin Elzie, who was suing the Clinton administration. The military had discharged the marine without benefits after he'd come out on national television. Impressed with Breuer, White House lawyers brought him on board as special counsel to the president. "I'm the only one to get a job at the White House by suing the administration," he liked to say.

He joined in the second Clinton term, when partisan battles over myriad scandals and pseudoscandals were bringing the president low. Breuer was regarded as a sharp and capable lawyer bent on adhering to the law. Charles Burson, who served as Vice President Al Gore's counsel and had been the Tennessee attorney general, recalled being impressed with the group's firepower. "I thought to myself, 'These are really good lawyers,' specifically Lanny," he says.

In one incident, the White House was going to send Congress material. To prevent it from being leaked, the team negotiated a protective order. The parties signed the protective order, and the White House delivered the first set of documents. No sooner had they reached Capitol Hill than the documents started being leaked to the press. All of them realized then, Burson says, that "it may look like there's a lot of law here, but it's all about politics."

During his time at the White House, Breuer met the other of the "Two Lannies," as they would come to be known: Lanny Davis, the bulldog lawyer and public relations man who lived on cable television in those years defending Clinton. In their first meeting, in the Oval Office, Davis and Breuer realized they had both been named after the same Upton Sinclair character, the Lanny Budd, a dashing sophisticate who popped up in moments of historical significance in a series of popular novels now largely forgotten. Davis remembers the day after their introduction, their mothers met to have lunch in Miami Beach. He and Breuer got along, though they could clash about public relations strategy. Davis was an advocate of getting more information to the media. He remembers Breuer holding back.

Breuer returned to Covington, and George W. Bush became president. He spent the next years working for several famous clients, including Sandy Berger, the former national security advisor who pleaded guilty to a misdemeanor for having taken and destroyed copies of classified documents from the National Archives, and counseled Roger Clemens, the former all-star pitcher, during his congressional hearing about his alleged use of performance-enhancing drugs.

Before taking his position as the head of the criminal division of the Justice Department, Breuer engaged in a clever round of coalition building and personal public relations, a classic element of the Washington game. He canvassed as many people as he could for advice about how to improve the criminal division. He spoke with every living head of the criminal division, deputy attorneys general and attorneys general—at least those who would take his calls. Most did. The message he heard from these worthies, the majority of whom were now in private practice on the defense side, was that the criminal division could be rolled in a negotiation. Obama's appointees saw the amateurism, scandal, mismanagement, and politicization that had riddled the Bush Justice Department. The criminal division needed an overhaul. He would remake it.

In his canvassing, Breuer had been told repeatedly that the criminal division's fraud section, which handles crimes such as securities and health care frauds, didn't have elite attorneys. They didn't do enough trials. Breuer discounted the trial expertise that was there, thanks to Hochberg and the Miami "mafia," led by Pelletier. Instead, he saw an office in chaos. "Indict and good things will happen." Breuer had heard that saying, and it soured his stomach. Bad things could happen, too. They had happened in the Ted Stevens case. The motto was cowboy talk—dangerous and ineffective bravado that got prosecutors into trouble. In their rush to indict first and ask questions later, they were prone to abuse their position or overlook holes that would destroy cases. Breuer and his crowd of precise and buttoned-down lawyers thought they could improve matters through importing the private bar's professionalism.

## THE TURTLE

Throughout 2009, it started to become clearer that the financial crisis wasn't just a paroxysm of capitalism, some kind of unforeseeable hundred-year flood. Fraud, it appeared, was rampant. The SEC and the Department of Justice began dozens of investigations. They covered Wall Street investment banks, commercial banks, regional banks, mortgage banks, giant insurance companies, small specialty mortgage insurers, credit rating agencies, hedge funds, and money managers. Every region of the country had potential targets. The probes covered mortgages and structured financial instruments but did not stop there. Did companies lie about the valuation of their assets? Did they misrepresent their books? As their firms were dying, did executives tell the public one thing but tell themselves another in private? Bankers had been reckless and stupid. Doubtless, some of the activities would prove merely aggressive business tactics but not illegal. As the government had done with Enron, prosecutors would now be required to sift through the actions. The job of investigating all the potential wrongdoing was too big, too broad, and too complex for any one US Attorney's Office or one SEC field office or for Main Justice alone.

One answer would be for the Justice Department to create a national task force. The Corporate Fraud Task Force that Larry Thompson helped start had become moribund—a body that held meetings and delivered statistics-dense reports no one read. A new national task force to tackle the financial crisis investigations might mobilize resources, make clear that such cases were a priority, and hand people responsibility for the prosecutions to come. Coordination problems plagued law enforcement, a perennial bugaboo.

The Obama administration inherited the Bush administration's decision about financial crisis investigations. Mukasey, Bush's last attorney general, and his deputy, Mark Filip, decided against creating a national task force for the crisis. They believed them to be slow moving and bureaucratic. Task forces can have flaws. Prosecutors are incentivized to bring cases, perhaps overreaching, to appear that they are doing something. Since the responsibility for assigning cases and adjudicating jurisdictional disputes falls to the deputy attorney general, Filip divided up the cases. He disbursed financial crisis cases around the country, often sending them to the local offices. The prosecutors in these offices often lacked corporate fraud expertise. A probe into mortgage bank Countrywide Financial went to Los Angeles and Sacramento, California. Washington Mutual (WaMu), a regional mortgage bank that collapsed in the fall of 2008, went to the Seattle office. When the probes weren't being conducted by inexperienced offices, turf battles delayed them. At least four Department of Justice offices—the District of New Jersey, the Eastern District of Virginia, the Eastern District of New York, in Brooklyn, and the vaunted Southern District of New York—opened investigations into the failure of Lehman Brothers, which had sparked the most acute phase of the financial crisis in September 2008.

Holder's Justice Department did not change the course Mukasey had set. David Ogden, Holder's first deputy attorney general, viewed the nation's law enforcement and regulatory structure as dysfunctional. Instead of cooperating, state and federal regulators competed, racing to be first to the press conference. It was a waste of resources and made for shoddy work. The Holder administration did not come close to fixing these problems. In its first year, the department was cautious and overwhelmed by political infighting. One former top official at Justice likened it to a soccer game with six-year-olds, where everyone clusters around the ball, and it never advances.

Breuer and Ogden squabbled. Political maneuvering between the deputy and the powerful criminal division head is common, and the two of them fell into the pattern. Typically, the deputy attorney general, not the head of the criminal division, articulates national goals and adjudicates jurisdictional disputes. But Breuer wanted to play a bigger role. Meanwhile, Ogden was having his own difficulties.

John Podesta, the Democratic power broker who headed up Obama's transition team, had pushed for Ogden to be hired. Holder resented him and in turn angered White House officials with his unmanageable streak. Holder had a middle-class upbringing in East Elmhurst, Queens. His father was a Barbados-born real estate broker, and his mother was a New Jersey native who worked as a telephone operator.[3] Some attorneys general serve a more political and ceremonial role, with the DAGs, as they are known inside the building, acting as chief operating officers. Holder wanted to be more active. He showed passion when it came to civil rights and national security, but he never evinced much interest in the financial crisis. When he suggested in a February 2009 meeting that financial fraud should be a priority of his Justice Department, he assigned Ogden to address the crisis by revamping the Bush-era Corporate Fraud Task Force.

A March 16 discussion draft memo outlined the "Proposed President's Financial Fraud Enforcement Council," with a to-be-named director reporting to Ogden, Breuer, and US attorneys around the country. A sprawling and unformed plan, it called for setting up groups to prosecute four categories: "Mortgage Fraud," "TARP/Rescue Fraud" (referring to the government's bailout efforts, known as the Troubled Asset Relief Program), "Securities Fraud," and "Commodities Fraud." Fraud by top executives at the large institutions would have fallen under the "Securities" umbrella, but was not emphasized. The category was listed third in the memo, and the "types of offenses" included Ponzi schemes and insider trading, crimes that had nothing to do with the calamity.

Through 2009, department officials volleyed different proposals and maneuvered for influence. Breuer supported the creation of a task force, housed in his criminal division, to address the financial crisis. He hoped to make it operational, to run investigations and take cases to trial. Ogden's office reacted suspiciously. They saw the ambitious Breuer's proposals as power grabs and attempts to hog the spotlight. Breuer's vision was that US Attorney's Offices would report to him, not to the deputy. The deputy's office scoffed that in his aspiration, Breuer had misunderstood the odd structure of the US attorney network. US attorneys didn't—and wouldn't—report to the head of the criminal division. While the criminal division has some national powers relating to investigations, US attorneys are a willful and ambitious bunch. Prosecutors had gained even more autonomy after the Bush administration's US attorney firing scandal. Breuer, new to the building, didn't grasp the complicated politics.

A more promising proposal came from within the fraud section. On July 13, 2009, Steven Tyrrell, the chief of the section who had gotten the role over Pelletier, and his assistant, Jay Lerner, recommended creating a Mortgage Fraud Strike Force to prosecute mortgage frauds. Mortgage losses were huge and impossible to ignore. Their memo noted the rise of "mortgage lending businesses" that "were not regulated, supervised, or audited by any of the primary financial regulators." Previous efforts had gone after borrowers who'd bilked banks. But Tyrrell and Lerner recommended going after the "most common suspect occupations associated with mortgage fraud," listing accountants, mortgage brokers, and lenders as the top targets. The memo outlined a plan for a specialized team of prosecutors, headed by a supervisor in the fraud section, to travel the country prosecuting mortgage fraud. The idea had promise. It would not have targeted Wall Street bankers or high-level executives initially. But such a team could have generated a body of evidence about the Wall

Street money machine. It might have helped prosecutors to work from the ground-level mortgages up to the Wall Street banks, which purchased mortgages, bundled them into securities, and sold them around the world. By the middle of the 2000s, these Wall Street creations were rife with fraud and misrepresentations.

On July 16, attorneys general and representatives from eight states, representatives from the Department of the Treasury and the Department of Housing and Urban Development (HUD), Breuer, Ogden, Tyrrell, Pelletier, and seventeen other Department of Justice representatives met in Washington to discuss financial crisis prosecutions. Breuer did nothing with Tyrrell's proposal. People in the fraud section thought he was unenthusiastic about ideas that were not his. In the end, the Justice Department prosecuted fraudsters for mortgage-related crimes, but almost all of them were small-timers. The department did not prosecute any top executives from a major mortgage lender.

Under public and congressional pressure, the Justice Department recognized it had to do something. Finally, in November 2009 President Obama announced his Financial Fraud Enforcement Task Force. On Friday, December 11, after an optional dinner the night before at Forlini's, a red-sauce staple in New York's Little Italy, top Justice Department officials from around the country met to outline the new task force's strategy. After Preet Bharara, the US attorney for the Southern District, and Ogden spoke, Breuer opined about "Real Time Investigations in Securities Fraud Cases." Staffers back at Main Justice rolled their eyes. At a quarter to three, the meeting was scheduled to finish. The agenda ended with a little touristy flourish: "Trip to the New York Stock Exchange (Potential)" as the last activity.

If the aim of the meeting was to help the Southern District get along better with Main Justice, it failed. After a promising start, the FFETF fizzled. Ogden left his post after less than a year, nudged out by Holder.[4] The task force had no operational powers to bring cases. The Justice Department struggled to staff it. It was just a coordinating committee to check in with offices around the country on their progress, with representatives from at least twenty-six federal agencies and departments, including the Department of Labor, the Social Security Administration, as well as state attorneys general, district attorneys, and "other state, local, tribal and territorial representatives." It would meet once a month, often with staffers calling into conference calls in their principals' steads.

If Main Justice was not going to create a serious task force, its responsibility to monitor the various cases that had been farmed out to far-flung offices became that much greater. Yet, the Holder administration did little. Just a few years earlier, Larry Thompson and Michael Chertoff understood the need to coordinate the cases, to move forward with investigations and prosecutions, to take regular stock of the progress of cases, and to administer the cattle prod when necessary.

Within the department, its new task force became the butt of jokes, called the "turtle," or derided with the vaguely Yiddish-sounding "Fuh-tuf-teh." Because of the failure, no one at Justice oversaw the entirety of the investigative effort. No one person was responsible. Every case was discrete. Any national push to combat the financial crisis died.

## "DO YOU LIKE GIVING TOASTS?"

Breuer wanted big cases and made those aspirations clear. But he didn't know how to bring them to fruition. His critics saw him chasing the issue of the day. If it was Southwest border control or foreign bribery, Breuer jumped on it. In April 2009, just as he got to the Justice Department, he testified in front of the US Senate Judiciary Subcommittee on Crime and Drugs about the disparity in sentencing for crack cocaine compared with the pure powder. (Dealing crack, a drug associated with urban African Americans, carried higher sentences than dealing cocaine, which was ubiquitous in affluent white circles.) Some staffers saw him as a glory hound.

Breuer saw it differently. He had so much to do. He changed the criminal division's human rights section. He set about revitalizing the public corruption department. He sped up wiretap approvals. He overhauled the organized crime section.

In his zeal to overhaul the place, Breuer alienated factions in the building. His critics claimed he surrounded himself with loyalists, including young lawyers steeped in corporate white-collar defense work, with limited experience in prosecuting criminals. Main Justice staffers dubbed his recruits the "Breu Crew." In October 2009 Steven Fagell, his deputy chief of staff, who also came from Covington, sent an email on behalf of his boss to the attorneys in the criminal division:

> Do you like giving toasts? Do you think it should have been you accepting the writing Emmy for *30 Rock*? Do you itch to work with the raucous crowd in the front office? If so, we need your wit, smarts, and gift for the written word! We're putting together a speechwriting team for the assistant attorney general, and we are looking for a small group of clever wordsmiths and humorists to assist the [assistant attorney general] in drafting his speeches across a wide range of topical areas.[5]

The building regarded the email with disdain. One former Justice Department official says, "You can't send that out to people doing serious work, trying to break up Los Zetas [a formidable Mexican drug cartel]. The reaction was: Are you fucking kidding me?" The notion that prosecutors longed to write speeches for the politicos? Laughable. Breuer also instituted a practice of conducting moot courts and had assistant US attorneys practice opening arguments and witness examinations. Many staffers felt patronized.

The experienced prosecutors bristled at Breuer's vision and notion that the place needed overhauling. When he met with Steven Tyrrell, the chief of the fraud section, Breuer told Tyrrell he wanted to compete with the Southern District of New York. Tyrrell was skeptical. Ultimately, he understood that Breuer had no use for him and decided to leave for private practice. Breuer told the *National Law Journal* he wanted to hire a "rock star" to replace him. Staffers got it. One former prosecutor from the office says, "The message was: you suck."

The Breu Crew looked to hire elites. They wanted graduates from the best law schools, who had clerked for prestigious judges and had worked at prominent firms. The Miami Mafia represented what was wrong with Main Justice; the résumés there were just not high-toned enough. Steve Fagell gathered people to a meeting to change how Main Justice recruited: "We all were on the hiring committee at Covington," he told the supervisors. "We know how to hire litigators." Most big law firms recruit from the Justice Department to get lawyers with litigation experience; the Breu Crew did the opposite.

Breuer admonished his prosecutors that "there's no way we can lose this." The sense was that even if he and his crew believed that a possible defendant was 100 percent guilty, but they had only a 70 percent shot to win at trial, they didn't want to pursue the case.[6] (Breuer rejected the notion that he was trepidatious. He believed he took on tough cases and maintained he had a strong record of white-collar enforcement, saying, "Where there were cases to bring, we brought them, and where there were not, we took a pass.") Gary Grindler, Breuer's first deputy, would emphasize to prosecutors that losing cases would reflect poorly on the front office. Grindler told Pelletier one day, "You know, if you lose this case, Lanny will have egg on his face."[7]

"I don't give a shit about that!" Pelletier yelled. The sentiment jolted him. He was apoplectic. "Nobody had ever said anything like that to me in more than twenty-five years of prosecuting federal cases. Whether someone might look bad in the event of a loss had never come up ever, ever, ever," Pelletier said.

Cases were not supposed to be about advancing the career prospects of the front office tourists in charge. Department of Justice leaders seek personal glory. The good ones win it through good cases, and by supporting and protecting their troops, rather than having their troops protect and support them.

Breuer recruited two men with big reputations: Denis McInerney, a partner with white-shoe firm Davis Polk, to replace Tyrrell as the chief of the fraud unit; and Greg Andres, who had been the chief of the criminal division in the US Attorney's Office for the Eastern District of New York, a top office. Andres joined as the deputy assistant attorney general overseeing the fraud section. As with Breuer's appointment, the question was whether these two men were right for the moment. Both had been involved in corporate white-collar cases that had helped to alter the culture of the Justice Department for the worse.

In the 1970s, McInerney had been a respected prosecutor in the Southern District. But he had spent the bulk of his career since then defending companies, including Arthur Andersen. The architect of that defense could hardly be expected to be an aggressive advocate of corporate indictments. He made it clear to the staff attorneys that he considered Andersen a major injustice that put the company out of business, throwing people on the streets needlessly.

Personable and gracious, McInerney urged his charges to pursue ambitious cases, but he was so cautious and deliberative that people wondered if he was setting a bizarrely high bar, requiring a level of proof and certainty that no one could ever reach. The joke was that McInerney would make a great line attorney if only someone could switch places with him. No one questioned how hard the guy worked. He left his family in New York and came down to DC, often putting in sixteen hours a day. He'd buy his meals in the CVS across the street and exercise on a stationary bike set up in his little apartment in the "Fraud Dorm," the building near the fraud section's offices. His office was a mess. He'd wander the halls disheveled, his shirt untucked, food stains on his clothing.

McInerney prepared cases like no one else. He memorized countless emails. The staff attorneys all had to prepare their binders for him. "It's Binders for Denis Day," one would say to another, preparing for an agonizingly late night. He ran the group like a giant law firm. Many staff prosecutors gloried in their entrepreneurial jobs and had sacrificed law firm pay for the freedom that comes with a Justice Department role. McInerney had them acting like associates, researching obscure lines of argument and precedents. Pelletier and his Miami mafia chafed under him. It was no way to manage a bunch of willful and accomplished prosecutors.

McInerney had been a career number two—more of a chief of staff than a chief of a Justice Department section. He had served Robert Fiske for years, both at Davis Polk and during Fiske's stint in 1994 as the Bill Clinton–era Whitewater scandal special prosecutor. Now he served Breuer. He often said he wanted to make Breuer look good. Breuer shared this desire.

Breuer's office was in the Main Justice building, on Pennsylvania and Ninth Street. The fraud section's offices were about a half mile away, on New York and Fourteenth Street. McInerney would spend his day yo-yoing back and forth between the buildings, attending meetings and carrying messages back from the front office. With each mile logged, the career prosecutors lost a little bit more respect. One time McInerney emailed an assistant prosecutor to ask him if he'd make the trek to Main Justice to escort Breuer over to a Justice Department training conference. Such requests got the pocket veto they deserved.

McInerney seemed to treat decision making like an experiment on a new and unknown virus—to be undertaken only with caution. Staffers reported he said, "Why make a decision today you can put off to tomorrow?" Or, preferably, why not punt and have someone senior make the decision? McInerney liked people to argue with him. In another supervisor, this quality might be admirable, indicating a willingness to hear differing points of view. With McInerney, colleagues felt, it was something different. He seemed to seek out nuances, complexities, and opposing arguments. They would paralyze him further, relieving him of the need to make a final call. Scarred by the Arthur Andersen indictment, he appeared to feel that prosecutors could too easily be precipitous and trigger happy. In 2013, when the office was considering resolving the case against the Royal Bank of Scotland (RBS), the British bank, over charges that employees had manipulated the key interest rate benchmark, LIBOR (an acronym for London Interbank Offered Rates), McInerney would ask prosecutors on the case, "What about the collateral consequences?"

Greg Andres also came with a tough reputation. When he was prosecuting the Mafia, the Bonanno crime family ordered a hit on him. (The assassination wasn't attempted.) But Andres, too, had been involved in a recent, headline-grabbing Department of Justice humiliation: the first major trial stemming from the financial crisis. The Eastern District of New York, where Andres was the chief of the criminal division, brought the case against two Bear Stearns executives who had run internal hedge funds at the investment bank.

The financial crisis, percolating since early 2007, accelerated with the collapse of two Bear Stearns funds that summer. Bear Stearns never recovered and was on the brink of collapse when JPMorgan acquired it in a fire-sale merger midwifed by a generous loan from the Federal Reserve. The trial of the executives, Ralph Cioffi and Matthew Tannin, started in Brooklyn in October 2009. It generated worldwide media attention. The trial lasted three weeks. After two days of deliberation, the jury acquitted the two managers.

The Department of Justice reeled. The prosecution team had been sloppy and hasty. It had built its case on a collection of seemingly damning emails, but overlooked others that complicated the executives' actions and motives. The judge in the case barred some of the most damaging messages from the trial. As had the Arthur Andersen and KPMG cases, the Bear Stearns trial loss had seismic reverberations. It eroded the department's confidence. The loss "was very damaging nationwide," says a top financial regulator. "It scared everyone." A former federal prosecutor says, "I felt it. You can't suffer a loss like that. It was a huge setback. People at the DOJ don't want to lose. The FBI became more cautious. The DOJ became more cautious. Yes, it put a chill on those cases."

Nevertheless, Breuer recruited Andres down to Washington only a few months after the loss. With that appointment, Breuer now had two top officials with indelible marks from two of the biggest corporate white-collar Justice Department fiascos of the past decade.

## BREUER GOES TO CAPITOL HILL

Timidity coursed through the Holder Justice Department. It was not isolated to Breuer's criminal division. In September 2010, a half dozen years after the trial, the Holder administration walked away from one of Kathy Ruemmler's top Enron victories. The prosecution carried significant symbolic importance: it was the only criminal case brought against Wall Street executives involved in the Enron fraud. That month, just days before a retrial had been scheduled, the Justice Department moved to drop charges against James Brown, a Merrill Lynch executive involved in the Nigerian barge case. In 1999 Enron had sold an interest in three energy-producing barges off the coast of the African country to Merrill, booking a profit. Enron promised Merrill that it would buy back the stock within six months at a predetermined profit. The reality was that it wasn't a sale at all but a loan. Merrill executives had described it internally as a "relationship loan."[8]

The case fell, a victim of one of the many rulings from appellate courts in recent years that have raised the bar on white-collar corporate prosecutions. In 2004 a jury found four bankers guilty and they went to prison. In 2006 the Fifth Circuit overturned the fraud and conspiracy charges against four of the five Merrill executives who had been found guilty at trial. (The fifth did not appeal his conviction.)[9] The Fifth Circuit had taken issue with the honest-services charge against the Merrill executives.

The appeals court ruled that the prosecutors had not demonstrated that the Merrill executives had been motivated solely to profit personally, as the indictment had alleged. Instead, the bankers and the Enron executives were worried, the lead judge on the decision wrote, that if the two parties did not close the deal, Enron would suffer. They were working in the best interests of the company, he determined. The "only personal benefit or incentive" for the executives "originated with Enron itself—not from a third party, as in the case of bribery or kickbacks." The judge, a Reagan appointee, contended that since top Enron executives had helped engineer the scheme, the company itself wasn't defrauded. *Fortune* dubbed the court decision the "too-crooked-to-defraud rule."[10]

When Ruemmler was principal associate deputy attorney general, she found Breuer serially reluctant to put up a fight. Any setback, and his criminal division would retreat, dropping the case. She would needle him, "How many cases are you dismissing this week?"

When the Justice Department dropped the remaining Nigerian barge charges, Ruemmler had already moved to the White House to be deputy counsel (later counsel) to President Obama. She was livid. Breuer was not the only timid Justice Department official. Nobody had even shown her the courtesy of telling her in advance that it was dropping the case. She had to read about it online. And it made little sense. The government had made the decision to pull the case on the eve of trial. Why had it waited so long and done so much preparation only to back out at the last moment?

She called Lisa Monaco, her replacement at the Justice Department.

"What the hell is this?"

Monaco stammered. She pleaded that the department was resource constrained. Then there was the kicker, a refrain that the criminal division sang frequently: the case was going to be difficult to win—maybe a fifty-fifty chance at best.

The jurors had no problem with the case originally, concluding that the conduct had been egregious and fraudulent. They hadn't been caught up in some anticorporate, anti-Enron fervor. The members had been thoughtful, carefully distinguishing between the defendants. They had voted to convict five of the six charged, while acquitting a woman executive in accounting who hadn't been implicated in any of the copious documentation that was so damning for the other executives.

The decision about the case came at a bad moment. The Supreme Court had just stung the Justice Department. In a June 24, 2010, ruling in *Skilling v. United States*, the court struck down aspects of the fraud convictions of Enron's Jeff Skilling and the newspaper tycoon Conrad Black, who had been convicted of looting his company, Hollinger International. Skilling and Black had been found guilty of depriving their shareholders of their honest services and were serving time. The high court narrowed the honest-services charge, assailing it as overly vague. Justice Ruth Bader Ginsburg wrote the unanimous decision. Justices Antonin Scalia, Clarence Thomas, and Anthony Kennedy wrote that they would have gone further and struck down the law entirely.[11]

But the Supreme Court ruling was no excuse to Ruemmler. The

Justice Department could have brought the case with more basic fraud charges. Sometimes you have to bring a case and risk losing to make a point, she thought. These guys were too scared to do that.

No doubt, resource constraints saddled the Obama Justice Department, too. Supervisors had to work around periodic hiring freezes, preventing managers from filling positions when people departed. The cutbacks affected the entire national network of US Attorney's Offices. Breuer complained about the constraints to Congress. Efforts to ameliorate the problem failed. In May 2009 President Obama signed the Fraud Enforcement and Recovery Act, designed to give $165 million to investigators and prosecutors to target financial fraud. Then-senator Ted Kaufman of Delaware, who had coauthored the law, intended it to bolster resources to go after crimes at the highest levels of the nation's financial firmament. In the end, Senator Barbara Mikulski, Democrat of Maryland, who chaired the Senate Appropriations Committee, allocated only $30 million. It was all the budget could spare, her office told Kaufman's staff.[12]

The Department of Justice exacerbated its problems by fighting with other bureaucracies. The era of the Southern District's cooperation with Stanley Sporkin was long over. In late 2010 Lorin Reisner, the deputy director of enforcement at the SEC, pressed the Justice Department for access to grand jury information and to wiretap info. Because grand jury information is confidential, the Justice Department cannot share it with regulatory agencies such as the SEC. This confidentiality damages investigations on multiple levels. It doesn't help the SEC learn new information and advance its own probes, which could end up helping federal prosecutors. In recent years, federal prosecutors have grown wary of using grand juries as evidence-gathering tools in corporate investigations. The Southern District, especially, uses grand juries less and less. Prosecutors don't like having witnesses under oath. They worry that the witnesses will change their stories, allowing defense lawyers to impugn their credibility. When Reisner made his request on behalf of the SEC, the Department of Justice perceived a threat, thinking the SEC wanted to horn in on its investigations. Top officials opposed it.

The Obama Justice Department did not seem to grasp how losing one tool after another—from the Thompson memo rollback to the honest-services clause—harmed its investigative and prosecutorial abilities. The courts increasingly found fault with white-collar prosecutions. The corporate lobby and defense bar had mobilized. Yet there was little analysis of the problem. Top Justice Department officials hardly discussed it publicly.

When the department did respond, it did so in blinkered fashion. On September 28, 2010, a few months after the Supreme Court ruling, Breuer testified in front of Congress to advocate for a statutory fix to the honest-services clause. At Main Justice, officials debated what had a better chance with Congress: asking for a restoration for public or private sector corruption, or both. Breuer took the more modest path. He recommended a fix only for public corruption cases. In neglecting to address the private sector aspects of the charge, the administration had absorbed the defense bar's view. As a defense attorney, Breuer heard the charge ridiculed when used in the corporate setting. He did not ask Congress to expand the statute to include private sector corruption. The administration believed there was no appetite in Congress for a private sector fix. But Breuer went so far as to offer an argument against it, telling the senators that it would be too hard to write a law covering private sector honest-services violations. Breuer told Congress, "Crafting appropriate language concerning undisclosed self-dealing in the private sector is more difficult than with respect to the public sector."[13]

Perhaps the Obama administration misread the political moment, for it remained preoccupied with limitations and constraints with every setback. But anger at the banks after the financial crisis reached an apex. Bailouts and bonuses infuriated the public. In 2009 the Democrats controlled both houses of Congress. They may have found an argument that prosecutors needed more weaponry hard to resist. Statutory reform to help prosecutors with corporate crime investigations might well have passed.

*Chapter Ten*

# THE LAW IN THE CITY OF RESULTS

IN 1919 A DEMOCRATIC POLITICAL OPERATOR AND an intellectual Republican came together to create the archetype for the revolving-door law firm: Covington & Burling. J. Harry Covington had been a Democratic Maryland congressman for three terms, from 1909 to 1914. He sponsored the bill that helped create the Federal Trade Commission. President Woodrow Wilson later made him a judge on what became the US District Court in Washington, DC. Edward Burling was a Bull Moose Republican, a short-lived progressive splinter of the Republican Party. Combining his reserved brilliance and Covington's contacts made for a formidable operation.

Soon enough, the firm's partners were moving from the firm into government and back again. Dean Acheson, who joined Covington in 1921, served Franklin Delano Roosevelt at the 1944 Bretton Woods Conference that molded the post–World War II global financial order, creating the International Monetary Fund. In 1949 Acheson became President Harry Truman's secretary of state. Covington partners have held top posts at the

Treasury Department, the IRS, and the Defense Department's Office of General Counsel. In 1971 a young star partner switched from representing food companies that were resisting a US Food and Drug Administration regulation to become the general counsel of the agency. While at the FDA, he continued to refer to Covington as "we." When he left four years later, another Covington partner replaced him.[1] And, of course, Covington lawyers populated the Department of Justice.

By the 1970s, Covington & Burling had become Washington, DC's, leading firm, with a client roster that included most of the top corporations in the United States, nearly all the major countries in the world, and almost every major trade association. It represented 20 percent of the Fortune 200, including IBM, DuPont, Exxon, and Procter & Gamble, specializing in tax advice and antitrust work. C&B lawyers were instrumental in securing passage of the Telecommunications Act of 1996, a sprawling deregulatory effort. Covington advised Exxon in its merger with Mobil in 1999. More recent clients have ranked among the top financial firms in the world: Goldman Sachs, JPMorgan Chase, Citigroup, Bank of America, Wells Fargo, and Deutsche Bank.[2]

Today Covington is a fixture in the unelected permanent governing class, though it doesn't carry the same special prestige as it once did. Nor is it uniquely powerful. In 1985 Covington had $49 million in revenue, making it the thirty-seventh-biggest firm in the country, and generated $215,000 in profits per equity partner, according to *American Lawyer*'s tally. Ten years of rapid growth later, in 1995, C&B brought in $135 million in revenue and generated $490,000 in profits per partner. Despite growth, it was then just the forty-fourth-largest firm.

Many other law firms and consulting operations have since joined its ranks. The DC rival WilmerHale is larger and more profitable. Consultancies and lobbying firms have won their fair share of business and new recruits. Washington became a big tent, capacious enough for all kinds of professionals to prosper. These firms lobby on behalf of clients; help write the laws that govern their clients; represent their clients in legal disputes and regulatory mishaps; consult with them; and help write their economic analyses to defend their merger proposals or fend off the government. Few people even know the names of these firms. The media hardly cover them, but reporters count many of their partners as sources. Legislators and regulators scrutinize them rarely because, generally, they are expecting to join them one day or receive campaign contributions from them.

Covington retained a particularly platinum reputation for tenacity and brilliance, tempered by understatement and modesty. Once, when a well-known partner began an argument by saying, "I don't mean to burden this court," the judge interrupted to say, "It's never a burden to listen to you speak."[3] The firm conferred standing on its lawyers, not the other way around. "Lawyers there are important not so much for their personal skills, which may be substantial, but precisely because they are at Covington & Burling," Mark Green, the future New York politician, put it in his 1978 book *The Other Government*, about the secret power of Washington law firms. Covington "exemplified the art of lawcraft as it is practiced in the City of Results."[4]

For decades, Covington & Burling, staid and steeped in reverence for its own culture, held a weekly firm luncheon at Washington's Metropolitan Club. In 1966, when founder Edward Burling Sr. was eulogized at the club, which did not admit women—and wouldn't for another twenty-two years—an interoffice memo stated that the women lawyers at C&B, and the wives of male partners, were forbidden to attend. The club accepted its first black member in 1972, in part because of the prodding of Edward Burling Jr., the son of the founder who was also a Covington partner. One firm partner remarked that the only way for a Jew to become a member of the Metropolitan Club was to be a senior partner at Covington.

Up through the 1970s, secrecy enshrouded the business of law. Covington partners turned down media interviews, citing the twin "canons": attorney-client privilege and the prohibition on soliciting employment through advertising. (The total ban on legal advertising was lifted after a 1977 Supreme Court ruling, *Bates v. State Bar of Arizona*.) H. Thomas Austern, a senior partner, explained C&B's reticence. "Our public work is in court or agency records," he said. "The rest of our practice is no one's business but ours, and we won't talk about it."[5]

By the late 1990s, the partners began to worry. The firm remained powerful. But it was insular, sleepy, and—unsurprisingly, given its history—predominantly white, male, and Protestant. To its credit, Covington remained less mercenary than the biggest firms, with an old-fashioned belief in pro bono work and professionalism. Big law firms, by contrast, were becoming much more commercial, merging with one another to become all-service shops. Covington, which preferred to cultivate its own talent, was falling behind. The firm's leadership realized it could no longer resist the changes in the business. Covington spent much of 1999 looking around for a merger partner before hitting on Howard, Smith & Levin. The upstart Manhattan firm, founded only in 1983, specialized in mergers-and-acquisitions (M&A) work. With the purchase of the practice, Covington kept its venerable name and added sixty lawyers. It became, in the words of a former partner, "twice as Jewish." Though it wasn't the sole aim, Covington now expanded its white-collar criminal practice and installed a Howard, Smith & Levin partner as its head. In 1999 the firm had $152 million in revenue, good for seventieth place in the country, and it made $485,000 in profits per partner. Just two years later, it had leapt to fifty-seventh place with $237 million in revenue and generated $655,000 per partner.[6]

By 2015, with both Obama's former attorney general, Eric Holder, and former criminal division head Lanny Breuer having returned to Covington, the firm ended the year with $709 million in revenue, jumping to forty-third-largest. Partners earned more than $1.3 million, on average. Marquee partners who had served at the highest levels of the government made much more. Breuer was set to make $4 million a year in his first year back at Covington.[7] When he was attorney general, Eric Holder made $199,700 a year. As a newly returned Covington partner, Holder, who in 1999 reportedly pulled in $2.5 million, including deferred compensation, when he left the firm to head up Justice, would make many times that.[8]

Covington's March 2013 press release announcing Breuer's return listed eighteen colleagues with law enforcement experience in this country and abroad, including two heads of the Justice Department's antitrust division and Michael Chertoff, who had been the assistant attorney general of the criminal division before heading the Department of Homeland Security. That didn't include all the former top regulators at the firm. After John Dugan left his position in 2010 as the head of the US Treasury's Office of the Comptroller of the Currency, a major banking regulator, he also rejoined Covington. And on and on.

The revolving door was not just a way for government employees to cash in. Both sides were changing the other—ultimately to the benefit of corporations. No one conceded, at least publicly, that the revolving door influenced the lawyers' work in government. "What people dismissively talk about as the revolving door allows people to be better public servants and private litigants," Breuer told the *New York Times*. "I believe I was a better assistant attorney general because of my deep experience in the private sector."[9]

## THE LOST LAWYER-STATESMAN

Prosecutors such as the Southern District's Peter Fleming, Rusty Wing, and Jed Rakoff began migrating to top law firms in the sixties and seventies. By the nineties, the trend had momentum. Almost every major firm in the country built or bought a substantial white-collar criminal defense practice. In 1986 the white-collar criminal defense bar tried to host its first annual meeting at the Boca Raton Resort and Club in Florida, but the resort rejected the group because it didn't want to be associated with "discussions of criminal activity."[10] Shifting to a new locale, seventy-five lawyers showed up. In the 1990s, Rakoff and his team moved to the New York law firm Fried, Frank, Harris, Shriver & Jacobson. Davis Polk had Bob Fiske but started building up its practice. Debevoise & Plimpton remained aloof, still outsourcing its criminal work to boutiques. Debevoise capitulated to the trend in earnest when it recruited Mary Jo White after she'd left her US attorney job.

White-collar criminal work was not just becoming plentiful, but also it provided healthy profit margins, with companies paying up for legal advice that could preserve their reputations. White-collar criminal lawyers began to be paid better, compared with specialists in antitrust, M&A, intellectual property, bankruptcy, and corporate securities. White-collar departments had higher ratios of partners to associates than other departments. And they, more than partners from other areas, shared a common trait: most white-collar criminal law partners were former government officials, especially federal prosecutors.[11] In 2016 the American Bar Association's National White Collar Crime Institute's thirtieth annual meeting hosted 1,034 attendees, an almost fourteen-fold increase from the original meeting. Today the government lawyers who cash in enter a business that has undergone a complete transformation in a few decades.

Rakoff, romantic about the past state of the business, worried about changes in the business of law. He'd grown up in the era of the lawyer-statesman and he had created a canyon of heroes to them in his chambers. Leon Silverman held a position of particular prominence. Silverman, who had been the head of Fried, Frank, where Rakoff practiced, was much more than a corporate lawyer. He'd served as president of the Supreme Court Historical Society and the Legal Aid Society, which provided lawyers for the poor.

Silverman and his other legal heroes, Rakoff believed, were the best exemplars of a generation of attorneys more interested in the law than in the business of law. Robert Gordon of Stanford Law School defined the lawyer-statesman as "the independent citizen, the uncorrupted just man of learning combined with practical wisdom." Rakoff saw lawyers as the natural guardians of the law and of society's morality. "They were a group of people whose view of the lawyer's role in society was much, much broader than anything that most lawyers have today. They vanished," the judge says. The statesmen had become endangered, done in by crude economics. They were luxuries firms could no longer afford.

Over time, competition in the legal business became fierce, and the old model fell away. Under the older oligopolistic model, partners did not live in constant fear of losing their long-standing corporate clients. Companies were more loyal. They had been clients for decades and expected to stay for decades to come. Law firms, secure in their clients, could give honest counsel. They could explain what was legal, what wasn't, and what was legal but not ethical. Lawyers could advise their clients on matters of judgment, ethics, and psychology, and not on narrow matters of the fine print, worried about losing a client to another firm. Today law firms are bigger and more profitable but more frenzied for business. If the client hears something it doesn't like, it seeks another opinion. That threat can prevent partners from being too strict with their clients. The new imperatives of this cutthroat world destroyed the old societal bond.

That, at least, was the story older lawyers told about their business. It was probably not an entirely accurate picture, but more true than not. The business had become much more commercial and more mercenary. Litigators had dominated the top ranks of firms in previous decades. Corporate transactional lawyers took over. They did deals, and they tracked the numbers and the bottom line. By the 2000s, law firms had imported the jargon and attitudes of business school.

Though the notion had been building for a while, by the 2010s, lawyers widely considered their profession in crisis. The growth in size of firms, their revenue, and their profits per partner had been strong. Yet uncertainty infused the model. The authors of a Harvard Law School essay about the ethical responsibilities of lawyers wrote: "There is widespread agreement that the legal profession is in a period of stress and transition; its economic models are under duress; the concepts of its professional uniqueness are narrow and outdated; and, as a result, its ethical imperatives are weakened and their sources ill-defined."[12] Firms obsessed over profits per partner even as overall demand for legal services overall was falling, a drop that accelerated after the 2008 recession. "Short-term economic goals seem to have overwhelmed the ethical imperatives and duties, resulting in widespread public mistrust of lawyers as a profession," they continued.

A symbiotic relationship developed between Big Law and the Department of Justice. The way government prosecuted corporate crime helped transform how private firms conducted their practice and their business. Big law firms in turn began to change how the government approached corporate investigations and prosecutions. The Department of Justice became a way station, a post-(law) doctorate course of study, a résumé builder for future partners of prestigious law firms. During the Obama years, the trend became only more pronounced. The transformation began when the government began to push to change corporate culture, not simply to punish individuals. The SEC's Stanley Sporkin had first pioneered the cooperation regime in the 1970s, but by the 2000s, regulators across the government—not just the Justice Department and the SEC—offered the cooperation-for-leniency bargain. Corporations hired law firms to conduct internal probes. One-off representations of individual criminal executives were not going to be an ongoing moneymaker. Internal audits, on the other hand, were. They employed many more lawyers and associates. And a large corporation might discover the need for another internal probe in the future.

Covington & Burling did its share of internal investigations. Adelphia, the cable company embroiled in post-Nasdaq-bubble-era accounting fraud, and the nonprofit United Way of New York City, which had been rocked by several instances of executives stealing from the charity, both retained Covington to conduct reviews.[13] In 2009 the mortgage giant Freddie Mac hired the firm to conduct a probe into whether its own lobbying campaign had helped quash new regulations on the company in the lead-up to the financial crisis.[14] When Hewlett-Packard needed to look into allegations that its CEO, Mark Hurd, had sexually harassed a former company contractor in 2010, the board hired Covington.[15] But the firm did not come close to dominating the business. Other major firms also had lucrative practices.

"The law treats the corporation as both criminal and cop, and uses the corporation as a vehicle for detecting, proving and punishing business crime," writes Samuel Buell, the onetime Enron and Arthur Andersen prosecutor who is now a Duke University School of Law professor, in his book *Capital Offenses: Business Crime and Punishment in America's*

*Corporate Age*.[16] The self-policing system has arisen in an ad hoc fashion, unplanned and little questioned, with far-reaching consequences for the ability to bring top executives to justice.

## EXCELLENT SHEEP

Before long, there began to be something of a chicken-and-egg question. A symbiotic relationship between the law firms and the DOJ and SEC arose. It became no longer clear whether the Department of Justice pushed investigations that turned out to be lucrative for the white-shoe big law firms or whether big law firms nudged prosecutors into conducting the types of investigation that required lucrative internal probes. The evolution could be seen in Foreign Corrupt Practices Act cases. Sporkin, who'd helped get the FCPA passed in 1977, had launched a revolutionary expansion of what a regulator could do. He wanted to police American corporations' moral behavior. His actions, coupled with his solid working relationship with the Southern District, succeeded.

After Sporkin, through the 1980s and 1990s, prosecutors put foreign bribery cases aside. Initially, they retained a bad smell from the Sporkin criticism. Three decades on, the Department of Justice set about reviving FCPA actions, starting around 2005. The department scored some necessary and important successes. In December 2008—predating the Obama administration—Siemens, the German industrial conglomerate, entered into the largest-ever FCPA settlement, at $800 million.[17]

In his first year as the head of Main Justice's criminal division, Lanny Breuer seized on foreign bribery cases. In 2009 Breuer and company appeared to worry that they didn't have any financial crisis prosecutions to parade in front of the public. Staffers started noticing that Breuer began to emphasize FCPA cases. He gave a muscular speech in November 2009, emphasizing how serious the Justice Department was about foreign bribery crackdowns.[18] He revisited the topic on multiple occasions. The Justice Department scored at least one success prosecuting a high-level individual from a top company. Albert "Jack" Stanley, who ran the American engineering and construction company Kellogg, Brown & Root (KBR), which until recently had been part of Halliburton, pleaded guilty to bribing Nigerian government officials. In February 2012 he was sentenced to two and a half years, making him the highest-ranking executive to go to prison in an FCPA case.[19]

After Siemens, the following nine largest-ever settlements were reached in the Obama era, between 2009 and 2016. All but three companies—KBR/Halliburton, Och-Ziff, and Alcoa—were foreign,[20] leading critics to wonder if the Department of Justice took a harder line on overseas entities or went relatively easy when investigations hit hometown companies. As one lawyer remarked, "It's fucked up that one of our priorities is crime in other countries. It's an area no rational person would put precious resources."

The Justice Department had embarrassments as well. In February 2012 a US District Court judge in Washington, DC, threw out a foreign bribery case involving African officials that had been built on a sting. Later that year, the Department of Justice dropped its appeal in its foreign bribery case against Lindsey Manufacturing Co., a maker of electrical transmission equipment. The previous December, a US district court judge had thrown out the convictions of the company—the first under the FCPA law—as well as its president and CFO. In a stinging rebuke, the judge condemned the prosecutors for their misconduct, finding that they had allowed false testimony to the grand jury, withheld important evidence from the defense, and put false information into search warrants, among other violations.[21]

More significantly, the FCPA may have served as a distraction from the bigger, more important investigations of the financial crisis. And FCPA cases became a cottage industry among Washington law firms—even something of a racket. Joseph Covington (not a partner at Covington & Burling), who had headed the Justice Department's FCPA efforts in the 1980s and then went into private practice advising corporations on foreign bribery, told *Forbes* magazine, "This is good business for law firms, this is good business for accounting firms, it's good business for consulting firms, the media—and Justice Department lawyers who create the marketplace and then get [themselves] a job."[22] A new boom for the defense bar meant a new door to revolve. Mark Mendelsohn, who had revived the FCPA enforcement effort at the Justice Department, left in 2010, driven out by Breuer's micromanaging. He began an FCPA practice at Paul, Weiss, the powerful firm, with an annual salary reported to be $2.5 million.[23]

The rise of the internal investigation had an unappreciated consequence. Setting up an enforcement regime based on cooperation and compliance hurt the government's ability to conduct investigations on its own. Prosecutors look upon sprawling multinationals in despair. They believe they cannot take on giant corporations without their compliance and cooperation. The law firms do the investigating. Prosecutorial skills erode. The government has outsourced and privatized work—to the misbehaving corporations themselves.

As they conduct their probes of their clients, corporate lawyers are often studiously incurious. Big Law's examinations lack rigor lest they risk putting their clients out of business by revealing the totality of the corruption. The investigations usually do not reach into the boardroom. The next time a corporate board is looking to hire a law firm, it will be reluctant to hire the one that just took out a chairman.

The law firms can't help but know that the client has certain desires. A person or a business line needs protecting. The reports tend to reflect that agenda. With internal investigations, "the play is called beforehand," says one partner for a major firm. In an internal investigation, there are dozens of judgment calls, not only about what to look at but how to interpret memos, emails, and decisions, and what to emphasize to the government with what phrases. The law firm understands the necessity of the appearance of an objective, unbiased, and thorough investigation. If there's a fraud at a foreign subsidiary, the reports condemn the subsidiary in fiery terms to demonstrate that the company has not held back. In casting as much firepower onto the subsidiary as possible, the firm shields headquarters as much as is feasible.

Because sprawling corporation investigations are so complex and difficult, and because the defense is so robust and well funded, prosecutors fell in love with settlements. The prosecutorial saying "Big cases, big problems" has an addendum: "Little cases, little problems, and no cases, no problems."[24] The department embraced deferred prosecution agreements with a fever. The fines rose, but the consequences remained the same. Companies could break the law over and over and still avoid serious penalties such as getting barred from government programs or losing operating licenses. Often the settlements lacked any detail. The government did not spell out what the company had done wrong. The Department of Justice frequently didn't appoint a monitor to oversee the agreements.

The Justice Department argued that the large fines signaled just how tough it had been. But since these settlements lacked transparency, the public didn't receive basic information about why the agreement had been reached, how the fine had been determined, what the scale of the wrongdoing was, and which cases prosecutors never took up. How could the public know how tough they were, really?

Moreover, one of the benefits of writing a gigantic check was that the company's lawyers could negotiate the findings to avoid calamitous civil collateral consequences. The Justice Department would furnish a draft agreement. The bank and its lawyers would request changes and negotiate, stripping out words that plaintiffs' lawyers would seize upon. The deferred prosecutions became stage-managed, rather than punitive.

As a matter of course, corporations pledged cooperation to the government as it conducted follow-on investigations into individuals after signing the agreements. But prosecutors almost never went on to prosecute individuals. Through the 2000s—with the Enron reversals, the Arthur Andersen backlash, the Thompson memo rollback, the KPMG case, the Bear Stearns trial losses—prosecutors began to focus less on investigations of individual executives. All the changes moved in one direction: to help big corporations and their top officials.

Investigations of companies are different from investigations of individuals. They run on separate tracks, at different speeds, for different lengths. If prosecutors are thinking from the outset (even subconsciously) that they are going to reach some kind of settlement with the corporation, they focus less on top executives. Investigations of top executives are more time consuming. They require better evidence, since the executives are much more likely to go all the way to trial rather than plead guilty. An executive can go to jail. A company cannot.

Prosecutors have a choice: they can work for years on a prosecution of individuals, who are going to fight through the trial because they have nothing to lose. Or the government attorneys can negotiate with a corporation, which must come to the table. When defense attorneys come to that table, they ruefully attempt to convince the government that no one executive—especially one at the top of the organization, with thousands under his or her purview—knew the full picture of the wrongdoing. They remind the government that in court it will be difficult to prove beyond a reasonable doubt that any individual knowingly and intentionally broke the law.

Of course, not all lifetime public servants were tough and not all candidates for the revolving door were weak, as defenders of the status quo pointed out. The common argument, echoed by every prosecutor, is that prosecutors have every incentive to show how tough they are. The bigger the takedown, the plumier the white-collar defense job that awaits. A corollary argument is that big law firms seek prosecutors for their trial experience, so prosecutors have every motivation to get some. But those arguments neglect how deferred prosecution agreements come into being and distort the incentive structure.

With deferred prosecutions and corporate settlements on the rise, new motivations have arisen. Big law firms may have once hired prosecutors because of their trial experience, but that is less and less true. These days, almost every defendant opts for a plea bargain rather than a trial. In federal criminal cases in 2015 (the vast majority of which were street crime), more than 97 percent of defendants pleaded guilty. The number of trials is dropping from even a few years ago. There were about 2,200 federal criminal trials in 2015, down almost 30 percent from just five years earlier.[25] Again, only a fraction of those were white-collar cases, and most of those covered small-time white-collar crime, not crime at large corporations.

As there have been more settlements and fewer trials, trial skill has become less valuable. What Big Law seeks now is an ability to negotiate the mega-settlements and the inside knowledge of the institution and the government hive mind, to glean what constitutes cooperation for the Justice Department and what settlement it would deem a win.

During settlement negotiations, the prosecutors want to appear tough to the defense lawyers on the other side of the table. They want to dazzle them with their knowledge of legal precedent, mastery of details, and bargaining skills. But young prosecutors also want their adversaries to imagine them as future partners. They want to be seen as formidable but not unreasonable. They want to demonstrate that they are people of proportion.

Even the rare prosecutions of individuals have become gamed by the defense bar. White-collar investigations of individuals have a ritualized gentility. Prosecutors call it the "dance." If they want to question a top corporate officer, they will typically first approach the executive's defense lawyer. These executives hire defense attorneys who are the prosecutors' idols and mentors; seasoned lawyers from the best law firms who are legends in the office where the prosecutors now work.

The defense lawyer will ask the prosecutor, who is usually significantly younger and less experienced, whether his client is a witness, subject, or target of the probe. There is an unwritten honor code among the defense and prosecution bars: they expect that the other won't mislead them (and are ethically barred from deceit). Then the lawyer will ask what the prosecutor wants to question the client about, and the prosecutor will tell him or her. The prosecutor may show the defense evidence that they have accumulated that the executive might know about. After this show-and-tell, the defense lawyer will request to come in alone, without his client, to discuss the case. The meeting is called a "lawyer proffer." The prosecutors will discuss the investigation, the issue at stake, and the evidence. Prosecutors almost never interview targets directly. For subjects and witnesses, only after all this waltzing will the defense lawyer bring them in for voluntary interviews. They are not under oath.

Prosecutors who push too aggressively court social discomfort, and few young assistant US attorneys are willing to do so. Young Justice Department hires are typically products of elite American educational institutions. They tend to be among the most ambitious students, their youths given over to endless hours slaving to achieve the highest grades, to please mentors and tutors, to get into the best middle schools, high schools, colleges, and law schools. Educators have begun to worry about this generation of students, which has been asked to learn more at an earlier age in an era of economic insecurity and heightened competition. They have "little intellectual curiosity and a stunted sense of purpose," as William Deresiewicz, the author of *Excellent Sheep: The Miseducation of the American Elite and the Way to a Meaningful Life*, put it. The students may be high achievers, but they lack imagination and an appetite for risk. A legal career has become the reliable route to an upper-middle-class life, analogous to working at IBM in middle management in the 1950s.

The top law students' hard work and sacrifices land them prestigious jobs at the Department of Justice. At that point, then, their formula for success has altered. They are not trying to please the powerful. If they do their job, they will displease them. To prosecute those sitting in corporate boardrooms, the young government litigators must become class traitors, investigating and indicting people very much like their mentors, peers, and friends. Criminally investigating top executives or partners at Fortune 500 corporations and their enablers at the most prestigious law firms, accounting firms, and consultancies means something different than going after Al Qaeda or a crooked politician. A corrupt politician excites in upstanding prosecutors a sense of outrage. By contrast, a well-mannered and highly educated executive seems like someone who wouldn't knowingly do something wrong.

"It's relatively easy to get corporate pleas and very hard to get convictions of individuals—and the combination is toxic," says David Ogden, who served as the deputy attorney general under Obama. "The department has tremendous leverage and power over corporate entities. It is able to get company pleas without fully developing a case or taking a risk of a loss in court—just by threatening them. That's bad. That rewards laziness. The department gets publicity, stats, and big money. But the enormous settlements may or may not reflect that they could actually prove the case."

Meanwhile, the incentive structure was changing outside the Justice Department as well. In the mid-1990s a prosecutor made about $100,000 and could live (though not lavishly) in New York or Washington. A top assistant prosecutor at the Southern District of New York or Main Justice today makes around $150,000 a year. In 2016 the government scale topped out at $160,300.[26] A top partner at a good firm can easily make $3 million to $4 million a year. In the meantime, the cost of living in the nation's most coveted and powerful cities has skyrocketed. A prosecutor's salary has become more difficult to live on, while in private practice a partner's income has dramatically outpaced inflation.

The Department of Justice needs diversity, but not just in the way the term is commonly understood in American society. The department needs geographic diversity: to hire from top law schools all over the nation and to break the hold that coastal elites from only the top institutions have on open positions. The department needs age diversity, so that a prosecutorial job is no longer a résumé booster for a future white-collar defense partnership but instead is a place that a retiring partner from a prestigious law firm can go to perform public service. They need to seek a diversity of experience, from class action and trial lawyers, from consumer protection lawyers and public interest lawyers. All these changes could help break the dominance that the defense bar holds over the pocketbooks and the imaginations of Department of Justice employees.

## *Chapter Eleven*

# JED RAKOFF'S RADICALIZATION

JUDGE JED RAKOFF LEANED BACK IN HIS CHAIR, appalled. Then he took a sip of his now-cold coffee (extra cream and Splenda) and grimaced. The cup tasted even lousier than what his clerks made for him, but he had no one to complain to. No clerks had come into the office this warm Sunday in August 2009. The judge sat alone with his bad thoughts and bad coffee.

With his white hair and beard and an impish grin, Rakoff sometimes looks like one of Santa Claus's thin cousins. In conversation and from the bench, he speaks efficiently but without haste, his gravelly voice working through the logic of his thoughts. Rakoff, avuncular and sweet natured in public, is always at the ready with self-deprecating jokes. One of his favorites is to respond, after a glowing introduction before a speech or panel performance, that'd he'd now like to bring in his wife for the rebuttal.

Rakoff gazed around his wood-paneled office in the district courthouse in downtown Manhattan—out the window, at the portraits of his wife and family on the wall, and back to his desk cluttered with papers, mementos, and baseball tchotchkes. Rakoff lined his expansive chambers not only with photos of his family and photos of himself ballroom dancing with his wife, but also *New Yorker* legal cartoons, paintings by friends, news clippings, his contributions to the Courthouse Follies, a private courthouse holiday celebration and satirical show, and portraits of his legal idols. His borscht-belt nature masked the indefatigable seriousness with which he approached his work.

That August weekend afternoon, Rakoff forced himself to focus again and started going over the agreement between the Securities and Exchange Commission and Bank of America one more time. Like many other district court judges, Rakoff grew accustomed to signing off on SEC agreements with companies—three or four a year—without thinking about them much. (Most government regulatory settlements needed a judicial okay.) He possessed confidence in the agency ever since he'd worked with Stanley Sporkin in the 1970s. Rakoff believed that SEC lawyers were tough and smart. What's more, the two sides in this case arrived at a settlement, so who was he to look askance at it? He just wanted to get matters off his docket and get on with his real cases and more important work. He'd made a name for himself by opposing death penalty cases; he'd traveled to war-torn Iraq to train judges; he was known for his eloquent and surprising decisions. Judicial reputations weren't won by spending time rubber-stamping SEC settlements. He wanted to dispense with them.

At first glance, the agency's case against Bank of America and its top officers appeared simple. The financial crisis crescendoed in September 2008. Bush Treasury secretary Henry Paulson seized mortgage giants Fannie Mae and Freddie Mac earlier that month. With the government as midwife, Bank of America and Merrill Lynch negotiated over the weekend of September 13 and 14. They announced the takeover on Monday—the same day that Lehman filed for bankruptcy. AIG was taken over by the government on Tuesday.

Without Bank of America's salvation bid, banks would have stopped lending to Merrill. The wounded investment firm was leaking tens of billions in losses, some of the biggest that any corporation has ever recorded. The investment bank would have been at the bottom of the ocean if not for the Bank of America takeover and generous government bailouts. In what now reads as unintended comedy, Bank of America's chairman and chief executive officer, Ken Lewis, called the deal the "strategic opportunity of a lifetime."[1]

As Bank of America raced to complete the deal to acquire Merrill in late 2008, with the global financial system teetering, Bank of America executives misled the public. The SEC alleged that Bank of America hadn't told its shareholders about bonuses to Merrill Lynch bankers, secretly paid out just ahead of the deal's scheduled closing date. (Later, the SEC would amend the complaint to allege that Bank of America had also hidden from the public how massive Merrill Lynch's losses were.)

This crime is appalling, Rakoff thought. And the remedy the agency sought? The bank admitted nothing. The SEC entered one of its typical no-admit, no-deny settlements. No-admit, no-deny didn't resemble punishment as much as being fanned with a palm frond. And that wasn't half as gross as the fine. The SEC sought to fine the bank—which had about $2 trillion in assets—only $33 million.[2] Not trillion, not billion, not even hundreds of millions. The sum was, Rakoff knew, less than trivial for Bank of America.

The fine contained an even more outrageous twist: the SEC alleged that Bank of America lied to its shareholders, but the agency was making shareholders pay the bank's fine. The victims of the scheme had to pay the penalty. The shareholders were getting screwed twice. Once by Bank of America and once by the SEC.

"Even now, I can't believe they did that," Rakoff says. After his second reading of the settlement agreement, the judge swiveled his chair around from his desk to his computer and started drafting an order for the parties to come see him. He had a naïve thought: maybe he was missing something. Maybe the SEC had written the agreement in code, with some reasonable explanation that couldn't be spelled out in a public document. He'd call the two sides in and have the lawyers explain it all to him.

## BE A JUDGE, BE A JUDGE, BE A JUDGE

Born in 1943, Rakoff grew up in Germantown, a middle-class neighborhood of Philadelphia with trim houses and lawns, attending public schools. He was the middle son, with a brother on either side. His father, Abraham, was a gynecologist and fertility specialist who had been one of the doctors whose early research led to the development of the contraceptive pill. Abraham had many grateful patients who came up to Jed to express their gratitude. He had treated Midge Rendell, the wife of Edward Rendell, who would serve as Pennsylvania's governor. Midge, a judge, would see Jed at a function, throw her arms around him, and declare in a loud voice for all to hear: "His father is responsible for my son!"

His mother, Doris, was an English teacher, with a wide-ranging intellect. It was a mixed marriage: Abraham's background was Polish Orthodox Jewish; Doris's was German Reform Jewish. Doris scored 182 on her IQ test—off the charts. (Rakoff had to be satisfied with his "mere" 154.) What Rakoff's father, he, and his two brothers had to reason to get to, she arrived at with blinding speed, which she dismissed as her intuition. She read widely, preferring mysteries for entertainment. Doris always read the last chapter first, preferring to know the solution so that she could trace how the author wove in the hints and clues.

Doris had been victimized repeatedly by the routine discrimination that women of her generation faced. When she was seven years old, the public school system steered talented children into careers in science. All the children were tested; Rakoff's mother made the top score. But her own mother wouldn't allow her to study science, contending that she'd never find a husband working in a lab. Later, she suffered age discrimination. Just before retiring from teaching, Doris decided to go to law school. She had graduated from the University of Pennsylvania at the top of her class and had earned her master's from Bryn Mawr College. She had a high LSAT score. She had her heart set on Penn Law School but didn't get in. When she inquired with the dean of admissions to find out why, he conceded that she did have higher scores and grades than other candidates.

But, he said, at most she would have only ten years of practicing law, while the younger applicants would have decades. Doris got into Temple University; however, Rakoff's father soon became sick, and she decided not to become a lawyer after all.

The Rakoff children had a classic secular Jewish upbringing of the 1950s, the kind of childhood that characters in a Philip Roth novel might have envied. They had strong Jewish identities without any piety or strictures. None of the boys was bar mitzvahed, because the parents felt the rite had become overly materialistic. Only too happy to forgo the ritual, Rakoff and his brothers chose to attend a camp in New Mexico instead. They celebrated Christmas with a tree, and Santa Claus visited their house. Doris and Abraham gave their sons first names that were not overtly Jewish: Jan for his older brother (pronounced with a hard *J*), Todd for his younger. But their parents made sure their middle names were the opposite: David, Saul, and Daniel. Todd recalls their mother told them they could switch if they wanted.

Their parents were socially conscious, but neither was overly political. Doris, active in interracial social work groups, was a fan of Truman but never a fire-breather. Todd still has his NAACP card from the 1950s. Abraham had even less explicit political views, though he had been so outraged when a colleague of his was blacklisted that he supported him financially for a while until the man found another position.

All the Rakoff boys attended Central High, a public school that required an admissions test. Jed graduated early and attended Swarthmore College. His brother Todd went to Harvard, aided in part by a glowing recommendation from a high school teacher for his championship debate skills. Except that the teacher had gotten confused, praising Todd for Jed's accomplishments.

After his successful career at the Southern District, Rakoff left in 1980. He went to the US attorney Bob Fiske, one of his mentors, to ask what he should do. Fiske suggested Mudge Rose. The suggestion took Rakoff aback. For one, it was Richard Nixon's old firm, and memories of Watergate were still fresh. Mudge Rose was also a tier below the most prestigious firms of the day: Cravath, Swaine & Moore; Sullivan & Cromwell; Davis Polk; Debevoise; Cleary Gottlieb Steen & Hamilton. But Rakoff wanted to start a white-collar practice, and Mudge Rose was looking for someone to do that.

As with the prosecutor's office, Rakoff knew he would have to make his name all over again in the private sector. He'd been prosecutor for about eight years. It took him twice that time as a defense attorney to achieve a similar level of success. Big cases came around less frequently. He faced more competition. Trials were rare. At Mudge Rose, he scored one of his highest-profile clients: Martin Siegel, a golden-boy investment banker who joined the pirate firm of Drexel Burnham Lambert after a successful run at Kidder, Peabody & Co., where he had been a prominent mergers-and-acquisitions advisor. While at Kidder, however, Siegel joined an insider trading ring with the arbitrageur Ivan Boesky. To make his first payoff for inside information, Boesky had him go to the Plaza Hotel. There Siegel exchanged code words with a hulking courier, who handed him a briefcase containing $150,000 in stacks of $100 bills.[3] When Rakoff first met Siegel, it impressed him that the investment banker did not deny wrongdoing. Siegel described everything, in detail. Siegel wanted to cooperate with the government. Rakoff facilitated his plea bargain.

Defense attorneys can become fond of clients, if they aren't the most hardened or sleazy of criminals. Rakoff did more than that with Siegel. They became friends. Rakoff found Siegel forthright and genuinely contrite.

Back then, after a plea agreement, the action came at the presentencing hearings. The prosecutors would tell judges that they left the terms entirely to their discretion. The defense attorneys would then make their appeals. At a presentencing hearing, Rakoff was masterful. He described all of the good that Siegel had done in his life. He explained how cooperative he'd been with the government's investigation, an assertion the prosecution verified. Rakoff didn't just choke up. Tears streamed down his face. He hadn't planned it. The display wasn't a turn for dramatic effect but a genuine outpouring of emotion. He had to turn away. He looked out the window for a good long moment. Then he recovered and went on.

At the sentencing, Rakoff and Siegel waited anxiously. Most observers expected the judge to give Siegel significant prison time. Judge Robert Ward began excoriating Siegel. He laid into him viciously for his betrayals and crimes. "After Mr. Boesky received a three-year sentence, I began to think about Mr. Siegel," the judge said. "I was of the view that a [prison term] of eighteen months to two years would be reasonable." Such sentences were long in those days.[4] Rakoff felt a wave of relief and thrill wash over him. He knew Ward's technique. When the judge was about to bring down a long prison term, he looked pained and went about his task gently. When he sentenced lightly, he brought his most unforgiving rhetoric. As Ward went on with all of his righteous fury, Rakoff knew he had won the argument. Siegel received two months of prison and five years' probation. Years later, Rakoff presided over the marriage of Siegel's daughter.

Sometimes loves that come later in life are the more ardent, and that was what Rakoff found with the law. Rakoff had loved being a prosecutor. He felt as if he were playing a crucial role in upholding the moral order. In a world filled with corruption, deception, and cynicism about the government, prosecutors made sure that truth won out on occasion. They put away bad guys. In making cases, prosecutors advanced the cause of justice, he felt.

Yet Rakoff made the transition from prosecutor to defender with ease, believing in the righteousness of his new job as well. He knew the terrifying apparatus of the state. He believed defense attorneys were champions of liberty, as the saying has it. To win against the government was a victory against all odds. He had represented people so unsavory that friends stopped talking to him. Winning when everyone was against him was the greatest thrill of all.

That is, until he became a judge. He put himself up to be a candidate for a judgeship, and then met with Daniel Patrick Moynihan, who, as the senior New York senator, had the prerogative of suggesting candidates to the president. Rakoff hit it off with Moynihan, bonding with the former ambassador to India about Indian history. In October 1995 President Bill Clinton nominated Rakoff to the federal bench. Later, he would contribute to the Courthouse Follies these lines about being a judge, set to the tune of Cole Porter's "Be a Clown":

> Don't just be a lawyer,
> It's nothing but a drudge;
> You'll feel more self-important
> If you get to be a judge . . .
> You can't become a doctor, you would wind up a quack,
> You can't become a porn star, you're no good in the sack,
> But you can be a judge because you're such a big hack.
> CHORUS: Be a judge, be a judge, be a judge.

Well, some of Rakoff's doggerel reflected his actual views more truly than others. A judgeship, he felt, was the best legal job of them all.

## A RAKOFF TRAGEDY

For the most part, lawyers liked arguing in Rakoff's court. He could be tough on them, but he was fair. If they had a good argument, he'd listen. He paid attention to the lawyering. He was not a pushover for the plaintiffs, defendants, or the prosecution. He moved his docket much faster than most judges. He made quick decisions and wrote clearly, without jargon or muddle. "He thinks he's the smartest guy in the court, and in almost every instance he's right," one lawyer said.[5] Remarked another, "His bravado and bravery are very alluring."

He came to understand the most important aspect of being a judge: "Both sides of an argument are really good, but you have to choose." And choose he did. Rakoff's judicial activism wasn't born fully formed, like Athena, after the 2008–09 financial crisis. He'd been willing to stake out new directions, wield bold arguments, and then—perhaps most controversially in the staid world of judicial chambers—talk about them publicly.

In 2002 Rakoff took one of his most imaginative stands, ruling the death penalty unconstitutional.[6]

In 2000 he was, as judges are, randomly assigned a case. It was the first federal death penalty case to come before the Manhattan bench in about fifty years. Congress passed new death penalty laws in the 1980s and 1990s, as part of the crackdown against rising crime rates. In 2000 the government charged a group of drug dealers in the Bronx with racketeering and narcotics violations. Two of them faced the death penalty for torturing and murdering a suspected police informant.[7]

The death penalty case preoccupied Rakoff more than usual. He understood its historic significance and wanted to take his time. He researched, turning over both the law and how he felt about the state's right to take life. At night, Rakoff read death penalty cases, mentally cataloging the cases with legitimate questions about a convicted criminal's innocence. As the new science of DNA evidence emerged, lawyers and activists turned up scores of cases that lead to multiple exonerations.

At the time, Rakoff was not against the death penalty. He had experienced a personal horror and family tragedy fifteen years earlier. At four o'clock on a midwinter morning in 1985, his brother Todd received a call from the Philippines. Jan, their older brother, had been murdered. Todd called his mother, who called Jed. He was at his home in Larchmont, New York, getting ready to go into the Mudge Rose offices. His mother was calm and businesslike, asking Jed to make the arrangements to bring the body home. Jed, also methodical, agreed, and went to her in Philadelphia right away.

Doris always said she loved her sons equally, but she had felt more protective of Jan. As a boy, Jed heard him awake in the middle of the night, howling from night terrors. Even though Jed was three years younger, he was stronger and more athletic than Jan, able to best him in fights. For years, Jan was closeted, coming out in the mid-1970s. Doris and Abraham did not mind, but their relationship with Jan was never as smooth as theirs was with Jed and Todd. Jan resisted their overprotectiveness.

Jan, brilliant and creative, did not have a steady or prominent career. After college, he spent several years trying to become an opera singer in Chicago. When that didn't work out, he founded a private school in Vermont, but he couldn't keep up the fund-raising, and it closed. Todd hadn't seen Jan in several years, and he'd been closer to Jan than Jed was. Jan was never good at keeping his opinions to himself. Once, when staying with Jed in his Manhattan home in the 1970s, he heard Jed, stressed from work, speak sharply to Ann, his wife. Jan told his brother he didn't treat his wife well. "Jan, that's none of your fucking business!" Jed cried, though he knew Jan was in the right.

Jed might have once shed tears in closing arguments for a client, but he did not for his brother—or for his father, Abraham, who had died in the hospital four years before Jan, after going in for a routine hernia operation. Jed didn't display his emotions that way. But he was grateful that after he had gotten into an argument with Jan about a year earlier, they had resolved it, and both said how much they had loved and admired each other. That was their last substantive conversation.

Jan had moved to the Philippines only a few months earlier to help the government there with its education policies. He moved into a gated community for foreigners, in a small bungalow. One evening, he hired a male prostitute. Afterward, he and the man haggled over the price. The argument became heated, and the prostitute picked up a pipe burner and an ice pick, bludgeoning and stabbing Jan to death. He was forty-four years old. When the mortician opened the casket to show the family the body, Jan's head was so disfigured, Jed hardly recognized him.

To cover his tracks, the prostitute set fire to Jan's house. Luckily, a security guard saw the smoke and detained him before he could escape. The prostitute confessed to the police. Jed realized soon that the prosecution was going wrong, convinced it was corrupt. At one point, the assailant escaped from jail, only to be recaptured. Another time, the prosecutor declared in court that his office had lost the confession. Fortunately, an American diplomat, attending that day, stood up to say he had a copy of it. The prosecutor was forced to continue with the case. After years, the murderer was found guilty but given only a three-year sentence. Since he had already served most of it, he got out in a matter of months.

Back then, Jed Rakoff—brother, husband, father, and lawyer in private practice—would have had little compunction had Jan's killer been sentenced to death. He was an evil man who had killed a wonderful man, Rakoff believed. In his judicial confirmation hearings, he was asked, like most nominees, about the death penalty. Legislators supported it overwhelmingly. Rakoff said he could support it, if necessary.

Now, years later, Judge Rakoff had been rethinking the issue and began changing his mind. He turned the opinion over and over, more than any other decision he'd made. He understood that this opinion would have serious consequences for his future. It was the only time he discussed a decision with Ann beforehand.

"Any chance for going up on the Second Circuit is going to be eliminated once I decide against the death penalty," he told her. "But I'm going to do it."

"Well, you're doing the right thing," she said.

In his preliminary ruling on the case, *US v. Quinones*, in April 2002, Rakoff introduced a novel theory against the death penalty. With the rise of new DNA science, the accused could now demonstrate their innocence beyond any doubt. Clearly, an innocent man who had been put to death could not appeal his sentence. He had no ability to seek redress. Despite that capital punishment has existed for centuries, Rakoff argued that society's notion of what the rights of the accused were throughout the legal process had changed. He contended the death penalty violated the accused's due process. Death penalty opponents more commonly argue that it violates the Eighth Amendment's ban on cruel and unusual punishments. Even activists and defense lawyers had not made Rakoff's point. It thrilled opponents and outraged some of his former prosecutorial colleagues, who believed in the most serious sanction for the worst criminals. Conservative media denounced him as an activist, but supporters showered him in praise. The renowned Harvard Law constitutional scholar

Laurence H. Tribe told the *New York Times*, "I've been thinking about this issue in a serious way for at least twenty years, and this is the first fresh, new, and convincing argument that I've seen."[8] Rakoff enjoyed the attention, both from allies and critics. In his office, he later put up two tabloid headlines next to each other. One read "Fed Judge KOs Death Penalty."[9] He paired it with another, from a different case. That one read "Rakoff, the Hanging Judge."

In professional settings, he had kept quiet about his own personal tragedy. But during this case, he opened up from the bench. At a June 2002 sentencing for a codefendant in the case, a prosecutor brought the victim's mother to the stand to address the perpetrator: "You have no idea the pain and agony you have caused me!" she cried out. "You took away my firstborn son." She moved Rakoff.

"Let me say," he began in an agonized voice, "that I understand more fully than you might realize the pain you feel." He explained to the mother, "Twenty years ago, my older brother was murdered in cold blood."[10]

Despite his emotional tumult, Rakoff finalized his ruling the next month. It did not stand. In December 2002 the Second Circuit Court of Appeals overturned his decision.[11] The panel of three judges wrote, "The District Court erred in looking to 'evolving standards' in conducting its due process analysis." The novelty of Rakoff's argument did not impress the appellate judges. They contended that many death penalty opponents have long raised the possibility that innocent people would be put to death. The Supreme Court was well aware of the argument, the appeals court wrote, but had not ruled the death penalty unconstitutional. The appeals court therefore ruled, circularly, that it wasn't.

The reversal disappointed Rakoff. "I had some hope it would get to the Supreme Court," he says. Two judges of the circuit court, who had not been on the panel that reversed him, told him independently that they had the same hope and thought his theory would have a shot. But the highest court passed. Still, Rakoff remains proud of the opinion, saying, "I am convinced to this day that if the Supreme Court ever rules the death penalty unconstitutional, it will be on the basis of my theory."

## HIGHFALUTIN BALONEY

For the public, Rakoff's death penalty case became his most famous ruling. He had cases related to the government's prison in Guantanamo Bay, Cuba, ruling the government had to disclose information requested under the Freedom of Information Act. He ruled against the FBI when the agency had abused lie-detector tests in a terrorism case after 9/11. In legal circles, Rakoff built his reputation in complex commercial litigation. He handled the WorldCom accounting fraud. He oversaw cases related to the Enron scandal. He observed his former colleagues at the Southern District and his former investigative partners at the SEC turn away from prosecutions of individuals, becoming obsessed with changing corporate cultures through their regulation and enforcement. The settlements with corporations troubled him.

Whether a corporation should be held criminally liable remains a controversial topic among legal scholars. The notion that one employee's wrongdoing implicates the entire company seems thin to many legal-world students. Europe has no analogous law. Scholars wonder if any company might be bold enough to challenge the notion in court, going up against the government and risking a prolonged legal struggle that might weigh on their reputation, profits, or stock price. How the current Supreme Court would respond to such a challenge is intriguing.

Rakoff complained that the resolutions were inadequate. Since fines came out of the pockets of shareholders, they were unjust. The shareholders were often the victims of the corporation's fraud—and then were victimized again by being made to pay for the crime.

Prosecutors argued that the government needed to charge corporations to change rotten cultures. Rakoff didn't know what such an aspiration meant. Of course, an institution could influence the behavior of its employees. "But it's vastly overstated. It's untestable. And because it's so nebulous, you can always claim, 'Oh, I've made a big difference, and I've changed the corporate culture of X because I've put in compliance programs or I got them to admit their mistakes' or whatever. A lot of it is just highfalutin baloney," he said.

Prosecutors argued that corporations were more complex than in Rakoff's day. They had a much more difficult task finding culpable individuals and proving their cases than he'd had during his time in the Southern District. The judge regarded this argument as ahistorical nonsense. Want complexity? he'd argue. Try an organized crime network or a narcotics distribution ring based overseas. Yet the government routinely charges people at the highest levels for those crimes.

Or take a look at the structure of corporations from the nineteenth century, he'd contend. The structure of modern companies was nothing like what the complexity and opacity of the big trusts that dominated the American economy back then. Jay Gould, John D. Rockefeller, J. P. Morgan —all incorporated maddening *matryoshka* dolls of overlapping ownership, designed to defeat scrutiny. Yet the government managed to break them up.

After the financial crisis and during the Bank of America–Merrill Lynch case, Rakoff began to regard prosecutorial arguments about their approach to corporate criminality as worse than baloney. They built the machinery of injustice. In emphasizing changing the culture of an organization, prosecutors neglected to pursue individuals for their wrongdoing. Would anyone say, "We're not going to prosecute bank robbers; we're going to change the culture of the bank robbery system"? he asked. It would be absurd.

Instead, he believed in trials of individuals. Rakoff loved a trial. He always felt disappointed when the parties, on the eve of trial, settled on the courthouse steps, even though such capitulations are commonplace. In a well-run trial, he thought, the truth comes out. The jury mostly gets it right.

No doubt taking more top executives to trial would be more difficult. It would cost the government money and time, and it would sometimes lose. But victories would be more meaningful. One top executive would be worth ten deferred prosecution agreements. The government needed to become more assertive and less worried. The dangers of governmental overreach were minimized in this area of criminal enforcement because, unlike for the poor, the executives had access to great lawyers.

## "HALF-BAKED JUSTICE AT BEST"

On November 3, 2008, Merrill Lynch filed a proxy statement, the official filing necessary to describe the important information about the takeover by Bank of America. The proxy failed to mention, in any of its 222 pages, that Merrill could lavish up to $5.8 billion in employee bonuses for 2008. Merrill Lynch ended up with an operating loss of $28 billion in 2008 and paid out bonuses of $3.6 billion. The investment bank normally paid out bonuses for the previous year in January, but Merrill chief executive John Thain moved up the payouts to December, just days before the merger was finalized. Within weeks, the government poured $20 billion in additional funding into Bank of America to shore it up, on top of the $25 billion invested in October. A flabbergasted public met the news of the bonuses with fury.

Not even dismal performance and a spectacular implosion, it seemed, could change Wall Street compensation culture. The government bailed out financial firms, and they funneled the money to reward executives who had run their companies asunder. As the public raged, the banks dissembled, and the main regulators reacted lackadaisically. Bank of America initially claimed that Merrill's board and CEO had made the decision to pay the bonuses independently. This claim was false. In truth, Bank of America had not only known about the plans but also had negotiated the bonuses months earlier when it agreed to take over the investment bank, requiring changes to the compensation.

Andrew Cuomo, then the New York State attorney general, opened an investigation into whether Bank of America misled the public about what it knew about the payments. Ben Lawsky, a young and ambitious lawyer in Cuomo's office, headed the probe. As a federal prosecutor in the Southern District, Lawsky attended Jim Comey's famous Chickenshit Speech, and drew inspiration from its message. Cuomo, briefly, replayed the Eliot Spitzer dynamic, pushing the federal regulators through aggressive enforcement. The attorney general's probe pressured the SEC. Embarrassed, the agency followed with its own probe.

After a financial panic, the country looks to the Securities and Exchange Commission for guidance and correction. The agency employs the finest financial-markets and securities law experts in government. Unlike the banking regulators, the Federal Reserve and the Office of the Comptroller of the Currency, the SEC had been a tough regulator in the past.

But Sporkin's SEC no longer existed. President Bush's last chairman of the agency had been Christopher Cox, an undistinguished congressman and deregulation champion. He became chairman in the summer of 2005, doing little to combat the credit or housing bubbles and the increasing speculation and leverage in the markets. During the frenzied bailouts of autumn 2008, the SEC was noteworthy only for its chairman's absence.

The case before Rakoff was one of the agency's first regulatory responses to the crisis. On August 3, 2009, less than a year after the height of the panic, the SEC announced with a whimper that Bank of America would have to pay $33 million to settle charges it had misled the public about Merrill's bonuses. After a season of trillions of global capital market losses and billions in bailouts, people had almost lost the ability to grasp the meaning of such small numbers. The great postcrisis crackdown had begun bizarrely.

After having reviewed the settlement, on August 10, 2009, Rakoff brought in the SEC and Bank of America to explain how they had arrived at this settlement. The type of settlement the parties were seeking required the court's approval. He wanted to know why he should give it. The hearing focused on the bonuses. Rakoff felt the settlement materials contained laughably bare detail about what had happened.

Rakoff couldn't believe how unconvincing the SEC lawyers were. They stammered. They couldn't remember facts. They couldn't explain how the agency had arrived at the fine. Rakoff laid into the SEC lawyers. The lead attorney attempted to explain why the regulator had brought an action in the first place. He said the Merrill bonuses were "clearly something that shareholders would have wanted to know in advance of the vote."

Rakoff leapt in. "What you are saying, if I understand it, is that Bank of America and Merrill effectively lied to their shareholders about a highly material matter."

Well, the SEC lawyer couldn't come right out and admit that. In its settlement, the agency wasn't saying that anyone lied—a much more serious securities law violation. It was merely accusing the bank of having been negligent. Lying had to be intentional. The SEC attorney interjected to explain.

"What we are saying—"

"Is that right?" Rakoff interrupted.

"That is essentially correct," the attorney said, in trouble now. "We are saying they made representations—"

"So who at Bank of America and Merrill was responsible for that?" Rakoff asked.

"We have not alleged any individual misconduct."

Rakoff was on. "Was this some sort of government that performed these actions, or were there human beings that wrote these documents?"

"There were indeed human rogues who wrote these documents."

"Were there human beings who made the decision?"

"Yes, there were human beings who made the decision."

"So who were they?"

Here was the issue. Rakoff kept his judicial calm, but he was infuriated and baffled. Under his probing, an SEC lawyer conceded that the chief executives of the two institutions, Ken Lewis of Bank of America, and John Thain of Merrill, signed off on the proxy statement. Yet the regulator hadn't managed to query them adequately, much less charge them for misleading shareholders. The SEC was merely asking approval for a settlement, without an admission, with a faceless, monolithic "Bank of America" that existed only as an abstract entity in incorporation documents.

Rakoff turned to the Bank of America lawyer, Cleary Gottlieb's Lewis Liman.

"I would like to know," Judge Rakoff said, "whether you admit or deny it."

Liman hesitated, telling the judge he didn't want to violate the settlement. Rakoff told him to answer.

"The Bank of America's position is that it did not violate the proxy law or any other federal securities law," said Liman.

So much for settlement. Not only was Bank of America refusing to admit that it had misled shareholders, but also it was denying it. Rakoff couldn't figure out why he should approve the settlement. If the SEC's version of events was correct, the fine was inadequate, and there should be some charges against top executives. If the bank was right, it was throwing money at the problem to make it go away. And why should the government force any entity to do that? "Well, it seems to me that I need a lot more material from the parties before I can assess whether this is a fair and reasonable settlement and meets the requirements of law for my approval." Rakoff went on: "It's the truth, not the stick, it's the truth, not each party's adversarial position, that is the warp and the woof of the legal process, and I need to know more before I can approve this settlement."

As the case progressed, it became clearer that the SEC's investigation had been pathetic. It had reached its initial settlement without having done much investigating at all. The agency had not taken depositions of almost any of the key executives. Bank of America was claiming its attorney-client privilege for much of its materials. In keeping with governmental timidity following the Thompson memo, the SEC hadn't bothered to get the bank to waive it.

At one point in court, the SEC explained to Rakoff that it had moved quickly on this probe, as if that were much of a defense: "Normally, in cases of magnitude such as this, it is not uncommon for it to take years for the commission to bring claims."

Rakoff shot back, "That certainly is the commission's reputation."

"We are working on it," the SEC lawyer replied sheepishly.

At another hearing, Rakoff parried with the defense. "If anything," Liman said at one point, trying to explain the pay disputes, "Bank of America's pay practices were too stringent and were—"

"Compared with Merrill's," Rakoff interrupted slyly.

"Right."

"Maybe not compared with China's, for example."

Jed Rakoff had started to grasp something awful: the SEC was no longer the agency he once admired. This incompetence would never have happened under Sporkin. It wouldn't have happened throughout the 1980s and 1990s. He recalled Richard Breeden, the chairman of the SEC under the first George Bush, once declared that he wanted to see corporate executives who violated the securities laws "naked, homeless, and without wheels."[12] Now the agency was scared. It didn't want to look like it was doing nothing, but it didn't want to take tough adversaries to trial. "They haven't given me any adequate answers," Rakoff thought. "The SEC has allowed the engine of a big bank and a big firm to overwhelm them." His beloved SEC was in more trouble than he had realized. Unlike those shareholders getting defrauded by Bank of America, Rakoff had the power to do something about it.

On September 14, 2009, Jed Rakoff broke with zombified judicial tradition. He refused to sign off on a settlement that he regarded as a sham. He labeled it "a contrivance designed to provide the SEC with the facade of enforcement and the management of the bank with a quick resolution of an embarrassing inquiry."[13] It was a remarkable revolt. Judges did not reject such agreements. They were required to show deference to the government. But judges had become overcoats that the agency and the companies walked over to prevent their shoes from being covered in mud. Rakoff wanted it to end.

"The proposed Consent Judgment is neither fair, nor reasonable, nor adequate," he wrote. Rakoff shredded the SEC's arguments and rationale. He was outraged that the agency was making Bank of America shareholders pay. That "does not comport with the most elementary notions of justice and morality," he wrote. He attacked the SEC for not having identified wrongdoing executives or lawyers. He concluded: "All this is done at the expense, not only of the shareholders, but also of the truth." He set February 1, 2010, as the trial date.

The public, revealing its fury about the financial crisis, showered Rakoff in letters of praise. "Only you have had the courage to stand up to the abusers!!! Why has none of these bank CEOs or Wall Street executives gone to jail?" a woman from Massachusetts wrote to him. A geology professor in Brazil commended him, as did a former CEO of publicly traded companies. "Finally, a jurist who lives up to our highest aspirations for our judges and our judicial system," wrote a doctor from Beverly Hills, while a fellow US district judge wrote, "You've just elevated the federal judiciary another notch."

That September, the same month Rakoff rejected the SEC settlement, Cuomo's investigators threatened to bring charges against Bank of America executives. They complained that the bank was thwarting their probe by denying them access to certain information, claiming protection under attorney-client privilege.

Cleary Gottlieb, Bank of America's law firm on regulatory matters, made miscalculations. The firm appeared not to grasp how frustrated Rakoff was. At one point, Rakoff chastised the Cleary lawyers and the SEC for draping a proposed order related to the attorney-client privilege dispute in legalese with a first sentence that spanned two and a quarter single-spaced pages and featured, he wrote, "no fewer than nine recitations of the word 'whereas.'" Cleary, along with another New York law firm, Wachtell, Lipton, Rosen & Katz, which had advised on the Merrill acquisition, and the bank's management, also seemed to have misread the dangers of a looming class action suit about the Merril acquisition. The bank began to realize its exposure looked staggering, perhaps as much as $15 billion.

In October Bank of America brought in a new law firm, Paul, Weiss. The three firms and the bank argued about which concessions to make or whether to make any at all.[14] Soon the bank waived attorney-client privilege for the investigations, a move to placate government investigators.

Paul, Weiss also offered to increase the size of the SEC settlement and suggested some corporate governance improvements. The bank and the Paul, Weiss lawyers would not, however, agree to any SEC charges against individuals. The commission had no problem agreeing.

On February 4, 2010, the SEC and Bank of America upped their settlement to $150 million.[15] That same day, Cuomo filed civil fraud charges against the bank's former CEO, Ken Lewis, and ex-CFO Joe Price for misleading shareholders about the bonuses. It added explosive new details to allegations that the bank and its executives had misled shareholders about the size of the losses at Merrill. Cuomo's complaint also accused Lewis of blackmailing the government into injecting $20 billion more into the bank by threatening to walk away from the acquisition.[16]

According to Lawsky's investigation for Cuomo, Bank of America executives wrestled over whether to tell investors about the mounting Merrill losses. On November 13, 2008, the bank's general counsel, Timothy Mayopoulos, and its outside lawyers decided that the numbers would have to be disclosed in a Securities and Exchange Commission filing, as stated by the complaint. Then they consulted with Price and decided to reverse their decision.

On December 3, 2008, the CFO knew that the losses had breached the threshold that Mayopoulos had laid out as the benchmark for requiring disclosure. The shareholder vote went ahead without any filing. Then six days later, Mayopoulos listened while Price told the board that Merrill was going to lose $9 billion in the fourth quarter. This statement was not accurate. Merrill had already lost $9 billion and expected to lose billions more before the quarter was over. After the board meeting, Mayopoulos tried to discuss the losses with Price. He was unavailable.

The next morning, the bank fired Mayopoulos, marching him out of the building. Bank of America installed another top bank executive, Brian Moynihan, as general counsel, though Moynihan hadn't practiced law in fifteen years. His legal career was such an afterthought that he had let his bar membership lapse. He would go on to become the chief executive of the bank.

Mayopoulos wasn't alone in his concerns. Merrill's auditors, Deloitte

& Touche, told Bank of America that it "might want to consider" informing shareholders of the losses, according to the complaint. Bank of America's corporate treasurer, urging the bank to disclose, said in a conversation with Price that he did not want to be talking about Merrill's losses "through a glass wall over a telephone."

Under pressure from Cuomo, and seeking to resolve the matter before a trial, Bank of America and the SEC agreed to give Rakoff facts. The bank tried to get everyone, including Rakoff, to consider the findings to be "nonbinding": in other words, that they wouldn't be stipulating to them for the purposes of any future legal proceedings. At a hearing on February 8, 2009, Rakoff grilled the SEC over why it had such a different set of facts and interpretations than the New York attorney general.

"Are you in disagreement, then, with the attorney general's conclusions?" he asked lead lawyer George Canellos.

"Let me be a little bit roundabout in saying—" the man began to respond.

"It won't be unheard of in this litigation," Rakoff interjected.

"I apologize for being a little circuitous," Canellos stammered.

The SEC, desperate to avoid the appearance that it had neglected to examine much of Bank of America's wrongdoing, had tried to shoehorn these new allegations into a new complaint, but Rakoff disallowed it because their efforts came too late for the trial date. (The SEC did roll allegations that Bank of America misled investors about the size of the Merrill losses into the revised settlements soon to be presented to Rakoff.)

The SEC disputed the notion that Mayopoulos was fired because he advocated that the bank disclose the size of the Merrill losses before the proxy vote on the merger. The real reason the general counsel was pushed out, the SEC asserted, was because Moynihan was about to leave, amid the uncertainty of the merger. The board scrambled to give him a new position to retain him.

Rakoff ended up thinking Cuomo's complaint was overheated—longer on rhetoric and shorter on facts than it should have been. But the judge believed there was some serious wrongdoing. Top officers of Bank of America knew about giant, surprising Merrill losses and about how it had agreed to bonus payments but did not disclose them promptly or precisely to the board or shareholders. They cut out people who advocated disclosing the information. That sure seemed like a lot of smoke. The SEC was content to think the failures to disclose were negligence, not intentional wrongdoing.

At least one regulator thought otherwise, that the matter merited a criminal investigation. The Office of the Special Inspector General for the Troubled Asset Relief Program (TARP) referred the case for criminal investigation to the United States attorney's office in Manhattan. Raymond Lohier, who was then the chief of the Securities and Commodities Fraud Task Force at the Southern District, took charge of the investigation personally, but reluctantly. Colleagues thought he viewed the charges skeptically. The Federal Reserve, both a regulator of Bank of America and one of its potential victims because it was lending to the bank, contended that it did not consider the losses material.

Mary Jo White, now one of the premier defense lawyers in the country at Debevoise & Plimpton, represented Ken Lewis. White passionately defended her clients, unafraid to use her sterling reputation as a former Manhattan US attorney to her advantage. The future SEC head blasted the Cuomo effort, saying the decision to bring the charges was "a badly misguided decision without support in the facts or the law" and there was "not a shred of objective evidence" to support the case.[17]

The Southern District received such complaints only too receptively. Justice Department officials in DC and Southern District officials in Manhattan reacted furiously to Cuomo's effort, seeing it as political grandstanding. Typically, in such investigations, lawyers from different offices are loath to share materials out of parochial self-interest. They want the glory of the investigation. Cuomo's office, to make peace, decided to share its materials with the Department of Justice. Lohier pledged to look at them. Mayopoulos, the fired general counsel, never implicated his former bosses. Lohier and the Southern District did little investigation, conducting no significant interviews that anyone could see. President Obama soon appointed Lohier to become a judge on the Second Circuit. The Justice Department brought no charges in the case.

On February 22, 2010, Rakoff signed off reluctantly on the SEC's revised settlement with Bank of America. The agency's attorneys took depositions and examined the documents. Under pressure, the SEC investigated. Rakoff wasn't satisfied or convinced it had been thorough. But the judge had spurred the agency to issue details to the public.

Rakoff wrote, "The proposed settlement, while considerably improved over the vacuous proposal made last August in connection with the Undisclosed Bonuses case, is far from ideal . . . While better than nothing, this is half-baked justice at best."

Obviously wrestling with what to do, Rakoff wrote that if he could, he would reject the agreement again. He called the fine "paltry." Legally, however, he believed he was obligated to show deference to the government now that it had furnished him with more information about what went into the settlement. And Rakoff wanted to hold himself back. He wrote: "In the words of a great former justice of the Supreme Court, Harlan Fiske Stone, 'The only check upon our own exercise of power is our own sense of self restraint.' In the exercise of that self-restraint, this Court, while shaking its head, grants the S.E.C.'s motion and approves the proposed Consent Judgment."

Given the facts he'd pushed the agency to produce, Rakoff put a number of them into his opinion. Going further than the SEC was willing to go, he suggested that Bank of America had violated securities laws as it took over Merrill Lynch. Bank of America and Paul, Weiss were chagrined. So much for the facts being "nonbinding." Rakoff's opinion proved valuable in the class action lawsuit, which was settled for $2.4 billion in September 2012.[18] The huge payment put the SEC's efforts even more to shame.

Andrew Cuomo moved on to become governor of New York. With his departure, the New York attorney general case fizzled. The state moved too slowly to finalize the case. Since the bank had settled with the shareholders before the state could resolve its own case, a law precluded the state from getting a significant settlement itself. In March 2014 Ken Lewis received a modest penalty of $10 million, paid for by his former employer, and a temporary ban from the banking industry. Given that he was retired, this punishment resembled the bite from a no-see-um. He did not admit or deny any of the charges. Bank of America paid $15 million to New York.[19] The settlement the following month with Joe Price wasn't much, either. The state fined him and barred him from being a corporate officer or director of a public company for a year and a half.

## A NATIONAL SCANDAL

The financial crisis and the Bank of America case radicalized Rakoff. For many years, he focused his energies more narrowly. "What really gets him upset is fraud and unfairness, as opposed to a broader social theory," says his brother Todd, a professor at Harvard Law School. "At the time, I was more focused on the pain working people had been subjected to [after the 2008 meltdown]. People losing their jobs. I hadn't begun to focus on the causes of the financial crisis. This case got me focused on the causes," he says.

American justice operated under a shroud, opaque, in plea bargains and corporate settlements. "A trial is nearly the only place where the entire criminal justice system is put to the test of truth: Do you have the proof of guilt, or don't you?" Judge Rakoff told a reporter. "A system of justice that chiefly operates behind closed doors will sooner or later be a system that leads to abuse."[20]

As Obama started making his judicial appointments, Rakoff was curious about whether he might yet get nominated to the Second Circuit Court of Appeals, despite his death penalty ruling from years earlier. The new administration appeared to have an age test for its judicial appointees. Rakoff was sixty-five. He would never be an appellate judge.

Rakoff realized it was for the good. He remembered his wife's wisdom when he'd been mulling his death penalty decision. As an appellate judge, he'd be one voice of many. His job would be to seek compromise and tamp down his strong opinions. He could pick legal battles more readily from the district court bench. Indeed, now he had a chance to express those opinions more boldly. With the financial crisis, all the country's institutions had failed: politicians, regulators, the banks, the capital markets—and now prosecutors. He had a duty and nothing constraining him. Jed Rakoff was free.

## *Chapter Twelve*

# "THE GOVERNMENT FAILED"

NEW PRESIDENTIAL ADMINISTRATIONS APPOINT new US attorneys. The Obama administration, based on a recommendation from the powerful New York senator Charles Schumer, picked Preet Bharara to be the next US attorney for the Southern District of New York. Nominated in May 2009 and sworn in in August, Bharara began overseeing the more than 220 prosecutors. Bharara had been a staff attorney in the Southern District and after that, Schumer's chief counsel.

Schumer was known as "the senator from Wall Street," friendly to the major industry of New York City. Not so much an outright enemy of regulation, he subtly undermined it. In the bubble years, Schumer argued that New York might lose out to London as a financial world capital if it didn't further loosen Wall Street's regulatory shackles. Veteran prosecutors worried that Bharara won the appointment over more seasoned and qualified rivals. Would Bharara take on the most powerful industry in New York?

Preetinder Singh Bharara's life story has appeal. He was born in the northern Punjab region of India to a Sikh father and Hindu mother. He had married a woman whose father was Muslim and mother was Jewish. Their four different families practiced four different faiths, and all had fled religious oppression. He'd often joke, "Even when my wife fasts for Yom Kippur, and my father-in-law fasts for Ramadan, I get to stuff my face with samosas all day."[1]

Bharara grew up in Monmouth County, New Jersey, and was valedictorian of his high school class. He graduated magna cum laude from Harvard in 1990 and Columbia Law School three years later. He worked at a top law firm but had clear political inclinations. The summer after graduating from law school, he volunteered for liberal Mark Green's campaign for New York City's public advocate. Bharara became a prosecutor in the Southern District and then, thanks to his friend and colleague Ben Lawsky's recommendation, went to work as a staffer for Schumer. There he investigated the Bush administration's firing of US attorneys, which culminated in Alberto Gonzales's resignation as attorney general.

Bharara looks older than his age, with dark circles under his eyes and thinning black hair. But his eyes gleam in conversation, attentive and amused, which restores youthful energy to his appearance. Bharara preens in front of a crowd, cracking self-deprecating jokes and moralizing. He dazzled audiences with passages from legal texts, often quoting from memory his hero Clarence Darrow's 1926 defense summation from *The People v. Henry Sweet*, a hallmark civil rights trial. Bharara spoke quickly as if to keep the crowd from noticing his didacticism.

He courted the media, both on the record and off, and lectured the subjects of his enforcement. He railed against New York State's political corruption and Wall Street's business culture. His speeches reflected careful tailoring for the audience. "Is corporate culture becoming increasingly corrupt?" he asked, talking tough in a 2011 speech to New York financial journalists. "[Is] ethical bankruptcy on the rise?"[2]

When Bharara arrived, the Southern District had major insider trading cases in development. Investigators had wiretaps on hedge fund managers and Wall Street research firms. Insider trading cases, especially when there is hard evidence from recorded phone calls, are easier to investigate and prove to a jury than cases concerning financial deals of dizzying complexity. Financial crisis cases might take years to investigate, and after all that, a prosecutor might determine no crime had been committed, let alone a provable one.

Bharara had no easy choices. He could have his prosecutors chase after leads where they weren't sure crimes had been committed and they didn't have targets. Or they could go after insider trading, where they knew what the infractions were and who committed them. Investigating esoteric financial instruments like collateralized debt obligations, or CDOs, could take three years or more. Insider trading cases could go much more quickly.

Staff prosecutors gravitated to the easier cases.[3] They had tapes of bad guys conspiring. Listening to the wiretaps felt like they were inside the rooms hearing the secret thoughts of every hedge fund manager in the city. They tracked young, rich, and cocky men plotting to destroy evidence by tossing pieces of their phones in Dumpsters in the middle of the night. They had engaged FBI agents to doorstep suspects at five o'clock in the morning. They flipped people before they lawyered up. Each dramatic twist of the cases—breakthroughs, arrests, trials—made front-page news in the *Wall Street Journal* and elsewhere.

In comparison, the evidence from the financial crisis cases sat dead on the page. There were millions of documents to wade through describing credit default swaps, BBB-rated mortgage-backed securities, super-senior tranches, CMBS,[4] RMBS,[5] CDX index, ABX index. Each had more impenetrable jargon than the last. The insider trading evidence had the perverse effect of making the financial crisis evidence seem inadequate and paltry. The young prosecutors worried how they would ever make a jury see any of it. But it didn't even get that far. The prosecutors themselves weren't seeing it. Their bosses weren't making them.

The insider trading cases became the path to further one's career. At one point, the office was 85-0 on insider trading cases.[6] In the office's biggest coup, it sent Raj Rajaratnam, who managed the multibillion-dollar fund Galleon Group, to prison. The media noticed. The *New York Times* celebrated that the Southern District was "back" in action after lackluster years under previous US attorneys. *Time* put Bharara on its cover, with the headline: "This Man Is Busting Wall St." *Fortune* headlined its profile "The Enforcer of Wall Street." The *New Yorker*, for its online version: "The Man Who Terrifies Wall Street." Almost alone among US attorneys in his class, Bharara had achieved celebrity status, even appearing at events such as the *Vanity Fair* Oscar Party.

But Preet Bharara wasn't taking on Wall Street. He might castigate corporate culture in a speech, but he was busting insider traders at hedge funds, a different beast altogether. Hedge funds were generally small firms. Each was a discrete entity, raising little possibility of systemic consequences if it were closed.[7] Though their principals were wealthy, they had few employees and little in the way of political power. Insider trading was a minor offense, a tilting of the seesaw. The victims, to the extent there were some, were often corporations or other big investors. The financial crisis and bank wrongdoing immiserated tens of millions of Americans.

The Southern District did not bring criminal charges against big investment and commercial banks. The office did not take on the power structure of American finance. Bharara did not charge top executives at the biggest companies. After the biggest bubble and financial crisis in generations, bankers at the biggest institutions sold defective products, misrepresented them, played games with their own finances, and almost crashed the global financial system, save for a multitrillion-dollar taxpayer bailout. The most important prosecutorial office in the country took on hedge funds. It was a prosecutorial non sequitur.

"The government failed," says a former top prosecutor in the Southern District, in a sentiment echoed by several former assistant US attorneys in the office. "We didn't do what we needed to do." Another former prosecutor who worked on insider trading cases said, "They made my career, but they don't change the world. They are not events that affect the public. If Raj Rajaratnam trades on a merger, who gives a shit at the end of the day?"

The staff understood the risks, rewards, and incentives of the Southern District. "It's a hell of a thing to tell someone they will spend the next three years of their life where we have virtually no evidence, whereas you can work on case where do have evidence," said the prosecutor who worked on insider trading cases. "If someone had come to me to say, 'We are going to take you off this case to have you toil on this hole,' I wouldn't have been happy about that. That's the human reality of all organizations."

Southern District top officials assigned financial crisis cases, but these were never the office priority. The leadership never tried to change the staff attorneys' calculus. The few cases that the office did catch were distributed piecemeal, with little plan or coordination. The Southern District prides itself on its entrepreneurialism. When one Southern District star got assigned a case on a dodgy Morgan Stanley residential mortgage-backed security, the prosecutor couldn't get the FBI interested. Then the office lost a turf war, and the San Francisco US Attorney's Office got the case. Main Justice seized investigations into interest rate and foreign exchange rate manipulation. Since when did the vaunted Southern District lose turf wars on securities fraud cases? Since its priorities now lay elsewhere.

The Southern District passed on the case that would become the first trial of the financial crisis: the Bear Stearns hedge fund case, in which two of the investment bank's employees were accused of misleading investors about the state of their mortgage investments. The Brooklyn US Attorney's Office picked it up. In November 2009, when a jury acquitted the two hedge fund managers, some Manhattan prosecutors felt private vindication. Others boasted that they would have won the case. But prosecutors around the country drew an unfortunate lesson from the experience: that the evidence required in these cases was almost insurmountable.

In the spring of 2010, Raymond Lohier, then the Southern District's chief of the Securities and Commodities Fraud Task Force, made the rounds in Washington as part of his confirmation process to become a judge on the Second Circuit Court of Appeals. Senator Ted Kaufman of

Delaware asked him what the Manhattan US Attorney's Office's priority was. Lohier told the gathering: "Cybersecurity." He didn't cite the financial crisis.[8] The audience was aghast. (Bharara later told the staff that did not accurately reflect the office's priorities.)[9]

Lohier was a few years older and more experienced than Bharara, and not one of his loyalists. To replace him, Bharara chose a younger staff attorney. Bharara preferred young unit chiefs. He viewed them as energetic. And they would owe him their loyalty.

When Lohier left, even by that early stage, there were almost no financial crisis investigations being pursued anymore. The securities fraud unit had generally about fifteen or twenty prosecutors at any one time. Most of the hotshots in the office chose to work on insider trading cases. A handful worked the Bernie Madoff Ponzi scheme case.

The office scored one success in a financial crisis prosecution; an accomplishment that serves to underscore its failure otherwise. The Southern District had prosecuted a supervisor at Credit Suisse named Kareem Serageldin. In 2007 Serageldin oversaw traders who lied about the value of their residential mortgage-backed securities as their value plummeted. Serageldin knew it and passed along the faulty valuation. He pleaded guilty. (One of the lower-level traders was spared prison for cooperating in the investigation. Another fled the country.) Serageldin went to prison with a thirty-month sentence. Such mismarking was commonplace. Traders had every incentive to lie, as did their supervisors and the top officials at the banks. Few, if any, Wall Street traders, bankers, or prosecutors believe that Serageldin's traders were the only ones who lied and covered up mismarked portfolios. The Department of Justice could not uncover any similar major cases at top banks.

The Madoff investigation was a higher priority at the Southern District, but even that moved agonizingly slowly. Prosecutors had gone after Madoff, whose fraud collapsed in late 2008, and then they seemingly stalled. By 2015, the government had prosecuted some of his colleagues and accountants. But what about Madoff's enablers on Wall Street? The Ponzi schemer had decades of help from major financial institutions.

JPMorgan Chase appeared guilty. It had been Madoff's primary banker for more than two decades. There were loads of incriminating documents. One employee wrote that Madoff's returns were "possibly too good to be true" and warned of "too many red flags." Another executive noted that there was a "well-known cloud over the head of Madoff and that his returns are speculated to be part of a Ponzi scheme." Bankers in the London offices attempted to create a derivative to match Madoff's performance—and couldn't. The unit even filed a suspicious-activity report. It pulled out money.

JPMorgan lawyers, both in-house and at outside firms, received emails alerting them to concerns about the money manager. In 2008, before the crisis and the Ponzi's collapse, the bank's global head of equities suggested "disclosure to US/UK regulators" about their concerns about Madoff, and said he assumed that the bank's general counsel would have to be a part of the "ultimate decision" because of Madoff's importance as a customer and the seriousness of the suspicions. JPMorgan's lawyers did not alert any authorities.[10]

The Southern District dithered. Because divisions within the bank communicated few of their Madoff concerns with one another, the government feared it couldn't make criminal cases against individual bankers. JPMorgan had loose oversight and warning systems, but prosecutors struggled to tie that to any one crime by any one person. In a way, JPMorgan insulated itself from criminal charges through its own lack of adequate internal oversight. No one group or person saw enough of Madoff's activities—at least that was what the prosecutors came to believe.

JPMorgan's lawyers helped prosecutors arrive at that conclusion. Give white-collar defense attorneys time, and they can muddy any investigation. As the Madoff probe dragged on, JPMorgan had time to prepare. There were civil suits. There were investigations of Madoff himself. The bank and its lawyers knew what documents the government had. They were ready. In the post–Thompson memo world, white-collar defense attorneys coordinate closely with the other lawyers representing other institutions and individuals, often forming joint defense agreements. They glean a full picture of the government's strategy. When the government interviews well-coached witnesses, they have mastered the materials the government lawyers ask about. If the government inquires about something that isn't in black and white on the page, memories go blank and knowledge dries up.

One of the main fights that JPMorgan and the government waged was over privileged materials. Bankers told investigators they were relying on the advice from their attorneys. Defendants can use an advice-of-counsel defense only if they provide a complete and accurate record to their lawyers about the matter under investigation. To demonstrate that is the case, the subjects of an investigation have to produce the full documentary record for the prosecutors to assess. JPMorgan and its attorneys at Wachtell, Lipton fought the requests. The government and the bank eventually agreed to a partial waiver. Then prosecutors requested to talk to witnesses. Wachtell said no. They battled, almost went to court, and then compromised at the last moment. But the government never got as free a hand to probe into JPMorgan regarding Madoff as it wanted.

Such fights over privilege in corporate investigations are now routine, since the government capitulated on attorney-client privilege. Prosecutors are at a terrible disadvantage. The defense bar knew that even though the government would threaten to litigate, prosecutors rarely did so. The government had been accused of being overzealous, most damagingly in the KPMG case. The law requires the government to argue to a judge that the documents it seeks are important factual material (which should not be protected) and not just full of lawyerly advice (which is protected). That's a difficult task when the prosecutor doesn't know what is in the documents. As one Southern District official says, "You are going into a gunfight. But you don't have any bullets. You are supposed to say, 'We suspect those are full of facts, Judge'?"

Having failed to prosecute any individual JPMorgan bankers, the Southern District moved to negotiate the bank's punishment. Bharara talked defiantly. He warned JPMorgan that there was enough to charge it criminally. He was posturing. The Southern District did not charge the bank, nor did it win many concessions. The parties settled. The bank did not plead guilty, instead entering into a deferred prosecution agreement in January 2014—the first with an American bank after the financial crisis. JPMorgan paid a $1.7 billion penalty to the Department of Justice (with another $350 million to the Office of the Comptroller of the Currency). Madoff's investors lost about $20 billion in the scam.

The Southern District's weak corporate settlements—no weaker than the rest of the Department of Justice's but no stronger, either—extended to industries beyond banking. In March 2014 the office entered into a deferred prosecution agreement with Toyota, charging that the car company concealed and misled the public about how its vehicles suffered from unintentional acceleration. The automaker had reassured the public that it had fixed the problem. However, subsequent accidents killed people. The office poured resources into the investigation. In its agreement with the Southern District, the car company paid $1.2 billion, which the office considered a hefty sum. In some ways, it was a triumph. The Department of Justice had never brought such an action against a car manufacturer.

But Toyota had not cooperated fully with the Southern District's investigation. It had not made Japan-based executives available for interviews. In light of the lack of full cooperation, the office might have been justified in taking much more serious action: making the company plead guilty, taking it to trial, or attempting to indict individual executives. The Southern District did not do that.

## "THIS WONDERFUL CHART"

Without a national task force to tackle the financial crisis investigations, all the US Attorney's Offices were left on their own in 2009 and beyond. They liked it that way. Top officials from Washington weren't calling every week, so they could set their own office's priorities without paying any bureaucratic cost. The Southern District of New York should have conducted the most serious probes of the most important banks. Instead, the only major financial crisis investigation that the most important

US Attorney's Office in the country conducted was into the September 2008 collapse of Lehman Brothers. The Lehman investigation may be the highest-profile casualty of Bharara's insider trading priorities.

Press accounts described the Justice Department as snapping into action almost immediately. By late October 2008, investigations into whether executives had misled the markets and whether the firm engaged in accounting fraud had begun. The probe was split among three offices: the Southern and Eastern Districts of New York, and the New Jersey office. According to a story in the *New York Times* that month, the offices were cooperating with one another and making progress.[11]

The Lehman investigation provided an embarrassment of rich targets for the government. The investment bank had had months of warning as the subprime credit crisis brewed. It had precarious finances and was desperate to find lenders and investors to take pieces of the company. Could top executives have misled anyone in its final, desperate months, weeks, and hours? The sprawling possibilities would require resources. Something on the order of ten FBI agents and five prosecutors dedicated full-time might have done it. No one office dedicated nearly those numbers.

The offices all got off to slow starts. Despite the notoriety of Lehman's collapse and the repeated Justice Department insistence that the case was important, the investigation received limited resources. The Brooklyn and New Jersey offices hardly did anything at all. Southern District attorneys puzzled over why the probe generated little of the usual watercooler talk. This pursuit was not aggressive.

In January 2009 the law firm Jenner & Block won the job to be Lehman's bankruptcy examiner. Courts appoint examiners to investigate fraud or mismanagement. Anton Valukas, the chairman of the firm and a former US attorney in Chicago, took an active role. He gathered a handful of partners in a room. "Tell me what your investigative work plan is in the next couple of days," he said, giving what seemed to the partners an unreasonable and extremely tight deadline. Valukas worked hard and efficiently and wanted everyone else to do so, too. The Jenner & Block lawyers split into four teams, each taking a piece of the mystery.

Jenner & Block partners learned that Main Justice had no involvement in the probe. The law firm had no contact with Eric Holder, his deputies, or Lanny Breuer. Lawyers from the firm soon made the courtesy rounds with all three US Attorney's Offices supposedly investigating the collapse. These months later, the government was not far along at all. Jenner & Block lawyers realized the prosecutors didn't understand much about what had happened.

Jenner & Block continued to see little progress out of the US Attorney's Offices. The lawyers submitted requests to prosecutors of names of Lehman executives with whom they wanted to speak. They anticipated being told no, an indication that prosecutors were using those witnesses for their own cases. Though they had to wait on occasion, Jenner & Block eventually interviewed everyone it requested. Valukas sat in on the major interviews, drilling down into the important matters.

Jenner & Block had about 130 lawyers working on the Lehman case for more than fourteen months. The firm conducted the kind of all-encompassing investigation the government cannot do anymore, given its choices over how to allocate people and time. These lawyers probed more deeply and thoroughly. Their firm put more money into it, organizing documents and breaking down the tasks into manageable pieces. Jenner & Block had a special motivation to uncover wrongdoing. As bankruptcy examiner, it sought to recoup losses for creditors. It could sue culpable entities for damages. Law firms hired by boards of directors lack that motivation. They want to appear cooperative to the government and protect their clients.

Ultimately, it seemed to the Jenner & Block team that the federal investigation, despite the three offices and various securities and banking regulators involved, fell to one person: Bonnie Jonas, a dogged assistant US attorney in the Southern District. Jonas had help here and there, but she shouldered the bulk. And she didn't work on Lehman full-time. (The Southern District says it devoted multiple people and ample resources to the investigation.)

White-collar prosecutors have more control over their schedules than the narcotics and gang specialists who have to respond to random acts of violence and crime. Supervisors rarely oversee their daily activity, and they don't have a lot of imposed deadlines from their bosses. A prosecutor's day usually starts on the late side, around nine thirty or ten. Typically, they'll work until eight at night. They almost never work on only one case at a time, dividing their attention among several matters. When they work on a trial, the days last much longer. "The shorter the trial, the longer the hours," goes the saying. Jonas worked longer hours than most. Most of the offices have windows at One St. Andrew's Plaza. The least desirable face a municipal jail, with its roof filled with concertina wire. When prosecutors work late into the night and peer out the window, sometimes they feel like prisoners themselves.

Jonas, who had been in the office for over a decade at that point, came on the investigation in the fall of 2009. Several Southern District prosecutors had already been assigned the case but had either left the office or moved off the case. A respected veteran, Jonas had a sharp memory and a fierce work ethic. She was deliberate. She wanted to know everything and never, ever wanted to be surprised. "If you were involved in a complicated set of facts and you were innocent, you'd want her investigating your case," a colleague says.

By the autumn of that year, the Southern District had narrowed its probe to two matters: whether Lehman had lied about the valuations of its commercial real estate portfolio, and a maneuver called Repo 105. With Repo 105, Lehman moved assets off its balance sheet at the end of quarters to make the bank look healthier, with less debt. When Jenner & Block lawyers brought up the name of a Lehman whistle-blower who raised concerns with US attorneys about Repo 105, the prosecutors warned the law firm to stay away—and not because they wanted to keep the witness for themselves. They told the law firm they didn't find the witness credible. An assistant US attorney told Jenner & Block that the whistle-blower was a "kook." Jenner & Block lawyers disagreed. Perhaps the man wasn't a saint, but he'd gotten it right.

For months, Jonas would trudge up to Jenner & Block's offices in

Midtown Manhattan to look through the Jenner & Block database of interviews, sifting through the voluminous materials. Occasionally, she brought colleagues, but most of the time, she came on her own. Prosecutors from the Eastern District and New Jersey offices never did. By the time Jonas started in the fall of 2009, Brooklyn and New Jersey seemed to have wound down their efforts. Prosecutors agonized that Lehman executives had received plenty of advice from lawyers and accountants. Of course, modern business works no other way. Good prosecutors did not stop there. Jenner & Block had much greater resources, but prosecutors continue to have investigative powers that private actors lack.

Some Jenner & Block lawyers couldn't understand what happened to the investigation into what Lehman executives had told the public about how much cash it had, known as liquidity. Misrepresenting a bank's liquidity is a time-honored tradition to stave off a run. The saying is that corporations die of cancer, but financial firms die of heart attacks. Banks can suffer crises of confidence, and then it's all over. Lehman executives knew the importance of cash and confidence. In an interview with financial journalist Maria Bartiromo in March 2008 after Bear Stearns had gone down, Lehman Brothers's then chief financial officer, Erin Callan, said, "Liquidity is the thing that will kill you in a moment."[12] Lehman was especially dependent on short-term financing, even more so than similar investment banks. Liquidity was, therefore, even more important for Lehman than for other, more stable financial firms. Prosecutors knew how to bring such cases. In the mid-2000s, Southern District prosecutors had convicted executives of Refco, a major commodities broker, in part for lying about the firm's liquidity on the eve of its failure.

But the Southern District did not take that part in the investigation, and the Brooklyn office, reeling from Bear Stearns, never probed the liquidity representations thoroughly. Jenner & Block did. Lehman executives appeared to have misled the public and regulators about the bank's liquidity position.

At the end of the first quarter of 2008, Lehman reported to the public that its liquidity pool was $34 billion. During the next few months of choppy markets and frightened lenders, Lehman reported that its position strengthened. By the end of the second quarter, the investment bank said it had $45 billion. By the third quarter, the bank said its position remained strong, at $42 billion. Lehman executives gave daily updates on the number to the SEC and the New York Fed.

Internally, Lehman seemed to acknowledge that the figures were misleading. Employees produced a chart that broke down the $42 billion figure under the heading "Ability to Monetize." It divided the money into three categories: high, mid, and low. Throughout the summer before its failure, Lehman deposited and pledged tens of billions of dollars at other banks to reassure them and to continue doing business with them. Retrieving that money would not have been easy. Of the $41 billion, $15 billion of it was in the "low" category, generally because it had been pledged as collateral to other banks. If something is truly liquid, it should not be difficult to monetize. At least two executives objected to how Lehman represented its liquidity, including the investment bank's international treasurer, Carlo Pellerani. But Lehman officials kept counting that money as part of its liquidity.

Trouble with Lehman's lenders started in June 2008. Citigroup demanded that Lehman put some money on deposit at the bank if it wanted Citi to continue as a trading partner. Lehman handed over $2 billion. Lehman continued to include this amount in its liquidity pool, because it had the right to call it back. Paolo Tonucci, the firm's treasurer, understood the reality. Tonucci told a New York Federal Reserve overseer that "even though Lehman 'technically' has access to the $2B [Citigroup deposit], if they [Lehman] pull it or a major portion thereof, Citi will stop" working with Lehman, crushing its business. That money was not unencumbered. It was not, therefore, liquid.

As investors panicked, the CEO Dick Fuld ousted CFO Erin Callan and elevated Ian Lowitt, a Rhodes scholar who had been a longtime executive at the investment bank, to the position. Lowitt said on a June 16, 2008, conference call that Lehman had "significantly increased . . . our liquidity pool." Neither he nor anyone else from the investment bank disclosed the $2 billion on deposit with Citigroup. By the time Lehman issued its second-quarter SEC filing on July 10, the investment bank had also pledged $5.5 billion to JPMorgan. It disclosed neither in its quarterly SEC filing. Lehman said in the filing that it had "strengthened its liquidity position" and represented the liquidity pool as "unencumbered." Lowitt signed the certification.

Over the next few months, Lehman's relationships with trading partners devolved. Despite its haggling with banks across the world and despite having tied up billions in agreements to placate them, Lehman executives told the bank's board of directors that everything was fine. In a September 9 meeting of the finance and risk committee of the board of directors, Tonucci said that the bank "was able to broadly maintain the status quo" for its liquidity. On September 10, 2008, five days before the investment bank would declare bankruptcy, Lowitt told shareholders on a conference call that Lehman's liquidity "remains very strong." He did not mention any of the assets on deposit at other banks. Nor did he tell investors that Lehman and JPMorgan agreed to more protection for JPMorgan's exposure that morning. Some in the market believed the firm. On September 11 one Wall Street research analyst wrote in a research report, "[L]iquidity risk appears low."

Regulators, credit rating agencies, and Lehman's outside lawyer had no idea that the liquidity pool wasn't, in fact, liquid. The SEC was unaware of the extent the firm was using pledged collateral until just before Lehman's bankruptcy.[13]

Attorney Lewis Liman, of Cleary Gottlieb, represented Lowitt. He prepared an elaborate defense of his client, presenting it to the SEC. Liman also spent several hours with Jenner & Block. Liman insisted that Lowitt had not intended to mislead anyone. He said his client wasn't a numbers guy. Yes, he was the investment bank's chief financial officer, but he was not an accountant. He had been relying on what his underlings told him, and no one raised red flags to him.

That may be a reasonable defense, but it does not appear that prosecutors and federal investigators made a serious attempt to test how much Lehman's chief financial officer or any other top executives knew about the bank's financial position. Prosecutors did not work their way up through lower-level employees to get to the top Lehman executives. Multiple midtier Lehman executives and some regulators involved in the bank's desperate attempts to keep itself liquid were never even interviewed by any federal government officials about the collapse. And, while he was interviewed by the Jenner & Block team, no federal prosecutor ever interviewed Lowitt.

In March 2010 Jenner & Block issued a blockbuster 2,200-page report on Lehman's collapse. The firm highlighted the Repo 105 transactions. Jenner & Block believed the transaction merited at least civil claims. The report included new, damning facts about Lehman's liquidity misrepresentations, but did not recommend bringing civil claims. As for Lehman's CFO, "although there is some evidence that Lowitt knew that the liquidity pool contained clearing-bank collateral," examiner Valukas wrote, he did not believe any legal claims could be brought against him for making misrepresentations or omissions about the investment bank's liquidity. Prosecutors at the Justice Department told the law firm that they had looked into liquidity representations but that they didn't think Lowitt, or any of the other top executives, had any firsthand knowledge of the key facts. Whatever the validity of this conclusion, some Jenner & Block partners and Lehman executives, at least privately, thought that crimes had been committed.

The SEC debated whether to bring civil charges over Repo 105 and to charge Lehman's auditor, Ernst & Young. It passed on both. The role that regulators played during the collapse may have contributed to the stymied investigations. The SEC, which was responsible for the investment banks, had blown its oversight. The Fed, which regulated the big banks but not investment banks like Lehman, had not given much attention to Lehman's precariousness.

US attorneys gave up on every probe they took up regarding the failure of Lehman Brothers. No office brought civil or criminal charges against the company or any Lehman executive.

## *Chapter Thirteen*

# A TOLLBOOTH ON THE BANKSTER TURNPIKE

On July 29, 2009, Jim Kidney left his townhouse in southwest Washington, DC, got onto the Metro train, and went to work at the SEC. In the summer heat, he felt grateful that he needed to be outside only for about a block during his commute. The agency's new building, built a few years earlier, was standard General Services Administration: new, clean, and unremarkable. The government had tucked it into a side street, attached like a barnacle to the backside of Union Station.

Kidney went to his orderly office and stood at his custom-made mahogany desk, a gift from his wife. When the agency had moved in, his office overlooked a parking lot. He checked on the progress of the new building now going up there. It wasn't improving his view. Kidney, a grizzled and experienced trial lawyer, was a good soldier at the SEC. As a litigator, he received cases that the staff developed, then came up with a compelling narrative to present to a jury of laymen unfamiliar with the intricacies of finance. He delivered his arguments in a raspy voice, cutting through jargon and distilling complicated concepts. Epigrammatic phrases spilled out of him. His soft eyes and carefully groomed gray hair gave him the air of a good-natured grandfather, belying his ornery and stubborn disposition.

Then a nineteen-year vet at the agency, Kidney took pride in the SEC, but in recent years, he'd become worried about what was happening at his shop. The regulator had suffered under Chairman Christopher Cox in the late Bush years and was still struggling to recover its reputation. Today he looked at his in-box. His boss asked him to take on a case. Kidney took a look at it and thought, "This could be it."

After a few months of investigation, the SEC was preparing to take action against Goldman Sachs for wrongdoing in the lead-up to the financial crisis. A top team of SEC staffers, charged with investigating Wall Street fraud, had warned Goldman that it was contemplating charges and preparing memos to put in front of the five-person commission that runs the SEC. The commission must okay every enforcement action. Kidney read the staff's Wells notice, the legal document the SEC sends to people and entities that it is considering charging with securities violations.

The charges stunned him. Throughout late 2006 and early 2007, Goldman had arranged a complex mortgage deal called Abacus 2007-AC1 for Paulson & Co., the hedge fund run by John Paulson that made about a billion dollars when US housing prices fell. Paulson placed "the big short"—the bet—made famous by the Michael Lewis book of the same name, that the real estate market was an epic bubble that would soon collapse.

Abacus was a collateralized debt obligation made up of derivatives, or side bets, on mortgage securities. Paulson shorted the $1 billion deal, betting that the bonds would crater in value. Paulson's point man, Paolo Pellegrini, had also essentially picked the bonds that would underpin Abacus. The hedge fund was not only betting on which horses would lose the race but also getting to pick the lame and infirm ones.

Abacus would pay off big if people began defaulting on their mortgages. Goldman was responsible for selling the deal to investors. It marketed the investment to a bank in Germany willing to take the opposite side of the bet—that housing prices would rise or remain stable. Cautious, the bank, Industriekreditbank, or IKB, asked that Goldman hire an independent manager to assemble the deal and look out for the interests of the investors.

Goldman did not tell IKB anything about Paulson's role in picking the assets. To assuage IKB's concerns, Goldman chose ACA Financial Guaranty Corp. to act as the independent "portfolio selection agent" for the assets that undergirded the deal. But the financial firm was anything but independent, effectively outsourcing its choices to Paulson & Co. What's more, the SEC discovered that Goldman had misled ACA about key aspects of the deal.

The day after he was given the case, on July 30, 2009, Kidney emailed Reid Muoio, the SEC official heading up the investigative team, expressing his enthusiasm. "I have been reading online stuff about Paulson," he wrote. "They are really big fish. If they rigged the cards against Abacus and ACA by picking the portfolio and then betting against it with Goldman's help, this is a really great case."[1]

In scrutinizing Goldman only months after the peak of the 2008 financial crisis, the SEC outpaced all the other regulators. The firm still retained its glittering reputation. Goldman almost certainly would have gone under had the government not bailed out the financial system and injected capital into the investment bank. Its short on the market would not have saved it, though Goldman Sachs would contend otherwise. Goldman was still nicknamed Government Sachs for its ability to stock regulatory agencies and presidential cabinets with its former executives. The US Senate had not yet put executives through embarrassing hearings. *Rolling Stone* magazine's Matt Taibbi had not yet written one of the most memorable phrases to emerge from the financial crisis: that Goldman was "a great vampire squid wrapped around the face of humanity, relentlessly jamming its blood funnel into anything that smells like money."[2]

As excited as he was, Kidney also read the Abacus memos with concern. The agency contemplated charging only Goldman Sachs itself and no individuals. That charge: Goldman omitted material information when selling Abacus. Pretty weak for the allegations, he thought. More worrisome, the investigation seemed incomplete. The SEC staff had not taken testimony from any top executives in Goldman's mortgage businesses or any top Goldman officials. It had not interviewed the German bank, the supposed victim. More bizarre still, the SEC hadn't even taken John Paulson's testimony. The SEC could not know if it was charging the right people with the right securities law violations, Kidney felt. The agency conducted much more extensive investigations in small-time insider trading cases. Recently, he had tried a case where the last guy charged was a fifth-level "tippee"—that is, the guy who got a tip from a guy who got a tip from a guy who got a tip from a guy who got a tip from the guy with the information. The whole lot of them had reaped only $1 million in ill-gotten gains, yet the agency brought out the B-52 bombers.

Here was one of its first and biggest investigations of the financial crisis, and it was against the marquee bank on Wall Street. Over the next nine months, Kidney would wage a battle within the SEC, making the same accusations internally that wouldn't emerge in public until much later. Kidney came to believe that the big banks had captured his beloved regulator—that it went after only minor actors and was cautious to the point of cowardice.

## "AN UNBELIEVABLE FRAUD"

On August 14, a little more than two weeks after having started on the Goldman case, Kidney sent a memo to lead investigator Muoio's team. His group was readying an enforcement action memorandum to send to the commissioners, who vote on every enforcement action. Action memos lay out the staff's case to the commission: what the SEC's findings are, who the agency is prepared to sue, and sometimes why it is not suing others. Within the bureaucracy of the agency, they assume elevated importance. Sometimes the staff writes forty or fifty drafts of such memos. Often the commission sends them back with comments. The staff toils on its replies and returns them. Then the commission votes.

Kidney tried to get Muoio's team to hold back on sending the action memo until it had done more on the probe. He suggested charges for individuals, including the Paulson & Co. executive who spearheaded the deal, Paolo Pellegrini, and a low-level Goldman banker named Fabrice Tourre. He called for more investigation of other Goldman bankers. He said the SEC should allege "scheme liability" for the fraudulent conduct and aiding and abetting. Charging them with scheme liability was a bold idea. Kidney thought the agency should argue that Paulson and Goldman had entered into an illegal "scheme": a conspiracy to build a product to fail, which had then been sold to unwitting buyers. Instead, the SEC picked the narrowest charge it could find: that Goldman had omitted material information. Kidney thought the charge was not only weak but also didn't depict what had happened. To him, it felt false.

Kidney had been thinking for a while that the SEC neglected to go after big targets. Here it was happening again. During his career, Kidney had never lost a trial. In 1989 he'd handled the agency's first trial of an insider trader that went before a jury. He'd won a case against KPMG accountants who had enabled Xerox to violate accounting rules. His bosses had framed some cheesy news clippings from his various victories. He'd put them up on the walls of his office. In 2001 he won the agency's Irving M. Pollack Award, named after the first head of enforcement at the agency and Stanley Sporkin's mentor, for his dedication to public service. He shrugged off his record, however, as the SEC didn't bring that many cases to trial. "I don't want to make too much of that because you settle a lot and have to know when to fold 'em," he says.

A native Washingtonian, born on the same day as Hillary Clinton, Kidney joined the SEC in 1986. He was already thirty-nine. He'd started out as a reporter. His father had also been a reporter. He had worked for the United Press International wire service, where he covered the Supreme Court. Kidney joked that he became a lawyer because the hard-drinking life of a reporter might lead to an early death. In reality, he thought it would make him a better legal reporter. And he wanted to take advantage of the GI Bill. His draft number had come up early—007—and he enlisted in December 1969, at the height of the Vietnam War. He served—"heroically," he'd say—in Kansas City, Missouri, at the Army Hometown News Service, mostly writing captions for photographs.

Once, Kidney left for a nongovernment job, but after four years, he returned to the agency. Kidney's mother had instilled in him a pride in civil service. She had been a pioneer who had risen to become a commissioner at the US Bureau of Labor Statistics at a time when few women had such prominent roles. Public service was worth the inevitable financial sacrifices, she taught him. When Kidney arrived at the SEC in the mid-1980s, the "steam was elevated" at the place, he says. Young lawyers were told to go after impressive cases, and they did in those early years: junk bond king Michael Milken, insider trader Ivan Boesky, investment banker Martin Siegel. But the place changed over the decades, as the SEC recruited more lawyers from big firms such as WilmerHale and from Wall Street banks.

The unspeakable marked James Kidney. More than a decade before the Abacus case had begun, he and his wife suspected that their young son was suffering from depression. But they could not get the attention of the multiple professionals they approached about him. One night in late October 2000, their son hung himself. He was twelve years old. Kidney wrote later that their faith in those professionals was "horribly misplaced."

Kidney went to work only days after the tragedy but remained in a fog that did not lift for months. Later, he started a website for parents of depressed children, where he posted a quote from Philip Roth's novel *American Pastoral.* It held terrible resonance:

> He had learned the worst lesson that life can teach—that it makes no sense. And when that happens the happiness is never spontaneous again. It is artificial and, even then, bought at the price of an obstinate estrangement from oneself and one's history . . . Stoically he suppresses his horror. He learns to live behind a mask. A lifetime experiment in endurance. A performance over a ruin.

Though scarring, the event did not, Kidney felt, change his approach to work. Kidney never wanted a promotion. He liked being a litigation jockey. Perhaps it amplified his central professional trait: a kind of reverse ambition. He did not need approval from his bosses. He did not put his trust in their judgment. He did not yearn for prestige. He wanted to remain able to say what he thought. And he wanted to do his job.

After getting the Abacus case, Kidney pressed the team to take what he thought were obvious investigative steps. A staff attorney in the group informed him that Muoio had vetoed the idea of calling John Paulson to testify. They hadn't even subpoenaed his emails yet. What could they be thinking? The SEC should interview him and the head of the group that Tourre was in, Jonathan Egol, yesterday. How could they know what happened, and who knew what and when? It turned out that the SEC was making little use of its subpoena power for the investigation—a sign of how gingerly the agency treated major investigative targets.

Muoio did not agree with Kidney. He wrote in an email, "I continue to have serious reservations about charging Paulson on our facts. And I worry that doing so could severely undermine and delay our solid case against Goldman. That said, I am committed to reconsidering the issue." Muoio was a low-key but bright SEC veteran who was serving as the deputy chief of the structured products unit. He'd been at the agency about a decade, having worked in private practice and graduated from Yale Law School.

Another attorney in the group, however, came to Kidney's defense: "Our theory of the case, as I understand it, is that Paulson and Goldman conspired to structure a transaction that was meant to rip off their ultimate counterparties, in this case [German bank] IKB. In other words, the case is more about *stealing* than about *lying*," underlining the words for emphasis. He went on: "It would be more than a little odd for the complaint not to name the primary architect and beneficiary of the scam. Not only odd, but it would undermine our case before the jury . . . And if we are going to argue that the case is about stealing, the jury is going to wonder why the hell Paulson isn't there."

Pleased to find an ally, Kidney seconded him: "If this is not scheme liability, I don't know what might be in a securities context. In any event, we should bring cases like this that challenge status quo thinking. We should do it on very strong facts. We have all that here, though I don't think it is much of a stretch legally."

The following week, Kidney emailed his boss Lou Mejia to voice his concerns in the event that the Goldman case came up while he was on vacation. "I am getting the sense that there is a desire to fast track a complaint against Goldman, presumably to show we are after these deals with synthetic swaps, CDOs, and other crap," he wrote. "This appears to be an unbelievable fraud. I don't think we should bring it without naming all those we believe to be liable."

## "GOOD PEOPLE WHO HAVE DONE ONE BAD THING"

As the weeks went by, Kidney and the staff traded damning bits of evidence and debated expanding the investigation and the charges. On September 14, 2009, a staff attorney referred to a 2007 Goldman email that circulated to the entire mortgage desk, in which a Goldman mortgage securities executive praised Paulson's work: "I would also note that paulson [*sic*] did a great job with the names they selected." Williams understood that Paulson & Co. had expertly picked dogs that made the hedge fund money. Abacus had been completed and sold to investors in early 2007. Less than a year later, the ratings agencies were downgrading the underlying bonds, turning Paulson's investment into a winner. The email confirmed further that Paulson, and not the selection agent, ACA, had driven the choices of what went into Abacus and that many Goldman executives knew what was going on. Kidney wanted to know: How many people at Goldman understood how Abacus had worked? The SEC had no idea.

The commission decided at last to charge an individual in the Abacus matter: Fabrice Tourre. They had a cornucopia of imprudent material from Tourre, a French citizen who lived in London and who was in his late twenties when the deal was created. Tourre had joked about selling the doomed deal to "widows and orphans." On January 23, 2007, he sent what would become an infamous email:

> More and more leverage in the system, the entire system is about to crumble any moment . . . the only potential survivor the fabulous Fab . . . standing in the middle of all these complex, highly levered, exotic trades he created without necessarily understanding all the implications of those monstruosities !!! [*sic*]

Tourre had not been in charge. He was an easy target, but charging him was not likely to send a signal that Washington was serious about cracking down on Wall Street's excesses.

On September 16, 2009, Kidney sent an email to the group with the subject line "splainin to do": "I think we will need to explain to the Commission why we are or are not recommending an action against" other Goldman executives.

An SEC staff lawyer responded: "Egol and Lehman were there, but not actively pushing the deal, from my perspective."

Kidney replied: Tourre "could not do it without their approval, however. It's always the lowest guy's deal when it comes to litigation."

Muoio, the investigation's leader, was implacable. On the morning of Saturday, September 19, 2009, Muoio sent a congratulatory email about the investigation, but with a note of caution. He had reviewed their work to make sure they had gotten the right guy:

> Ten years into this, I have seen the devasting [*sic*] impact our little ol' civil actions reap on real people more often than I care to remember. It is the least favorite part of the job. Most of our civil defendants are good people who have done one bad thing.

The email agitated Kidney. How did Muoio know they had done only one bad thing? Could he look into their souls to know whether they were decent folk or not? He stewed. Kidney waited out the weekend. He went to work on Monday and managed to hold off for hours before responding. Then, trying to keep a measured tone, he wrote:

> I think we should talk about a couple of the others. I am in full agreement that when we sue it can be devastating, and that we have sued little guys way too often on flimsy charges or when they have been punished enough. But I'm not at all convinced that Tourre alone is sufficient here.

Then Kidney sent an alarmed email to his boss: "This is sort of the problem in a nutshell." Was this the right mind-set for a regulator? Street criminals were hardly afforded such assumptions about their character. Since the agency was in the middle of a bunch of investigations of the CDO business and multiple Goldman deals, maybe this incident wasn't just one bad occurrence but something much worse: systemic fraud on Wall Street.

Mejia backed his subordinate and encouraged him. "If you want me to escalate, let me know. Commission is going to have a lot of questions if this goes up without individuals," he wrote to Kidney on September 25.

In a meeting with the group to discuss taking the testimony of Tourre's superior Jonathan Egol, Muoio said, "We know what he is going to say: he was too busy to pay attention." Kidney went ballistic: "That's a cardinal sin in an investigation! You can't assume what somebody will say!"

The staff sought direct evidence, as it had against Tourre. The SEC wanted something incriminating that John Paulson, Paolo Pellegrini, or Goldman Sachs executives had written down somewhere—and embarrassing emails such as "Fab"'s would be a bonus. But high-level Goldman executives were savvy about communications. When topics broached sensitive territory in emails, they would often write "LDL": let's discuss live.

Kidney emailed Mejia with resignation:

> There is no way that the staff will go along with suing Paulson or anyone at Paulson & Co. unless his emails [contain] admissions about scheming to defraud which are wholly unrealistice [*sic*] to expect. Theis [*sic*] staff wants

> an extraordinary amount of direct evidence before bringing any claim against anyone, and are very satisfied to just sue Goldman.

The lack of direct evidence did not bother Kidney. The SEC could rely on inferences the buyers made. In its defense, Goldman was going to argue that sophisticated investors stood on the other side of Paulson. Kidney explained the SEC could flip that argument to its advantage. Because of its relative sophistication, ACA assumed Paulson was investing in the deal, not against it. IKB assumed ACA would act in its interest. Yes, IKB could see the portfolio of bonds that made up Abacus, but the bank didn't know anything about the origin or the construction process. The SEC uncovered evidence that IKB discussed needing a selection agent like ACA on the deal to act in its interest. The German bank told Goldman it would decline to invest in the deal otherwise. Had it understood that Paulson and Goldman had suborned ACA, as it did later, it would not have put in the money. In other words, the information was material.

Kidney continued to believe Goldman and the hedge fund had entered into a conspiracy. On October 21 his boss emailed him, "I back the theory" of scheme liability and wrote that he "share[d your] concerns" about the lack of charges for more individuals. But Kidney's argument to bring a scheme liability charge was getting nowhere. Muoio cited bad legal precedent. The major setback to scheme liability law had come in the *Stoneridge Investment Partners, LLC v. Scientific-Atlanta, Inc.* case in 2008. The Supreme Court ruled that private investors could not sue a secondary participant in a fraud scheme, unless that participant had made misleading statements directly to the plaintiff.

Stoneridge was the most important securities fraud ruling in years. The case involved two large companies: the cable giant Charter Communications and Motorola. Charter, worried about meeting its earnings estimates, came up with a way to inflate revenue and earnings. The company bought cable set-top boxes from Scientific-Atlanta for a low price—say, $25 a box. The cable company went to its vendors and told them it would be willing now to pay, say, $50 a box. In exchange, the vendors would pay $25 back to Charter in advertising revenue. Charter could increase its advertising revenue but had no corresponding cost. Eventually the market realized what had happened, and the stock crashed.

A hedge fund investor in Scientific-Atlanta, called Stoneridge Investment Partners, sued the company, saying it had entered into a scheme with Charter to defraud the public. (When the companies came up with this transaction, Charter backdated documents to make it appear as if these were two unrelated transactions, for the purchase of set-top boxes and a separate advertising buy, to avoid detection by the auditors.) A majority of Supreme Court justices took the position that Scientific-Atlantic and other vendors were not responsible for what Charter told its investors.

Through the 2000s and into the 2010s, as courts ruled against the Justice Department and the SEC in corporate and securities fraud cases, the government responded inadequately. The government did not retry Kathy Ruemmler's Enron case against Merrill bankers. Lanny Breuer and the Obama Justice Department did not seek to restore the honest-services charge. Remarkably, the Justice Department and former SEC commissioners went one step further in the Stoneridge case. They helped the Supreme Court reach its conclusion. The Justice Department and fourteen commissioners of the SEC wrote briefs in support of Charter. Both briefs argued against allowing private actors to hold parties such as the vendors in the case liable. The Bush-era Justice Department, reflecting the conservative hostility to such lawsuits, wrote in its brief: "[P]rivate securities actions can be abused in ways that impose substantial costs on companies that have fully complied with the applicable laws."

The Supreme Court did not prevent the SEC or the Department of Justice from bringing such suits. But the ruling hurt the enforcers nonetheless. By 2009, as the SEC considered bringing charges against Goldman over Abacus, the Supreme Court ruling, which the agency helped nudge to fruition, now constrained the enforcement lawyers. They worried they could not win a scheme liability case.

Muoio, by now, appeared exasperated. He found Kidney unsophisticated and wasn't impressed with his record. Undefeated at trial? Sure, but that was for chickenfeed matters. Muoio didn't display his emotions, but he'd put up his record against Kidney's any day. Muoio specialized in what the agency considered the big blockbuster cases against the major banks and he thought his judgment had proven spot on. That they were settlements—no-admit, no-deny ones, at that—didn't matter. Muoio counted them as wins nonetheless.

Debating Abacus, Muoio would explain to Kidney, "It's just a trade!" The general Wall Street attitude about transactions such as Abacus was that there were buyers and sellers, making a trade. Buyers didn't know why sellers were offloading, and neither had any obligation to explain their reasoning. Nor did the investment bank facilitating the transactions. Muoio told Kidney he was concerned about "being laughed at" on Wall Street if the SEC charged Paulson, because it would look naïve about trading.

But Abacus was nothing like buying or selling stock. Goldman arranged the deal, acting more like an underwriter. The entire transaction was predicated on keeping Paulson's role and aims quiet. If the buyer had known the true circumstances, it would not have bought the CDO. Kidney felt that Goldman executives didn't need to say these sentiments out loud or write them in an email. It was all understood. Goldman and Paulson had teamed up to make something designed to fail. Kidney posted a slogan at his desk, to help him simplify and encapsulate the deal: "Satisfy the long and sell to the short is legal. . . . Satisfy the short and sell to the long is fraud."

For its part, Paulson & Co. and Goldman said there was never any "scheme." And they said Abacus was never "designed to fail." Paulson & Co. maintained throughout the investigation and afterward that ACA was free to reject its suggestions and said that it never misled anyone in the deal. The hedge fund did not instruct Goldman what to disclose to investors and said it did not know what the bank was telling investors. The investment bank argued that the precipitous collapse in the value of Abacus resulted from the broad decline in the housing market that afflicted all securities related to real estate, not because of flaws in the product.

On October 21 Kidney circulated a long memo arguing that the SEC should consider charging Paulson & Co.; John Paulson himself; the employee responsible for the deal, Pellegrini; and Goldman's Egol:

> *Each of them knowingly participated, as did Goldman and Tourre, in a scheme to sell a product which, in blunt but accurate terms, was designed to fail. An important part of the scheme was, of course, not to inform investors the product was designed to fail and, further, to lull them into confidence about the offering by promoting the participation of a supposed independent entity to select the underlying assets which dictated the performance of the offering. This was intentionally done to disguise the participation and veto authority of Paulson & Co. in selecting the assets. In other words, the current and possibly additional evidence suggests they should be sued for securities fraud because they are liable for securities fraud.*

Kidney argued to the SEC that under Section 10(b) of the Exchange Act, it is unlawful "to employ any device, scheme, or artifice to defraud" and "to engage in any act, practice, or course of business which operates or would operate as a fraud or deceit upon any person." Kidney premised the case on a simple notion: "Paulson and Goldman created and offered a deceptive product. It was in connection with the purchase and sale of a security. Nothing more is required to find them liable for a deceptive scheme."

If the SEC pressed the case and won, the agency could widen the securities law in its favor. The current SEC case fell, Kidney conceded, "within accepted legal maxims," he wrote. But he argued for ambition.

## "DAMAGE TO THE REPUTATION"

By the fall of 2009, Kidney was furious with the staff, and the staff seemed fairly well fed up with him. After Kidney wrote an insulting email about Muoio—and then inadvertently fired it off to Muoio himself—he apologized and tried to explain why he was so passionate: he loved the SEC and worried about the institution where he'd spent his career, referring, as SEC lawyers do, to the commission as their "client."

"The damage to the reputation of the client in the last few years and the decline of the institution are very troubling to me," he told Muoio.

Kidney saw the chance to rehabilitate that reputation slipping away. He started to get aggressive. No one could mistake Kidney for having bureaucratic acumen. On November 6 he did something audacious: he sent an email to Robert Khuzami, the director of enforcement at the SEC. Before taking this role, Khuzami had been the general counsel of the American division of Deutsche Bank, the major German bank. Deutsche Bank had a vast structured finance business and had been neck-deep in the CDO business. Since Paulson had shopped his idea to Deutsche Bank as well as to Goldman, Kidney suggested that Khuzami think about recusing himself. He conceded that his boss had warned him off making this entreaty, writing that Mejia had told him "it should be not mentioned and that you would know whether to recuse yourself."

But Kidney explained, "There may be debate" after the SEC charges Goldman about whether the charge was right and sufficient. "Given all our recent problems," he wrote, the SEC doesn't want critics claiming it had a conflict of interest, especially since it wasn't going to sue Paulson.

Khuzami was politely dismissive. He said he would forward the concern to the proper channels but replied, "Can't say I see a basis for recusal under the recusal principles as I know them." The ethics czars at the agency agreed. Khuzami stayed involved with the case.

Frustrated by the overarching theory of the case, Kidney pressed another issue: charging more individuals. He argued the SEC should charge Jonathan Egol, Tourre's superior. "He was on most of the most incriminating emails, was Tourre's boss, and is more prominent in structured finance circles than Tourre," Kidney wrote. Tourre was just a piker, he explained. A small-time gambler.

Kidney laid out the evidence: Egol created the first Abacus structure and had been one of two lead Goldman representatives on two earlier Abacus trades involving a hedge fund called Magnetar Capital and Deutsche

Bank as the shorts. Egol knew Paulson was investing in Abacus and that Paulson was shorting the market. Egol reviewed all of the materials that had been prepared to create and sell the deal, including the three key documents the SEC was relying on to make its false-statement-and-misrepresentation case.

When he couldn't persuade Muoio and his team, Kidney tried to take himself off the case. He emailed a deputy to chairwoman Mary Schapiro, explaining that he had withdrawn as litigation counsel. "Maybe I have lost professional distance somehow (though in my heart, I don't think so)," he despaired. "In good conscience, I cannot put my name on the current draft being circulated." The complaint "is woefully inadequate. My fear is that the Commission will lose the chance to show it is a tough regulator worthy of public trust and instead look like chumps."

Mejia told Kidney that Khuzami wanted him to stay on the case. So he relented. He had prevailed on the Egol interview, so the staff postponed its meeting with the commissioners to get their approval for the enforcement action until after it had the Goldman executive's testimony. The SEC still hadn't interviewed the primary victim: the German bank Industriekreditbank. A top official forced a reluctant Muoio to fly to Germany to interview IKB officials. They ended up saying they had no idea how the deal had come about or the extent of Paulson's involvement. But for reasons that were never clear to the SEC, the German bank refused to send someone to the States to testify. That hurt the case.

As 2009 ended, Muoio not only resisted Kidney's view but almost seemed like he was making Wall Street's case rather than the SEC's. On December 30 he wrote another congratulatory email to his team: "Now that we are gearing up to bring a handful of cases in this area, I suggest that we keep in mind that the vast majority of the losses suffered had nothing to do with fraud and the like, and are more fairly attributable to lesser human failings of greed, arrogance, and stupidity, of which we are all guilty from time to time."

Muoio's note echoed bankers' favored explanation of the crisis. Wall Street had captured Kidney's agency. Enforcement officials are not required to figure out causes of crises. They are responsible for enforcing against fraudulent activity. If Muoio meant his message just for Kidney, well, Kidney wasn't making a sweeping argument about the losses from the financial crisis. He was making a narrower point: on a deal the SEC *did* believe was fraudulent, more than the lowest drudge at Goldman might be guilty. Kidney emailed a warning to a top SEC official: "We must be on guard against any risk that we adopt the thinking of . . . Wall Street Elders."

Kidney and Muoio dueled into January 2010. One SEC staffer wrote that they had testimony but little documentary evidence that Egol reviewed the Abacus documents. "The law surely imposes liability on others besides the literal scrivenor [*sic*], or we are in big trouble. How did we get Mike Milken?" Kidney lamented in an email. "Why are we working so hard to defend a guy who is now a managing director at Goldman so we can limit the case to the French guy in London?"

Muoio fired back,

> I am sure you are not suggesting we charge Egol because of his position within the company, as we have previously discussed with you our concerns with that approach to our charging decisions. Nationality is also clearly irrelevant, and I hope that's the last we hear from you on that subject. Tourre admits he was principally responsible for the problematic disclosures.

The staff interviewed Egol later in January. Muoio would eventually tell the SEC inspector general, "We didn't lay a glove on him." But Kidney felt differently: Egol had confirmed he had reviewed all the documents that the SEC contended were misleading. That made Egol responsible, he believed.

The SEC readied its complaint against Goldman and Tourre. Kidney found it constipated and filled with financial arcana. Wall Street used complexity as a cover, and the SEC had fallen victim. He tried to offer edits. "Unless the complaint is intended for an audience of CDO brokers,

I think the opening is way too full of jargon and will be incomprehensible to most people. This is more than a cosmetic or publicity issue. Goldman's defense will rely heavily on making this sound like a really complex deal. This complaint plays right into that," he wrote.

Finally, Kidney got help. A top official in the SEC's litigation department wrote a memo enumerating the evidence against Egol and explaining the state of the law. The official concluded, "Given Egol's participation in the preparation of the offering materials, outlined above, it might behoove us to consider whether we should recommend a charge of primary liability and allege aiding and abetting in the alternative."

On January 29, 2010, after months of investigation and debate, the SEC sent a Wells notice to Jonathan Egol. His attorneys started their negotiations by attacking the long delay, asking for more time. On February 2 the lawyer responded, "This investigation began in the late summer of 2008, and the formal order was issued in February 2009. Mr. Egol's involvement . . . was perfectly obvious from the beginning, yet the staff did not even ask for his testimony until November 2009, over a year after the beginning of the investigation. After Mr. Egol testified on January 4, 2010, it took the staff three weeks, until January 28, to decide that it was considering an action against him, and until January 29 to provide us with a Wells call."

Muoio took a tough line at first. Three days later, Egol's lawyer took his complaints to senior SEC officials. Two weeks after that, on February 19, a sheepish Muoio backed down. The agency agreed to extend the deadline. When Egol's lawyers did respond, they disputed everything the SEC contended: the deal was not fraudulent, and, at any rate, Egol had little responsibility for it. The attorneys argued that the offering hadn't been misleading in the first place; that Egol himself did not make any misleading statements to anyone; and—in what they thought was a killing blow—that not only had Goldman not shorted Abacus, but also it had kept a piece and lost money on the deal. The last point did not persuade the SEC. Goldman never had plans to buy a piece of Abacus. It simply wasn't able to unload all of it.

The Egol response underscored to Kidney the error of the SEC's narrow approach. The agency could avoid battling over the minutiae of Egol's specific role if it charged them all with a scheme.

Reid Muoio hadn't seen the point in interviewing Egol in the first place, and now he believed that Egol's lawyers had the better argument. On March 8 he made the case against charging Egol. He wrote that Egol did not know that Tourre misled ACA, did not communicate directly with the buyers or ACA, and had only one conversation with Paulson. He contended that Egol did not "approve" the transaction. That was done by Goldman's Mortgage Capital Committee. The marketing materials had been approved not by Egol but by the legal and compliance departments. Egol was not even Tourre's supervisor, nor did he suggest to anyone that Paulson's role in the transaction be concealed. Muoio wrote: "I put our chances of surviving a motion to dismiss at 25 percent. Odds of winning at trial drop to 10 percent for a variety of reasons, including, among other things, the quality and experience of defense counsel and my expectation that Egol will strike most jurors as a nice, likable, down-to-earth family man."

If the Mortgage Committee had approved it, maybe the SEC needed to be charging more than Egol, Kidney thought. Here was Chickenshit Club thinking. Stubborn and pissed off, Kidney forwarded on a sardonic reply to a colleague: "I guess Reid is relying on his deep experience as a staff attorney and gofer at a big NY law firm for his estimate of surviving a motion to dismiss. I will forbear from crystal ball gazing."

On March 22 the team assembled in Khuzami's office for an afternoon meeting. Kidney and two others, including the deputy director of enforcement, voted in favor of suing Egol. Muoio remained against, as did others. Most of the lower-level staffers stayed quiet. The following day, Khuzami emailed the group with his decision:

> I am a no on Egol. An extremely difficult call, but in the end, the record does not for me reflect the necessary level of comfort that he knowingly provided substantial assistance in this violation to warrant proceeding against him. I am not substituting my judgment for that of judge or jury, but applying my view of

> our obligations as an enforcement authority as to what we need to see before we should file a case. The lack of consensus among our group is itself, for me, confirmation of this conclusion. There are lots of other secondary considerations, some for and some against, but in the end, the fundamental principle has to be whether in my heart of heats [*sic*], he meets this standard. For me, he does not.
>
> The case against Tourre and Goldman is a good case and an important one to bring. The decision on Egol does not change that.

Kidney had lost. The top officials offered him the job of handling the experts during the trial but he knew what that meant. He'd been demoted. He declined.

## ANSWERS LOST TO HISTORY

On Friday, April 16, 2010, the SEC stunned the markets by suing Goldman Sachs, charging the firm with omitting information that would have been crucial to investors in Abacus. The agency brought a charge against Tourre as well. They were the first against firms that capitalized on the housing bubble and its collapse. Goldman's stock dropped 13 percent that day, erasing $10 billion from its market capitalization.[3]

For the SEC, the tactic was tough. It rarely sued and mostly settled. But it wasn't tough enough for Kidney. As he had feared, the public reception to the suit was mixed, at best. The tabloid *New York Post* accurately headlined its story about Tourre "Goldman Fall Guy."[4]

"Sadly, it will not suffice to offer up Fabrice Tourre as a ritual sacrifice," Michael Lewis, the author of *The Big Short* and a columnist for Bloomberg, wrote several days after the SEC announced its complaint. "No one is going to accept a then twenty-seven-year-old Frenchman, whose job was apparently to keep sweet the patsies on the other end of your trades, as the world's authority on your trading positions. His name isn't even on the top of the list of Goldman traders on the $2 billion Abacus deal for which you are being sued. The name on top of that document is 'Jonathan Egol.'" Lewis concluded, "The public eventually will ask: Who is Jonathan Egol and what exactly was his game?"[5]

Kidney had been right.

On April 27, 2010, Senator Carl Levin's Permanent Subcommittee on Investigations (PSI) held hearings on the role that investment banks played in the financial crisis. One of its reports examined Goldman's CDO business and found that the bank had deceived and taken advantage of its customers. Relieved that the firm had managed to offload it to some credulous buyers, a top Goldman executive referred to a CDO as "one shitty deal." On one occasion, Goldman had marked, or recorded, slices of a CDO at one low price and sold those same slices the same day for much higher prices. Lloyd Blankfein, Goldman's CEO, testified before the PSI. Levin and the investigators believed that he had misled Congress. The committee referred its report to the Department of Justice for criminal investigation into Goldman's CDO business and its representations to Congress.

Blankfein hired star defense attorney Reid Weingarten. One of Eric Holder's close friends, Weingarten thought the case was bullshit and going nowhere. When Goldman's board of directors wondered if it should cut Blankfein loose, Weingarten argued that it should not. He guaranteed that the CEO would not be indicted. The board did not need much convincing to heed Weingarten's advice. The Department of Justice didn't seem active. The Southern District of New York had done a cursory investigation of some Goldman CDOs. The investigation didn't seem hot at all.

Now the head of Main Justice's criminal division, Lanny Breuer, reopened the matter. He did not give the investigation to the fraud section. Instead, Breuer assigned one of his staffers, Dan Suleiman, to review the evidence. Suleiman was a member of the Breu Crew, who, like the others, had been a young associate at Covington. And, like several of the others, Suleiman had no prosecutorial experience. Weingarten and Lanny Breuer were acquaintances. Both had children at Georgetown Day School, a posh private school in the capital. Weingarten had a series of conversations with Breuer about the case. He would call up periodically to wheedle and bellow, "Close this fucking case, will ya?"

The Justice Department found nothing criminal in Goldman's actions. In July 2013 Suleiman rejoined Covington. Lanny Breuer's staffers had boosted their résumés with government experience and now revolved back into the private sector. On August 9, 2012, the department put out an unusual statement, clearing Goldman in the Abacus case.

Abacus was a fulcrum point. Had the government taken a different tack, enforcement following the financial crisis might have looked different. If Kidney had prevailed, the SEC would have brought fraud charges against numerous individuals as well as Goldman and Paulson & Co. With the major regulator bringing such fraud charges, the Department of Justice might have found it easier to make a criminal case in Abacus. The Abacus case might have provided a framework for other SEC civil charges against individuals and Justice Department criminal cases.

Instead, the SEC stumbled. The Abacus case illustrates how debilitated the government's investigative skills had become by 2009. Like Gresham's law, where copper coins drive more valuable gold coins out of circulation, the agency's focus on corporate accountability (an obsession shared by the Justice Department) drove out the good investigations of individuals. The two kinds of investigations should have aided each other but didn't. The investigators who were skilled and motivated to go after the human beings behind corporate bad actions suffered. To the SEC staff's mind, bringing charges against Goldman and Goldman alone was fine.

Publicly, Goldman expressed outrage and innocence about the PSI's and the SEC's allegations. But the pressure forced the firm to the negotiating table. Three days after the SEC sued, on April 19, Khuzami sent around a note: "Settlement possibilities have been raised; pls come prepared to think about terms. RK." There would be no trial. A couple of months later, on July 15, 2010, the SEC settled with Goldman for what appeared to be a sizable fine of $550 million. Goldman Sachs did not admit any wrongdoing. The SEC wrung an apology out of the bank, which it perceived as a victory. Critics perceived it as comically inadequate. The bank issued a statement:

> Goldman acknowledges that the marketing materials for the Abacus 2007-AC1 transaction contained incomplete information. In particular, it was a mistake for the Goldman marketing materials to state that the reference portfolio was "selected by" ACA Management LLC without disclosing the role of Paulson & Co. Inc. in the portfolio selection process and that Paulson's economic interests were adverse to CDO investors. Goldman regrets that the marketing materials did not contain that disclosure.[6]

Where had the SEC gone wrong? The staff was blinkered. It failed to understand Goldman's overall mortgage and CDOs business. Senator Levin's committee, by contrast, did take a sweeping view. It uncovered the entirety of the bank's mortgage views and business. The PSI found that in late 2006, Goldman's top executives worried that the American housing market and mortgage securities, including CDOs, would crash. The firm pivoted to short the market, selling as much as it could. The PSI found numerous dodgy deals, but the SEC did not fully grasp this context as it analyzed the Abacus deal. The SEC staff hadn't interviewed enough people at the bank. The staff, except for Kidney, was staring too hard at the Abacus documents.

Not only did the Abacus investigation suffer, but so did the other SEC investigations into Goldman CDOs. Goldman understood that if it settled Abacus, the SEC wouldn't bring any more cases. The SEC appears to have wrapped up all of the settlements into one. The SEC never brought any other charges against the firm over CDOs. A $550 million payout for one CDO was a lot, dwarfing the bank's fees on the deal. But if it implicitly covered all of its mortgage securities transgressions, the fine was much smaller as a percentage of its overall revenue and profits that the business had generated during the bubble.

Kidney, meanwhile, was disillusioned. In late 2013 his wife went into the hospital for routine hip replacement surgery. Having suffered continuous health problems since their son's suicide, she acquired an infection and spent six weeks on life support before dying. She was two months shy of her sixty-ninth birthday. Six months later, Kidney decided he didn't need to struggle with the bureaucracy anymore. He retired. At his retirement, in 2014, he gave an impassioned going-away speech: "It is no surprise that we lose our best and brightest as they see no place to go in the agency and eventually decide they are just going to get their own ticket to a law firm or corporate job punched. They see an agency that polices the broken windows on the street level and rarely goes to the penthouse floors," he said. "For the powerful, we are at most a tollbooth on the bankster turnpike. We are a cost, not a serious expense."

The speech leaked, and Kidney had a moment of media attention. He went on National Public Radio and Bloomberg Television. Then nothing happened.

After he left, he toyed with going public with his story but felt torn out of loyalty to the SEC. He penned a long, anonymous letter to the *New York Times* and sent it. No one seemed to receive it. (He'd sent it to an old address.) He wondered if anyone cared anymore. Kidney reflected on what had gone wrong at the SEC and with securities law enforcement. The oft-cited explanations—campaign contributions and the allure of private sector jobs to low-paid government lawyers—played a role. But to Kidney, the driving force was something subtler. Over the course of three decades, the public and the civil servants working in the agency lost belief in the good that comes from enforcement and regulation. Regulatory capture was a psychological process. Officials become timorous in the face of criticism from their bosses, Congress, and the industry the agency is supposed to oversee. Regulators don't pursue leads. Prosecutors don't open cases. The enforcers never make Wall Street executives explain their actions.

In 2013 the SEC took Tourre to trial and won.[7] By that point, the view that the government had gone soft on financial crisis crimes had crystallized, and the victory did nothing to dispel it. Tourre was found liable and ordered to pay more than $850,000. He went on to become a PhD candidate at the University of Chicago. In early 2016 the Justice Department settled a case with Goldman, charging that the bank had misrepresented mortgage-backed securities (investments that differed from CDOs). The bank had to pay a headline figure of $5 billion, though various sweeteners in the settlement meant that Goldman would pay far less. The Justice Department did not charge any individuals.

"I was a believer in the SEC. A subpoena from the SEC meant something when I started," Kidney says. "I still believed [in] it until I saw how this case and the subsequent cases were handled." But, he adds, "The answers to unasked questions are now lost to history as well as to law enforcement. It is a shame."

*Chapter Fourteen*

# THE PROCESS IS POLLUTED

"WE'RE FUCKED, BASICALLY."[1]

Just over a year before the financial crisis peaked, on July 11, 2007, Andy Forster, an executive at AIG Financial Products, worried aloud over the phone to Tom Athan, his subordinate. Forster had worried for some time now about the subprime mortgage market—and now those fears were being realized. On July 3 Forster told Athan, "If we actually mark it, we would physically have to take that hit." In other words: if they accepted what the market deemed the value of their investments to be, AIG Financial Products would, in Wall Street lingo, have to record those lower values on its books, to "mark" the value of its investments down. The losses were—well, there was only one conclusion: they were fucked.

Over the next several months, AIG's losses mounted. The firm fought with trading partners. Executives grappled with how to value the collapsing positions and fretted about what to tell the top AIG executives and the public. Paul Pelletier and some of his colleagues at the Department of Justice came to believe that during this anxious period, AIG executives committed crimes.

On July 27 Goldman Sachs came calling: the investment bank wanted money from AIG Financial Products. Goldman had been on the other side of AIG FP as its main trading partner. AIG FP had been selling insurance, in the form of derivatives called credit default swaps, on the supposedly safe portions of collateralized debt obligations. Goldman paid AIG a little bit on a regular basis for the insurance, and AIG had an obligation to pay out large amounts if the CDOs collapsed in value. The contracts contained an unusual feature: if the price of the securities dropped, the likelihood that AIG would have to pay rose, and AIG had to give money to Goldman as collateral. If the price moved back up, Goldman would give money back. Now, with the markets collapsing, Goldman wanted AIG to honor the contract. The investment bank did not want a little bit of money; it asked for $1.8 billion—a big number but nothing that would have come close to putting the insurer at risk of collapse.

The implications were clear. Forster told Athan that he was going to tell the big boss, the head of AIG FP, Joseph Cassano, exactly how clear. On August 2 Athan reported to Forster about a "tough call" he had with Goldman. He told Forster that they needed Cassano to "understand the situation 100 percent and let him decide how he wants to proceed." Athan complained, "This isn't what I signed up for—where are the big trades, high fives, and celebratory closing dinners you promised?"

If Goldman's estimate of the value of its positions was right, AIG, the parent company to AIG Financial Products, faced a loss of around $1 billion to $2 billion on its derivatives portfolio. Its top executives did not know about this loss. Indeed, they were telling the public quite the opposite: that all was fine. On August 9, AIG executives held a conference call with investors. The parent company's chief risk officer played down the tumult in the subprime market, telling investors, "The risk actually undertaken is very modest and remote." Joe Cassano, who was also on the call, went further, making a comment that would become infamous as AIG imploded: "It is hard for us, without being flippant, to even see a scenario within any kind of realm of reason that would see us losing one dollar in any of those transactions."

That evening, Forster, who served at Cassano's right hand, and Athan had a conversation. The call had gone over well with Wall Street; analyst notes afterward had been positive. Athan marveled that most analysts seemed to believe that AIG had high-quality investments and that it could handle its subprime losses.

"Yeah, but it's not right, right?" Forster replied.

"Well, I know that, but," Athan responded, "it doesn't seem like everybody . . . knew it."

Over the next several weeks, the problems mounted. In August and September, at least four more parties demanded collateral from AIG. In August, Elias Habayeb, the CFO of AIG's financial services division, to which AIG Financial Products notionally reported, began to raise questions about the potential losses. Cassano, a power unto himself within the behemoth AIG, cut Habayeb out of the discussions, ordering his own chief financial officer not to talk to him about valuations. "They are fish way out of their depth," he wrote in an email. Cassano, an authoritarian boss, badgered his employees and sought control over information flow. "Why are you talking to Elias?" he yelled at the AIG vice president of accounting policy, Joseph St. Denis. "You don't work for that fat fuck!" During the third quarter of the year, Cassano took over a project to value the positions, excluding his own CFO.

AIG may not have made public the demands from trading partners, but that didn't stop those demands from continuing. When the French bank Societe Generale made a request for collateral, Athan emailed Forster on September 6: "Our only option is to delay and then dispute." St. Denis, who felt bullied by Cassano, tried to resign, worried that the firm hadn't been clear about the losses. Cassano dismissed it to colleagues as "[a]ll very dramatic." He refused to accept St. Denis's resignation and prevailed on him to stay. But a couple of weeks later, Cassano blew up at St. Denis, telling him, "I have deliberately excluded you from the valuation" process "because I was concerned that you would pollute the process."

By September 11, 2007, AIG had received multiple collateral calls. That day, Forster and Athan discussed the potential for losses in the "catastrophic-type numbers." They said they needed to "hold off the accountants." The day after that, Habayeb met with Cassano and Forster. He advised them that they had to take the hit and mark down the portfolio to reflect the losses. Cassano and Forster argued against it. They contended that Wall Street was wrong and they were right about how to value the esoteric securities. Since the securities weren't trading on an open market, everything had to be done with complex models. Cassano argued that AIG's positions were special. They were more secure and more difficult to value because the other CDOs were made up of real bonds: cash instruments. But AIGs were derivatives. The differences between the two, he contended, required differing estimates.

Cassano also maintained they differed given that AIG FP wasn't trading the securities but holding them like an insurance contract. An insurer holds a homeowner's policy and makes money if the home never has a fire. Same arrangement here. AIG FP only needed to adjust for the chance that the values would collapse (that the fire would wipe out the building), and not add in any liquidity risk (that it would be forced to sell at a time not of its choosing). Anything that is illiquid and hard to sell requires a discount. But Cassano said AIG's positions didn't need that discount because they were never going to try to sell them.

Still, the executives kept returning to the incoming truth. On September 19 Athan discussed with another colleague the potential losses, worrying they would be about $5 billion. A few days later, however, on September 26, AIG FP executives and auditors from its accounting firm PricewaterhouseCoopers met to discuss how to value AIG FP's positions. Cassano played down the Goldman collateral dispute and said that no other calls had been made, which was not true. His lawyer would later tell prosecutors that the executives and accounting discussed Goldman only briefly in the meeting, almost as an afterthought, and that Cassano and his employees emphasized that Financial Products had not finished estimating the values.

On October 3 Athan told a colleague that AIG FP's losses were "a couple of billion," saying that Forster and Cassano knew it. That day, Forster made his stress apparent, exclaiming, "Fuck, this is an ugly portfolio!" The model the company was using to value its positions was "hokey" and "too made up," he said.

In October AIG Financial Products executives met to discuss the problem. They determined the division had a minor loss on the portfolio, on the order of $45 million. That was nothing for a behemoth the size of AIG. The insurer had exposure to $34 *billion* worth of pre-2006 CDOs at the time. (As of the end of 2007, AIG had credit default swaps of $527 billion, of which $78 billion were written on CDOs.)[2]

In a conference call with executives and outside accountants on November 1, the accountants learned for the first time that Goldman was now requesting $3 billion and that other firms had made collateral calls. Cassano now reported to the top executives that his group's estimates of the losses had risen, to somewhere between $45 million and $350 million. The next day, PricewaterhouseCoopers told Cassano that the $45 million figure was too low. He reran the estimates and arrived at $352 million.

By now, banks from all over were demanding money from AIG FP. Forster and Athan worried about the insurer's liquidity, wondering if it could actually come up with the cash to give its trading partners. On November 6 PricewaterhouseCoopers learned that AIG FP had received collateral calls from Merrill Lynch, JPMorgan Chase, French banks Societe General and Calyon, Swiss bank UBS, and Morgan Stanley. It was a pile-on. In early November AIG Financial Products received $6.5 billion worth of collateral calls, another indication of how many billions in losses AIG faced.

On November 14 Cassano and Forster spoke by phone and discussed how big the write-down was looking. "We're gonna end up with about—my guess is about a $4 billion write-down, right?" Cassano said.

"Yeah, slightly more, I think, actually," Forster responded. It depended, they agreed, on what the model spit out.

A few days later, Cassano found out from the top executives that he would have to make a presentation about the credit default swaps portfolio during a December 5 meeting AIG held for investors. On November 17 Forster and another executive discussed the rapidly escalating collateral calls, now estimating that they had reached as much as $16 billion.

Some executives at AIG understood that losses were serious. In an "early warnings and lessons learned" memo to top executives, Kevin McGinn, AIG's chief credit officer, wrote, "Not all credit events are foreseeable; this housing correction was, in my judgement. And we saw it, perhaps before anyone else and warned the business units accordingly. Some paid heed; others did not. But no one can suggest that they were not told." Yet the top AIG management still did not know how bad the situation was.

On November 23 AIG transferred $1.55 billion to Goldman as "good faith" collateral. That was it. An acknowledgment of losses, an admission of the truth. Cassano told Habayeb the opposite, that this deal should have no effect on the valuations because there was no "science" to the amount. The number was the product of haggling between the two disagreeing firms.

Meanwhile, Athan had an ongoing battle with Merrill Lynch over its collateral call. He began to lose that fight, too. The bank "called our bluff," he wrote to Forster. He was going to see "if there is some way to wiggle some right to dispute on a technicality." The same day, Cassano emailed a report on the collateral calls to top management, stating "all of the counterparties are understanding and working with us in a positive framework."

On November 29 the top AIG executives held a conference call to plan for the investors' meeting. All the senior corporate officers, including AIG's CEO, Martin Sullivan, and its CFO, Steve Bensinger, along with auditors from PwC were on the line. During the call, Cassano tried to explain why his division's valuations differed so starkly from the much lower valuations Goldman was using as a basis for its collateral call, which now was $3 billion. Cassano explained that if AIG used Goldman's methodology, AIG's loss would be $5 billion. The estimate stunned the group. After a moment, Sullivan said that loss would "eliminate" the quarter's profits. Using AIG's own methodology, Cassano attempted to reassure the gathered executives, would reduce the loss to $2.5 billion.

Immediately after the conference call, the two senior PwC partners took aside AIG's CEO and CFO, telling them they were concerned about the company's lack of understanding about how Cassano's valuation model worked. The accounting firm warned top officials that the problems could be so serious that it would have to classify them as a "material weakness," an accounting term meaning that a corporation's numbers cannot be relied upon. The partners cited AIG's "managing" of the valuation process—a damning phrase suggesting that the company was gaming the numbers to make the problem seem smaller than it was.

After the call, Cassano scrambled with his lieutenants to adjust how it valued the portfolio. He met a few days later with executives, who came up with a new way to estimate the value of its losses. One technique put the loss at $5 billion. Another pegged it at "only" $1.49 billion.

The amount was still unacceptably high. Then the executives did something that government prosecutors would eventually regard as devastating actions. The AIG FP executives came up with a valuation trick. Changing valuation measures to prettify a loss when a market turns against a position can be, but is not always, criminal. The executives called it the "negative basis" adjustment. "Negative basis," in the technical jargon, means that the bond bought with cash is less valuable than the bond created through derivatives; in this case, credit default swaps. Why would that be? To buy a bond with cash, the purchaser had to come up with that money. That often meant borrowing. However, a buyer could go "long" a credit default swap with no money down, or at least with little cash. The borrowing raised the cost of owning the cash bond. Therefore, in normal times, the derivative was slightly more valuable by a fraction—mere hundredths of a percent, which are called "basis points." AIG FP's bonds were all derivatives and therefore supposedly more valuable. With the new valuation technique, the company could reduce its loss by overlaying a bit of juice, a boost, because they were derivatives. The Financial Products executives took the losses and then reduced them by a percentage they selected themselves. If the losses were a billion, and AIG decided the negative basis was worth 10 percent, the loss would shrink to $900 million.

Just as AIG was fumbling for a way to reduce the estimates of its losses, the market was coming to the opposite conclusion. Many traders were skeptical about the housing market, and betting against it with credit default swaps. Given the demand for the derivatives, the market was flipping. Investors and traders began to treat the derivatives as less valuable than the cash bonds, not more so. Just as AIG was granting itself a "negative basis" adjustment, the credit market was signaling that an opposite "positive basis" adjustment was needed.

Some top executives got suspicious. Habayeb, skeptical for months, bore in. On Saturday, December 1, he emailed Cassano, pounding him with a series of questions. He asked directly if AIG Financial Products's valuation methodology had changed. Cassano replied that his unit had used various models to estimate the losses and they "have come in within a range of each other." In fact, they had a wide disparity. One had produced the $1.49 billion loss, while the other had come up with an estimate of $5 billion in losses. Cassano implied that the loss estimates were up to the minute, when they had not taken into account the latest market drops. He elided the specifics of the "negative basis" magic. Prosecutors and government investigators came to regard the exchange as one of the most damning interactions that took place in the days, weeks, and months before AIG's crisis.

Cassano and Forster understood that the trading partners—Goldman, Merrill, Societe Generale, UBS, Morgan Stanley—posed the problem. As more banks claimed AIG owed them money, their insistence that AIG Financial Products wasn't facing significant losses became ever more incredible. On December 3 Forster relayed instructions he said came from Cassano: Athan was to withdraw a collateral offer AIG had made to Merrill. Forster explained that the auditors might force them to use it as a basis to value the entire portfolio, creating an immense loss. Athan said he would continue to try to stall.

On December 5 AIG held the investors' meeting. Martin Sullivan reassured the shareholders and the public that AIG was confident in its derivatives valuation processes. The CEO also said that management understood how much subprime risk the insurer had. On the call, Cassano told investors that the losses in November were in the $500 million to $600 million range and that they stood at about $1.5 billion for the year. Neither Sullivan nor Cassano specified just how many billions in collateral calls AIG had received, though Cassano dismissed the requests as "drive-bys." An analyst asked a question about how the firm was estimating its position, because by his estimate, using the public indexes, the losses would be more than $5 billion—much closer to the number that AIG had come up with internally using the more accepted techniques, when not using the negative basis adjustment. Cassano replied that the question was "nonsensical."

Over the next several weeks, Cassano and his group continued scrambling to value its assets—if you believed the account the executives would give later. Forster admitted to Athan in a phone conversation that AIG would be "lucky" to be able to continue to reduce its losses through its negative basis adjustment.

By January 30, 2008, Habayeb had figured out how much trouble they were in. He now understood how much Cassano and his team had used the negative basis technique to reduce its estimates of the losses. He brought it to the attention of a top partner at PricewaterhouseCoopers. The auditing firm stopped permitting AIG FP from using the technique, as Forster and Athan had feared. Habayeb then called CFO Steve Bensinger. AIG's top executives could no longer pretend. The giant insurer had to reveal the devastation to the markets.

Bensinger told Habayeb to ask Cassano whether he had been aware of how bad the loss was before the December 5 investors' call and to ask why he had not disclosed it to corporate officers. Habayeb called Cassano. "Who is asking?" Cassano said. When Habayeb told him "Steve," Cassano said he had to go and hung up.

On February 4 AIG senior management and the outside auditors from

PwC met with Cassano and Forster. The two AIG FP executives attempted to justify how they had valued the positions, but convinced no one. Martin Sullivan talked with Cassano on February 8 and suggested he "retire." A week later, on February 11, AIG came clean to the public: its December 5 disclosures had been erroneous; it had understated its losses by $3.5 billion, and PwC had determined that AIG had "a material weakness" in its internal controls.[3] AIG's stock fell 12 percent. It would continue plummeting.[4]

A year and a half later, by the fall of 2009, at Main Justice, Paul Pelletier and Adam Safwat had assembled that narrative of the AIG Financial Products collapse. Government agents and prosecutors had gathered emails, pored over documents, listened to hours and hours of taped calls, and talked to witnesses. Pelletier supervised Safwat, other prosecutors from Main Justice, and the postal inspectors who worked on the investigation. They had been on this case since February 2008, right after AIG had made its shocking confession to the markets. If this was not a white-collar crime, what was? AIG FP executives knew they were facing huge losses, had motive to hide them, took steps to do so, made erroneous statements, and misled investors.

Nevertheless, everyone on the probe always knew it would be a tough criminal case to bring. They had no doubt that Cassano had tried to fool the top executives and the auditors. But he had been artful. He dropped subtle mentions of what his group was doing. He'd been cute in answering questions from top management, which had no idea what he meant. He'd been smart not to put anything in email.

But, in Cassano, the prosecutors felt they had one of the great villains of the crisis to present to a jury. *Vanity Fair* had labeled him "the man who crashed the world." Along with Lehman Brothers CEO Richard Fuld and Countrywide CEO Angelo Mozilo, Cassano ranked in the first tier of most-despised figures of the financial crisis. He had ruled the unit through terror and intimidation. He repeatedly pronounced Habayeb's name incorrectly, a reflection of his haughty disdain, which the prosecutors expected to exploit.

Was it enough? Could they prove Cassano lied to anyone? What about Forster and Athan? Would they flip if indicted? Pelletier believed in the case. So did Safwat and James Tendick, the postal inspector doing the investigation. The government should bring the indictments based on their evidence, present the facts to a jury, and let it decide. According to the *US Attorneys' Manual*, if the prosecutors believe in good faith that the evidence shows wrongdoing, they are justified in bringing the case.

But the criminal division's leadership did not agree. In the spring of 2010, Lanny Breuer and his lieutenants resolved not to bring any case against AIG executives. The consequences of this decision wouldn't become clear for a while. Each time top government officials had a difficult choice, they did not take the risk and did not bring charges. By shying away, they created a moral hazard, making bankers more likely to take risks the next time. It was also a moral failure.

## "THE MAYOR OF THE BUILDING"

In the fall of 2008, the government effectively nationalized AIG, investing $182 billion (originally putting in $85 billion and more than doubling it later) and taking a stake in the company of 79.9 percent.[5] More than $75 billion of that passed through to AIG's trading partners—mainly Goldman Sachs and Societe Generale, the banks on the other side of Cassano's fateful contracts.[6] The government conducted a backdoor bailout of the banks that had taken advantage of AIG. Public fury about the bank bailouts peaked in March 2009 when it came out that AIG had paid out $165 million in bonuses to employees.[7] After bailouts in the trillions, this relatively small number set off the public.

The US House of Representatives held angry hearings and readied a bill to tax the bonuses at 90 percent.[8] New York Attorney General Andrew Cuomo announced an attempt to seize the bonuses. Senator Charles Grassley of Iowa suggested that AIG employees should, like the Japanese, either resign or commit seppuku. President Obama denounced their greed.[9]

Safwat, Pelletier, and others at Main Justice worked the investigation through 2008, in the waning years of the Bush administration, without interference from a checked-out front office. They interviewed the auditors at PricewaterhouseCoopers as well as third parties such as the Goldman bankers who had tangled with AIG over collateral.

By the fall of 2008, they had a working theory of what the accounting fraud had been. They homed in on the three executives at the Financial Products division—Cassano, Forster, and Athan—believing that they had misled auditors, management, and the public about the true value of the company's assets. The investigative theory had three prongs:

One, Cassano shared information with only a close circle of executives, while terrorizing his employees to make them stop asking questions. People who needed to know information didn't get it and were afraid to ask. Two, the executives took steps to avoid making the collateral calls. They did not tell the complete truth to the auditors or top management about the size and seriousness of those demands. Three, when they could no longer do so, they changed their valuation techniques, using the negative basis adjustment without fully disclosing to anyone its impact.

## TOO BIG TO JAIL

Pelletier's and Safwat's problems started when the Obama administration came in. Early in his tenure, in March 2009, Attorney General Eric Holder wanted an update on the investigation into AIG. Holder stayed calm to the point of evincing boredom. Corporate prosecutions didn't fire his emotions. He kept his feelings to himself. Noting that the insurer had reached both a deferred prosecution agreement and a nonprosecution agreement in recent years with the Justice Department, Holder said, "We ought to be considering a charge" to the corporation if the case materializes.

The head of the fraud section, Steven Tyrrell, spoke up. The taxpayers now owned the majority of the company. An indictment of AIG might shut down the insurer, handing the new owners—American taxpayers—a massive hit. They couldn't indict AIG. They couldn't reach another deferred prosecution agreement that saddled taxpayers with the penalties. "Oh," said Holder, appearing to remember.

Main Justice would, by necessity, have to pursue individual executives, which Pelletier preferred. As he and Safwat pressed forward, the administration resisted. The investigation became a flashpoint within Main Justice; a clash between the old, aggressive cowboy culture personified by Pelletier, and the new, cautious one with Breuer as its figurehead. Breuer disliked Pelletier When Breuer arrived, Pelletier seemed like the mayor of the building. Many staff prosecutors had been inspired by Pelletier. In May 2009, as a young line attorney, Sam Sheldon attended one of the white-collar training sessions that Pelletier ran with a colleague down at the DOJ's National Advocacy Center, where prosecutors go to learn how to manage investigations and trials, in South Carolina. Pelletier mesmerized Sheldon, who was coming from Laredo, Texas, where assistants handled a "rocket docket": a furious load of three hundred to four hundred cases a year dealing with crimes related to guns, drugs, and illegal immigration. Pelletier contended that white-collar cases, while obviously more complicated, should be treated with similar urgency and efficiency, harkening back to Larry Thompson's and Jim Comey's credo of "real-time" prosecutions. He urged prosecutors not to neglect circumstantial evidence, which has the same standing in court as direct evidence. If prosecutors were 100 percent convinced of their target's guilt, it would be okay to take the risk of a difficult trial.

Sheldon wanted to get to Main Justice and join Pelletier. But to the Breu Crew, Pelletier was a puzzle they didn't bother to solve. They saw him as an out-of-control maniac who could blow up a case, taking his and their careers with them. It wasn't just Pelletier; after Andersen, KPMG, Ted Stevens, and Bear Stearns, they sought to avoid overly zealous prosecutions at all. A victory in court was golden, but a humiliating loss damaged prosecutors more than a win boosted them. It could crush careers, as the KPMG case showed.

Pelletier, however, did not worry about losing if he thought the case was just. It requires an unusual person to lack regard for one's future viability. Most people husband their credibility both within the bureaucracy, which prizes collegiality and hierarchy, and with the outside professional world, which values success. The same forces push people to reject others who aren't as politic or ambitious. Pelletier might have been dangerous. He was a rebuke, forcing others to confront their own cowardice. In the new, cautious order, those who are not conscious of their reputations at all times are so unusual that they are dismissed as cranks, their exhortations regarded as rants.

Lanny Breuer was not the only one at the Department of Justice fearful of prosecuting top executives or corporations. The entire institution, laboring under the legacy of Arthur Andersen and the fight over the Thompson memo, became even charier following the financial crisis. Almost immediately after taking power, the new administration faced a decision about what to do about a major bank. In early 2009, just months after the financial crisis reached its apex, the Obama White House deliberated over serious misconduct by UBS, the Swiss bank. The IRS had sued the bank for names of wealthy American clients suspected of offshore tax evasion. Now the Justice Department was negotiating over a settlement and to get the names. Delivering the names might violate Swiss law, however. The case fell to the new Obama Justice Department officials. Breuer had yet to arrive. Holder was recused, since Covington had represented the bank.

The Swiss government had bailed out UBS the previous October. The bank still teetered. The Department of Justice did not want to make the decision alone. The Treasury Department consulted. "There were policy-level deliberations about whether or not [to indict] and whether whatever penalties UBS faced would impact the fragility of the bank itself, but more importantly, systemic risk," says a former top Obama official, "as there should be." It was a "very precarious situation," this person says. Prosecutors believed they could not indict any of the big global banks. On February 18, 2009, UBS entered into a deferred prosecution agreement, on charges of conspiring to defraud the United States by impeding an IRS investigation.[10] While the media covered the UBS negotiations extensively, the Justice Department's settlement instead of an indictment or a guilty plea generated little criticism.

Three years later, public opinion about the Department of Justice's soft treatment of the big banks had shifted. The Holder administration had not recognized the change. The department was trying to resolve a six-year investigation into HSBC, a British bank that had flouted money-laundering rules. HSBC had become the preferred bank for Mexican and Colombian drug cartels, had financed banks with links to terrorism, and had conducted transactions with countries under American sanctions, including Iran and Libya. The amounts reached into the trillions.

HSBC executives repeatedly ignored internal warnings of its shortfalls. At one point, Mexican law enforcement officers told the head of HSBC's Mexico unit that they had a wiretap of a drug cartel leader saying that his bank was the preferred money-laundering destination. The bank did nothing. The cartels even had especially wide boxes to fit into the deposit windows at local Mexican branches to facilitate their cash deposits.[11] The HSBC investigation was not about arcane mortgage securities or arguments about how to value assets on its balance sheet. Here was a simple, straightforward case that would be understandable and outrageous to jurors. The staff pushed for criminal charges.[12]

Holder and Breuer deliberated. By 2012, markets had stabilized, so the worry about disruption from a tough sanction should have receded. As the department worked to resolve the investigation, Breuer sought advice to understand whether the Justice Department could indict a bank of HSBC's size without collateral consequences to the financial markets and global economy. He surveyed Washington regulators. He flew to London to consult regulators there. He had sleepless nights. It troubled him that no regulator discounted the possibility that markets might be disrupted. Meanwhile, George Osborne, the United Kingdom's Chancellor of the Exchequer, and the UK banking regulator, the Financial Services Authority, reached out to their counterparts in the States. Osborne wrote to Ben Bernanke, the chairman of the Federal Reserve, and Treasury Secretary

Timothy Geithner to warn that charging HSBC criminally could lead to a "global financial disaster."[13]

Breuer also canvassed a lawyer who had a direct interest in the outcome: H. Rodgin Cohen, one of the preeminent banking attorneys in the country. Cohen, a partner at Sullivan & Cromwell, was representing HSBC. Breuer pulled Cohen aside during a meeting and asked, "Is any bank too big to indict?"

Cohen, soft-spoken and courtly, replied, "That cannot be the rule."

The Sullivan & Cromwell partner then outlined the questions he would ask if he were assessing whether to indict: Had the company made serious efforts to fix the problem and prevent it from reoccurring? Had it removed the responsible senior managers or punished them? If so, no indictment should be necessary. As it happened, HSBC had taken those steps. This was from the standard defense counsel playbook. Davis Polk's Bob Fiske had used it in the Andersen case, Skadden, Arps's Bob Bennett had done likewise in the KPMG matter, as had countless defense lawyers representing corporations. Emphasize the guilty company's cooperation, remorse, and remediation, the rule goes.

Breuer believed his department was getting tough on the bank, telling Cohen, "The era of banks no longer getting indicted is over." Concerned, Sullivan & Cromwell drafted a press release outlining dire consequences for the bank and told prosecutors it would be made public if HSBC was charged criminally. The statement said other financial institutions would no longer do business with HSBC, forcing the bank to leave certain markets. The implications were clear: indict HSBC, and global finance markets will be disrupted—and HSBC would fan the disruption by putting out the press release.

But the era of avoiding indictments was not over. The staff debated it but never recommended bringing charges or asking for a guilty plea, instead opting for a DPA. Holder and top officials went along. In December 2012 the Justice Department entered into a deferred prosecution agreement with HSBC. The bank paid a sum that seemed spectacular to DOJ officials: $1.3 billion in forfeited profits and $665 million in penalties. The bank agreed to management changes, to make large investments in oversight and compliance, and to have a monitor oversee the agreement.[14]

Not only did the Justice Department not charge HSBC itself, but also it did not charge a single employee. The news was met with public outcry. Department officials explained later that it was too difficult to single out responsible individuals, since the behavior had gone on for so long and had been overseen by so many. They defended the reforms that HSBC had undertaken, but even those were flimsy. By April 2015, the special monitor assigned to oversee them assailed the bank's progress as "too slow."[15]

In testimony in front of the Senate in March 2013, Attorney General Holder acknowledged the problem. "I am concerned that the size of some of these institutions becomes so large that it does become difficult for us to prosecute them when we are hit with indications that if you do prosecute—if you do bring a criminal charge—it will have a negative impact on the national economy, perhaps even the world economy. I think that is a function of the fact that some of these institutions have become too large," he said, adding, "It has an inhibiting impact on our ability to bring resolutions that I think would be more appropriate." He had acknowledged the truth. But then, in response to widespread opprobrium, Holder walked back the remarks.

## "AN ORANGUTAN COULD PROSECUTE STANFORD"

As the AIG Financial Products probe continued throughout early 2009, Paul Pelletier worked on another investigation, into the R. Allen Stanford Ponzi scheme case. Stanford had run a financial services company called Stanford Financial Group that had in actuality been a $7 billion fraud—not quite as big as Bernie Madoff's but still massive. Pelletier had tried to get the FBI to intervene in August 2008, but he couldn't persuade any agents. Stanford collapsed on its own early the next year, and the authorities—lamentably, serving as archeologists rather than detectives—swooped in.

As Pelletier worked on the investigation, Obama won the presidency, and his appointees came into the building. Almost right away, the front office worried both about the case and Pelletier. Once, after a briefing on Stanford, Breuer, now the head of the criminal division, demanded, "Now everybody tell me about the admissible evidence." He regarded Pelletier as a bullshit artist. Gary Grindler, then Breuer's number two, rode Pelletier. In May 2009 Grindler forwarded a news report of a governmental filing, asking if Pelletier and his boss, Steve Tyrrell, the head of the fraud section, had reviewed it. "We need to be apprised of the positions that are being taken in this matter," he wrote. Pelletier responded that he'd reviewed it and was "truly confused as to what you need to be apprised of," adding that the government had not taken any new position. Grindler explained that since it was such a high-profile case, the front office required constant updating. Pelletier pushed back. "Sorry, sorry, sorry," Grindler replied. "Does this place such a large burden on you?"

Pelletier felt so. He'd never seen a front office dun him with petty requests and nettlesome tasks. They chastised him on small details and raised alarms at any possible hint of negative press coverage. The micromanagement was annoying enough. But the Breu Crew's behavior raised a worse specter. The Main Justice staff believed that the front office—the political appointees—shouldn't get involved in cases to that degree of detail; it increased the potential for political meddling.

In June 2009, after weeks of delay, Pelletier urged Breuer and the front office to give a thumbs-up or thumbs-down on the Stanford indictment. Breuer called Tyrrell, Pelletier, and the other prosecutors involved to his office, where his inner circle surrounded him. The new assistant attorney general of the criminal division appeared unhappy to be put in this position so early in his tenure.

"These are my first months on the job, and you guys have me in a tough position," he said. "You are advocating bringing this case very strongly, and my back is really up against the wall. I am going to remember this. I am not going to forget this."

Pelletier was barely four feet outside Breuer's office when he said loudly, "Holy shit!" Breuer cared, he thought, about his image. If something went wrong, Breuer would exact revenge. Pelletier was on notice.

Pelletier would say, "An orangutan could prosecute Stanford." His crimes were obvious and easy to prove. When Pelletier and a colleague trained prosecutors at the National Advocacy Center, they explained a white-collar conviction is only half the job. Then comes restitution. To help make Stanford's victims whole, Pelletier wanted to go further: to look at the lawyers, banks, and all the Stanford enablers. He wanted to go after Societe Generale, which had done banking for Stanford. Greg Andres, who replaced Grindler as the number two in the fraud section, told him, "I don't give a shit about Stanford II," meaning the follow-on cases. The Main Justice front office passed on investigating the French bank further. The Obama administration Department of Justice was demonstrating its preference for cases against the scammers who made the headlines rather than pursuing the larger, systemic actors who allowed crimes like Stanford's to flourish. The Enron Task Force, by contrast, had gone after Merrill Lynch and NatWest bankers. Up in the Southern District of New York, Madoff prosecutors took years to go after his enablers at the banks and never charged individual executives from firms that helped him.

Fed up with Pelletier, Breuer pushed him off the case in August 2010. In March 2012 the Department of Justice won at trial against R. Allen Stanford. A jury convicted him of fraud and obstruction charges. A judge sentenced him to 110 years in prison. The government never pursued any enablers of his Ponzi scheme.

## FRONT OFFICE MEDDLING

The Obama administration's cautious attitude worked to the advantage of the AIG Financial Products executives. AIG executive Andrew Forster's lawyers managed to protect many of his materials, saying they were subject to attorney-client privilege. After the withdrawal of the Thompson memo, prosecutors had little ability to fight the assertions. Forster's attorneys kept at least eight of the executive's phone conversations, which they said contained "legal advice" about the derivatives contracts and collateral calls. The defense pressed in other ways. The government would have a conversation with the company's counsel. Then it would hear that the lawyers for the executives knew what had been said. In the old days, prosecutors would have scolded the company's lawyers and might have prevented those conversations. Now they weren't allowed to object at all.

In early 2009 Pelletier and Safwat began telling defense attorneys that some executives were "targets," including Cassano, Forster, and Athan. They particularly thought that Athan might flip. Like many prosecutors, Pelletier and Safwat believed that witness testimony makes white-collar cases. Documents are often technical and dry. To some less aggressive government types, calling Athan a "target" this early in the investigation violated unspoken white-collar mores. In Justice Department parlance, people who testify fall into one of three categories: "witnesses," who may have observed something prosecutors want to discuss; "subjects," who may have been involved more directly; and "targets," who prosecutors believe could be indicted based on the current evidence. Investigations are supposed to proceed slowly. An early threat is viewed as just not cricket. The Breu Crew felt Pelletier and Safwat had been too aggressive.

Tom Athan would prove no pushover. He had a powerhouse legal team protecting him: Debevoise & Plimpton's Mary Jo White and Andrew Ceresney, the same pair that had represented Bank of America chief executive Ken Lewis. Tyrrell heard that White was complaining about Pelletier, concerned that Main Justice had already come to its conclusions about the case. She succeeded in coloring how the case was viewed within the Justice Department.

Concerned, Rita Glavin, a front office official, sat in an interview (known as a proffer) with Athan. White and Ceresney accompanied him. Pelletier, Safwat, and Tyrrell were outraged. The front office's micromanagement during Stanford was one thing, but this meddling took it a step beyond. Such active front office participation in investigations was highly unusual.

White and Ceresney laid out their arguments for why Athan was not culpable. Glavin interrupted Safwat and asked questions that seemed to those closest to the investigation as sympathetic to White's and Ceresney's positions. In one melodramatic moment, Glavin pulled Tyrrell, Pelletier, and Safwat out of the meeting to chastise them. She found White convincing and exited the Athan interview even more discomfited than she'd entered it. She viewed Pelletier's and Safwat's conduct as unprofessional. They were overreaching. In her view, Pelletier and Safwat kept representing their case as stronger than it was. She warned Breuer that the case was weak.

## "NOT A SCINTILLA OF DOUBT"

By early 2010, Breuer and Andres and the front office had lost faith in the AIG FP case. The micromanagement hurt the case. The front office received too many updates, seeing the investigative ups and downs. Pelletier understood that every complex investigation took a natural course. The government gathered information, developed theories, and then sometimes discovered new information that made the conclusion less clear. At each new turn, the front office grew more worried. Officials were upset that no one at AIG had yet pointed the finger directly at Cassano. The government had no damning emails from Cassano himself. Perhaps he was too clever. Top AIG officials had been incurious about the state of Financial Products's business and had let Cassano skate with vague reassurances too often. Sometimes Justice Department officials would mock Safwat and Pelletier for the case's lack of direct evidence, as if that were the only way to make a case.

By late 2009, the AIG investigation case shifted. Early on, auditors from PricewaterhouseCoopers insisted that Cassano and AIG Financial Products never told them about the negative basis adjustment. But now the government found out that wasn't exactly true. Investigators found a handwritten note in the margin of a document from the PwC auditor suggesting that Cassano had briefed the accountants on how AIG Financial Products was booking its credit derivative positions. The scribbled note suggested at least one auditor understood something about the negative basis technique. This raised the possibility that Cassano hadn't been entirely misleading, as auditors had told prosecutors initially. AIG FP's defense lawyers viewed the note as reasonable doubt in and of itself.

But this piece of evidence was only one elliptical handwritten piece of marginalia. The partner couldn't say why he wrote it down, who said it, or what the person had meant. Was this truly an investigation killer? People conducting the probe didn't think so. The note did not change that AIG Financial Products executives had resisted taking losses or reaching collateral deals with counterparty banks in order to avoid losses and then had taken steps to hide their actions and mislead people. James Tendick, the postal inspector who worked the case, found the decision confounding. "We still saw red flags of accounting fraud," he says. If the office shrunk from complex investigations in the face of one problematic fact, nothing or nobody would be indicted, he believed.

The prosecution team held heated debates about it. Some worried about the evidence, but others favored indictments, with Pelletier as the strongest advocate. But if that wasn't forthcoming, then he, Tendick, and the agents wanted to continue their investigation—at the least. Sometimes the Department of Justice needed to bring a case even if victory wasn't assured. The AIG cases were righteous prosecutions. Good things happen when you indict, they argued.

The defense lawyers sensed weakness with the DOJ's potential case. In a series of meetings, defense lawyers argued that Athan and Forster had certainly struggled with valuing the difficult-to-understand securities but never misled anyone. As Kathy Ruemmler had known when she worked the Enron case for the Justice Department's task force, more often than not, white-collar suspects truly believe they have done nothing wrong. Their defense lawyers reinforce those beliefs. Cracking them takes time and effort and pressure. If defense attorneys can see that the government is split or sense any vulnerability, flipping becomes almost impossible.

That spring, Breuer and Andres discussed the case with Pelletier, Safwat, and the team several times. The higher-ups probed the prosecutors on the evidence. They asked about their chances of winning. Chances of winning? Pelletier had never been asked that! No other boss had been concerned with trying to estimate the likelihood of victory. "You can always undermine a case in white-collar when you are required to guarantee a win," he reflects. "If all they do is sit down to hear Athan's attorneys give the closing argument and conclude the case is weak, the front office is creating an overwhelming burden. What they wanted was a perfect, airtight case. With these kinds of cases, you're never going to get that."

Pelletier did not want to provide an answer to Breuer. Juries and judges were unpredictable. Any white-collar case can be lost at trial. This case was even more complicated than usual, and with excellent defense attorneys.

Pelletier started to realize what had dawned on so many prosecutors before him: "These motherfuckers will never authorize the case," he thought, "and if we somehow get them over that hurdle and we lose, I will be fighting for my job." Pelletier and Safwat knew what had happened in the Ted Stevens case. He felt the front office had blamed the staffers for their mistakes. "I knew that the end was coming soon for me," he says. "I knew I couldn't stay in the department in the kind of high-stakes litigation we were doing; that with the first fuck-up, my career was over anytime. You are trying to make a difference, pushing the envelope; you are just doing your job, bringing hard but righteous cases. Things can go bad in a thousand ways, many of which you could never imagine and most of which you have little control over."

Pelletier thought he had no choice but to undersell the case. If he didn't, and they lost, he and Safwat would be dead men at the Justice Department. Pressed, Pelletier answered that they should bring the case. It was a righteous prosecution, but he'd put the chances of winning at 40 percent. That was all Breuer and Andres needed to hear. The Justice Department would abandon the investigation.

It's possible that Breuer was right. Perhaps no provable crimes had been committed. Alternatively, perhaps Pelletier and Safwat hadn't set their sights high enough. The Financial Crisis Inquiry Commission, the body Congress set up to examine the causes of the crisis, had the opposite interpretation: that the Justice Department should have gone after AIG's top executives. The FCIC believed AIG's top executives had misled the public and referred that case to the Justice Department.[16] If Cassano had disclosed the methodologies and the losses, higher management should have been investigated more thoroughly. Pelletier and Safwat didn't believe they had uncovered strong enough evidence that upper management knew of the problems and covered them up. Andres and Breuer certainly never pushed that line of inquiry. The FCIC made multiple criminal referrals covering a variety of financial firms involved in the 2008 financial crisis. All withered away without any significant attention paid to them at all.

Pelletier took one last desperate gambit. Andres, acting on Breuer's order, told Pelletier to have Safwat write a memo explaining why they were going to decline to prosecute. Pelletier had Safwat fill the memo with all the details and evidence to compose a prosecution memo in the guise of a declination memo. Pelletier wanted to demonstrate just how much evidence they had in the case and to put it in the record. The front office would have to reckon with all of it before making a final decision to wind up the probe. Safwat wrote what both thought was a knockout twenty-six-page document. Andres took a look at this long document and flipped out. He insisted they cut it way down for Breuer's benefit. They rewrote it, reducing it to four pages. The Justice Department officially passed on a prosecution.

Pelletier believes today that Cassano should have been indicted. "He conspired to mislead the American public about AIG's losses. Period. Not a scintilla of doubt." In May 2010 the Department of Justice dropped the AIG Financial Products investigation.

Passing on one investigation is understandable; passing on every single one starts to speak to something else: a cultural rot. Adam Safwat saw it more clearly than most Justice Department staffers. In addition to investigating AIG Financial Products, his job was to keep track of the financial crisis investigations across the country for Main Justice. Safwat made the rounds to prosecutors across the country: to New York to get an update on the Lehman investigation; to Los Angeles to get up to speed on Countrywide; to Seattle to hear about Washington Mutual. The Feds dropped plenty of subpoenas on banking officials, but that was more or less it.

Clearly, there wasn't a commitment to digging in. One by one, the financial crisis criminal investigations fell to the decision not to take the risk: Countrywide, Washington Mutual, CDO wrongdoing, mortgage-backed securities transgressions, Lehman Brothers, Citigroup, AIG, valuation games, Bank of America, Merrill Lynch, Morgan Stanley. There were no indictments.

The aftermath of 2008 called for aggressiveness. The people demanded it. The politics were favorable. The Department of Justice had chances to bring cases against companies and executives. Public trials would have presented the evidence. Juries would have decided if crimes had been committed. That this fear of failure took hold when it did is tragic.

*Chapter Fifteen*

# RAKOFF'S FALL AND RISE

ON OCTOBER 19, 2011, THE SEC ANNOUNCED WITH a flourish that it had reached a $285 million settlement with Citigroup over charges that the bank misled investors about a mortgage investment.[1] Citigroup had created the instrument, called Class V Funding III, in early 2007 and filled it with bad assets that the bank wanted off its books as the housing bubble burst. Then the bank sold them to unwitting investors. The bank lulled investors into a false sense of confidence by assuring them the deal would be handled by a supposedly independent firm, similar to ACA in the Abacus case. In truth, Citigroup had foisted the rotten assets onto the firm, which went along with it because it received a fee. Citigroup made $160 million on the deal. Investors lost hundreds of millions.

The Citigroup agreement was the SEC's third settlement with banks over bad behavior in the market for collateralized debt obligations. The SEC had settled with Goldman over Abacus and JPMorgan over another deal. It brought no other cases against either but merely scolded the banks and moved on, searching for one bad deal at other major firms. Now the agency had come to Citigroup for its own one-and-done settlement. Brad Karp, the chairman of Paul, Weiss, whose firm had been brought in on the Bank of America case in front of Judge Jed Rakoff, represented Citigroup.

As he negotiated for Citigroup, the Paul, Weiss team studied the previous SEC settlements. When Goldman settled the Abacus charges, the investment bank made a show of contrition by issuing a statement of apology and paying up beaucoup bucks—at least from the investment bank's perspective. JPMorgan Chase had gone second and paid a penalty of $133 million ($154 million total, including disgorgement). That was the number for Citigroup to beat. In addition, JPMorgan settled only under a charge of negligence. Citi, too, wanted to avoid a stronger charge. Every detail mattered in a settlement. Even though the bank wouldn't be admitting wrongdoing, what it wasn't admitting was important.

Born in 1959, Karp has boyish features and knowing eyes. He speaks softly and so genially that people couldn't help but feel as if he enjoyed their company. Since he was so frank (or expert in giving the appearance of frankness), they couldn't help but enjoy his. His outward manner served his fierce negotiating skill. When Karp met with the SEC, he defended his client deftly. Citi was hardly a master criminal, he insisted; in fact, it was the biggest victim of the CDO business by far, having lost $30 billion on the investments. Citigroup was the schmuck at the poker table.

Despite occasional tough SEC talk, Karp and Paul, Weiss got what they wanted. Citi agreed to pay a $95 million penalty (on top of $160 million in disgorged profits), less than JPMorgan. The bank scored a negligence charge, a lesser charge than Goldman's. Citigroup, of course, did not admit any wrongdoing; that was beyond habit at the agency. It almost had morphed into religious ritual. The SEC also charged a low-level banker and none of his superiors, just as it had done in the Abacus case with Fabrice Tourre.

Now, as with every one of this type of settlement in the Southern District, the case had to be assigned randomly to a judge. The day it happened, a colleague came into Karp's office at Paul, Weiss and said, "You are never going to believe this." Who should have gotten the Citigroup case but Judge Jed Rakoff. Karp understood the implications. Rakoff was not going to be happy with the settlement at all. And Rakoff fever was spreading on the bench. In 2010 Citi had been "Rakoffed" by a federal judge in the DC circuit over an SEC settlement. Now it looked as though it would get Rakoffed by the original article. Karp did not want to see all of his good work for his client undone. He began planning for the worst.

Jed Rakoff may not have had the inside view that James Kidney had of the SEC, but from the outside, the situation reeked. Three years after the financial crisis, no top executives had been charged with any crimes. The SEC had barely brought any actions and mainly charged low-level, tangential miscreants. Rakoff's first salvo, against the Bank of America settlement, created the beginnings of a movement. But since the parties had revised the terms so quickly, it had stalled. The judge was not done. He could take another shot at the intellectual bankruptcy of the no-admit, no-deny settlements.

As soon as they learned Rakoff had been assigned the case, Paul, Weiss lawyers called the SEC. When they were negotiating the settlement, the agency and the bank had been adversaries. Now they were allies, determined to defend their agreement in united fashion against the judge. When Rakoff put questions to both parties about the settlement, they both worked up responses. The two teams talked on the phone about how to answer.

Rakoff moved his docket with alacrity. The next month, on November 9, 2011, the judge held a public hearing with the SEC and Karp. With the press scrum and associates from law firms all over the city filling his courtroom, Rakoff, obviously pleased, couldn't help but begin the hearing coyly: "I'm reminded of Humphrey Bogart's famous comment in *Casablanca*: 'Of all the joints in the world, you chose to come here.' But I'm delighted to have you all."

Rakoff made it clear how unhappy he was with the weak settlement. The SEC's knocking knees could be heard from the press release. He dove right into questioning an SEC lawyer, Matthew Martens. A former clerk for then Supreme Court chief justice William Rehnquist, Martens had been put in a difficult, almost ludicrous position. Rakoff discussed the four criteria on which he was supposed to judge settlements: the settlements must be fair, reasonable, adequate, and in the public interest. Now, the SEC, in its responses, seemed to argue that settlements did not, as a matter of law, have to be "in the public interest." Martens had to defend this line of argument.

Rakoff raised another case the SEC had brought in front of him. In that matter, the SEC itself contended its settlements were—and were required to be—in the public interest. Which was it? Martens gamely explained that his own agency had been incorrect earlier.

"So are you saying that if I found that a settlement was—giving due deference to the SEC—fair, reasonable, and adequate, but, still looking at the equities, did not serve the public interest or even disserved the public interest, that I would be compelled" to okay it? Rakoff asked.

While of course the agency believed that all of its settlements were in the public interest, Martens said, he went on to explain that the judge did not get to decide: "I do not respectfully believe that's part of the analysis." Fair, reasonable, and adequate were it.

"It's an interesting position," Rakoff mused. "I'm supposed to exercise my power but not my judgment."

The judge continued, complaining about the no-admit, no-deny language. How was one supposed to interpret whether the allegations were true or not? "You make very serious assertions," he said. "Your own complaint labels them securities fraud. And yet your adversary is not in any legally formal way admitting those. They remain unproven in a court of law."

Martens countered: "Citi has agreed to pay a substantial sum of money in response to our allegations. And they have not denied the allegations. We don't believe in that instance that the public is left wondering what occurred in this case."

"Let's find out," said Rakoff. "Let me ask Mr. Karp. Do you admit the allegations?"

Karp stood up and stepped forward. "We do not admit the allegations, Your Honor," Karp said in a low, even voice. He went to sit back down, paused, and then added: "But if it's any consolation, we do not deny them," he added. The courtroom tittered.

"I understand that. And I won't get cute and ask you what percentage of Citigroup's net worth is $95 million because I don't have a microscope with me."

When Rakoff probed about the consequences to Citigroup from this settlement, Karp explained they were minimal. Citigroup could deny the charges where it mattered—in court—if it had to defend itself in any private litigation based on the transaction or similar ones. The bank could present the facts as it saw them, not as the SEC claimed. The SEC settlement, Rakoff was pointing out, was toothless.

Karp parried the notion that the settlement was without consequence, but Rakoff was skeptical. When Karp listed off the reforms the bank had agreed to—that Citigroup had new management and had overhauled its practices, its compliance structures, and its oversight—the judge couldn't help but snap, "I'm glad to know that Citigroup had such a remarkable change. And I'm sure the economy might have benefited from it having come sooner."

Then Rakoff moved on to skewering the SEC about the flimsiness of the negligence charge. He noted that the agency, in the separate action against the low-level Citigroup banker whom it charged in conjunction with the bank settlement, used language indicating that Citigroup undertook its actions knowingly and intentionally.

"Your complaint says that Citigroup marketed the securities being picked by Credit Suisse as having various attributes; but, in fact, there was a portion of real dogs that were picked by Citigroup, and Citigroup had turned around as soon as they had completed the sale or as soon as the offering had begun and started dumping those dogs on the investors." The judge had given a near summary. "So how can that be negligence?"

Martens gave an answer encapsulating the central weakness with its investigations. It couldn't figure out how to identify wrongdoing by high-level executives. "The problem, Your Honor, is identifying an individual who both had the relevant information and who was involved in the disclosure process." The Citigroup employee, a low-level banker named Brian Stoker, was the only one who both had full knowledge of the deal and was in a position to object to the disclosures, but didn't, the agency's lawyer contended. No other Citigroup employee, according to the SEC, had the same view.

During the hearing, Rakoff made it clear that he hadn't missed the effects of Karp's advocacy on behalf of his client. The SEC's complaint contained allegations that were tougher than those it made against Goldman in the Abacus transaction. Yet the agency entered into a softer settlement. What did the SEC and the public achieve from this settlement besides a "quick headline"? Rakoff wondered. Not much. The fine was "pocket change." He pointed out that Citigroup was a recidivist, noting the SEC did little to punish repeat offenders.

The SEC and Karp came out of the hearing convinced that Rakoff would reject the settlement. They assumed the judge would ask them for more facts about how they reached the agreement. Karp resolved to resist, having learned from past experience. He wasn't going to have Citi furnish more facts. Bank of America had been burned when Rakoff put facts in his opinion, because the plaintiff's lawyers used them in their class action suit, winning an enormous $2.4 billion settlement.[2] Citigroup couldn't afford a similarly disastrous judicial finding as had befallen Bank of America. The potential exposure Citi faced was much worse, perhaps on the order of tens of billions.

Citigroup now needed to make an ally of its ostensible overseer, the SEC. Paul, Weiss had a series of conversations with agency officials, including the head of enforcement, Rob Khuzami; his deputy, Lorin Reisner; and a few others. Rakoff had set a trial date for the two parties. The bank did not want to give any admissions.

The SEC assured Citigroup's lawyers it would not cave to Rakoff. (After a stint at the Justice Department, Lorin Reisner joined Paul, Weiss.)

Rakoff didn't take the intermediate step to request more information. He felt the two parties were blowing him off. He decided to skip right over it.

## MINDLESS AND INHERENTLY DANGEROUS

The ruling came easily to Rakoff. He'd been thinking about the issues for a couple of years now. He did most of his thinking and writing on the weekends and at night, but this draft took only an afternoon. Good judges keep the societal context out of their rulings, focused on the narrow legal issue before them. Rakoff tried to put the crisis and recession out of his mind. He had read an infuriating *New York Times* story pointing out how many times Citigroup was a repeat offender. He concluded he could not grant his okay when he was not presented enough evidence.

His younger, verbose days were long past. Rakoff now kept his rulings short. This one came to fifteen pages, pithy even by his standards. He ran it by his clerks to check the citations. After a quick second look the next day, November 28, he issued the ruling.

Rakoff could not approve the settlement "because the court has not been provided with any proven or admitted facts upon which to exercise even a modest degree of independent judgment." He explained: "An application of judicial power that does not rest on facts is worse than mindless, it is inherently dangerous.

"When a public agency asks a court to become its partner in enforcement," Rakoff wrote, "the court, and the public, need some knowledge of what the underlying facts are: for otherwise, the court becomes a mere handmaiden to a settlement privately negotiated on the basis of unknown facts, while the public is deprived of ever knowing the truth in a matter of obvious public importance."

He then exposed the central problem with the settlements: they undermined any notion that justice had been served. The regulator could claim victory, but the corporation could just as easily claim it was making a nuisance payment to make the government go away. A settlement "that does not involve any admissions and that results in only very modest penalties is just as frequently viewed, particularly in the business community, as a cost of doing business imposed by having to maintain a working relationship with a regulatory agency, rather than as any indication of where the real truth lies."

As much as Judge Rakoff claimed to have put the financial crisis out of his mind when coming to his decision, it clearly informed his pen. "In any case like this that touches on the transparency of financial markets whose gyrations have so depressed our economy and debilitated our lives, there is an overriding public interest in knowing the truth," he wrote.

Rakoff arrived at a view of the problem with corporate law enforcement. The government did not hold companies and executives accountable. The settlement culture had corroded the Department of Justice and the SEC. As Rakoff says, "When you can settle cases so easily, you lose your edge. You lose your ability to go after the really tough cases and to penetrate the really sophisticated frauds because you haven't been put to the test" of a public trial.

The public went wild, or as wild as it can get over a judicial opinion. The press profiled Rakoff. Letters of support poured in, more than in the Bank of America case and more than in his death penalty case. Rakoff viewed the centerpiece of his argument as a request for facts. He was not calling for an abolishment of the SEC's mode of settlement. The press, however, focused on the settlements.

## A NARROW VIEW OF THE LAW

Citi and Paul, Weiss were now worried. Rakoff set a trial date for July 2012. Hoping to avoid an ugly public airing of the entire case, which would be a PR problem even if Citi prevailed, the law firm appealed. It needed the appellate court to act fast. They needed to figure out the right legal argument to get the circuit's attention, and get the appeals court to stay the decision. Routine defendants, even those with legitimate constitutional issues to put before an appeals court, can wait years for responses. If it had merely desired to lay down a legal principle, the appeals court could have just as easily waited for the trial and then made a ruling later. But one of the most prominent law firms in the country working for one of the largest and most powerful corporations in the world managed to generate fast results from the court.

On March 15, 2012, a Second Circuit Court of Appeals panel stayed Rakoff's decision, delaying the trial. The panel laid into Rakoff's reasoning, dismissing it. "The scope of a court's authority to second-guess an agency's discretionary and policy-based decision to settle is at best minimal," the panel wrote.[3]

Rakoff's critics read into the fairly standard legalese of the ruling a tone of harsh personal rebuke. Rakoff felt it, too. He professed to not taking things personally but couldn't help feel a little twinge. "I was bothered by the tone," he says. The judge who authored it "obviously decided I was a dumbbell and wrote the opinion accordingly. That hurt."

Being overruled generates complex feelings. "If you're never reversed on appeal," Rakoff told a reporter, "you probably have taken too narrow a view of the law."[4] Once judges worry about reversals, Rakoff felt, they were lost. They no longer were trying to do what they thought was right. "The glory of the penal court is independence," he says.

He may have respected the court system, but it didn't mean he couldn't poke fun. Back in 2001, Rakoff wrote "The Court of Appeals" for the Courthouse Follies, to the Irving Berlin tune "A Couple of Swells" from the movie *Easter Parade*. His stage direction was for three hobos to enter and go through a garbage can, bring out black robes, and put them on. Then they began to sing:

> We're the Court of Appeals.
> We're very, very big deals.
> We're not the sort
> On District Court,
> To us, they are just schlemiels.
> Circuit judges are we.

The pride of judic'ary
We work
We do?
From ten to two,
At least every week in three.
Those district judges leave things such a mess.
Thank God it's we who get to second guess.
Second guess.
We would vote for affirming 'em,
But their thinking's rather light.
We would vote for affirming 'em,
But it just would not be right.
We would vote for affirming 'em,
But it wouldn't be much fun.
So, we'll keep on reversing 'em,
Yes, we'll keep on reversing 'em,
Oh, we'll keep on reversing 'em
Till they're done.

Now again, Rakoff took solace in doggerel. Though he hadn't lost his sense of humor, others were not so amiable. After his Citigroup ruling, with another Southern District reunion coming up, Rakoff proposed to Rob Khuzami, his longtime friend who was now the head of enforcement at the SEC, that they sing a song together. He had written lyrics based on the Irving Berlin tune "Anything You Can Do," from the musical *Annie Get Your Gun*. In the original, Annie Oakley says to marksman Frank Butler, "Can you bake a pie?"

Frank Butler says, "No," and then she says, "Neither can I."

Rakoff's version was, "Can you bake a pie? Don't admit or deny." Khuzami was game initially. But in vetting the proposal, the drudges in the government vetoed his participation.

Rakoff did build a bridge with Brad Karp. One day a call came in to Karp's office. Rakoff was on the line. The judge said, "I know I've been ruling against you, but you are an excellent lawyer." They talked amiably, and then Karp suggested dinner.

Rakoff loved to collect younger lawyers as friends and contemporaries. Karp, sixteen years younger, and Rakoff began having dinner every several months, often with their wives and other lawyers, at restaurants around Manhattan: Il Gattopardo, the Leopard, Telepan. Karp would join Rakoff and another federal judge, Denise Cote, as guest lecturer at a class up at Columbia Law School taught by Rakoff's close friend, the prominent securities law professor Jack Coffee. Karp even sent a snow globe with a caricature of Rakoff to the judge, which he placed on his crowded desk.

Given the sharp tone of the court's stay, Citigroup and Paul, Weiss figured they were in the clear. The actual appeal, they assumed, would be anticlimactic. They were right. Though the parties had to wait years and received a little scare during a subsequent argument in front of the Second Circuit, on June 4, 2014, the appeals court reversed Rakoff.

To some extent, Judge Rakoff had boxed himself in. A logical conclusion of his opinion was that the government should or could never settle cases without getting admissions of wrongdoing first. While agencies had become addicted to settlements without admissions, settlements serve a purpose. But the appeals panel did not make this point. Instead, it sought to ratify that a judge was, indeed, nothing much more than a rubber stamp. The district court had "abused" its "discretion by applying an incorrect legal standard."

"The primary focus of the inquiry," the court wrote, "should be on ensuring the consent decree is procedurally proper."

Rakoff didn't agree. "Boy, is that nonsense!" he says. The standard includes the words *fair* and *reasonable*. "Is 'fair' about procedure only? Is 'reasonableness' about procedure at all?" he says. "They took all the lifeblood out of the standard. I went further in one direction. They went further in the other direction."

On August 5 he grudgingly approved the settlement. The appeals court "has now fixed the menu, leaving this court with nothing but sour grapes," he wrote.[5]

## THE BUSINESS FRIENDLY COURTS

The Citigroup ruling was of a piece with how the courts have been ruling on securities enforcement for years. The business of law had changed. The incentive structure of the prosecutors at the Department of Justice had changed. And the judiciary had changed as well. The Supreme Court turned more sympathetic to business and more skeptical of government regulation and enforcement. The shift began in the 1970s, during the Warren Burger court, but accelerated in the court of John Roberts, who became chief justice in 2005.

The Roberts court is the most business friendly since World War II, according to a study looking at about two thousand decisions from 1946 to 2011.[6] The 2010 *Citizens United v. Federal Elections Commission* case, in which the court ruled that corporations were allowed to spend unlimited amounts in elections, is perhaps the best known of the group of rulings that widened corporate rights and protections. But the high court has also moved to protect corporations from class actions and human rights lawsuits; increasingly granted summary judgment, where the court decides quickly, without a full trial, in favor of corporations; and ratcheted up the scientific standards upon which claims against businesses can be made. Over a series of rulings, the Supreme Court has allowed companies to put clauses in their contracts to force customers into arbitration, a forum that favors large companies, rather than the court system. In *Wal-Mart Stores, Inc. v. Dukes et al.*, in 2011, the high court raised the bar on discrimination class action suits. Another ruling, *Comcast Corp. et al. v. Behrend et al.*, in 2013, made certain class actions almost prohibitive.[7]

On social issues, the views of liberal and conservative justices diverge cavernously. On economic and corporate issues, the two sides have much less daylight between them. The Supreme Court upheld abortion rights, affirmative action, and marriage equality, but expanded corporate rights and narrowed prosecutorial power. In the wider world of politics, conservatives have stirred the social anxieties of their base for decades as a smokescreen to mask their aid to big business. Liberals made a political choice to favor social reform over resistance to business impunity.

The Second Circuit Court of Appeals, the most influential appellate court for securities law, has similarly turned friendlier to business. The court has become, in recent years, less sympathetic to securities fraud cases. The Second Circuit has a storied history of pioneering rulings on social issues, but it has not been a lionhearted populist court when it comes to reining in Wall Street. New York, the Second Circuit's major city, is a company town that manufactures paper: instruments such as stocks, bonds, and derivatives. The Second Circuit has hometown bias for Big Finance.

By the 2000s, a shift to the right began to become clearer. The Second Circuit started to become a more reliably pro-business, pro-defendant court. The appeals court gave more skeptical receptions to the government, district court judges who ruled harshly against white-collar defendants, and private lawyers who took on large corporations. No court, though, was pro–criminal defendant. The government still won the majority of its cases, and the appeals courts affirmed the vast majority of the rulings. But lawyers discerned a change.

In 2006 the court overturned the conviction of star technology investment banker Frank Quattrone because the lower court's jury instructions allowed the jury to reach a verdict without finding enough evidence against him. The Second Circuit upheld Judge Lewis Kaplan's ruling in *United States v. Stein*, the KPMG case in 2008.[8] The court threw out Pelletier and Safwat's convictions of the Gen Re executives. And now it had upheld the SEC's ability to make namby-pamby settlements.

What explains the courts' shift? Big business, seeing a crisis as it became more regulated in the 1960s and 1970s, counterattacked. In 1971 Lewis Powell, a partner at a Richmond, Virginia, law firm, wrote a memo for the US Chamber of Commerce calling for American business "to wake up and tell their story and that of the free enterprise system." The corporate world faced threats from government oversight and activists such as Ralph Nader. Powell called for responses not only in the courts but also in academia, the media, and the Washington world of think tanks and lobbyists.[9] Just two months later, President Richard Nixon appointed Powell to the Supreme Court, where he authored rulings that began to expand free speech protections beyond the realm of politics and into the commercial world.

Over time, the Powell initiative reaped success. A new right-wing faction arose: the antigovernment libertarian. Starting in the 1970s, the conservative movement funded legal efforts at think tanks and through lobby groups, such as the Business Roundtable and the US Chamber of Commerce. The legal world, especially, was deluged with these new conservatives. Classic conservatives were more deferent to government power. Liberals leaned pro-defendant, but more for the poor, indigent street criminals. That left corporate criminals with money but less power and few true friends. Then came the rise of the libertarian judge. The Democratic Party shifted, too. Democrat-appointed judges more often came now from private practice, where they had represented corporations. These new judges might be socially liberal yet willing to give corporations more sympathetic hearings.

The government backed down from fights to preserve its powers and retain verdicts. Despite this lack of assertiveness, the courts seem to worry about the opposite problem: that prosecutors are too aggressive and abusive. The Second Circuit appears to want to provide a countervailing force to ambitious US attorneys. Southern District US attorney Rudolph Giuliani propelled himself into New York's Gracie Mansion in 1993 by parlaying a series of tough and media-friendly prosecutions of mobsters, politicians, and Wall Street bankers, traders, and lawyers in the eighties and early nineties. Higher courts largely affirmed Giuliani's early prosecutions. In later years, though, he began to get reversed more often. Giuliani had become hubristic, but it also seemed that the appellate court appeared to want to lean against this government aggressiveness. The same sentiment seemed to arise with Preet Bharara, who has served from 2009 through the present day. He was another top federal prosecutor who roused cries of abuse from the defense bar and alleged white-collar miscreants. In 2014 the Second Circuit in *United States v. Newman and Chiasson* overturned Bharara's marquee convictions of two hedge fund managers, ruling that the fund managers were too removed from the source of the insider information and did not know that the source was deriving a personal benefit. The decision threw insider trading law into disarray.

## RAKOFF FEVER

For Rakoff, the Second Circuit's sympathy for the corporation had resulted in a public spanking. He had lost the battle, at least in the courts. But in between his initial ruling and his reversal, Rakoff had emerged victorious. He had become a celebrity. In his chambers, he hung up a framed article with the headline "'Rakoff Fever' Sweeps the Federal Bench." A "Rakoff effect" swept the courts. He inspired at least seven federal judges to raise questions about SEC government settlements or to reject them outright. Another judge laid into a settlement with the Federal Trade Commission.[10]

Judge Rakoff first noticed the change in an opinion from Eastern District Court federal judge Fred Block. Reading a law blog, Rakoff saw that Block used the words "chump change" to refer to the paltriness of a particular SEC settlement—a reference to Rakoff's "pocket change."[11]

Judges had the power to review most settlements. Despite the Second Circuit's Rakoff rebuke in the Citigroup case, judges were not going to stop scrutinizing them. Facing more skeptical judges, regulators began seeking tougher settlements, if gingerly. (In another, less salutary effect of Rakoff fever, the SEC and the Justice Department also began to develop settlements that did not require judicial reviews.)

After the Second Circuit's stay but before its final ruling, on October 3, 2012, SEC chairwoman Mary Schapiro invited Judge Rakoff to speak with enforcement lawyers at the agency. That same year, the House Financial Services Committee held a hearing on the no-admit, no-deny practice. In May 2013 Massachusetts's liberal firebrand Senator

Elizabeth Warren, who began to make lax regulatory enforcement a cornerstone of her political message, wrote a letter to the new chairwoman of the agency, Mary Jo White, excoriating the habit. White wrote back defending it.

Then, in an abrupt turn a month later, in June 2013, White announced a change in policy. No longer would the SEC treat no-admit, no-deny settlements as the only option; it would now seek guilty pleas. She explained the agency would seek such admissions only when the misconduct was egregious. Such were the times that this incremental and commonsense change seemed momentous, especially to those announcing it.

Both the SEC and the Department of Justice, as much or more out of political pressure than true conviction, began to seek admissions in a small handful of cases. The Department of Justice wrung guilty pleas out of several major financial institutions, including Credit Suisse and UBS. A group of banks pleaded guilty to manipulating foreign exchange rates. The SEC also scored a handful of admissions. The admissions had a disappointing quality. The Department of Justice canvassed regulators to make sure they wouldn't be compelled to do anything drastic in response to an admission of guilt, such as pull a bank's license. Regulators assured prosecutors that they would not do so. So the wrongdoers were insulated from the consequences of their bad behavior, even as they admitted it. The reputations of the malefactors did not seem to suffer. After they admitted wrongdoing, bank stocks usually rose in response. Investors considered the problem resolved. The government worded the admissions and guilty pleas in a manner that insulated the entities from private lawsuits. In the past, regulators had seen private lawsuits as an adjunct to their mission. Now they were entering into settlements that undermined those suits.

Rakoff always had a different view of what a judge could be than many of his colleagues did. When he'd worked for the government as a prosecutor, he couldn't easily speak his mind. On the defense side, he'd often take positions that were the exact opposite of what he believed. But a judge can speak his or her mind. Despite this freedom, few did. In his years on the bench, the legal profession turned ever more inward, valuing complexity, jargon, and specialization. Rakoff was, by contrast, turning expansive.

He had long ago given up ambitions to rise to a higher court. Only a handful of judges talk to the press and write for lay audiences. Rakoff had long understood the importance of the media and public perception. He had always given speeches and sat on panels, and expressed himself with his typical commitment to bluntness. In 2004 he'd written for the American Bar Association's journal, *Litigation*, an article titled "Is the Ethical Lawyer an Endangered Species?" But he had usually been addressing legal audiences. Now Rakoff felt like he should begin to express himself publicly. "The judicial code in no way discourages judges from speaking out about general issues," he says. "Indeed, the code of judicial ethics actually encourages judges to speak out."

He could be more influential as a public intellectual. And it was more fun. He kept up a grueling schedule of speeches, appearances, and advisory roles. In addition to training Iraqi judges, he served as the cochair of a National Academy of Sciences committee on science and the law. If the firms no longer had lawyer-statesmen, nothing prevented him from becoming one.

Having seen the SEC in action and waited in vain for the Department of Justice to bring high-profile cases, Rakoff decided to speak out publicly on the topic of corporate enforcement. In May 2013 he gave a speech in Australia examining why there had been no criminal indictments of high-level bankers after the financial crisis. After he returned, he went onto the website of the *New York Review of Books*, his favorite publication, found the email address, and submitted a version of the speech blind. To his delight, Robert Silvers, the long-serving editor of the *Review*, published it in its January 9, 2014, issue.

Others had written on the topic, but Rakoff's hit the hardest in the circles that mattered. He questioned the Department of Justice's assertions that the cases were so hard to prove. He asked why prosecutors had not considered charging executives with "willful blindness," a well-established legal doctrine making it illegal for people to consciously avert their eyes from bad behavior. Rakoff skewered Lanny Breuer for having mischaracterized the criminal law. In an interview on the PBS show *Frontline*, Breuer had said that prosecutors had to prove not only that a party made a false statement but also that those on "the other side of the transaction relied on what you were saying."

Rakoff explained that this assertion "totally misstates the law. In actuality, in a criminal fraud case, the government is never required to prove—ever—that one party to a transaction relied on the word of another. The reason, of course, is that that would give a crooked seller a license to lie whenever he was dealing with a sophisticated buyer."

No one of Rakoff's stature had spoken out in this way. Through his jurisprudence and his public writings, the judge had lost in the courts, but enforcement policy had changed. The Justice Department's argument that it had looked as hard as it could for criminals and evaluated cases on their full merits no longer convinced.

## *Chapter Sixteen*

# "FIGHT FOR IT"

It was Cinco de Mayo. May 5, 2011. "How fitting," thought Paul Pelletier. The holiday commemorates the Mexican army's 1862 victory over France at the Battle of Puebla during the Franco-Mexican War of the 1860s. Pelletier, of French and French-Canadian heritage, nursed his defeat. The Breu Crew had forced him out of his beloved Department of Justice. Tonight was the wake, a classic DOJ going-away party and roast. The turnout was so overwhelming that they spilled out of the restaurant and into an adjacent atrium. Maybe two hundred had come. "How amazing was that?" Paul marveled.

Pelletier looked up and saw people in the balcony. People gathered around the fountain. His family was there. His sister and her husband came. His old US attorney from Miami made the trip up. People flew in from all over the country. The party had maybe the broadest grouping of agents any prosecutor had ever managed to gather in one place—and those guys didn't like mingling with one another. The FBI, the US

Department of Health and Human Services Office of the Inspector General, the Postal Service, and the Secret Service all sent agents. Even Lanny Breuer, ever the politician, came.

Aside from Breuer, however, the front office and power class of DC had passed. The attendees weren't looking to make an appearance to further their Washington careers. Though Pelletier's going-away party wasn't well attended from the top-down at the Justice Department, it was thronged by the bottom-up: secretaries, paralegals—anyone who had worked for him over the years. Guys who had put thirty years in at the department and knew what the government was losing came to see him off. These were people who felt love and loyalty toward Paul Pelletier.

It was a rousing night. One of the Miami mafiosi who had joined Pelletier up at Main Justice emceed the affair. Every time they anticipated profanity, the children were hustled out of the room. "Send the kids away for this one!" someone would say, to another round of laughter. The emcee started in with his PowerPoint presentation, with some innocuous pictures of the Pelletier brood. Then he showed a photo with the washed-out, overexposed colors of the 1970s: Paul with blond hair to his shoulders, in a green plaid tuxedo with black lapels as wide as vulture wings, awaiting his prom date. Still another had Paul in his cop's uniform, giant mustache over a ridiculous grin, reaching for his gun. The presentation was peppered through with Pelletierisms: "Don't be a p%$$y!"; "Do your J.O.B.!"; "Keep doin' what you're not supposed to be doin'!"

Speakers made paeans to his supervisory ability and his love of public service. One slide read: "There is a simple Paul Axiom—one that defies all other laws of physics and science: If Paul is on your side, anything can be accomplished. If he is not—you are screwed."

Pelletier held off drinking too much. He wanted to take it all in and be lucid for his speech, which came at the end. At last, his friend handed Pelletier the microphone. He looked up to the balcony and around. He began by giving out presents to colleagues and supervisors. To Denis McInerney, the cautious head of the fraud section who had so tormented him with his passivity, he produced a white cue ball and told him, “Here. This is my left nut.” After the round of joke presents, he launched into his farewell speech.

“The best piece of advice my father ever gave me,” he began, “was: ‘Never argue to crazy people.’ ” Everyone laughed. “That really prepared me to work at Main Justice . . . particularly the front office.”

But Pelletier had some serious points to make. “Everyone talks about wanting to do the right thing,” he said. Whenever there was a tough decision around these hallways, that was the mantra. Every prosecutor had been told many times, “Do the right thing.”

“I don’t know what the fuck that means,” he said with a shrug. People laughed. Something might be “right” to one person and not to another. How can you tell? Too often, it was an empty platitude at the Department of Justice. Well, you can tell if you are willing to take a risk. “If you are prepared to fight for it, then it’s probably the right thing,” he said. But the corollary was true, too: “If it’s the right thing, then you have to fight for it. If you are not willing to fight for it, then don’t give me that bullshit.”

The fighting man of Main Justice presented a gift to the Department of Justice. As he put it, “The department is dispossessing its history.” He wanted to remedy that. His voice choked, and his eyes watered.

“The department,” he said, “gives so much to us; we need to give something back.” He gave the department two giant photographs. “They cost me a fortune,” he assured the crowd.

One photo contained all the attendees for the fortieth anniversary party for the fraud section. The second depicted everyone who had come to the fiftieth anniversary. The department is about the people who staff it. The politicians come and go. The honor belongs to the people and the mission.

The night had been so emotional and had gone so fast. That weekend, Paul Pelletier cleared out his office.

## BEYOND THE FINANCIAL CRISIS

The Department of Justice does not merely struggle to prosecute top bankers. The problems go beyond the financial crisis and beyond the financial sector. Even corporate prosecutions that do not involve powerful banks face profound problems. In April 2012 the *New York Times* ran a blockbuster story by star investigative reporter David Barstow. He had uncovered that Walmart's Mexican operation had carried out a "campaign of bribery to win market dominance." Walmart found through its own internal investigation at least $24 million in suspicious payments. The lead agent on the probe determined that American and Mexican laws had probably been broken. Then, the report went on to demonstrate, Walmart's leaders, including then CEO H. Lee Scott Jr., kiboshed the investigation. Barstow won a Pulitzer for the stories the following spring.[1]

After the *New York Times* approached Walmart but before the story came out, the company reported itself to the Department of Justice for possible violations of the FCPA. The retail giant had known about the bribery allegations but had shown little inclination to reveal itself to the government until the *Times* forced the matter. The Feds initiated an investigation. The Walmart investigation generated a cornucopia for law firms. The retailer spent upward of $700 million on legal advice and compliance improvements.[2]

All that money was well spent. The Justice Department's probe proceeded slowly. The government was frequently stymied. Many of the allegations involving Mexico were old. The statute of limitations had run out. The Mexican government barely cooperated, ignoring the Department of Justice's official requests for assistance for years.

Walmart seemed to have had troubled operations in other countries as well. Justice Department officials investigated its activities in India, China, and Brazil. The department tried to put resources into the case. There were two prosecutors from the Eastern District of Virginia and three from Main Justice. But early on, prosecutors couldn't get the FBI or the IRS engaged. The agencies did not prioritize the case.

Part of the Big Law playbook when corporations are under federal investigation is for them to appear as if they are taking the allegations seriously. Companies ease out culpable executives. Prosecutors tend to look favorably on such earnestness. After two years, Walmart eased out at least eight executives who had been involved in the suspicious activities or had been alerted to them. Their retirement packages, however, remained intact. The Department of Justice probe lasted years but slowed dramatically by 2015. In October of that year, the *Wall Street Journal* reported that the federal investigation found no serious violations.[3] That Walmart made its changes and avoided any charges or even a deferred prosecution settlement suggested that the gentle farewells had been carried out with at least the tacit approval of the government. One of the biggest corporate scandals in years faded away to nothing.

Similar problems plagued the corporate investigations into Toyota (for the unintended acceleration problems with its cars) and General Motors (faulty ignition switches). Toyota did not cooperate fully with the Southern District's investigation. As for GM, the Department of Justice could not identify any executives who had the full picture of the carmaker's problems and responsibility for fixing them.

Even dedicating resources does not bring success. After the Deepwater Horizon platform exploded in 2010, killing eleven people and causing the largest oil spill off the US coast in history, Lanny Breuer gathered together a task force to investigate. BP paid $4 billion in criminal penalties and pleaded guilty. But by early 2016, the task force had come up almost entirely empty against individuals. It had started by charging low- and midlevel executives with a variety of crimes, but began withdrawing charges and dropping executives from its cases as courts ruled against it. The government ended up withdrawing manslaughter charges against two midlevel supervisors. Some of the cases were dismissed. Finally, the Justice Department lost three trials against executives.[4]

Even supposed triumphs against corporate executives often underwhelm. In late 2015, the Justice Department brought coal baron Don Blankenship, CEO of Massey Energy Company and a power in West

Virginia, to trial for his role in creating unsafe conditions at the Upper Big Branch mine, the site of a terrible explosion that killed twenty-nine miners in 2010. The jury found Blankenship guilty, the first conviction of a top executive for a workplace safety violation.

But the success was tempered. Massey was not in the Fortune 500 and presented an easier target than, say, a Goldman Sachs or JPMorgan executive. More troublingly, the jury found Blankenship guilty only on one count of conspiracy, a misdemeanor for breaking federal safety rules, and exonerated him on two other felony counts.[5] Even with a local jury made up of people supposedly sympathetic to dead miners, such cases don't go smoothly. The judge sentenced Blankenship to one year in prison, the maximum allowed by law. People hailed the result, relieved that at least yet another CEO wasn't getting off. But for a man who had been so cavalier about jeopardizing the lives of his employees, one year seems paltry.

Defenders of the Department of Justice maintain that these failed corporate investigations did not indicate a lack of will or skill. They highlighted, these people argue, the inherent difficulties with prosecuting corporate crime. Corporate responsibility is diffused; the top leadership of giant corporations make few day-to-day decisions and none without the advice of lawyers and accountants. They say that prosecutors didn't make cases because there were not cases to make.

But then the Department of Justice started changing its corporate investigative practices and policies. In making these shifts, the department tacitly admitted that its past actions were indeed wanting. The age of deferred prosecution agreements gave way to what we have today: prosecutors and the SEC, responding to criticism from Judge Jed Rakoff, academics, the media, lawmakers, and activists, made companies admit wrongdoing and plead guilty.

The government now assigns corporate monitors to oversee its settlements more frequently. By early 2016, the 2008 crisis had resulted in nearly $190 billion in fines and settlements from forty-nine separate financial institutions.[6] These new arrangements are no more satisfying than the previous period's. The fines continued to hit the shareholders, not the wrongdoing executives. Prosecutors almost never named any individuals. Portions of the penalties often were tax deductible (since they were partially disgorging profits). All the big banks lined up to make mea culpas over mortgage securities misdeeds. For mortgage securities abuses, JPMorgan paid $13 billion, Bank of America paid $8.5 billion, and others paid giant sums. The big banks paid up for foreclosure abuses; for manipulating interest rates and foreign exchange rates; for trading with sanctioned countries; for money-laundering-monitoring failures; and for conflicts of interest in their research activities.[7]

But many of these settlements became less impressive once the particulars came out. The banks could earn credit for building affordable housing or helping mortgage holders, earning bonus dollars for each dollar actually spent. Perhaps worst of all, the department's statements of fact that went along with these settlements were terse documents that contained little detail about who did what to whom and when. The banks wrote checks and in exchange won the ability to shield their executives from punishment and the specifics of their activities from the public eye.

The government celebrated its admissions of wrongdoing and guilty pleas, but they are little more than a semantic change. Prosecutors took extreme measures to minimize the regulatory consequences for a guilty plea. Regulators did not pull licenses. They did not ban them from government programs. The guilty pleas had only symbolic value. They lacked force just as much as the old settlements did.

## REVERSING THE HOLDER ERA

The Eric Holder era at the Justice Department ended in April 2015. He rejoined Covington & Burling in July. The nation's first African American attorney general had the third-longest tenure in history. Mythili Raman, the acting head of the criminal division, who had been in the role since Lanny Breuer left in early 2013, departed in the spring of 2014 to reunite with Breuer at Covington. James Cole, the deputy attorney general, left in early 2015 to join another top white-collar defense firm in Washington.

The regime of new attorney general Loretta Lynch moved to fix the flaws of Holder's term. Few, if any, would admit as much publicly. Leslie Caldwell, who headed up the Enron Task Force, became the chief of the criminal division. She brought in her old friend and colleague from the task force, Andrew Weissmann, to be the chief of the fraud section. Weissmann had spent several years after Enron as a zealous advocate for his corporate clients at Jenner & Block, but he retained his reputation as a tough prosecutor.

As chief of the criminal division, Caldwell remained guarded both in public and private. But she told friends that she found the post-financial-crisis investigations puzzling. She thought it was a failure that the department did not prosecute Angelo Mozilo, the chief executive of Countrywide. The case had been given to the Sacramento office, with an assist from the Los Angeles office. According to Caldwell, the offices didn't have the skill or experience to bring the case to a successful indictment.

For Lynch's new deputy attorney general, the Obama administration chose Sally Yates, the US attorney general for the Northern District of Georgia. Confirmed in May 2015, Yates did not fit the model of early Obama administration clubby Beltway types. She was a career prosecutor, having worked for the Justice Department for twenty-six years. Yates had gone to the University of Georgia School of Law, not an elite institution. Four months later, she published the Yates memo. The memo was the first overhaul of the Department of Justice's corporate prosecutorial policies of the Obama administration.

The Yates memo was seen for what it was: an implicit critique of the previous Holder administration and a tacit admission that it had not done enough to prosecute top executives. Yates created new policy: the department had to go after individuals again. The key element of a corporation's cooperation, the memo stated, was to identify individuals who had done something wrong. Without naming the people responsible, a company could not get credit for cooperation and softer penalties.

Some critics welcomed the new policy but with caution. What

individuals would corporations be required to finger? How would the Justice Department prevent a company from scapegoating some low-level schnook? In the SEC case on Abacus, the agency had been satisfied to go after Fabrice Tourre and no one else. Time and again, the government went after only one low-level employee, a "lone gunman theory" of corporate crime. Would the Yates memo change this practice? Would the department's investigations go high enough, to the boardroom and the top corporate offices? Would prosecutors still be overly reliant on Big Law's internal investigations of its clients?

The department even undermined these minor improvements. At the same time that it issued the Yates memo, Main Justice also set up a compliance office to vet corporate cooperation. The ostensible aim was to determine whether companies were cooperating or not and whether they were receiving due credit. The effect would be to add to the bureaucracy. The move added yet another layer of evaluation for investigations, making it harder to bring cases against either corporations or high-level individuals.[8]

The Yates memo suggested that the Justice Department's policy had changed, but had it altered the way the department conducted business? The answer soon appeared to be no. In the first year of the Yates memo, the DOJ scored few obvious successes. When it brought a civil action against Goldman Sachs in 2016 for mortgage-related wrongdoing in the lead-up to the financial crisis, the Department of Justice named no individuals. The government charged individual executives from Volkswagen for having faked its emissions tests, but it did not appear likely to charge top officials at the German carmaker.

Despite its fanfare, the Yates memo lacked ambition. Implying a criticism of past practices is not the same as making one out loud. The Justice Department did not reckon publicly with its corporate white-collar prosecution problem. It had not conducted any serious analysis of whether it had lost crucial prosecutorial tools over the last several years or had devoted insufficient resources. It did not grapple with whether staff prosecutors have the incentive or skills to work on long cases against well-fortified defendants. There is no sign that the Justice Department thinks it should recruit different types of lawyers to bring cross-fertilization and a wider range of experience: older and more experienced lawyers; those with public interest law backgrounds rather than those from private practice; those from less prestigious institutions. The government has not grappled with how dependent it is on Big Law's internal investigations for its own probes. The government gave no indication it understood it needed fewer insiders and more outsiders. The Justice Department published no reports about the issue. The department made no request from Congress for new statutory powers to prosecute white-collar criminals. The lack of public introspection doomed the policy change.

## BACKLASH

A broad coalition of corporate interests had led a fight against prosecutorial power in the post-Enron period. After Enron, Arthur Andersen, WorldCom, Adelphia, and Tyco, corporations, their lobbyists, and the white-collar defense bar revolted. They forced the Department of Justice to roll back the Thompson memo, depriving the government of tools and techniques to push corporate investigations. They won in courts, especially at the appellate level. They took advantage of the prosecutorial abuses and overreach. Over the decade, these interests changed the way the government enforces the corporate criminal code.

Now the same forces gathered again to fight the Obama administration's initiatives. Modest as the corporate guilty pleas and the Yates memo were, the corporate lobby recognized a new danger: the government understood how inadequate its corporate investigations were. And so, in response to the reforms of the post-financial-crisis era, the same interests tried to roll out the same campaign from more than a decade earlier. Why shouldn't the defense bar go back to the exact same playbook it had employed then? It had worked.

Former members of the Obama administration, now working for corporations, attacked the Yates memo, just as former Department of

Justice officials had assailed the Thompson memo. In November 2015, two months after the memo was issued, two former high-level officials in Obama's Justice Department went public with criticisms. Both had just moved to private practice. Mythili Raman, the former acting head of the criminal division and now a partner with Lanny Breuer at Covington & Burling, feigned hurt at what the Yates memo was saying about her tenure. "I was surprised, a little, that there was even an implicit acknowledgment that there weren't sufficient prosecutions brought against individuals, which, in my view, wasn't necessary to say," she said. "You bring cases if you have the evidence, and if you don't, you don't. That's about as plain as I can say it."[9]

Yates's direct predecessor, James Cole, attacked the new memo more forcefully. In a speech at a meeting of the American Bar Association, he revived the same argument levied at the Thompson memo: the Department of Justice was attacking the sacred attorney-client privilege. He went on to argue that with the Yates memo in effect, corporations will clam up to their lawyers. Executives won't cooperate with investigations. The new Justice Department policy will backfire, he warned.

Yates denied that the department had any interest in violating attorney-client privilege, just the way that Larry Thompson had walked similar hallways at similar conferences making similar arguments. Cole responded to Yates with condescension: "With all due respect, I'm not sure she entirely understands."[10]

The defense bar worked the government refs almost every week in the nation's capital and in New York. Prosecutors gathered with white-collar defense attorneys at cocktail parties, conferences, dinners, and meetings where they heard about the mistakes they were making. In the real world, the public saw a pandemic of corporate misconduct and a lack of accountability. At these gatherings, however, white-collar defense lawyers of Washington insisted that their clients were the real victims. They had been bent to their knees beneath the weight of the government's arbitrary, capricious, and harsh punishments.

Whether they have faux Louis XVI gold leaf moldings or bare beige walls suitable for thumbtacks, whether they serve cantaloupe and honeydew of the same pale color and tastelessness or acai smoothies with chia seeds, all Washington conference halls are the same. Lawyers, politicians, policy makers, and lobbyists gather to practice the genteel art of public influence. At the Securities Enforcement Forum in the fall of 2014, held in the capacious halls of the Four Seasons Hotel in the Georgetown district of Washington, DC, top regulators gathered with defense bar worthies. The marquee panel included Andrew Ceresney, the enforcement director of the Securities and Exchange Commission, and five of his predecessors. Four of those former SEC officials now represented corporations at prominent white-collar law firms: Robert Khuzami, President Obama's first enforcement director, who now plied his trade at Kirkland & Ellis; Linda Chatman Thomsen, who served at the George W. Bush–era SEC and now worked for Davis Polk & Wardwell; William McLucas, the longest-serving agency enforcement director, who was now at WilmerHale; and George Canellos, who'd just left the Obama SEC to work for Milbank, Tweed, Hadley & McCloy. Even the legendary Stanley Sporkin sat at the end, leaning back in his chair with his legs spread before him, seemingly nodding off on occasion but clearly still attentive.[11]

The conference turned into a free-for-all as the defense attorneys hammered away at regulators about how unfair they had been to their clients, some of America's largest companies. In a subsequent panel, Brad Karp, the chairman of Paul, Weiss, who had won the Citigroup case against Judge Rakoff, laid into the agency about how onerous the punishments have been. There is a "profound sense in defense circles," he said, that there is a scrum of various regulators and enforcement bodies: the SEC, the Justice Department, state attorneys general, the New York State financial regulator, and so on. Karp said that these enforcers had become increasingly politicized and were trying to one-up one another. They "cannot be too tough," "penalties cannot be too large," and there was a "tremendous push toward increasing all of the sanctions," he said, complaining that there was "no consistency other than that penalties and sanctions are much more draconian."

The government representative on the panel, Scott Friestad, the number two enforcement officer at the SEC, was a target of Karp's indignation. In response, Friestad took a shot at other government bodies, saying that he was proud that the SEC wasn't as politicized as other offices and agencies. He noted the SEC didn't do things such as hold news conferences when it issued subpoenas. That could be read as a dig at state officials and the Department of Justice, particularly Lanny Breuer and Preet Bharara, both famous for seeking podiums in front of the press. Then Friestad sympathized with Karp's complaint. "Not to say you don't have a valid point," he said, adding, "It's very tough for a company to navigate those waters." In comments the next day, he had to do the classic Washington retreat, explaining further his concerns that too many regulators around the world were "piling onto" the banks.[12]

Some reformers hoped to expand prosecutorial power when it came to white-collar crime. They discussed extending statutes of limitations and expanding the criminal code. In health and public safety, prosecutors can charge responsible corporate officers criminally (with a misdemeanor). It does not matter if they were not aware of the problems. Some argued to expand that into other sectors, such as finance. Bank failures could cause job losses and economic devastation. Perhaps bankers who drove their institutions to disaster merited such punishment. None of these proposals made progress.

Companies recognized the threat. When a movement arose to respond to the country's mass incarceration problem, corporations spotted an opportunity. They pressed their congressional friends to wring concessions out of the reformers. House Republicans attempted to raise the burden of proof for certain crimes committed by corporate executives.[13] The right-wing Heritage Foundation penned a white paper on the need for such "mens rea" reform, referring to the legal term for having conscious intent.[14] Instead of expanding the responsible corporate officer doctrine beyond health and safety violations, the new House language would roll back the ability to make such charges. The law did not pass, but the risk that the Department of Justice would lose more tools against corporate crime remained high.

With Donald Trump in office, corporations have an even friendlier Washington despite his populist rhetoric and pitch as the champion of the working class. He fired Sally Yates, the architect of the DOJ's attempt to improve its prosecution of corporate crime, for a separate reason. She had determined the DOJ could not defend his immigration executive order effectively banning Muslims from entry to the United States. His appointees came from corporate boardrooms and Wall Street, especially Goldman Sachs. Meanwhile, Republicans moved to gut regulations, especially those reining in the banks, seeking to eviscerate the Consumer Financial Protection Bureau and roll back Dodd-Frank. Jefferson Beauregard "Jeff" Sessions III took over the DOJ, promising to pull back on its aggressive civil rights enforcement and go after voter "fraud," a Republican obsession and vehicle for voter suppression. The incoming SEC chairman, the Sullivan & Cromwell partner Walter J. "Jay" Clayton, boasted Goldman Sachs as a loyal client and had few public views on securities enforcement, except that the government had gone too far in pushing the FCPA antibribery law, passed in the wake of Stanley Sporkin's enforcement push in the 1970s. Any hope for tougher corporate enforcement appears laughably misplaced.

In January 2013, when Rob Khuzami left the SEC for the law firm of Kirkland & Ellis, the *New York Times* wrote a laudatory article about his tenure.[15] Breuer congratulated him, writing, "Really nice article. You deserve it. I'm glad for you and proud of you."

Khuzami wrote back, "Thx. Make sure the reporters call me when your article is being written."

The articles about Breuer's departure did not hit the same glowing notes. Breuer and his supporters believed he had overseen a significant upgrade in talent, recruiting a class of attorney that Main Justice hadn't been able to secure in the past. He had commanded the first guilty pleas from banks in decades, overseen investigations into currency and interest rate fixing, guided major public corruption cases, and set up the BP Task Force in the wake of the Deepwater Horizon disaster, which supporters praised for having won a guilty plea and large fine from the company itself.[16]

He received little credit for any of those measures, however. In a maddening turn of events for him and his loyalists, Breuer left the Justice Department having become the face of the department's inability to bring cases against Wall Street. That was unfair. The problem was much greater than one man. Yet despite his Washington skills, Breuer was ill-suited to take on such a profound financial and economic crisis. He brought professionalism and caution when the times required audacity and vision. The moment called for a Ulysses S. Grant, but with Lanny Breuer, the country had gotten a George B. McClellan.

Today Breuer works the corridors of power from his post as the vice chairman of Covington & Burling, after one of the longest tenures as criminal chief in department history. The Breu Crew largely went back into private practice, mostly at Covington, and thrived. Greg Andres went to Davis Polk. Denis McInerney returned to join him at the firm. Gary Grindler joined King & Spalding. The Southern District star prosecutors who had taken on high-profile insider trading cases all collected lavishly paid partnerships at the best law firms in New York.

Breuer may have stood out for blame, but few emerged from the post-financial-crisis era of enforcement with enhanced reputations. After returning to Covington, Eric Holder launched himself into political work, fighting for voting rights and against President Donald Trump's anti-immigration push. But he also stood ready to take on corporate work, and signed on with Uber to investigate charges of endemic sexual harassment at the Silicon Valley ride-hailing upstart. In September 2013 James Comey, who had talked so bravely about not being chickenshits at the beginning of the century, took a job as Obama's FBI head. His interventions during the 2016 presidential campaign soiled his hard-won reputation, perhaps permanently. In July of that year, he gave an unusual press conference chastising Hillary Clinton for her handling of her email scandal, while explaining why he wasn't recommending criminal charges in the matter. Prosecutors were appalled, viewing it as a grandstanding spectacle. Good prosecutors do not explain their declinations publicly. To smear the subject of an investigation while passing on charges is regarded as unethical. But the department had been oversharing for years now. The Justice Department had, in less detailed fashion, started to comment publicly when it closed investigations, as it did with AIG and Goldman.

Then Comey reopened the Clinton email investigation eleven days before the election, after the FBI had found new emails—which were not even on her computer, but disgraced former Congressman Anthony Weiner's, who was married to Huma Abedin, a Clinton aide. Comey alerted Congress before agents had reviewed the emails, violating long-standing FBI and Justice Department policy not to go public about investigations right before elections. The FBI closed the matter soon after as the email trove contained nothing new. But the damage to the Clinton campaign was done. (Comey's actions, which helped Trump win the election, provided the pretext for the president to fire him in May 2017. The ouster came during the FBI's investigation into possible Trump campaign collusion in Russian meddling in the election, leading to fears of a coverup and a constitutional crisis.)

Bad judgment, acts of prosecutorial abuse, fears of losing—all could be seen as products of the eroded investigative skills. A senior official goes rogue, as Comey did, because he doesn't have enough faith in the customs of his institution. Abuses happen when a prosecutor doesn't have a strong enough case but goes forward anyway. Senior officials take a pass on indictments because they are too inexperienced to judge the evidence. As the abilities of the FBI, SEC, and Justice Department corrode, they make blunders. The blunders make them more reluctant to pursue riskier paths such as prosecutions of powerful and well-defended individual corporate executives, which leads to more mistakes.

Those who fought hard against the large corporations incurred costs, not rewards. They often left with diminished status and did not alight on such prominent perches as Breuer's. The people who broke with the prevailing culture, such as Paul Pelletier and James Kidney, were pains in the ass and made life difficult for their bosses. Often the people who do so—the whistle-blowers at companies and the prosecutors who take on the powerful—share a character flaw: they don't play exactly by the unwritten rules, they lack diplomatic skills, and they don't understand how to preserve their viability, either within the bureaucracy or for their next job. Their righteousness offends others. Most people act in their own self-interest. They do not. A reputation for toughness was not its own reward.

Justin Weddle, who had suffered public criticism from a judge in the KPMG case, struggled to find work in private practice. Stanley Okula, also a key prosecutor in the KPMG case, stayed at the Southern District—a lifer whom defense attorneys felt free to criticize because he had been assailed by judges. Shirah Neiman, the long-serving and unrelenting government lawyer, was pushed out of the Southern District of New York. Though she was in her seventies, she was not one to retire, so she started a consulting firm. After a long career, Jim Kidney left the SEC and in retirement grew steadily angrier about the agency's shortcomings. Adam Safwat landed a job at the prestigious firm Weil, Gotshal & Manges. Paul Pelletier joined a firm, but he did not take easily to private practice and nursed a hope to return to government service. He never stopped referring to the Justice Department as "we."

Those who took on the large financial institutions from other government roles also suffered. Sheila Bair, who had headed up the FDIC and challenged the Obama administration over its bank bailouts, could not land a prominent corporate or administration position. She became the president of Washington College in Maryland. Ben Lawsky, the former Southern District prosecutor who had risen to become the head New York State financial regulator and had miffed his fellow regulators and the banks with his aggression, did not take a job at a top law firm. One chairman of a major New York firm said the New York bar had blackballed him. Lawsky held out his own shingle as a consultant and attorney.

Corporate whistle-blowers had it even worse. Their lives were never the same. They faced divorce, financial ruin, and joblessness. They wondered whether it had been worth it. They wondered why they had been disbelieved so often by government investigators—when they had been interviewed at all.

Judge Jed Rakoff had a tough time as well. His rulings faced legal setbacks. In 2016 a panel of the Second Circuit Appeals Court threw out a verdict in a civil fraud trial that Rakoff had presided over. The Southern District had brought charges against Countrywide Home Loans, the mortgage bank, for deceptive mortgages it had sold to mortgage giants Fannie Mae and Freddie Mac. The government had also brought charges against one midlevel executive. The jury found the company, now owned by Bank of America, and the executive liable. In reversing the jury, the appellate panel criticized Rakoff's jury instructions. It determined that the judge had erred in his definition of fraud. The panel wrote that since Countrywide had not intended to commit fraud at the time the contracts with Fannie and Freddie were written, the government had not met the standard of proof. Countrywide had intentionally breached its contracts, but that did not constitute fraud.[17] Prosecutors at the Southern District and Rakoff found the decision ridiculous. The Southern District petitioned the panel to review it, a request the higher court rejected.

Rakoff remained undaunted. Now a senior judge, he had more prominence and pluck than ever. He sat as a visiting judge on the Ninth Circuit in California and happened to get a case on insider trading. Rakoff had long wanted insider trading law either resolved by the Supreme Court or clarified by Congress. The Second Circuit in New York had recently overturned some of Preet Bharara and the Southern District's key insider trading convictions. Rakoff took the other side of the argument in his own ruling, setting up a dispute between appellate courts. Rakoff's opinion was full of sly references to a sister circuit, as if he were a dispassionate judge sitting across the country on the other coast rather than a frustrated district court judge right on the home circuit's turf. The Supreme Court picked up the case and resolved it in Rakoff's favor, a triumph.

The higher courts had often been wrong on Rakoff, but the public embraced him. He branched out to write on other judicial topics. After Rakoff had written a *New York Review of Books* article criticizing his fellow judges about their lack of outcry at mass incarceration, a colleague of his, Judge Barrington Parker Jr. of the Second Circuit, complimented him and sent him a present: a blown-up 1906 photograph of a chain gang. Black prisoners in striped jumpsuits work cornfields and stare into the camera. On closer inspection, the prisoners turn out to not be men but boys, with some looking impossibly young. Their cheeks are still full of baby fat, their eyes wet and wide, and their prison suits are far too big for their bodies. The country has continued to put young black men behind bars at alarming rates. Judge Rakoff has cried out about the injustice of the system. He has played a role to change the way the country addresses corporate criminals. But today his United States remains unable to punish the powerful. They still have impunity.

# ACKNOWLEDGMENTS

THIS BOOK HAS ITS GENESIS IN THE 2008 FINANcial crisis, an event as cataclysmic and indelible for my generation as the Great Depression and World War II were for that of my grandparents. Without it, we might not have had the first black president of the United States and we surely would not have Donald Trump and Trumpism.

As a financial journalist, I have lived with the crisis for well over a decade. With only a dim understanding of what I was writing, I warned about it before it happened in articles for the *Wall Street Journal* and *Condé Nast Portfolio*. I wrote about it as it tore the global banking system asunder and devastated lives. After it passed and we were living among the wreckage, I investigated what bankers did to make it worse and profit from it.

After I wrote that series of stories on the collateralized debt obligation market for ProPublica with my colleague Jake Bernstein, I waited for the government to charge bankers with criminal wrongdoing. And waited. The indictments never came.

By late 2010 I was puzzled enough about that bizarre outcome to write a column for ProPublica and the *New York Times* about what I termed a "white-collar slump." The problem nagged at me, and I pitched an article to my editor at ProPublica, Mark Schoofs, that delved into what was going wrong. Stephen Engelberg, the editor in chief, supported it enthusiastically. Eventually we pitched Hugo Lindgren, then the editor of the *New York Times Magazine*, on a piece about why no bankers had been prosecuted after the financial crisis.

Mark edited early, messy drafts of what became the magazine story, never wavering in the belief that I had something important to say. Jon Kelly, the editor at the magazine, put the finishing touches on it, shaping it into a narrative. That story ran in April 2014 but I believed there was more to find out and more to say.

My editors and colleagues at ProPublica have been enormously helpful throughout this process. I'm grateful that Paul Steiger and Steve Engelberg rescued me from unemployment in 2009 with a job offer. Steve stayed with me as I pursued my obsession, teaching me to lift my eyes from the financial minutiae and widen my lens. When I asked for a leave of absence, he and Dick Tofel graciously granted the request.

My agent, Chris Calhoun, buoyed me with his enthusiasm and helped me polish and expand the idea into this book. I'm thankful that Jonathan Karp and Ben Loehnen bought into the vision I had for it—and stuck with the title. Ben gave me meticulous and thoughtful edits. I've learned more about writing from Ben than I had in my previous twenty-odd years of working as a reporter.

New America was generous enough to give me a fellowship. For that I thank Peter Bergen, Kirsten Berg, Fuzz Hogan, and Konstantin Kakaes.

My parents were early and keen readers of the draft. Other early readers and advisors include Jesse Drucker, Chris Leonard, Jennifer Taub, and K. Sabeel Rahman.

I'm grateful for the support and advice I received from Anat Admati, Serge Avery, James Bandler, Neil Barsky, Seth Bomse, Sam Buell, Peter Eavis, Robin Fields, Andrew Foote, Brandon Garrett, David Grais, Peter

Goodman, Scott Klein, Peter Lattman, Carrick Mollenkamp, Fiachra O'Driscoll, Frank Partnoy, Michael Powell, Tom Purcell, Guy Rolnik, Tim Sutton, Eric Umansky, Tracy Weber, Jon Weil, and Leanne Wilson.

Sara Morrison helped with crack research. My excellent fact-checkers Michelle Ciarrocca and Beatrice Hogan saved me from many embarrassing mistakes. Any that remain are mine and mine alone.

I am especially grateful to the many people who spent hours upon hours with me, walking through their experiences and helping me understand the fine points of corporate investigations, prosecutions, and the law. Without their patience, help, and courage, I would not have been able to write this.

Finally, thank you to my wife, Sarah, for her unstinting support and love. My first and best reader, she refined my ideas and added grace to my prose.

# NOTES

## INTRODUCTION

1. Chris Smith, "Mr. Comey Goes to Washington," *New York*, October 20, 2003, http://nymag.com/nymetro/news/politics/n_9353.
2. Jean Eaglesham and Anupreeta Das, "Wall Street Crime: 7 Years, 156 Cases and Few Convictions," *Wall Street Journal* online, last modified May 27, 2016, www.wsj.com/articles/wall-street-crime-7-years-156-cases-and-few-convictions-1464217378.
3. *United States Attorneys' Annual Statistical Report* (Washington, DC: US Department of Justice), www.justice.gov/usao/resources/annual-statistical-reports.
4. Brandon L. Garrett, *Too Big to Jail: How Prosecutors Compromise with Corporations* (Cambridge, MA: Belknap Press, 2014).
5. Brandon L. Garrett and Jon Ashley, Federal Organizational Prosecution Agreements, University of Virginia School of Law, http://lib.law.virginia.edu/Garrett/prosecution_agreements/home.suphp.
6. *Justice Department Data Reveal 29 Percent Drop in Criminal Prosecutions of Corporations* (Syracuse, NY: Transactional Records Access Clearinghouse [TRAC], Syracuse University, October 13, 2015), http://trac.syr.edu/tracreports/crim/406.

7. Ryan Knutson, "Blast at BP Texas Refinery in '05 Foreshadowed Gulf Disaster," ProPublica, last modified July 27, 2010, www.propublica.org/article/blast-at-bp-texas-refinery-in-05-foreshadowed-gulf-disaster.
8. *Federal White Collar Crime Prosecutions at 20-Year Low* (Syracuse, NY: Transactional Records Access Clearinghouse [TRAC], Syracuse University, July 29, 2015), http://trac.syr.edu/tracreports/crim/398. See also *White Collar Crime Prosecutions for 2016* (Syracuse, NY: Transactional Records Access Clearinghouse [TRAC], Syracuse University, September 1, 2016), http://tracfed.syr.edu/results/9x7057c8a7ee9c.html.

## CHAPTER ONE: "THERE IS NO CHRISTMAS"

1. Bethany McLean and Peter Elkind, *The Smartest Guys in the Room: The Amazing Rise and Scandalous Fall of Enron* (New York: Portfolio, 2013), 219.
2. Pamela H. Bucy et al., "Why Do They Do It? The Motives, Mores, and Character of White Collar Criminals," *St. John's Law Review* 82, no. 2, art. 1 (2012): http://scholarship.law.stjohns.edu/lawreview/vol82/iss2/1.
3. McLean and Elkind, *Smartest Guys in the Room*, *xx*, 239.
4. Kurt Eichenwald, *Conspiracy of Fools: A True Story* (New York: Broadway Books, 2005), 180.
5. "Where Are the Faces of the Enron Trial?," Fuel Fix, November 28, 2011, http://fuelfix.com/blog/2011/11/28/the-defendants-of-the-enron-era-and-their-cases.
6. District attorneys are local-level, elected prosecutors who prosecute state crimes and have no connection with the Justice Department, which prosecutes federal crimes. Under longtime district attorney Robert Morgenthau, the Manhattan DA's office had a successful track record of taking on corporate crime.
7. Dan Morse, Chad Terhune, and Ann Carrns, "HealthSouth's Scrushy Is Acquitted," *Wall Street Journal* online, last modified June 29, 2005, ww.wsj.com/articles/SB111702610398942860.
8. Jonathan Stempel, Reuters, "Former HealthSouth CEO Scrushy's Bribery Conviction Upheld," July 15, 2013, www.reuters.com/article/us-healthsouth-scrushy-conviction-idUSBRE96E0TQ20130715.
9. Eichenwald, *Conspiracy of Fools*, 642.
10. Samuel W. Buell, *Capital Offenses: Business Crime and Punishment in America's Corporate Age* (New York: W. W. Norton, 2016), 185.
11. Samuel W. Buell, interview with the author, April 17, 2015 and August 24, 2014.
12. Edward Iwata, "Enron Task Force Faces Big Pressure to Deliver," *USA Today*

website, last modified August 21, 2002, http://usatoday30.usatoday.com/money/industries/energy/2002-08-21-enron-task-force_x.htm.

13. Jeffrey Toobin, "End Run at Enron," Annals of Law, *New Yorker*, October 27, 2003, 48–49.
14. Jonathan Weil, "The Other Shoe Has Yet to Drop in Enron Case," *Wall Street Journal* online, last modified August 5, 2002, www.wsj.com/articles/SB1028495391564229080.
15. "Transcript of News Conference with Deputy Attorney General Larry Thompson Wednesday, October 2, 2002," US Department of Justice, www.justice.gov/archive/dag/speeches/2002/100202dagnewsconferencefastow.htm.
16. Terry Maxon, "Ex-Enron Executive, Wife Plead Guilty," *Sun Sentinel* (South Florida), January 15, 2004, http://articles.sun-sentinel.com/2004-01-15/news/0401150112_1_lea-fastow-andrew-fastow-mr-skilling.
17. "News Conference on Indictment," C-Span video, 32:27, July 8, 2004, www.c-span.org/video/?182612-1/news-conference-indictment.
18. Mary Flood, "Experts See Lessons from Broadband Jurors," *Houston Chronicle*, July 22, 2005, http://www.chron.com/business/enron/article/Experts-see-lessons-from-broadband-jurors-1948046.php.
19. McLean and Elkind, *Smartest Guys in the Room*, 412.
20. Alexei Barrionuevo and Kurt Eichenwald, "In Enron Trial, a Calculated Risk," *New York Times*, April 4, 2006, http://query.nytimes.com/gst/fullpage.html?res=9C03E0D71330F937A35757C0A9609C8B63&pagewanted=all.
21. Peter Elkind and Bethany McLean, "Enron Trial: Devils in the Details," *Fortune* website, last modified March 15, 2006, http://archive.fortune.com/magazines/fortune/fortune_archive/2006/03/20/8371741/index.htm.
22. Ibid.
23. Barrionuevo and Eichenwald, "Enron Trial, Calculated Risk."
24. John R. Emshwiller and Gary McWilliams, "Testimony Links Skilling, Lay to Alleged Effort to Hide Losses," *Wall Street Journal* online, last modified March 1, 2006, www.wsj.com/articles/SB114114167255385382.
25. McLean and Elkind, *Smartest Guys in the Room*, 419.
26. Ibid., 415.
27. Ibid., 420.
28. Ibid., 421.

## CHAPTER TWO: "THAT DOG DON'T HUNT"

1. Eichenwald, *Conspiracy of Fools*, 642–46.
2. Jennifer L. O'Shea, "Ten Things You Didn't Know About Michael Chertoff," *U.S. News & World Report* online, last modified August 27, 2007,

www.usnews.com/news/articles/2007/08/27/ten-things-you-didnt-know-about-michael-chertoff.

3. Flynn McRoberts et al., "Repeat Offender Gets Stiff Justice," *Chicago Tribune*, September 4, 2002, www.chicagotribune.com/news/chi-0209040368sep04-story.html.
4. Greg Farrell, "Roll of Dice Pays Off for Justice," *USA Today* online, last modified June 16, 2002, http://usatoday30.usatoday.com/money/energy/enron/2002-06-17-chertoff.htm.
5. Barbara Ley Toffler with Jennifer Reingold, *Final Accounting: Ambition, Greed, and the Fall of Arthur Andersen* (New York: Currency, 2004), 20.
6. Reed Abelson and Jonathan D. Glater, "Enron's Collapse: The Auditors—Who's Keeping the Accountants Accountable?," *New York Times*, January 15, 2002, www.nytimes.com/2002/01/15/business/enron-s-collapse-the-auditors-who-s-keeping-the-accountants-accountable.html?pagewanted=all.
7. Susan Scholz, *Financial Restatement: Trends in the United States, 2003–2012* (Washington, DC: Center for Audit Quality, July 24, 2014), www.thecaq.org/docs/reports-and-publications/financial-restatement-trends-in-the-united-states-2003-2012.pdf.
8. Robert Kowalski, "Levitt Assails Accounting Industry for Fund Cuts for Oversight Board," TheStreet, May 10, 2000, www.thestreet.com/story/937042/1/levitt-assails-accounting-industry-for-fund-cuts-for-oversight-board.html.
9. Toffler with Reingold, *Final Accounting*, 157.
10. US Securities and Exchange Commission, "Waste Management Founder, Five Others Sued for Massive Fraud," news release, March 26, 2002, www.sec.gov/news/headlines/wastemgmt6.htm.
11. US Securities and Exchange Commission, "Arthur Andersen LLP: Litigation Release No. 17039," news release, June 19, 2001, www.sec.gov/litigation/litreleases/lr17039.htm.
12. Flynn McRoberts et al., "Civil War Splits Andersen," *Chicago Tribune*, September 2, 2002, http://articles.chicagotribune.com/2002-09-02/news/0209020071_1_andersen-partners-andersen-clients-tiger/7.
13. Toffler with Reingold, *Final Accounting*, 148.
14. Kathleen F. Brickey, "Andersen's Fall from Grace," *Washington University Law Review* 81, no. 4 (2003): 926.
15. Toffler with Reingold, *Final Accounting*, 152.
16. Emily Cartwright, "Taken on Faith," *60 Minutes*, July 30, 2002, www.cbsnews.com/news/taken-on-faith.
17. *Wrong Numbers: The Accounting Problems At WorldCom—Hearing Before the Committee on Financial Services, US House of Representatives*, 107th

Congress, Second Session, July 8, 2002, serial no. 107-74 (Washington, DC: US Government Printing Office, 2002), www.gpo.gov/fdsys/pkg/chrg-107hhrg83079/html/chrg-107hhrg83079.htm.

18. McLean and Elkind, *Smartest Guys in the Room*, 161.
19. Ibid., 147.
20. Ibid., 207–8.
21. Ibid., 146.
22. Flynn McRoberts et al., "Ties to Enron Blinded Andersen," *Chicago Tribune*, September 3, 2002, www.chicagotribune.com/news/chi-0209030210sep03-story.html.
23. Garrett, *Too Big to Jail*, 25.
24. Joe Berardino, "Enron: A Wake-up Call," Commentary, *Wall Street Journal* online, last modified December 4, 2001, www.wsj.com/articles/SB1007430606576970600.
25. Dan Morgan and Peter Behr, "Enron Chief Quits as Hearings Open," *Washington Post*, January 24, 2002, www.washingtonpost.com/archive/politics/2002/01/24/enron-chief-quits-as-hearings-open/488a9983-7b0a-490e-9e15-0509d8ab14be.
26. Eichenwald, *Conspiracy of Fools*, 642.
27. Mitchell Pacelle, Ken Brown, and Michael Schroeder, "Andersen Tries Deloitte, Others for a Sale, but So Far, No Deal," *Wall Street Journal* online, last modified March 11, 2002, www.wsj.com/articles/SB1015799139268944800.
28. Carolyn Lochhead and Zachary Coile, "The Enron Collapse: House Panel Slams Firm for Shredding Enron Papers—Andersen Officials Told They Could Be Charged," *San Francisco Chronicle*, January 25, 2002, www.sfgate.com/news/article/THE-ENRON-COLLAPSE-House-panel-slams-firm-for-2880281.php.
29. Flynn McRoberts et al., "Repeat Offender Gets Stiff Justice," *Chicago Tribune*, September 4, 2002, www.chicagotribune.com/news/chi-0209040368sep04-story.html.
30. Jonathan Weil and Alexei Barrionuevo, "Arthur Andersen Is Convicted on Obstruction-of-Justice Count," *Wall Street Journal* online, last modified June 16, 2002, www.wsj.com/articles/SB1023469305374958120.
31. The business wing of the Democratic Party, led by Bill Clinton's Treasury secretary Robert Rubin, certainly supported that financial deregulatory push. Under the influence of the Rubin caucus, the Democrats helped finally raze Glass-Steagall, the Depression-era law separating commercial and investment banking. Clinton signed the Commodity Futures

Modernization Act on his way out the door in late 2000, a law that prevented oversight of the emerging derivatives markets.

32. "Text: Bush on Corporate Reform, Terrorism Funds," On Politics, *Washington Post*, July 8, 2002, www.washingtonpost.com/wp-srv/onpolitics/transcripts/bushtext_070802.html.
33. Joel Roberts, Associated Press, "Senate Adopts Corporate Fraud Measure," CBS News online, July 10, 2002, www.cbsnews.com/news/senate-adopts-corporate-fraud-measure.
34. Brickey, "Andersen's Fall," 959.
35. Ibid., 941–42.
36. Gabriel Markoff, "Arthur Andersen and the Myth of the Corporate Death Penalty: Corporate Criminal Convictions in the Twenty-First Century," *University of Pennsylvania Journal of Business Law* 13, no. 3 (2013): 797–842, http://papers.ssrn.com/sol3/papers.cfm?abstract_id=2132242.
37. Toffler with Reingold, *Final Accounting*, 224.
38. "Interview with Mary Jo White, Partner, Debevoise & Plimpton LLP, New York, New York," *Corporate Crime Reporter* 48, no. 11: (December 12, 2005), www.corporatecrimereporter.com/maryjowhiteinterview010806.htm.
39. US Department of Justice, "Assistant Attorney General Lanny A. Breuer Speaks at the New York City Bar Association," news release, September 13, 2012, www.justice.gov/opa/speech/assistant-attorney-general-lanny-breuer-speaks-new-york-city-bar-association.

## CHAPTER THREE: THE SILVER AGE

1. Lawrence M. Friedman, *Crime and Punishment in American History*, 3rd ed. (New York: Basic Books, 1993), 290.
2. Joel Seligman, *The Transformation of Wall Street: A History of the Securities and Exchange Commission and Modern Corporate Finance*, 3rd ed. (New York: Aspen, 2003), 5.
3. Friedman, *Crime and Punishment*.
4. Seligman, *Transformation of Wall Street*, 71.
5. Ibid., 77.
6. The 2008 financial crisis recapitulated these arguments. Defenders pointed out that risky and opaque mortgage securities and derivatives were legal. They were, but it doesn't follow that common behaviors in the creation and sale of those instruments were always legal.
7. Victor Navasky, "A Famous Prosecutor Talks About Crime," *New York Times*, February 15, 1970.
8. David M. Dorsen, *Henry Friendly, Greatest Judge of His Era* (Cambridge, MA: Belknap Press, 2012), 237.

9. "The United States Attorneys for the Southern District of New York," compiled by the Committee for the Bicentennial Celebration (1789–1989) of the United States Attorney's Office (Southern District of New York), 316, August 2014.
10. Theodore A. Levine and Edward D. Herlihy, "The Father of Enforcement," *Securities Regulation Law Journal* 43, no. 1 (March 2015): 7–27.
11. Seligman, *Transformation of Wall Street*, 449.
12. Ernst & Ernst v. Hochfelder, 425 U.S. 185 (1976), 2016, accessed September 8, 2016, https://supreme.justia.com/cases/federal/us/425/185.
13. Levine and Herlihy, "Father of Enforcement."
14. Nathaniel C. Nash, "Washington at Work: For Judge in Keating Case, Being on the Bench Is Not Sitting on the Sidelines," *New York Times*, January 11, 1990, www.nytimes.com/1990/01/11/us/washington-work-for-judge-keating-case-being-bench-not-sitting-sidelines.html?pagewanted=all.
15. Kenneth B. Noble, "The Dispute over the S.E.C," *New York Times*, April 21, 1982, www.nytimes.com/1982/04/21/business/the-dispute-over-the-sec html?pagewanted=all.
16. Stanley Sporkin, interview with the author, April 1, 2015.
17. Jason E. Seigel, "Admit It! Corporate Admissions of Wrongdoing in SEC Settlements: Evaluating Collateral Estoppel Effects," *Georgetown Law Journal* 103 (2015): 433, http://georgetownlawjournal.org/files/2015/01/AdmitIt.pdf, Vol. 103:433.
18. Stephen Labaton, "Judge Rejects Keating Suit; Sees 'Looting' of Lincoln," *New York Times* August 24, 1990, www.nytimes.com/1990/08/24/business/judge-rejects-keating-suit-sees-looting-of-lincoln.html.
19. Robert S. Pasley, *Anatomy of a Banking Scandal: The Keystone Bank Failure—Harbinger of the 2008 Financial Crisis* (New Brunswick, NJ: Transaction, 2016).
20. Seligman, *Transformation of Wall Street*, 540.
21. Peter Clark, interview with the author, November 10, 2015.
22. Mike Koehler, "The Story of the Foreign Corrupt Practices Act," *Ohio State Law Journal* 73, no. 5 (December 7, 2012): http://ssrn.com/abstract=2185406.
23. A. Timothy Martin, "The Development of International Bribery Law," *Natural Resources & Environment* 14, no. 2 (Fall 1999): 97, www.rmmlf.org/Istanbul/5-Development-of-International-Bribery-Law-Paper.pdf.
24. Stanley Sporkin, interview.
25. Seligman, *Transformation of Wall Street*, 540.
26. Ibid.
27. David S. Hilzenrath, "Judge Jed Rakoff on Free Love, the Death Penalty,

Defending Crooks and Wall Street Justice," *Washington Post*, January 20, 2012, www.washingtonpost.com/business/economy/judge-rakoff-on-free-love-the-death-penalty-defending-crooks-and-wall-street-justice/2012/01/05/gIQAIGKrDQ_story.html.

28. Robert C. Koch, "Attorney's Liability: The Securities Bar and the Impact of National Student Marketing," *William & Mary Law Review* 14, no. 4 (1973): 883–98, http://scholarship.law.wm.edu/cgi/viewcontent.cgi?article=2641&context=wmlr.
29. Stephen Labaton, "Cortes Randell: Student Market Hoax," Archives of Business: A Rogues Galley, *New York Times*, December 7, 1986, www.nytimes.com/1986/12/07/business/archives-of-business-a-rogues-gallery-cortes-randell-student-market-hoax.html.
30. Skip McGuire, interview with the author, October 15, 2015.
31. Koch, "Attorney's Liability."
32. Margaret P. Spencer and Ronald R. Sims, eds., *Corporate Misconduct: The Legal, Societal, and Management Issues* (Westport, CT: Quorum Books, 1995).
33. Louie Estrada, "Anthony M. Natelli Dies," *Washington Post*, March 28, 2004, www.washingtonpost.com/archive/local/2004/03/28/anthony-m-natelli-dies/23ff418e-6819-4685-8955-879e4f1c3d64.
34. L. Ray Patterson, "The Limits of the Lawyer's Discretion and the Law of Legal Ethics: *National Student Marketing* Revisited," *Duke Law Journal* 6 (1979): 1251–74, http://scholarship.law.duke.edu/cgi/viewcontent.cgi?article=2725&context=dlj.

## CHAPTER FOUR: "UNITEDLY YOURS"

1. Rich Cohen, *The Fish That Ate the Whale: The Life and Times of America's Banana King* (New York: Picador USA, 2013).
2. Marcelo Bucheli, *Bananas and Business: The United Fruit Company in Colombia, 1899–2000* (New York: New York University Press, 2005), 71.
3. David J. Krajicek, "Going Bananas: Pan Am Building Suicide in Chiquita Scandal," *New York Daily News*, May 22, 2011, www.nydailynews.com/news/crime/bananas-pan-building-suicide-chiquita-scandal-article-1.143195.
4. Cohen, *Fish That Ate the Whale.*
5. Peter T. Kilborn, "Suicide of Big Executive: Stress of Corporate Life," *New York Times*, February 14, 1975, www.nytimes.com/1975/02/14/archives/suicide-of-big-executive-stress-of-corporate-life-suicide-of-a-top.html?_r=0.
6. Danforth Newcomb, *Digests of Cases and Review Releases Relating to Bribes to Foreign Officials Under the Foreign Corrupt Practices Act of 1977 (As of January 31, 2002)* (New York: Shearman & Sterling, 2002), 76, www.justice

.gov/sites/default/files/criminal-fraud/legacy/2012/12/03/response2-appx-a.pdf.

7. Walter LaFeber, *Inevitable Revolutions: The United States in Central America*, 2nd ed. (New York: W. W. Norton, 1993), 208.
8. Robert D. Hershey Jr., "United Brands Bribe Called 'Aberration': Inquiry Finds the Agreement Not to Be Part of a Pattern," *New York Times*, December 11, 1976, www.nytimes.com/1976/12/11/archives/united-brands-bribe-called-aberration-inquiry-finds-the-agreement.html?_r=0.
9. Newcomb, *Digests of Cases and Review Releases Relating to Bribes to Foreign Officials*, 76.
10. New York Central R. Co. v. United States, 212 U.S. 481 (1909), https://supreme.justia.com/cases/federal/us/212/481/case.html.
11. Garrett, *Too Big to Jail*, 34.
12. Ibid., 35.
13. Arnold H. Lubasch, "Guilty Plea in Foreign Bribe Case: United Brands Fined $15,000 in Plot Involving Honduran," *New York Times*, July 20, 1978, timesmachine.nytimes.com/timesmachine/1978/07/20/110896364.html?pageNumber=72.
14. Jeff Gerth, "S.E.C.'S Future Focus in Doubt," *New York Times*, January 29, 1981, www.nytimes.com/1981/01/29/business/sec-s-future-focus-in-doubt.html.
15. Noble, "Dispute Over the S.E.C."
16. Karen De Witt, "Stanley Sporkin Is on the Case," *Washington Post*, May 28, 1977, www.washingtonpost.com/archive/lifestyle/1977/05/28/stanley-sporkin-is-on-the-case/35db79b1-06e1-473d-a880-d1697067f50e.
17. Levine and Herlihy, "Father of Enforcement."
18. David Einstein, "The Judge Who Rejected Microsoft: Stanley Sporkin Is Known as Aggressive, Unpredictable," *San Francisco Chronicle*, February 16, 1995, www.sfgate.com/business/article/The-Judge-Who-Rejected-Microsoft-Stanley-3044564.php.
19. Dan Carmichael, United Press International, "Judge Criticizes Justice Department," March 12, 1991, www.upi.com/Archives/1991/03/12/Judge-criticizes-Justice-Department/1467668754000.
20. Dan Freedman, "Sporkin Built Reputation by Battling Big Business," *San Francisco Chronicle*, February 16, 1995, www.sfgate.com/business/article/Sporkin-built-reputation-by-battling-big-business-3151584.php.

## CHAPTER FIVE: THE BACKLASH

1. United States Sentencing Commission, *Guidelines Manual* (Washington, DC: US Government Printing Office, 1991), www.ussc.gov/sites/default

/files/pdf/guidelines-manual/1991/manual-pdf/1991_Guidelines_Manual_Full.pdf.

2. Scot J. Paltrow, "Prudential Firm Agrees to Strict Fraud Settlement," *Los Angeles Times*, October 28, 1994, http://articles.latimes.com/1994-10-28/news/mn-55889_1_prudential-securities.
3. Garrett, *Too Big to Jail.*
4. Paltrow, "Prudential Firm Agrees to Strict Fraud Settlement."
5. Dave Michaels, "Obama's SEC Pick Wary of Zealous Wall Street Prosecutions," Bloomberg, February 27, 2013, www.bloomberg.com/news/articles/2013-02-27/obama-s-sec-pick-wary-of-zealous-wall-street-prosecutions.
6. Andrew Longstreth, "A Memo Too Far," *American Lawyer*, January 2007, 13–15, www.americanlawyer-digital.com/americanlawyer-ipauth/tal200701ip?pg=12#pg12.
7. Timothy Harper, "Pepsi One—Larry Thompson Stands Behind an Iconic Brand," Super Lawyers, Corporate Counsel Edition, December 2008, www.superlawyers.com/new-york-metro/article/pepsi-one/944b6a83-f5a9-44da-b346-6bec2db0f317.html.
8. CNBC News, "Deputy Attorney General Larry Thompson Discusses the Fight Against Corporate Crime," June 23, 2003.
9. Julie R. O'Sullivan, "Does DOJ's Privilege Waiver Policy Threaten the Rationales Underlying the Attorney-Client Privilege and Work Product Doctrine? A Preliminary 'No,'" *American Criminal Law Review* 45 (2008): 1237–96.
10. Richard A. Epstein, "The Deferred Prosecution Racket", *Wall Street Journal* online, last modified November 28, 2006, www.wsj.com/articles/SB116468395737834160.
11. "An Informed and Forceful Critique of NPAs and DPAs by . . . Guess Who?," *FCPA Professor*, April 25, 2013, www.fcpaprofessor.com/an-informed-and-forceful-critique-of-npas-and-dpas-by-guess-who.
12. The letter, dated September 5, 2006, was included in the "Statement of the American Bar Association to the Committee on Judiciary of the United States Senate Concerning Its Hearing on 'Examining Approaches to Corporate Fraud Prosecutions and the Attorney-Client Privilege Under the McNulty Memorandum,' September 18, 2007," 31.
13. Carol Morello and Carol D. Leonnig, "Chris Christie's Long Record of Pushing Boundaries, Sparking Controversy," *Washington Post*, February 10, 2014, www.washingtonpost.com/local/chris-christies-long-record-of-pushing-boundaries-sparking-controversy/2014/02/10/50111ed4-8db1-11e3-98ab-fe5228217bd1_story.html?utm_term=.7208b6b20637.
14. US Department of Justice, "U.S. Deputy Attorney General Paul J. McNulty

Revises Charging Guidelines for Prosecuting Corporate Fraud," news release, December 12, 2006, www.justice.gov/archive/opa/pr/2006/December/06_odag_828.html.

## CHAPTER SIX: PAUL PELLETIER'S WHITE WHALE

1. Jeff Leen, "Mel Kessler: The Miami Drug Lawyer," *Miami Herald*, September 2, 1990.
2. Roddy Boyd, *Fatal Risk: A Cautionary Tale of AIG's Corporate Suicide.* (Hoboken, NJ: John Wiley & Sons, 2011), 130–31.
3. "The PNC Financial Services Group, Inc.: Admin. Proc. Rel. No. 33-8112/July 18, 2002," www.sec.gov/litigation/admin/33-8112.htm.
4. United States of America v. AIG-FP Pagic Equity Holding Corp., 15 U.S.C. §§ 78j and 78ff(a); 17 C.F.R. § 240.10b-5; and 18 U.S.C. § 2, Deferred Prosecution Agreement, November 30, 2004, 18.
5. Peter Lattman, "The U.S.'s Fly on the Wall at AIG," *Wall Street Journal* online, last modified March 27, 2009, www.wsj.com/articles/SB123812186477454361.

## CHAPTER SEVEN: KPMG DESTROYS CAREERS

1. United States v. Jeffrey Stein et al., Kaplan Opinion (S.D. N.Y, 2006), 2.
2. IRS, "KPMG to Pay $456 Million for Criminal Violations," news release, August 29, 2005, last modified July 16, 2014, www.irs.gov/uac/KPMG-to-Pay-$456-Million-for-Criminal-Violations.
3. *U.S. Tax Shelter Industry: The Role of Accountants, Lawyers, and Financial Professionals, Hearings Before the Permanent Subcommittee on Investigations of the Committee on Governmental Affairs*, US Senate, 108th Congress, first session, November 18 and 20, 2003, www.gpo.gov/fdsys/pkg/CHRG-108shrg91043/html/CHRG-108shrg91043.htm.
4. Charles D. Weisselberg and Su Li, "Big Law's Sixth Amendment: The Rise of Corporate White-Collar Practices in Large U.S. Law Firms," *Arizona Law Review* 53 (2011): 1274, http://scholarship.law.berkeley.edu/facpubs/1164.
5. David W. Chen, "Pirro Sentenced to 29 Months in U.S. Prison," *New York Times*, November 2, 2000, www.nytimes.com/2000/11/02/nyregion/pirro-sentenced-to-29-months-in-us-prison.html?_r=0.
6. Winnie Hu, "Husband Is Convicted, but Jeanine Pirro Is Topic," *New York Times*, June 23, 2000, www.nytimes.com/2000/06/23/nyregion/husband-is-convicted-but-jeanine-pirro-is-topic.html.
7. Larry D. Thompson, "Memorandum: Principles of Federal Prosecution of Business Organizations," US Department of Justice, Office of the Deputy Attorney General, January 20, 2003, www.americanbar.org/content/dam

/aba/migrated/poladv/priorities/privilegewaiver/2003jan20_privwaiv_dojthomp.authcheckdam.pdf.

8. Carrie Johnson, "9 Charged over Tax Shelters in KPMG Case," *Washington Post*, August 30, 2005, www.washingtonpost.com/wp-dyn/content/article/2005/08/29/AR2005082900822.html.
9. *Stein* et al., 24.
10. Lynnley Browning, "Documents Show KPMG Secretly Met Prosecutors," *New York Times*, February 9, 2015, www.nytimes.com/2007/07/06/business/06kpmg.html.
11. US Department of Justice, "KPMG to Pay $456 Million for Criminal Violations in Relation to Largest-Ever Tax Shelter Fraud Case," news release, August 29, 2005, www.justice.gov/archive/opa/pr/2005/August/05_ag_433.html.
12. Jonathan D. Glater, "8 Former Partners of KPMG Are Indicted," *New York Times*, August 30, 2005, www.nytimes.com/2005/08/30/business/8-former-partners-of-kpmg-are-indicted.html?_r=0.
13. "The KPMG Fiasco," Review & Outlook, *Wall Street Journal* online, last modified July 10, 2007.
14. Paul Davies, "Bench on Fire: KPMG Judge Grills Prosecutors," *Wall Street Journal* online, last modified August 5, 2006.
15. Weisselberg and Li, "Big Law's Sixth Amendment," 1278.
16. Amir Efrati, "Appeals Court Upholds Ruling to Dismiss KPMG Tax Case," *Wall Street Journal* online, last modified August 28, 2008, www.wsj.com/articles/SB121994701590180363.
17. Weisselberg and Li, "Big Law's Sixth Amendment," 1280.
18. *The Thompson Memorandum's Effect on the Right to Counsel in Corporate Investigations, Hearing Before the Senate Judiciary Committee,* September 12, 2006, www.americanbar.org/content/dam/aba/migrated/poladv/letters/attyclient/060912testimony_hrgsjud.authcheckdam.pdf.
19. Robert J. Anello, "Preserving the Corporate Attorney-Client Privilege: Here and Abroad," *Penn State International Law Review* 27, no. 2 (February 2, 2009): 291–314, www.maglaw.com/publications/articles/00259/_res/id=Attachments/index=0/Preserving%20the%20Corporate%20Attorney-Client%20Privilege%20Here%20and%20Abroad.pdf.
20. United States v. Monsanto, 491 U.S. 600 (1989), https://supreme.justia.com/cases/federal/us/491/600/case.html.
21. Caplin & Drysdale, Chartered, Petitioner v. United States, 491 U.S. 617 (March 21, 1989), www.law.cornell.edu/supremecourt/text/491/617.
22. Weisselberg and Li, "Big Law's Sixth Amendment," 1273.

23. Adam Liptak, "Justices Limit Use of Corruption Law," *New York Times*, June 24, 2010, www.nytimes.com/2010/06/25/us/25scotus.html?_r=0.
24. Longstreth, "Memo Too Far."
25. Paul Davies and Chad Bray, "KPMG Trial, Pared in Scope, Nears After Stormy Prologue," *Wall Street Journal* online, last modified October 12, 2007.
26. "Corrections & Amplifications," *Wall Street Journal* online, last modified November 27, 2007.
27. Charles Levinson, "Veteran Federal Prosecutor Moves to Law Firm Brown Rudnick," *Law Blog, Wall Street Journal* online, last modified April 28, 2014, http://blogs.wsj.com/law/2014/04/28/veteran-federal-prosecutor-moves-to-law-firm-brown-rudnick.

## CHAPTER EIGHT: THE HUNT FOR AIG

1. "A Chronology of the United States Postal Inspection Service," U.S. Postal Inspection Service, https://postalinspectors.uspis.gov/aboutus/History.aspx.
2. Boyd, *Fatal Risk.*
3. Timothy L. O'Brien, "Guilty Plea Is Expected in A.I.G.-Related Case," *New York Times*, June 10, 2005, www.nytimes.com/2005/06/10/business/guilty-plea-is-expected-in-aigrelated-case.html.
4. US Department of Justice, Office of the Inspector General, "Top Management and Performance Challenges in the Department of Justice—2007," last modified October 2016, https://oig.justice.gov/challenges/2007.htm.
5. *The External Effects of the Federal Bureau of Investigation's Reprioritization Efforts* (Washington, DC: US Department of Justice, Office of the Inspector General, September 2005), https://oig.justice.gov/reports/FBI/a0537/final.pdf.

## CHAPTER NINE: NO TRUTH AND NO RECONCILIATION

1. Marilyn Geewax, "It's Geithner vs. Warren in Battle of the Bailout," NPR online, last modified May 25, 2014, www.npr.org/2014/05/25/315276441/its-geithner-vs-warren-in-battle-of-the-bailout.
2. K. Sabeel Rahman, "The Way Forward for Progressives," *New Republic* online, last modified November 2, 2016, https://newrepublic.com/article/138325/way-forward-progressives.
3. Glenn Thrush, "The Survivor: How Eric Holder Outlasted His (Many) Critics," *Politico*, July/August 2014, http://www.politico.com/magazine/story/2014/06/the-survivor-108018?paginate=false.

4. Carrie Johnson, "Deputy Attorney General David Ogden to Leave Justice Department," *Washington Post*, December 4, 2009, www.washingtonpost.com/wp-dyn/content/article/2009/12/03/AR2009120301727.html.
5. Jesse Eisinger, "The Rise of Corporate Impunity," ProPublica, last modified April 30, 2014, www.propublica.org/article/the-rise-of-corporate-impunity.
6. Ibid.
7. Asked about the exchange, Grindler says the phrase doesn't sound like something that would come from him.
8. John R. Emshwiller, "U.S. Won't Seek Retrial of Former Merrill Lynch Official in Enron Case," *Wall Street Journal* online, last modified September 16, 2010, www.wsj.com/articles/SB10001424052748703743504575494551974075066.
9. John C. Roper, "4 Ex-Merrill Lynch Execs' Convictions Overturned," *Houston Chronicle* online, last modified August 6, 2006, www.chron.com/business/enron/article/4-ex-Merrill-Lynch-execs-convictions-overturned-1484942.php.
10. Roger Parloff, "Redefining Fraud: Judicial Opining," *Fortune* online, last modified August 22, 2006, http://archive.fortune.com/magazines/fortune/fortune_archive/2006/09/04/8384701/index.htm.
11. Liptak, Adam. "Justices Limit Use of Corruption Law," *New York Times*, September 16, 2014, www.nytimes.com/2010/06/25/us/25scotus.html?_r=0.
12. Jeff Connaughton, *The Payoff: Why Wall Street Always Wins* (Westport, CT: Prospecta Press, 2012).
13. *Statement of Lanny A. Breuer, Assistant Attorney General, Criminal Division, United States Department of Justice, Before the United States Senate Committee on the Judiciary Hearing Entitled "Honest Services Fraud"* (September 28, 2010), http://legaltimes.typepad.com/files/breuer-testimony-on-honest-services-fraud-final-9.23.10.pdf.

## CHAPTER TEN: THE LAW IN THE CITY OF RESULTS

1. Mark J. Green, *The Other Government: The Unseen Power of Washington Lawyers* (New York: W. W. Norton, 1978), 31.
2. Peter J. Boyer, "Why Can't Obama Bring Wall Street to Justice?," *Newsweek* online, last modified May 6, 2012, www.newsweek.com/why-cant-obama-bring-wall-street-justice-65009.
3. Green, *The Other Government*, 13.
4. Ibid., 15.
5. Ibid., 6.
6. Most of the data come from *American Lawyer* magazine's annual rankings. See also David Segal, "A May-December Marriage of Law Firms: Venerable

Covington & Burling, Thinking Young, Announces Merger," *Washington Post*, September 21, 1999.

7. Ben Protess, "Once More Through the Revolving Door for Justice's Breuer," DealBook, *New York Times* online, last modified March 28, 2013, https://dealbook.nytimes.com/2013/03/28/once-more-through-the-revolving-door-for-justices-breuer.
8. Boyer, "Why Can't Obama Bring Wall Street to Justice?"
9. Protess, "Once More Through the Revolving Door."
10. Peter Lattman, "For White-Collar Defense Bar, It's Happening in Vegas," DealBook, *New York Times* online, March 7, 2013, http://dealbook.nytimes.com/2013/03/07/for-white-collar-defense-bar-its-happening-in-vegas.
11. Weisselberg and Li, *Big Law's Sixth Amendment*, 1265.
12. Ben W. Heineman Jr., William F. Lee, and David B. Wilkins, *Lawyers as Professionals and as Citizens: Key Roles and Responsibilities in the 21st Century* (Cambridge, MA: Center on the 13. Legal Profession at Harvard Law School, November 20, 2014), 5, https://clp.law.harvard.edu/assets/Professionalism-Project-Essay_11.20.14.pdf.
13. Susan Pulliam and Robert Frank, "Inside Adelphia: A Long Battle over Disclosing Stock Options," *Wall Street Journal* online, last modified January 26, 2004.
14. Pete Yost, Associated Press, "Freddie Mac Investigates Self over Lobby Campaign," February 24, 2009.
15. Robert A. Guth, Ben Worthen, and Justin Scheck, "Accuser Said Hurd Leaked an H-P Deal," *Wall Street Journal* online, last modified November 6, 2010.
16. Buell, *Capital Offenses*, 173.
17. WilmerHale, "Siemens Agrees to Record-Setting $800 Million in FCPA Penalties," news release, December 22, 2008, www.wilmerhale.com/pages/publicationsandnewsdetail.aspx?NewsPubId=95919.
18. Dionne Searcey, "Breuer: Beware, Execs, the DOJ Will Take Your Fancy Cars," *Law Blog*, *Wall Street Journal* online, last modified November 17, 2009, http://blogs.wsj.com/law/2009/11/17/breuer-beware-execs-the-doj-wants-your-fancy-cars.
19. Laurel Brubaker Calkins, "Ex-KBR CEO Stanley Gets 2½ Years in Prison for Foreign Bribes," Bloomberg, last modified February 24, 2012, www.bloomberg.com/news/articles/2012-02-23/ex-kbr-ceo-albert-stanley-gets-30-month-prison-term-in-nigeria-bribe-case.
20. Richard L. Cassin, "Och-Ziff Takes Fourth Spot on Our New Top Ten List," *FCPA Blog*, last modified October 4, 2016, www.fcpablog.com/blog/2016/10/4/och-ziff-takes-fourth-spot-on-our-new-top-ten-list.html.

21. "Lindsey Manufacturing Case Officially Over," *FCPA Professor* (blog), May 25, 2012. http://fcpaprofessor.com/lindsey-manufacturing-case-officially-over.
22. Nathan Vardi, "The Bribery Racket," *Forbes* online, last modified June 7, 2010, www.forbes.com/global/2010/0607/companies-payoffs-washington-extortion-mendelsohn-bribery-racket.html.
23. Nathan Koppel, "Top U.S. Bribery Prosecutor to Join Paul Weiss," *Wall Street Journal* online, last modified April 14, 2010, www.wsj.com/articles/SB10001424052702303695604575182174285804354.
24. Buell, *Capital Offenses*, 187.
25. *United States Attorneys' Annual Statistical Report, Fiscal Year 2010* and *Fiscal Year 2015. United States Attorneys' Annual Statistics Report* (Washington, DC: US Department of Justice), www.justice.gov/sites/default/files/usao/legacy/2011/09/01/10statrpt.pdf and www.justice.gov/usao/file/831856/download.
26. "Salary Table 2016—NY," US Office of Personnel Management, www.opm.gov/policy-data-oversight/pay-leave/salaries-wages/salary-tables/pdf/2016/NY.pdf.

## CHAPTER ELEVEN: JED RAKOFF'S RADICALIZATION

1. Shawn Tully, "The Golden Age for Financial Services Is Over," *Fortune* online, last modified September 29, 2008, http://archive.fortune.com/2008/09/28/news/companies/tully_lewis.fortune/index.htm?postversion=2008092908.
2. US Securities and Exchange Commission, "SEC Charges Bank of America for Failing to Disclose Merrill Lynch Bonus Payments," news release, August 3, 2009, www.sec.gov/news/press/2009/2009-177.htm.
3. James B. Stewart, *Den of Thieves* (New York: Simon & Schuster, 1999), 97.
4. Ibid., 440.
5. Hilzenrath, "Judge Jed Rakoff."
6. Jerry Gray and Benjamin Weiser, "Judge Rules U.S. Death Penalty Violates the Constitution," *New York Times*, July 1, 2002, www.nytimes.com/2002/07/01/nyregion/judge-rules-us-death-penalty-violates-the-constitution.html?_r=0.
7. Benjamin Weiser, "A Legal Quest Against the Death Penalty," *New York Times*, January 2, 2005, www.nytimes.com/2005/01/02/nyregion/a-legal-quest-against-the-death-penalty.html.
8. Benjamin Weiser, "Manhattan Judge Finds Federal Death Law Unconstitutional," *New York Times*, July 2, 2002, www.nytimes.com/2002/07/02/nyregion/manhattan-judge-finds-federal-death-law-unconstitutional.html.
9. John Lehmann, "Fed Judge KOs Death Penalty," *New York Post*, July 2, 2002, nypost.com/2002/07/02/fed-judge-kos-death-penalty.

10. Weiser, "Legal Quest Against the Death Penalty."
11. "U.S. Court of Appeals for the Second Circuit: United States v. Quinones," Death Penalty Information Center, www.deathpenaltyinfo.org/us-court-appeals-second-circuit-united-states-v-quinones.
12. Donald C. Langevoort, "On Leaving Corporate Executives 'Naked, Homeless and Without Wheels': Corporate Fraud, Equitable Remedies, and the Debate over Entity Versus Individual Liability," *Wake Forest Law Review* 42, no. 3 (2007): 627–66, http://scholarship.law.georgetown.edu/cgi/viewcontent.cgi?article=1453&context=facpub.
13. Roger Parloff, "The Demise of the-Lawyers-Did-It Defense," *Fortune* online, last modified September 22, 2009, http://archive.fortune.com/2009/09/22/news/companies/sec_bofa_rakoff.fortune/index.htm.
14. Paul Davis, "B of A Move Shows Perils of Getting Many Opinions," *American Banker*, October 13, 2009, www.americanbanker.com/news/b-of-a-move-shows-perils-of-getting-many-opinions.
15. US Securities and Exchange Commission, "Bank of America Corporation Agrees to Pay $150 Million to Settle SEC Charges," news release, February 4, 2010, www.sec.gov/litigation/litreleases/2010/lr21407.htm.
16. Zachary A. Goldfarb and Tomoeh Murakami Tse, "N.Y. Attorney General Cuomo Charges Bank of America with Fraud," *Washington Post*, February 5, 2010, www.washingtonpost.com/wp-dyn/content/article/2010/02/04/AR2010020402146.html.
17. Stephen Grocer, "Lewis Rebuffs Cuomo's BofA Lawsuit: It Is 'Badly Misguided,'" *Deal Journal* (blog), *Wall Street Journal* online, last modified February 4, 2010, http://blogs.wsj.com/deals/2010/02/04/lewis-rebuffs-cuomos-bofa-lawsuit-it-is-badly-misguided.
18. Bernstein Litowitz Berger & Grossman, "Pension Funds Recover $2.425 Billion for Shareholders in Bank of America Securities Class Action: A Historic and Outstanding Result for Investors," news release, September 28, 2012, www.boasecuritieslitigation.com/pdflib/media_64.pdf.
19. Christie Smythe, Chris Dolmetsch, and Greg Farrell, "Lewis, BofA Reach $25 Million Pact with N.Y. Over Merrill," Bloomberg, last modified March 27, 2014, www.bloomberg.com/news/articles/2014-03-26/bofa-lewis-reach-25-million-pact-with-n-y-over-merrill.
20. Hilzenrath, "Judge Jed Rakoff."

## CHAPTER TWELVE: "THE GOVERNMENT FAILED"

1. William D. Cohan, "Preet Bharara: The Enforcer of Wall Street," *Fortune* online, August 15, 2011, http://fortune.com/2011/08/02/preet-bharara-the-enforcer-of-wall-street.

2. Preet Bharara (prepared remarks, New York Financial Writers Association, CUNY School of Journalism, New York, June 6, 2011), www.justice.gov/usao-sdny/speech/prepared-remarks-us-attorney-preet-bharara-new-york-financial-writers-association.
3. For this chapter, I relied on many hours of interviews with dozens of former Southern District employees, current and former prosecutors, and people familiar with the inner workings of the office.
4. "Commercial mortgage-backed securities," investopedia.com.
5. "Residential mortgage-backed securities," investopedia.com.
6. Sheelah Kolhatkar, "The End of Preet Bharara's Perfect Record on Insider Trading," Bloomberg, last modified July 8, 2014, www.bloomberg.com/news/articles/2014-07-08/rengan-rajaratnam-and-the-end-of-an-insider-trading-win-streak.
7. The late 1990s implosion of Long Term Capital Management, a fund with huge borrowings, is an obvious exception to that rule, since its collapse may have caused a systemic financial crisis had the New York Federal Reserve not forced Wall Street banks to bail out the fund.
8. George Packer, "A Dirty Business: New York City's Top Prosecutor Takes On Wall Street Crime," A Reporter at Large, *New Yorker*, June 27, 2011, www.newyorker.com/magazine/2011/06/27/a-dirty-business. See also Connaughton, *The Payoff.*
9. Connaughton, *The Payoff.*
10. Dan Fitzpatrick, "J.P. Morgan Settles Its Madoff Tab," *Wall Street Journal* online, last modified January 7, 2014, www.wsj.com/articles/SB10001424052702304887104579306323011059460.
11. Benjamin Weiser and Ben White, "In Crisis, Prosecutors Put Aside Turf Wars," *New York Times*, October 30, 2008, www.nytimes.com/2008/10/31/business/31street.html.
12. Interview with Maria Bartiromo, "Lehman CFO Erin Callan: Back from Ugly Monday," *BusinessWeek*, March 20, 2008, https://www.bloomberg.com/news/articles/2008-03-19/lehman-cfo-erin-callan-back-from-ugly-monday.
13. In addition to speaking with multiple people familiar with Lehman's inner workings, from regulators, former executives, prosecutors, defense attorneys, and investors, I relied on the Jenner & Block bankruptcy examination report, known as *The Valukas Report*, for many of the liquidity pool details. Lowitt declined to comment. Anton R. Valukas, Lehman Brothers Holdings Inc. et al., chap. 11 case no. 08-13555 (JMP) (U.S. Bank ruptcy Court, S.D. N.Y., 2010), 1401–80, https://jenner.com/lehman/VOLUME%204.pdf.

## CHAPTER THIRTEEN: A TOLLBOOTH ON THE BANKSTER TURNPIKE

1. This account was drawn from hundreds of internal SEC emails, investigative documents, and interviews with James Kidney and many others involved in the investigation, most of whom spoke on background.
2. Matt Taibbi, "The Great American Bubble Machine," *Rolling Stone*, April 5, 2010, www.rollingstone.com/politics/news/the-great-american-bubble-machine-20100405#ixzz41g9UL5eF.
3. Louise Story and Gretchen Morgenson, "S.E.C. Accuses Goldman of Fraud in Housing Deal," *New York Times*, April 16, 2010, www.nytimes.com/2010/04/17/business/17goldman.html?pagewanted=all&_r=1.
4. Mark DeCambre, "Goldman Fall Guy," *New York Post*, April 17, 2010, nypost.com/2010/04/17/goldman-fall-guy.
5. Michael Lewis, "Bond Market Will Never Be the Same After Goldman," Bloomberg, April 22, 2010, www.bloomberg.com/news/articles/2010-04-22/bond-market-will-never-be-same-after-goldman-commentary-by-michael-lewis.
6. US Securities and Exchange Commission, "Goldman Sachs to Pay Record $550 Million to Settle SEC Charges Related to Subprime Mortgage CDO," news release, July 15, 2010, www.sec.gov/news/press/2010/2010-123.htm.
7. Justin Baer, Chad Bray, and Jean Eaglesham, "'Fab' Trader Liable in Fraud," *Wall Street Journal* online, last modified August 2, 2013, www.wsj.com/articles/SB10001424127887323681904578641843284450004.

## CHAPTER FOURTEEN: THE PROCESS IS POLLUTED

1. The beginning of this chapter reflects to a significant extent the case as the DOJ prosecution team saw it. The entirety of the chapter relied on hundreds of pages of emails, transcripts, and other documents I obtained, as well as interviews with current and former Justice Department prosecutors, former AIG executives, defense counsel, and other people familiar with AIG and the investigation. My efforts to reach Forster and Cassano were not successful, but I spoke with people close to them. Athan declined to comment.
2. William D. Cohan, "The Fall of AIG: The Untold Story," *Institutional Investor*, April 7, 2010, www.institutionalinvestor.com/Article/2460649/The_Fall_of_AIG_The_Untold_Story.html#/.WKPHTlUrKUl.
3. "Form 8-K, American International Group, Inc.," United States Securities and Exchange Commission, February 11, 2008, accessed October 26, 2016, www.sec.gov/Archives/edgar/data/5272/000095012308001369/y48487e8vk.htm.

4. Alistair Barr, "AIG Stock Tumbles on Heightened CDO Concerns," MarketWatch, last modified February 11, 2008, www.marketwatch.com/story/aig-drops-12-as-auditor-spat-raises-cdo-concerns.
5. Leslie Scism, "Closing Arguments Loom in AIG Bailout Trial," *Law Blog* (blog), *Wall Street Journal* online, last modified April 21, 2015, http://blogs.wsj.com/law/2015/04/21/closing-arguments-loom-in-aig-bailout-trial.
6. Brady Dennis, "AIG Discloses $75 Billion in Bailout Payments," *Washington Post*, March 16, 2009, www.washingtonpost.com/wp-dyn/content/article/2009/03/15/AR2009031501909.html.
7. Sharona Coutts, "AIG's Bonus Blow-up: The Essential Q&A," ProPublica, last modified March 18, 2009, www.propublica.org/article/aigs-bonus-blow-up-the-essential-qa-0317.
8. Carl Hulse and David M. Herszenhorn, "House Approves 90% Tax on Bonuses After Bailouts," *New York Times* online, last modified March 19, 2009, http://www.nytimes.com/2009/03/20/business/20bailout.html?ref=business.
9. David Goldman and Jennifer Liberto, "Tug of War over AIG Bonuses," *CNN* online, last modified March 18, 2009, http://money.cnn.com/2009/03/18/news/companies/aig_hearing.
10. US Department of Justice, "UBS Enters into Deferred Prosecution Agreement," news release, February 18, 2009, www.justice.gov/opa/pr/ubs-enters-deferred-prosecution-agreement.
11. Carrick Mollenkamp, Reuters, "HSBC Became Bank to Drug Cartels, Pays Big for Lapses," December 12, 2012, http://uk.reuters.com/article/uk-hsbc-probe-idUKBRE8BA05K20121212.
12. Christopher M. Matthews, "Justice Department Overruled Recommendation to Pursue Charges Against HSBC, Report Says," *Wall Street Journal* online, last modified July 11, 2016, www.wsj.com/articles/justice-department-overruled-recommendation-to-pursue-charges-against-hsbc-report-says-1468229401.
13. Rupert Neate, "HSBC Escaped US Money-Laundering Charges After Osborne's Intervention," Guardian (US), website of the *Guardian* (UK), last modified July 11, 2016, www.theguardian.com/business/2016/jul/11/hsbc-us-money-laundering-george-osborne-report.
14. US Department of Justice, "HSBC Holdings Plc. and HSBC Bank USA N.A. Admit to Anti-Money Laundering and Sanctions Violations, Forfeit $1.256 Billion in Deferred Prosecution Agreement," news release, December 11, 2012, www.justice.gov/opa/pr/hsbc-holdings-plc-and-hsbc-bank-usa-na-admit-anti-money-laundering-and-sanctions-violations.
15. Jessica Silver-Greenberg and Ben Protess, "HSBC Is Deemed Slow to Carry Out Changes," DealBook, *New York Times* online, last modified April 1, 2015,

www.nytimes.com/2015/04/02/business/dealbook/us-says-hsbc-needs-to-step-up-on-compliance.html.

16. Aruna Viswanatha and Ryan Tracy, “Financial-Crisis Panel Suggested Criminal Cases Against Stan O’Neal, Charles Prince, AIG Bosses,” *Wall Street Journal* online, last modified March 30, 2016, www.wsj.com/articles/financial-crisis-panel-suggested-criminal-cases-against-stan-oneal-charles-prince-aig-bosses-1459330202.

## CHAPTER FIFTEEN: RAKOFF’S FALL AND RISE

1. US Securities and Exchange Commission, “Citigroup to Pay $285 Million to Settle SEC Charges for Misleading Investors About CDO Tied to Housing Market,” news release, October 19, 2011, www.sec.gov/news/press/2011/2011-214.htm.
2. Jessica Silver-Greenberg and Ben Protess, “Bank of America Settles Suit Over Merrill for $2.43 Billion,” DealBook, *New York Times* online, last modified September 28, 2012, http://dealbook.nytimes.com/2012/09/28/bank-of-america-to-pay-2-43-billion-to-settle-class-action-over-merrill-deal/?_r=0.
3. David S. Hilzenrath, “SEC Likely to Win Its Defense of ‘No-Admit’ Citigroup Settlement, Appellate Panel Says,” *Washington Post*, March 15, 2012, www.washingtonpost.com/business/economy/sec-likely-to-win-its-defense-of-no-admit-citigroup-settlement-appellate-panel-says/2012/01/30/gIQAnVcDES_story.html.
4. Hilzenrath, “Judge Jed Rakoff.”
5. Ben Protess, “Judge Rakoff Says 2011 S.E.C. Deal with Citigroup Can Close,” *New York Times*, August 5, 2014, http://dealbook.nytimes.com/2014/08/05/after-long-fight-judge-rakoff-reluctantly-approves-citigroup-deal/?_r=0.
6. Lee Epstein, William M. Landes, and Richard A. Posner, “How Business Fares in the Supreme Court,” *Minnesota Law Review* 97 (2013): 1431–72, www.minnesotalawreview.org/wp-content/uploads/2013/04/EpsteinLanderPosner_MLR.pdf.
7. Adam Liptak, “Pro-Business Decisions Are Defining This Supreme Court,” *New York Times*, August 9, 2014, www.nytimes.com/2013/05/05/business/pro-business-decisions-are-defining-this-supreme-court.html.
8. Ashby Jones, “Appeals Court Overturns Frank Quattrone Conviction,” *Law Blog, Wall Street Journal* online, last modified March 20, 2006, http://blogs.wsj.com/law/2006/03/20/appeals-court-overturns-frank-quattrone-conviction.
9. Michael J. Graetz and Linda Greenhouse, *The Burger Court and the Rise of the Judicial Right* (New York: Simon & Schuster, 2016), p. 237.

10. Seigel, "Admit It! Corporate Admissions of Wrongdoing in SEC Settlements."
11. "Judge Approves 'Chump Change' Settlement with Two Former Bear Fund Managers," *Securities Law Prof Blog*, June 22, 2012, http://lawprofessors.typepad.com/securities/2012/06/judge-approves-chump-change-settlement-with-two-former-bear-fund-managers.html.

## CHAPTER SIXTEEN: "FIGHT FOR IT"

1. David Barstow, "At Wal-Mart in Mexico, a Bribe Inquiry Silenced," *New York Times*, April 22, 2012, www.nytimes.com/2012/04/22/business/at-wal-mart-in-mexico-a-bribe-inquiry-silenced.html?pagewanted=all.
2. "Wal-Mart's FCPA and Compliance Related Expenses Stand at $738 Million—Expected to Grow to Approximately $850 Million," *FCPA Professor* (blog), February 23, 2016, http://fcpaprofessor.com/wal-mart-fcpa-and-compliance-related-expenses-stand-at-738-million-expected-to-grow-to-approximately-850-million.
3. Aruna Viswanatha and Devlin Barrett, "Wal-Mart Bribery Probe Finds Few Signs of Major Misconduct in Mexico," *Wall Street Journal* online, last modified October 19, 2015, www.wsj.com/articles/wal-mart-bribery-probe-finds-little-misconduct-in-mexico-1445215737.
4. Aruna Viswanatha, "U.S. Bid to Prosecute BP Staff in Gulf Oil Spill Falls Flat," *Wall Street Journal* online, last modified February 27, 2016, www.wsj.com/articles/u-s-bid-to-prosecute-bp-staff-in-gulf-oil-spill-falls-flat-1456532116.
5. Kris Maher, "Jury Convicts Former Massey CEO Don Blankenship of Conspiracy," *Wall Street Journal* online, last modified December 3, 2015, www.wsj.com/articles/ex-massey-energy-ceo-don-blankenship-found-guilty-on-1-of-3-counts-1449164466.
6. "Overview," Keefe, Bruyette & Woods, accessed October 17, 2016, http://www.kbw.com/research; Richard Bowen, "Goldman Sachs aka the Great Vampire Squid Rides Again!," Richard Bowen, last modified January 28, 2016, www.richardmbowen.com/goldman-sachs-aka-the-great-vampire-squid-rides-again.
7. Stephen Grocer, "A List of the Biggest Bank Settlements," *Moneybeat* (blog), *Wall Street Journal* online, last modified June 23, 2014, http://blogs.wsj.com/moneybeat/2014/06/23/a-list-of-the-biggest-bank-settlements.
8. Joel Schectman, "Compliance Counsel to Help DoJ Decide Whom to Prosecute," *Risk & Compliance Journal* (blog), *Wall Street Journal* online, last modified July 30, 2015, http://blogs.wsj.com/riskandcompliance/2015/07/30/compliance-counsel-to-help-doj-decide-whom-to-prosecute.
9. Evan Weinberger, "Ex-Prosecutor Says Yates Memo Knocks Post-Crisis

Cases," Law360, last modified November 17, 2015, www.law360.com/articles/728462/ex-prosecutor-says-yates-memo-knocks-post-crisis-cases.

10. Katelyn Polantz, "DOJ's 'Yates Memo' Goes Too Far, Former Deputy AG Says," *National Law Journal*, November 20, 2015, www.nationallawjournal.com/id=1202743031700/DOJs-Yates-Memo-Goes-Too-Far-Former-Deputy-AG-Says?slreturn=20160918124713#ixzz45YUGiCHq.
11. "Early-Bird Registration Now Open for Securities Enforcement Forum 2014—Oct. 14, 2014 in Washington, D.C.," Securities Docket, the Global Securities Litigation and Enforcement Report, last modified October 14, 2014, www.securitiesdocket.com/2014/02/28/early-bird-registration-now-open-for-securities-enforcement-forum-2014-oct-14-2014-in-washington-d-c.
12. Suzi Ring, "SEC Official Says Too Many Regulators Are 'Piling On,'" Bloomberg, last modified October 15, 2014, www.bloomberg.com/news/articles/2014-10-15/sec-official-says-too-many-regulators-are-piling-on.
13. "Conyers Goodlatte Mens Rea Reform Deal in the Works in House Judiciary Committee," *Corporate Crime Reporter* online, last modified November 13, 2015, www.corporatecrimereporter.com/news/200/conyers-goodlatte-mens-rea-reform-deal-in-the-works.
14. John Malcolm, *Crime and Justice: The Pressing Need for Mens Rea Reform* (Washington, DC: Heritage Foundation, September 1, 2015), www.heritage.org/research/reports/2015/09/the-pressing-need-for-mens-rea-reform#_ftn7.
15. Ben Protess. "Khuzami, S.E.C. Enforcement Chief Who Reinvigorated Unit, to Step Down," *New York Times,* January 9, 2013, http://dealbook.nytimes.com/2013/01/09/s-e-c-enforcement-chief-khuzami-steps-down.
16. Steven Mufson, "BP Settles Criminal Charges for $4 Billion in Spill; Supervisors Indicted on Manslaughter," *Washington Post*, November 15, 2012, www.washingtonpost.com/business/economy/bp-to-pay-billions-in-gulf-oil-spill-settlement/2012/11/15/ba0b783a-2f2e-11e2-9f50-0308e1e75445_story.html?tid=a_inl.
17. Ben Bedell, "Finding No Evidence of Fraud, Circuit Reverses $1.27B Verdict," *New York Law Journal*, May 24, 2016, www.newyorklawjournal.com/id=1202758444032/Finding-No-Evidence-of-Fraud-Circuit-Reverses-127B-Verdict?slreturn=20160918162729.

# INDEX